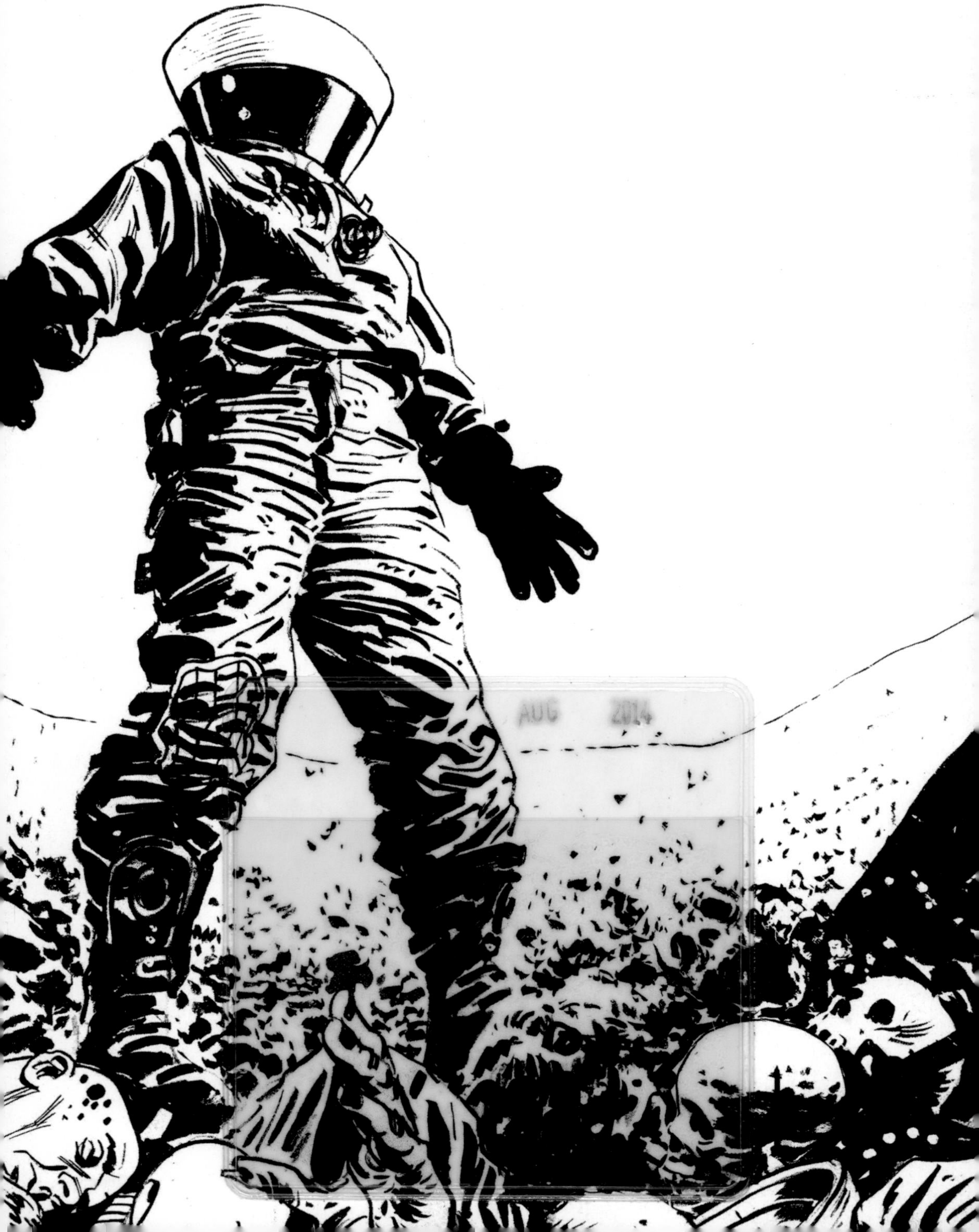

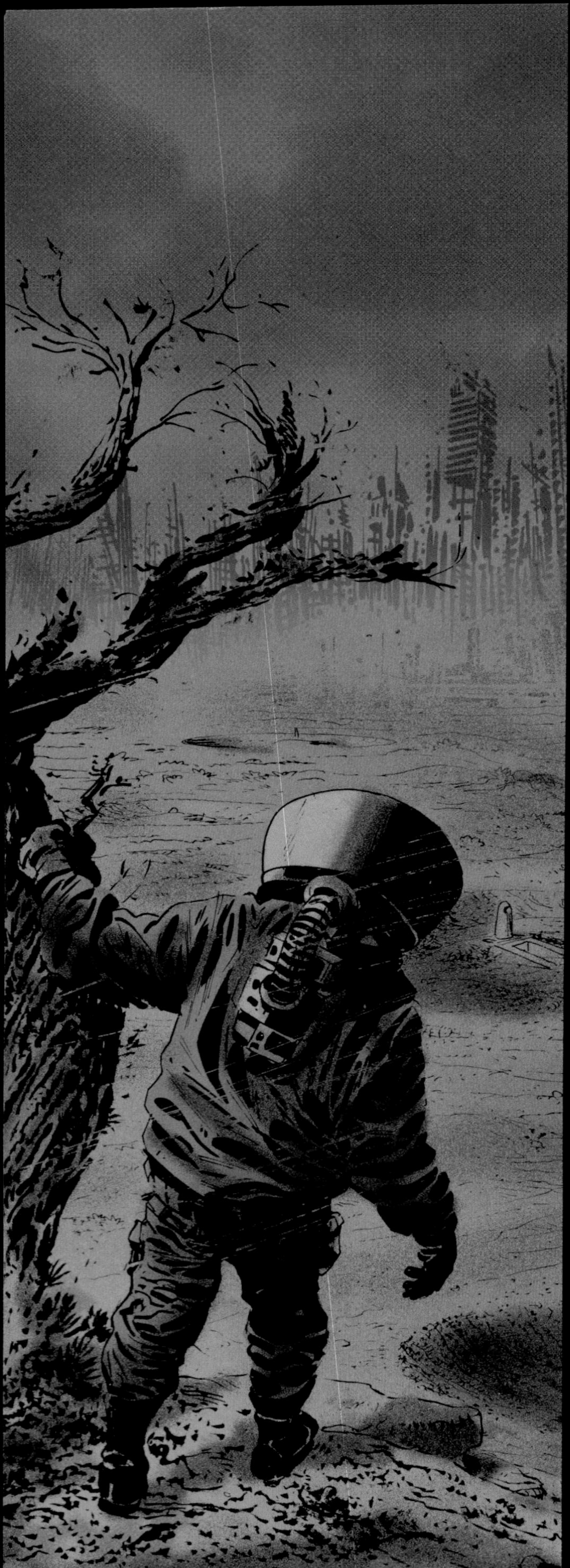

HUGH HOWEY'S

WOOL

Script by
JUSTIN GRAY &
JIMMY PALMIOTTI

Art by
JIMMY BROXTON

Letters by
BILL TORTOLINI

Cover by
DARWYN COOKE

Editor
MATT HOFFMAN

Omnibus Design by
DERON BENNETT

Senior Production Manager
JILL TAPLIN

Senior Collection Editor
ALEX CARR

JET CITY COMICS

Produced in association with
Cryptozoic Entertainment

WOOL: The Graphic Novel Omnibus. The characters and events portrayed in this book are fictitious. Any similarity to real persons, living or dead, is coincidental and not intended by the author.

Printed in the United States of America.

Published by Jet City Comics, Seattle
www.apub.com
ISBN-10: 1477849122
ISBN-13: 9781477849125
E-ISBN: 9781477899120

Artwork by Jimmy Broxton

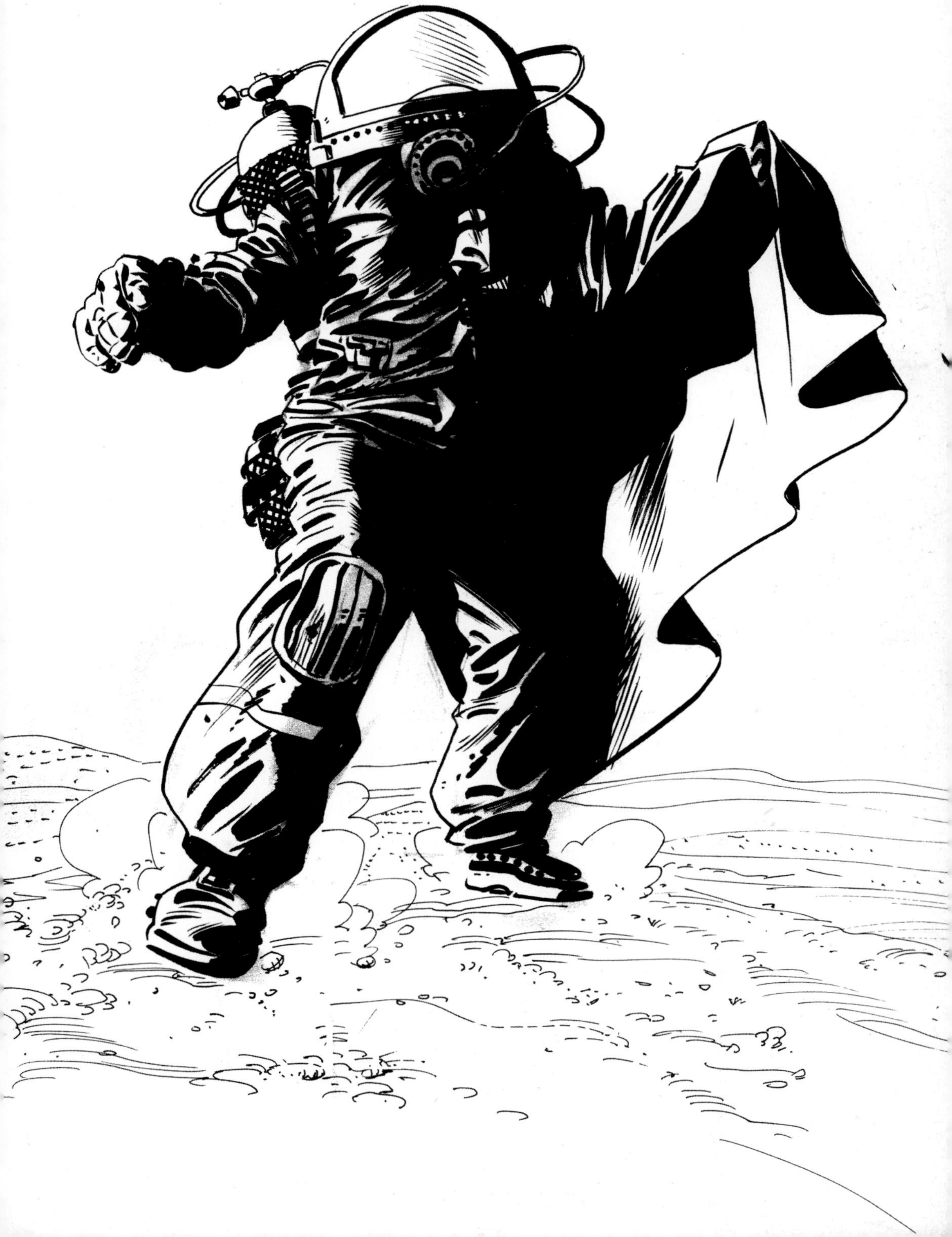

ISSUE 1

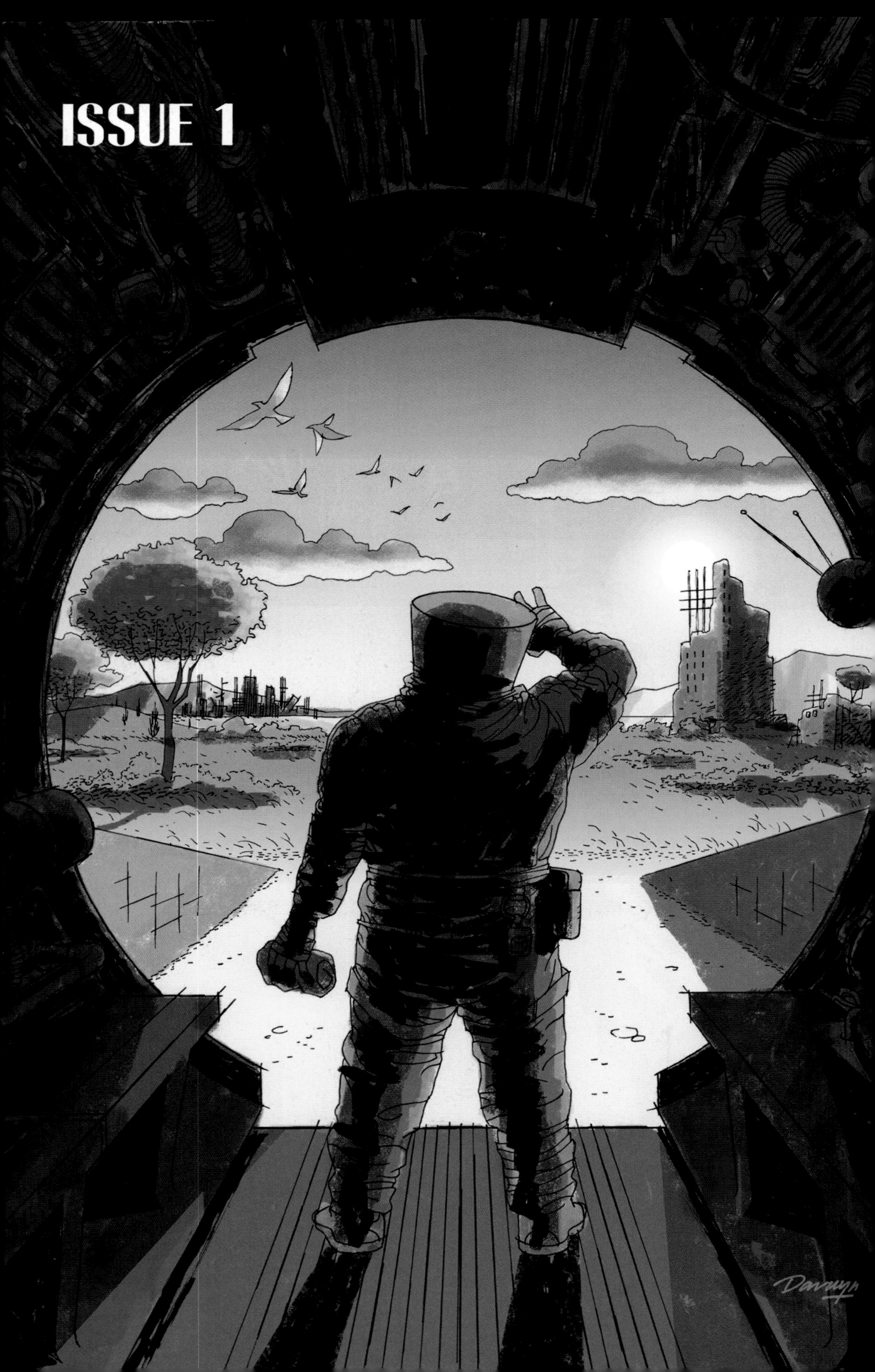

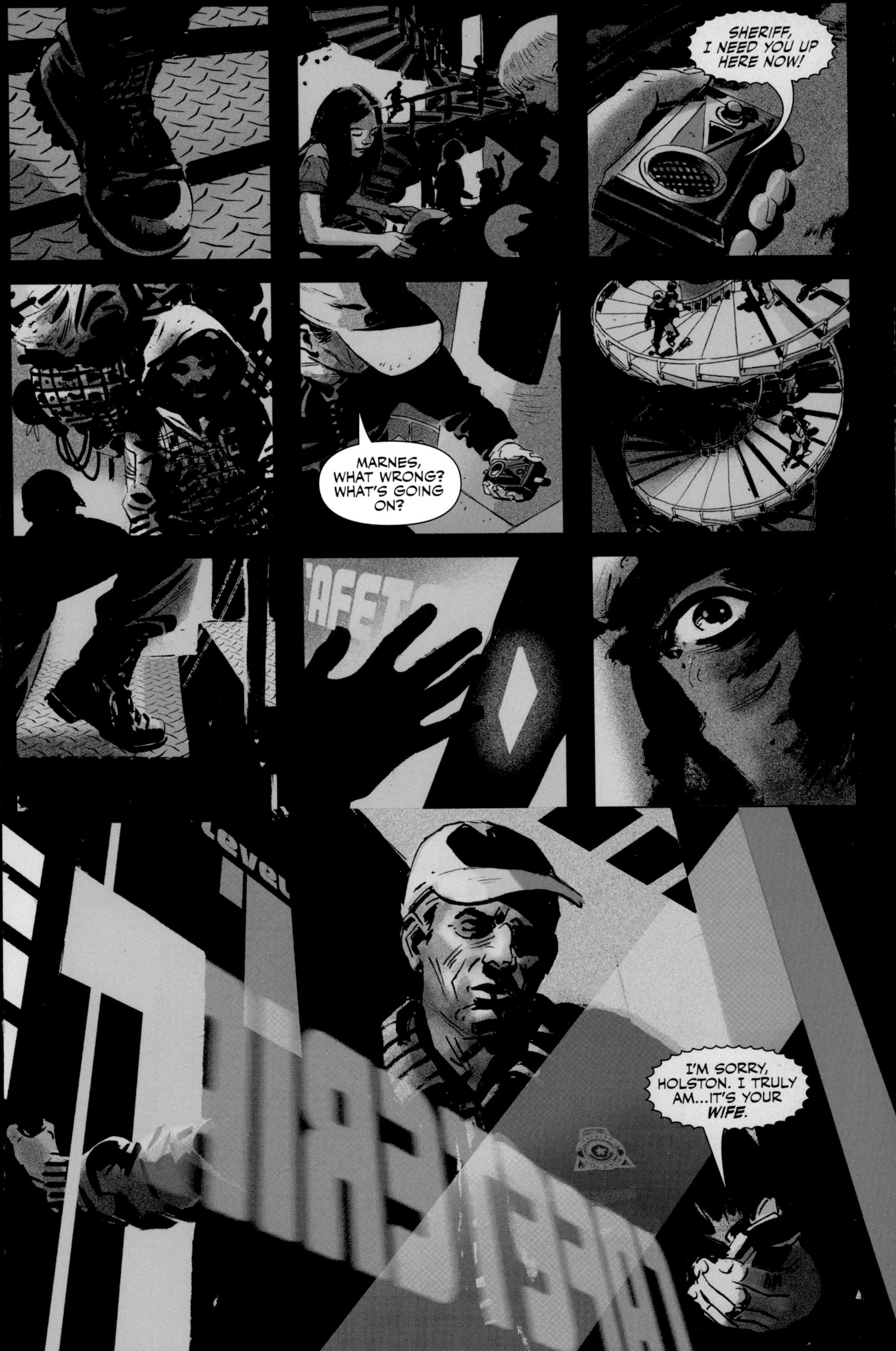
SHERIFF, I NEED YOU UP HERE NOW!
MARNES, WHAT WRONG? WHAT'S GOING ON?
I'M SORRY, HOLSTON. I TRULY AM...IT'S YOUR WIFE.

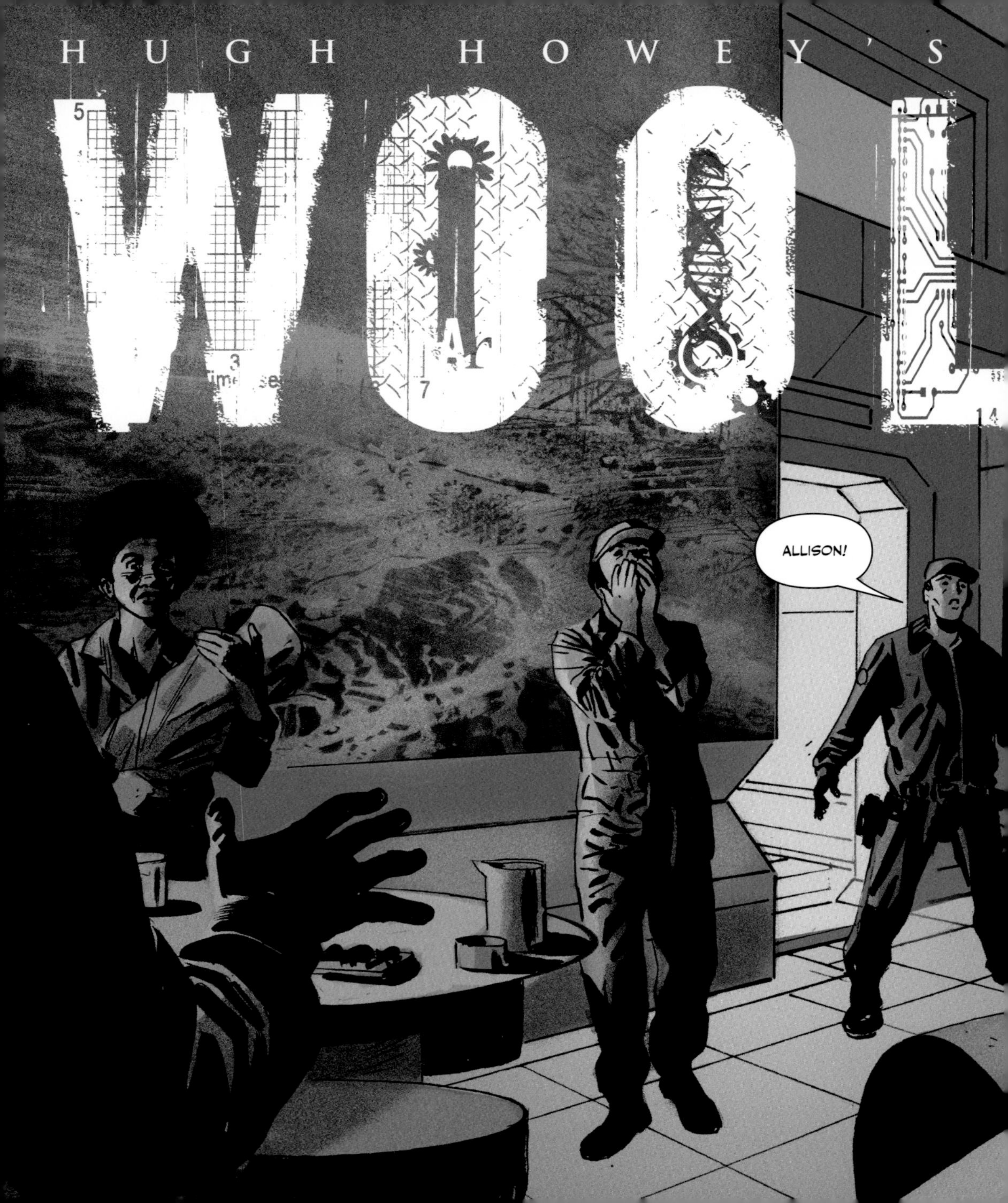
HUGH HOWEY'S
WOOL
ALLISON!

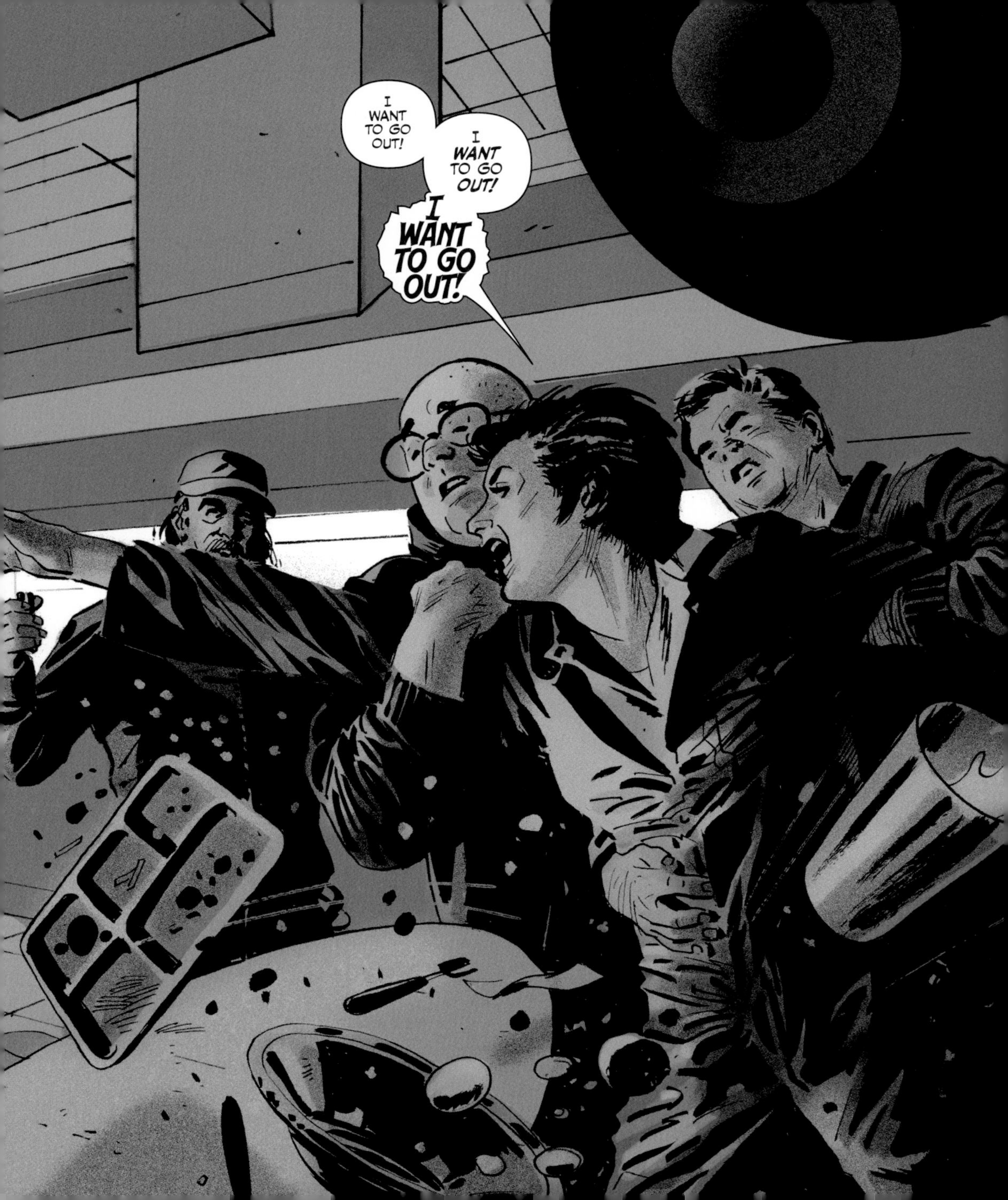
I WANT TO GO OUT!
I WANT TO GO OUT!
I WANT TO GO OUT!

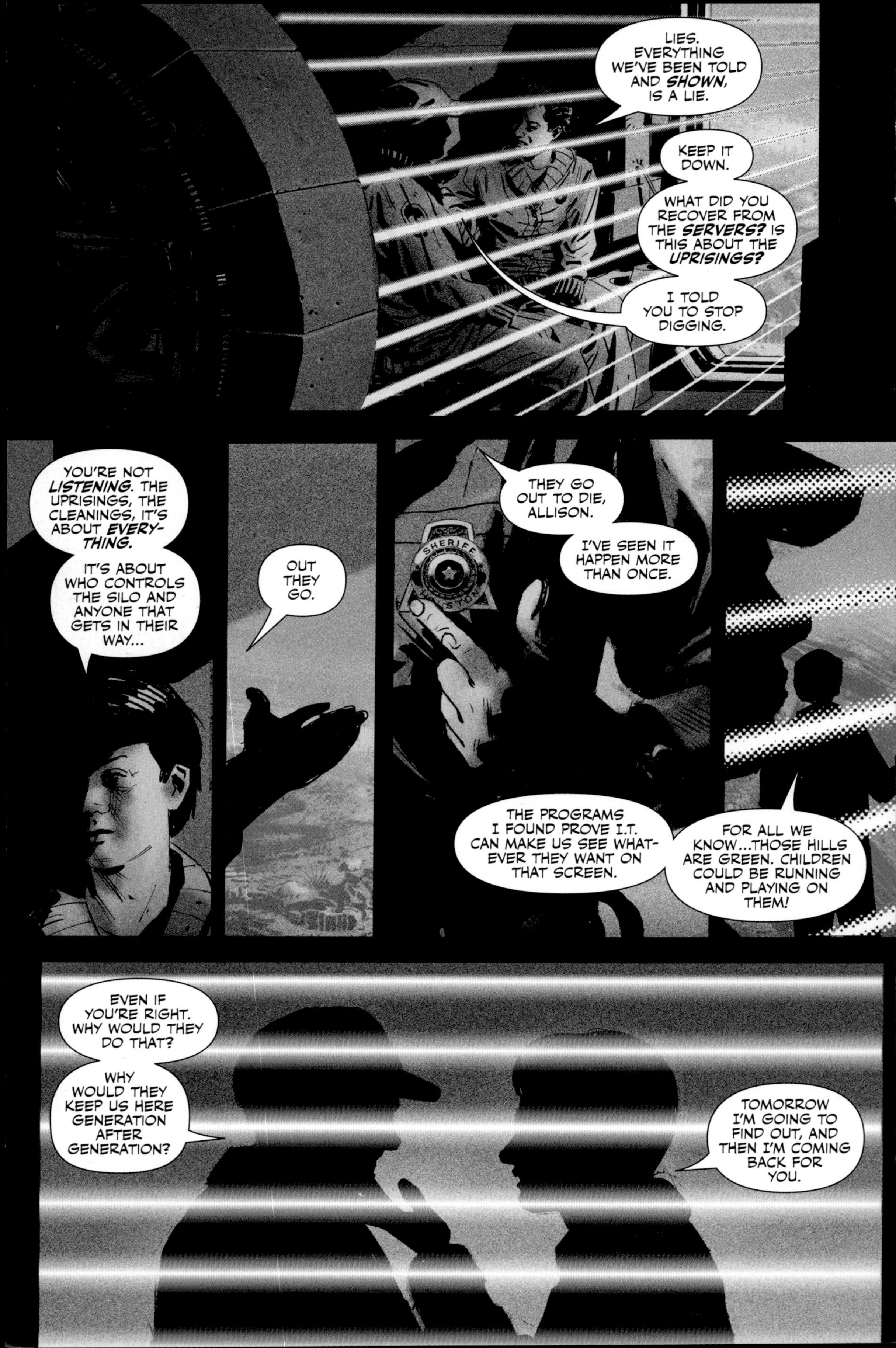
LIES. EVERYTHING WE'VE BEEN TOLD AND *SHOWN,* IS A LIE.
KEEP IT DOWN.
WHAT DID YOU RECOVER FROM THE *SERVERS?* IS THIS ABOUT THE *UPRISINGS?*
I TOLD YOU TO STOP DIGGING.
YOU'RE NOT *LISTENING*. THE UPRISINGS, THE CLEANINGS, IT'S ABOUT *EVERYTHING.*
IT'S ABOUT WHO CONTROLS THE SILO AND ANYONE THAT GETS IN THEIR WAY...
OUT THEY GO.
THEY GO OUT TO DIE, ALLISON.
I'VE SEEN IT HAPPEN MORE THAN ONCE.
SHERIFF
THE PROGRAMS I FOUND PROVE I.T. CAN MAKE US SEE WHATEVER THEY WANT ON THAT SCREEN.
FOR ALL WE KNOW...THOSE HILLS ARE GREEN. CHILDREN COULD BE RUNNING AND PLAYING ON THEM!
EVEN IF YOU'RE RIGHT. WHY WOULD THEY DO THAT?
WHY WOULD THEY KEEP US HERE GENERATION AFTER GENERATION?
TOMORROW I'M GOING TO FIND OUT, AND THEN I'M COMING BACK FOR YOU.

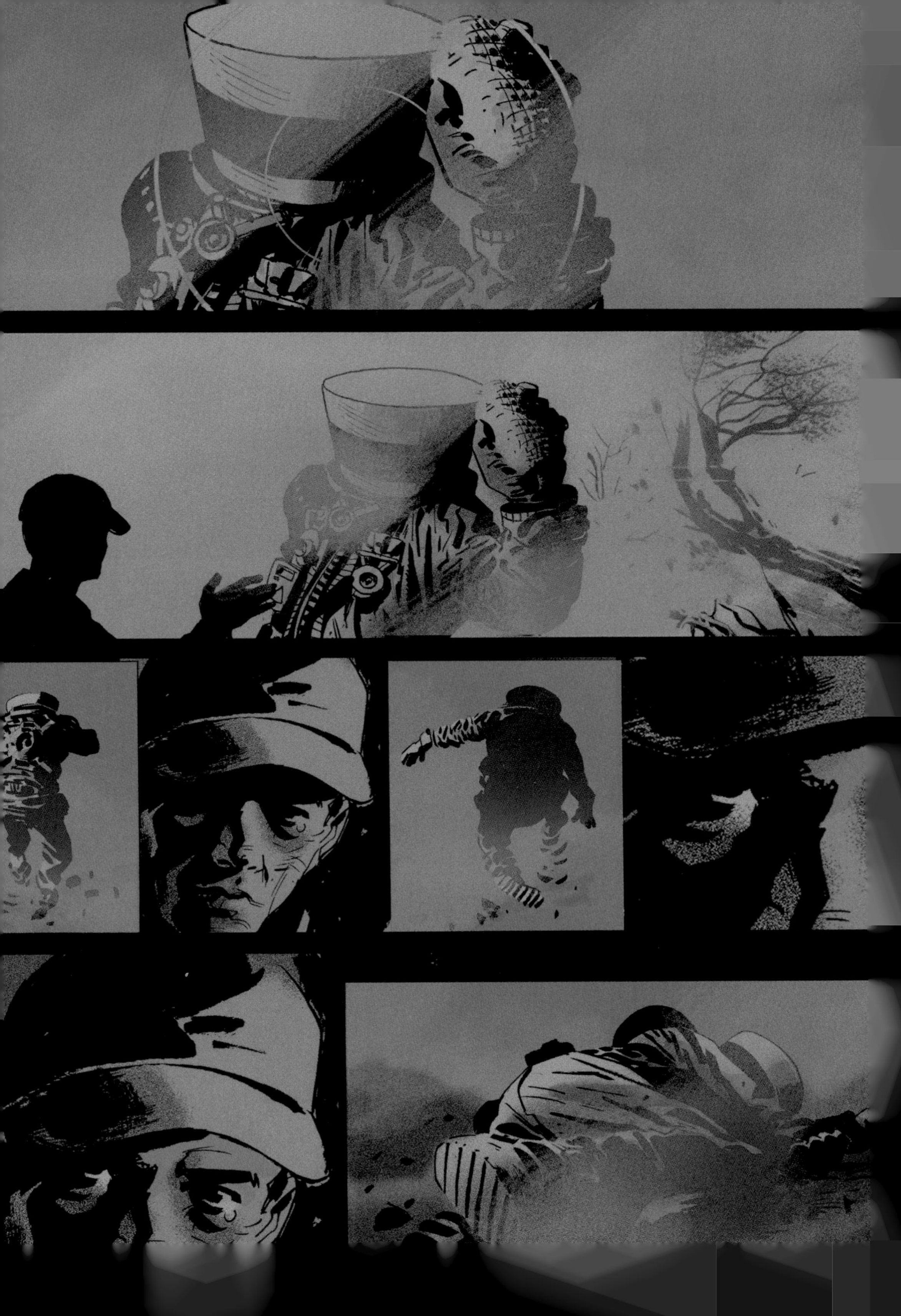

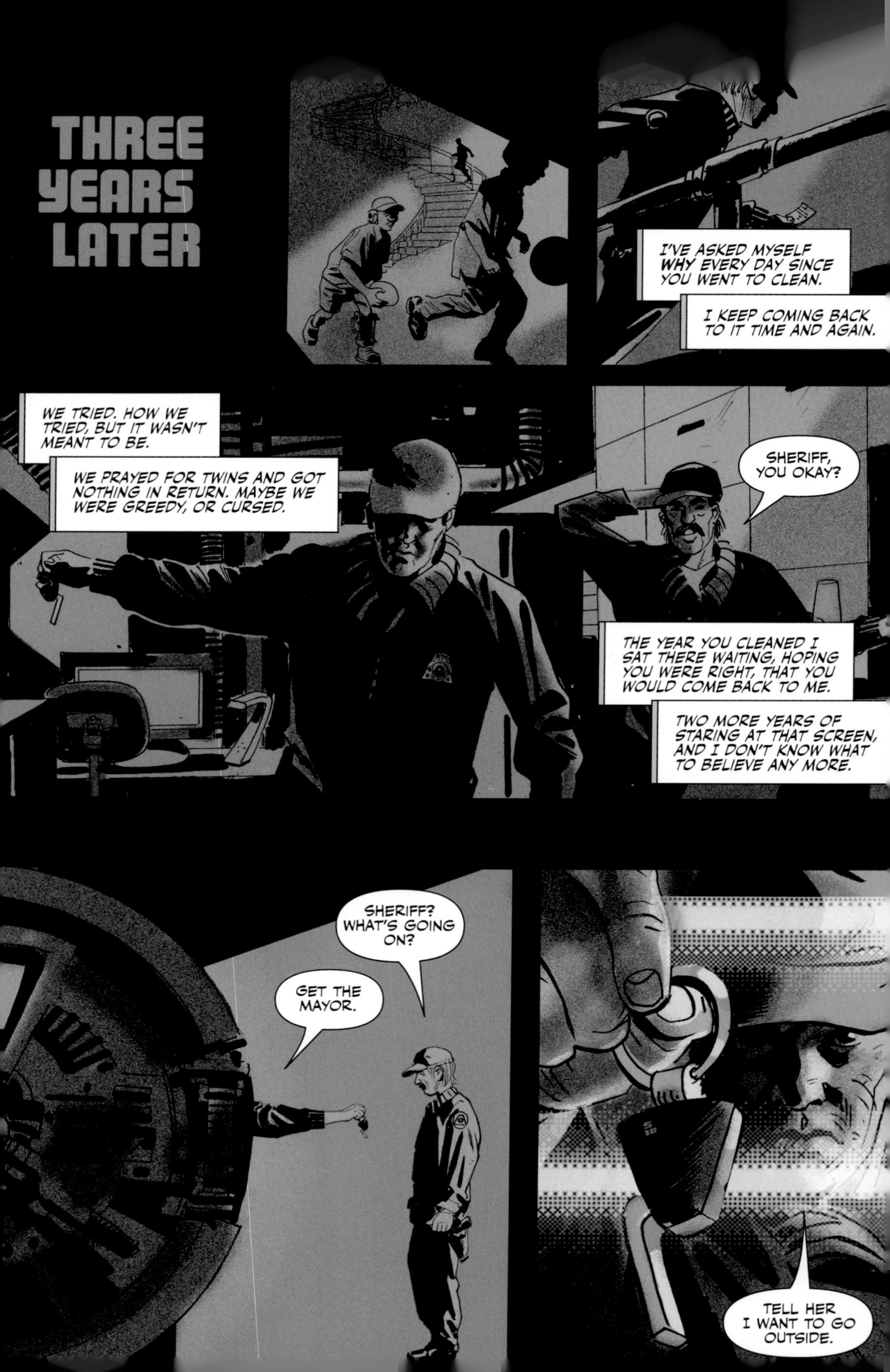
THREE YEARS LATER
I'VE ASKED MYSELF WHY EVERY DAY SINCE YOU WENT TO CLEAN.
I KEEP COMING BACK TO IT TIME AND AGAIN.
WE TRIED. HOW WE TRIED, BUT IT WASN'T MEANT TO BE.
WE PRAYED FOR TWINS AND GOT NOTHING IN RETURN. MAYBE WE WERE GREEDY, OR CURSED.
SHERIFF, YOU OKAY?
THE YEAR YOU CLEANED I SAT THERE WAITING, HOPING YOU WERE RIGHT, THAT YOU WOULD COME BACK TO ME.
TWO MORE YEARS OF STARING AT THAT SCREEN, AND I DON'T KNOW WHAT TO BELIEVE ANY MORE.
SHERIFF? WHAT'S GOING ON?
GET THE MAYOR.
TELL HER I WANT TO GO OUTSIDE.

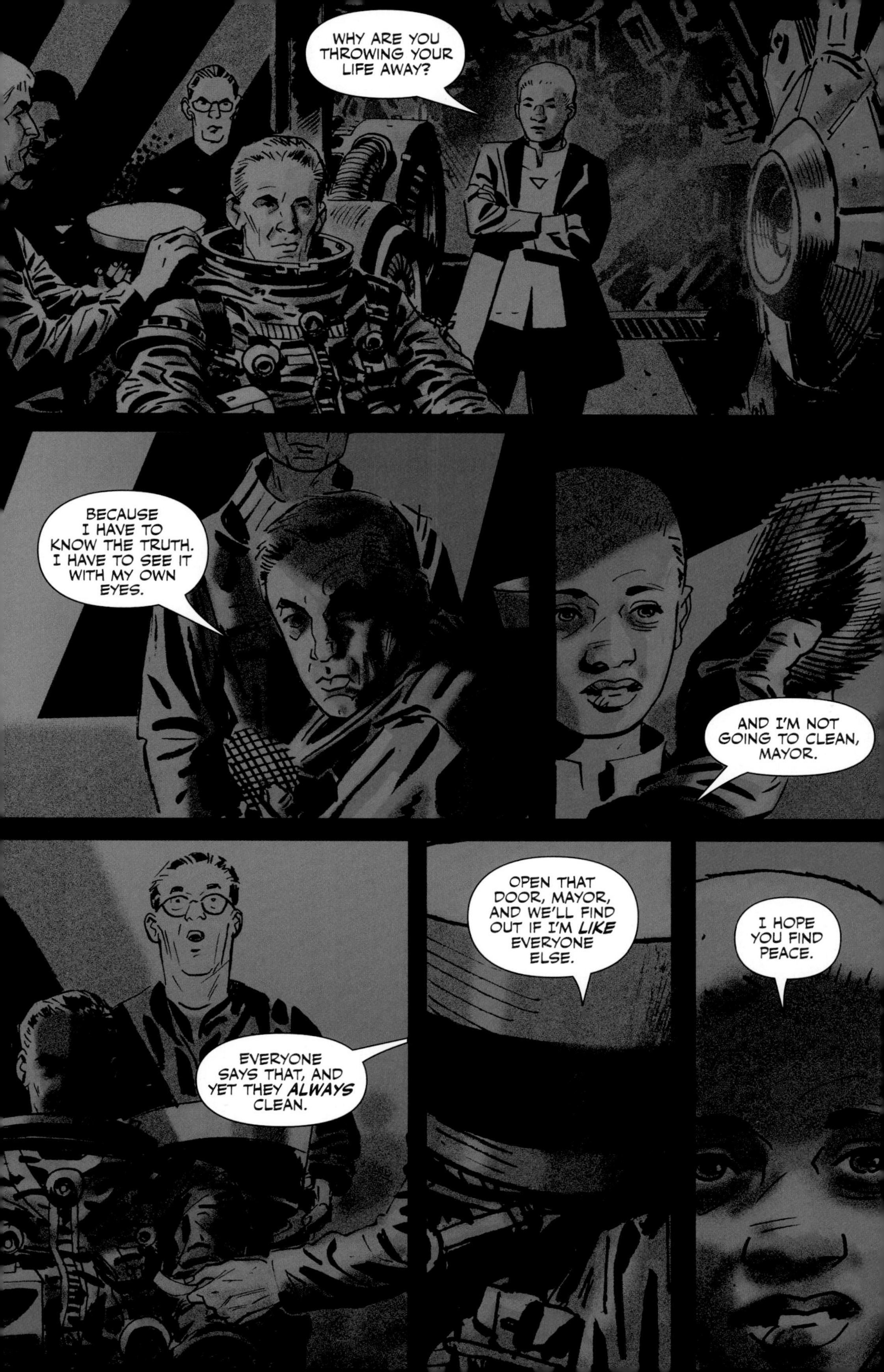
WHY ARE YOU THROWING YOUR LIFE AWAY?
BECAUSE I HAVE TO KNOW THE TRUTH. I HAVE TO SEE IT WITH MY OWN EYES.
AND I'M NOT GOING TO CLEAN, MAYOR.
EVERYONE SAYS THAT, AND YET THEY *ALWAYS* CLEAN.
OPEN THAT DOOR, MAYOR, AND WE'LL FIND OUT IF I'M *LIKE* EVERYONE ELSE.
I HOPE YOU FIND PEACE.

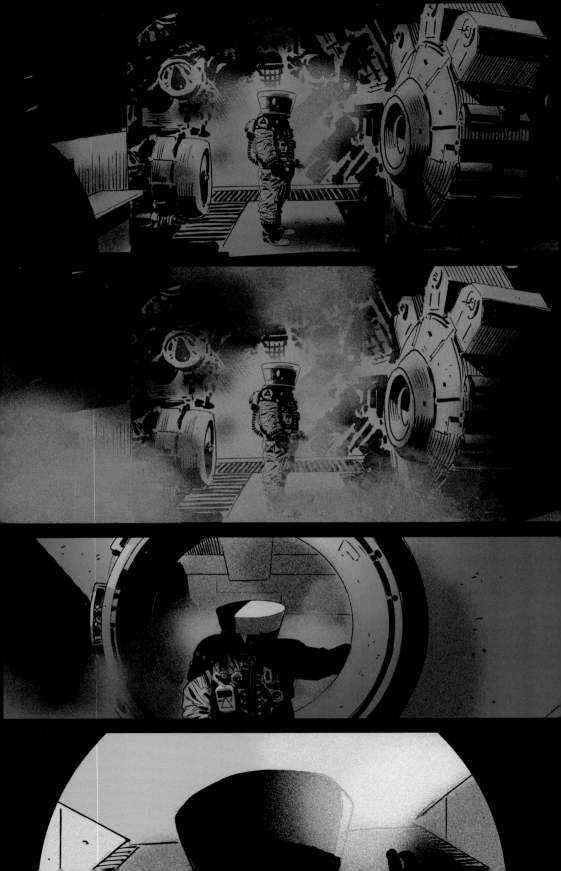

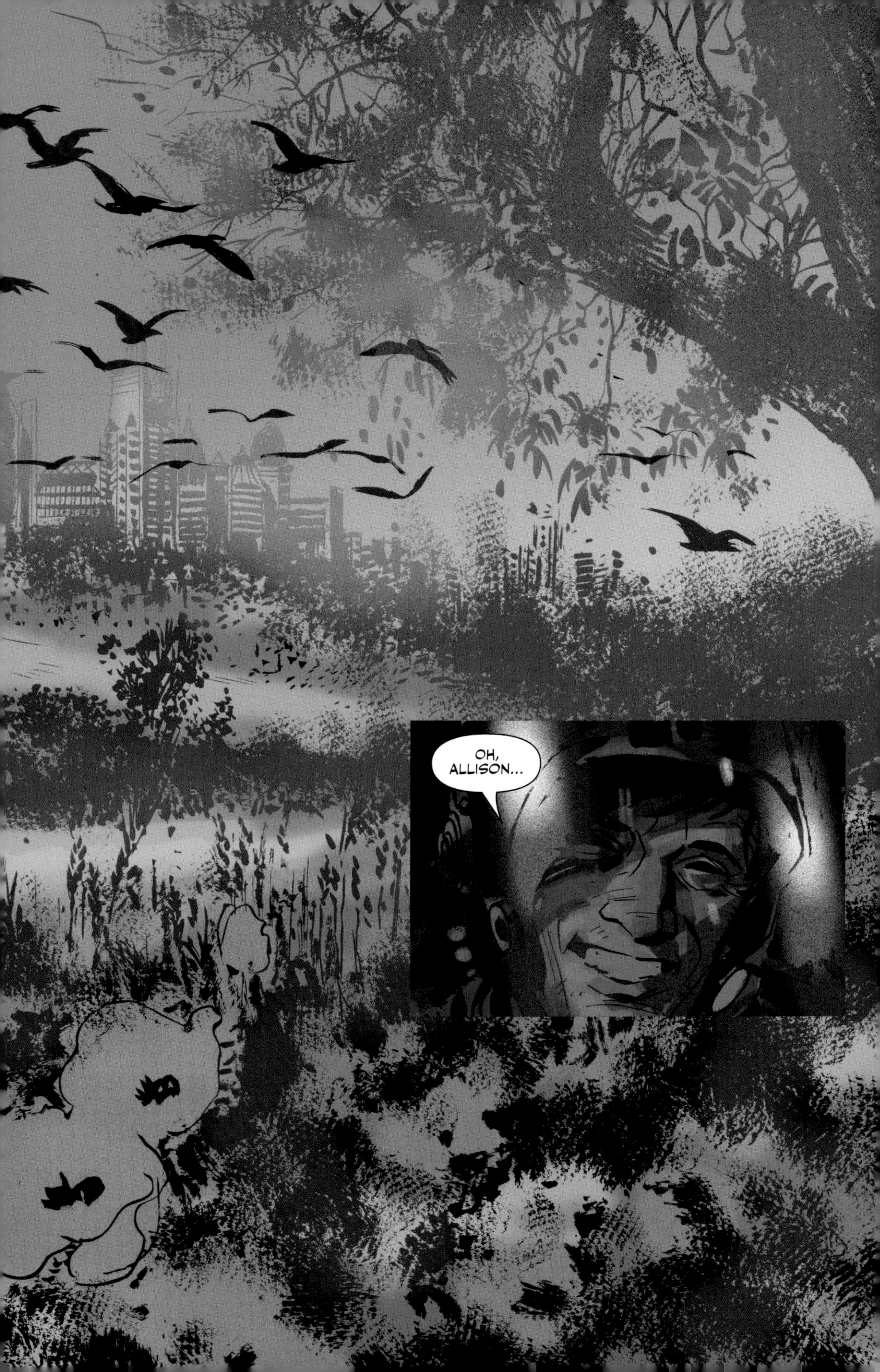
OH, ALLISON...

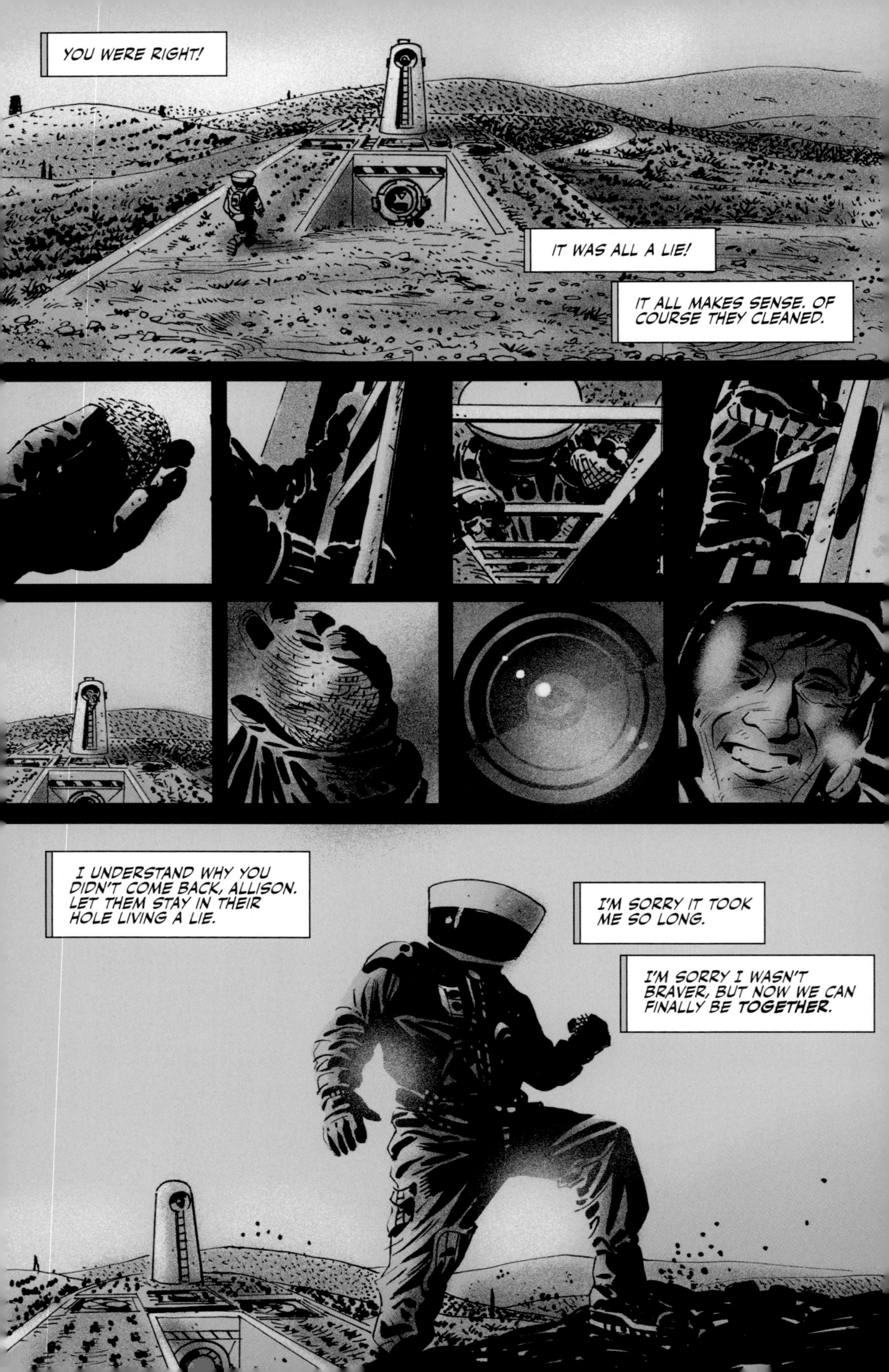
YOU WERE RIGHT!
IT WAS ALL A LIE!
IT ALL MAKES SENSE. OF COURSE THEY CLEANED.
I UNDERSTAND WHY YOU DIDN'T COME BACK, ALLISON. LET THEM STAY IN THEIR HOLE LIVING A LIE.
I'M SORRY IT TOOK ME SO LONG.
I'M SORRY I WASN'T BRAVER, BUT NOW WE CAN FINALLY BE TOGETHER.

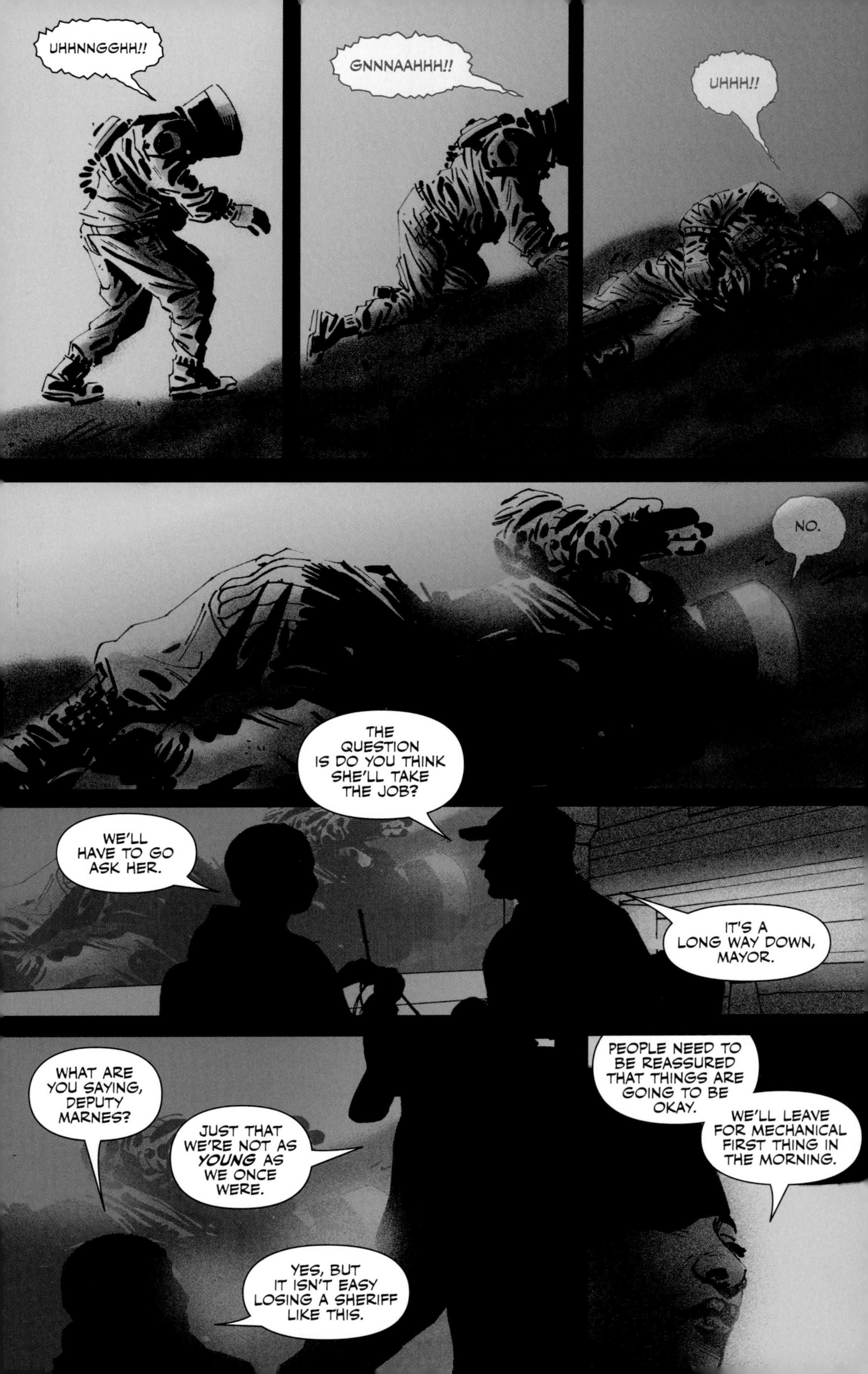
UHHNNGGHH!!
GNNNAAHHH!!
UHHH!!
NO.
THE QUESTION IS DO YOU THINK SHE'LL TAKE THE JOB?
WE'LL HAVE TO GO ASK HER.
IT'S A LONG WAY DOWN, MAYOR.
WHAT ARE YOU SAYING, DEPUTY MARNES?
JUST THAT WE'RE NOT AS *YOUNG* AS WE ONCE WERE.
YES, BUT IT ISN'T EASY LOSING A SHERIFF LIKE THIS.
PEOPLE NEED TO BE REASSURED THAT THINGS ARE GOING TO BE OKAY.
WE'LL LEAVE FOR MECHANICAL FIRST THING IN THE MORNING.

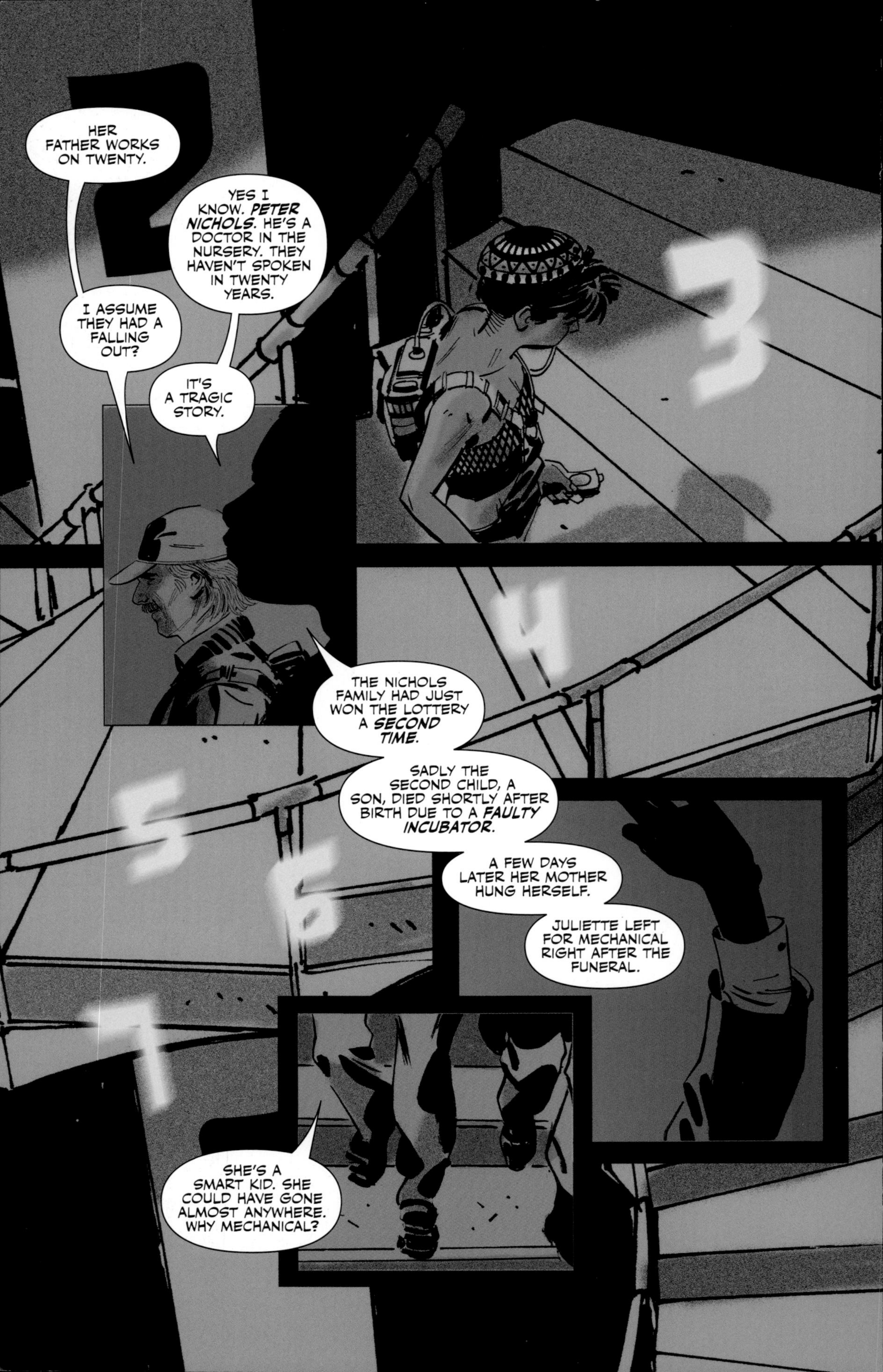
HER FATHER WORKS ON TWENTY.
YES I KNOW. PETER NICHOLS. HE'S A DOCTOR IN THE NURSERY. THEY HAVEN'T SPOKEN IN TWENTY YEARS.
I ASSUME THEY HAD A FALLING OUT?
IT'S A TRAGIC STORY.
3
4
THE NICHOLS FAMILY HAD JUST WON THE LOTTERY A SECOND TIME.
SADLY THE SECOND CHILD, A SON, DIED SHORTLY AFTER BIRTH DUE TO A FAULTY INCUBATOR.
5
6
A FEW DAYS LATER HER MOTHER HUNG HERSELF.
JULIETTE LEFT FOR MECHANICAL RIGHT AFTER THE FUNERAL.
7
SHE'S A SMART KID. SHE COULD HAVE GONE ALMOST ANYWHERE. WHY MECHANICAL?

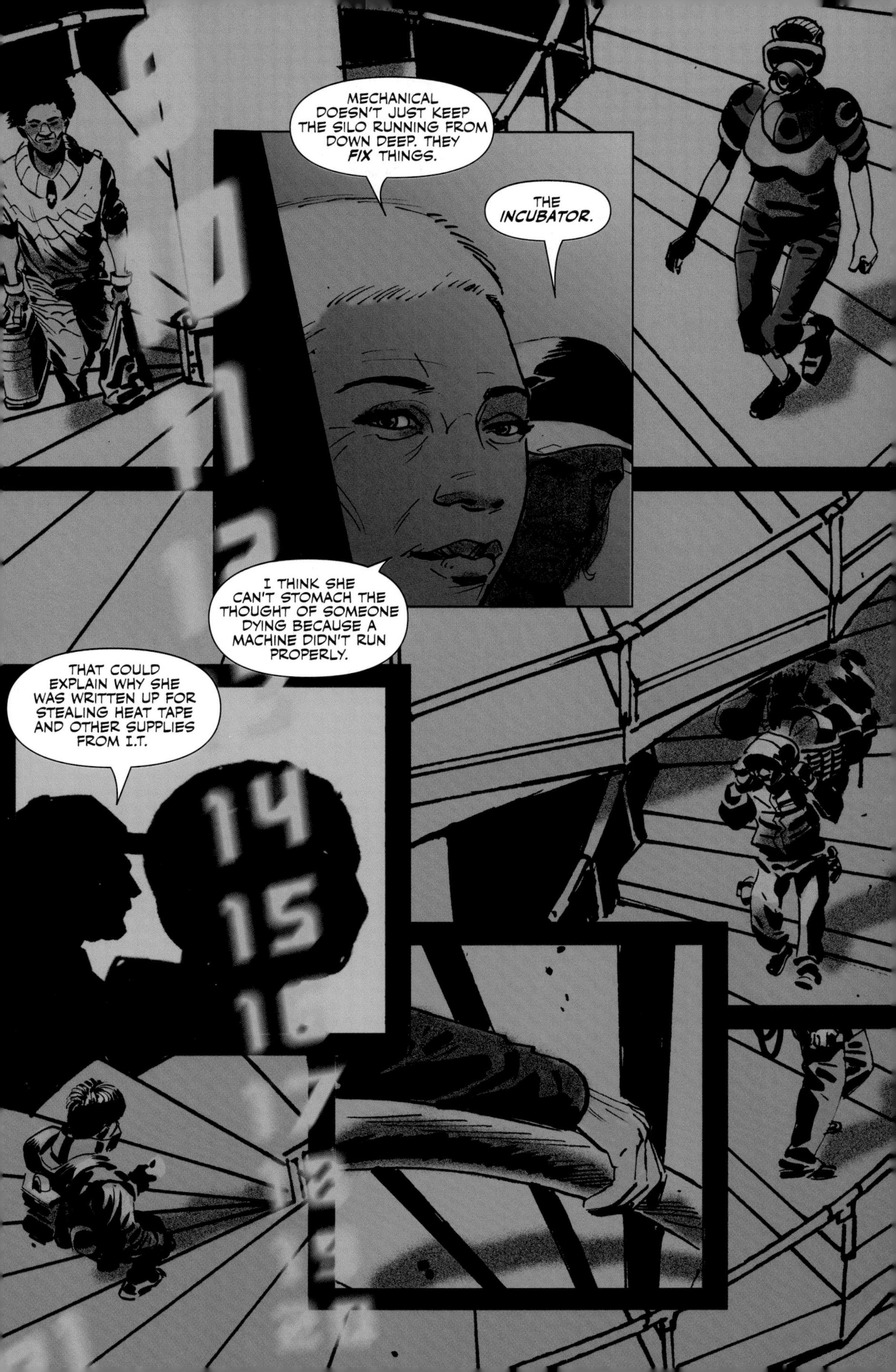
MECHANICAL DOESN'T JUST KEEP THE SILO RUNNING FROM DOWN DEEP. THEY *FIX* THINGS.
THE *INCUBATOR*.
I THINK SHE CAN'T STOMACH THE THOUGHT OF SOMEONE DYING BECAUSE A MACHINE DIDN'T RUN PROPERLY.
THAT COULD EXPLAIN WHY SHE WAS WRITTEN UP FOR STEALING HEAT TAPE AND OTHER SUPPLIES FROM I.T.
14
15

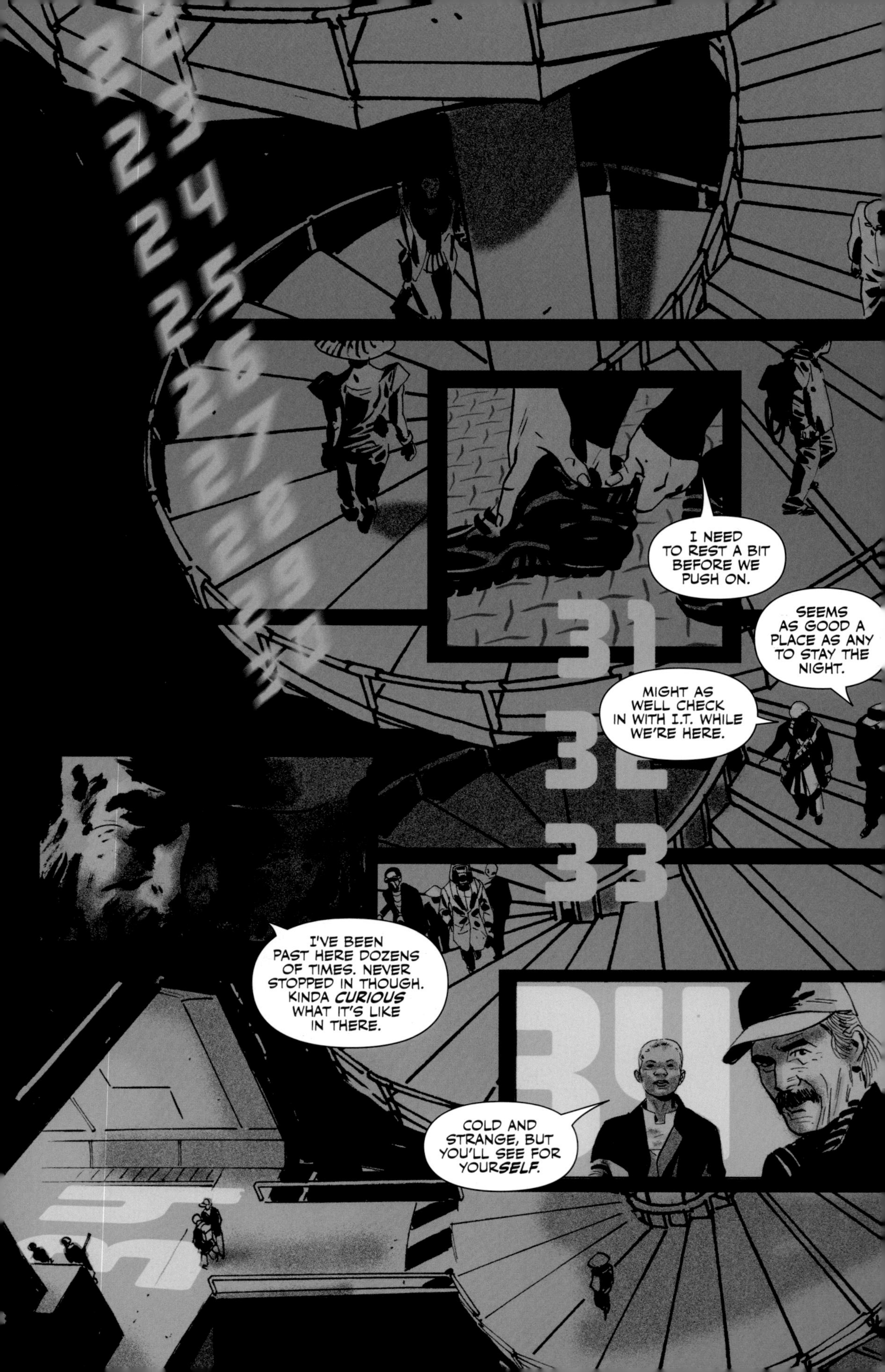
23
24
25
26
27
28
29
30
I NEED TO REST A BIT BEFORE WE PUSH ON.
SEEMS AS GOOD A PLACE AS ANY TO STAY THE NIGHT.
31
MIGHT AS WELL CHECK IN WITH I.T. WHILE WE'RE HERE.
32
33
I'VE BEEN PAST HERE DOZENS OF TIMES. NEVER STOPPED IN THOUGH. KINDA *CURIOUS* WHAT IT'S LIKE IN THERE.
34
COLD AND STRANGE, BUT YOU'LL SEE FOR YOUR*SELF*.

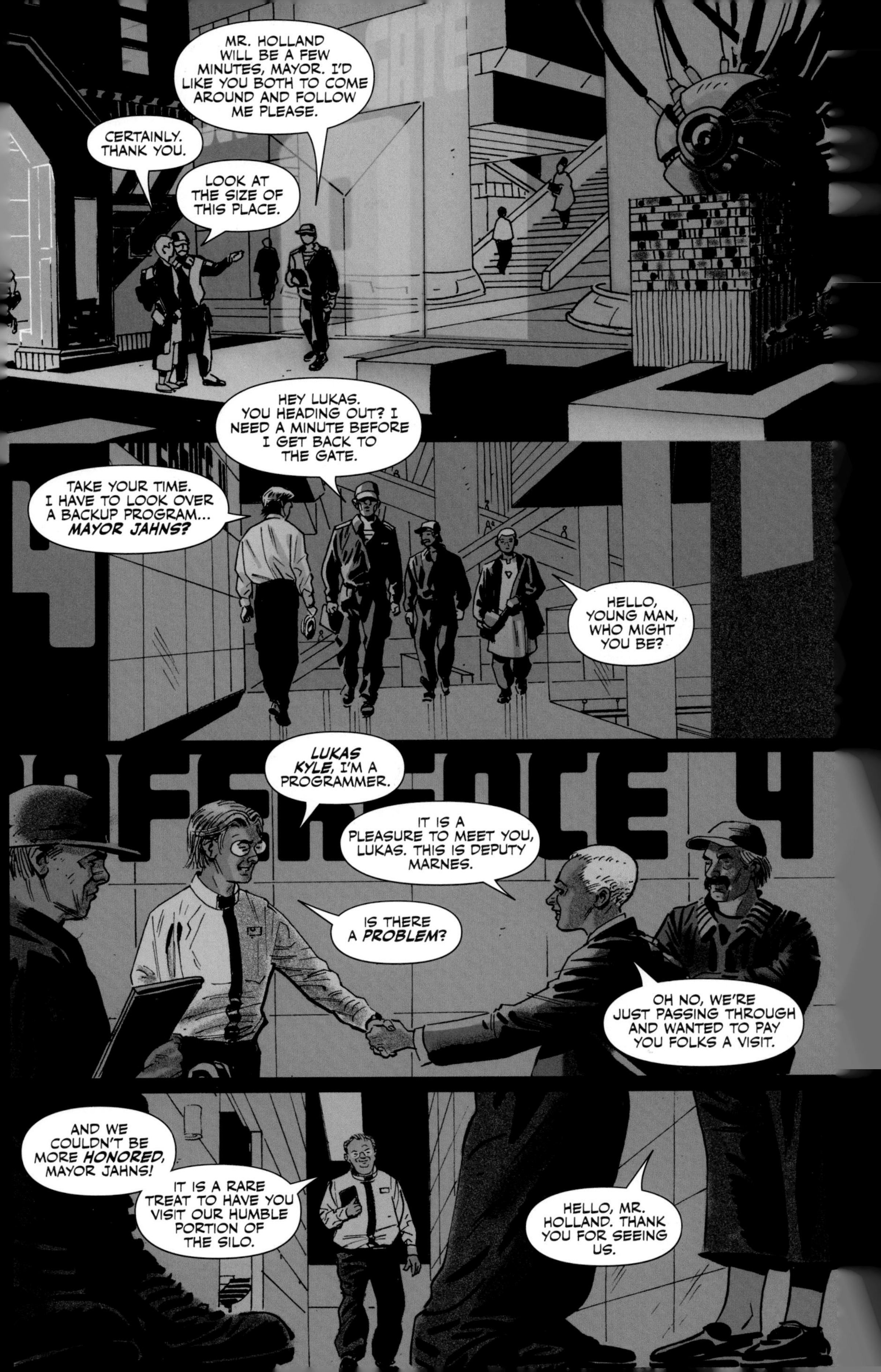
MR. HOLLAND WILL BE A FEW MINUTES, MAYOR. I'D LIKE YOU BOTH TO COME AROUND AND FOLLOW ME PLEASE.
CERTAINLY. THANK YOU.
LOOK AT THE SIZE OF THIS PLACE.
HEY LUKAS. YOU HEADING OUT? I NEED A MINUTE BEFORE I GET BACK TO THE GATE.
TAKE YOUR TIME. I HAVE TO LOOK OVER A BACKUP PROGRAM... *MAYOR JAHNS?*
HELLO, YOUNG MAN, WHO MIGHT YOU BE?
LUKAS KYLE, I'M A PROGRAMMER.
IT IS A PLEASURE TO MEET YOU, LUKAS. THIS IS DEPUTY MARNES.
IS THERE A *PROBLEM*?
OH NO, WE'RE JUST PASSING THROUGH AND WANTED TO PAY YOU FOLKS A VISIT.
AND WE COULDN'T BE MORE *HONORED*, MAYOR JAHNS!
IT IS A RARE TREAT TO HAVE YOU VISIT OUR HUMBLE PORTION OF THE SILO.
HELLO, MR. HOLLAND. THANK YOU FOR SEEING US.

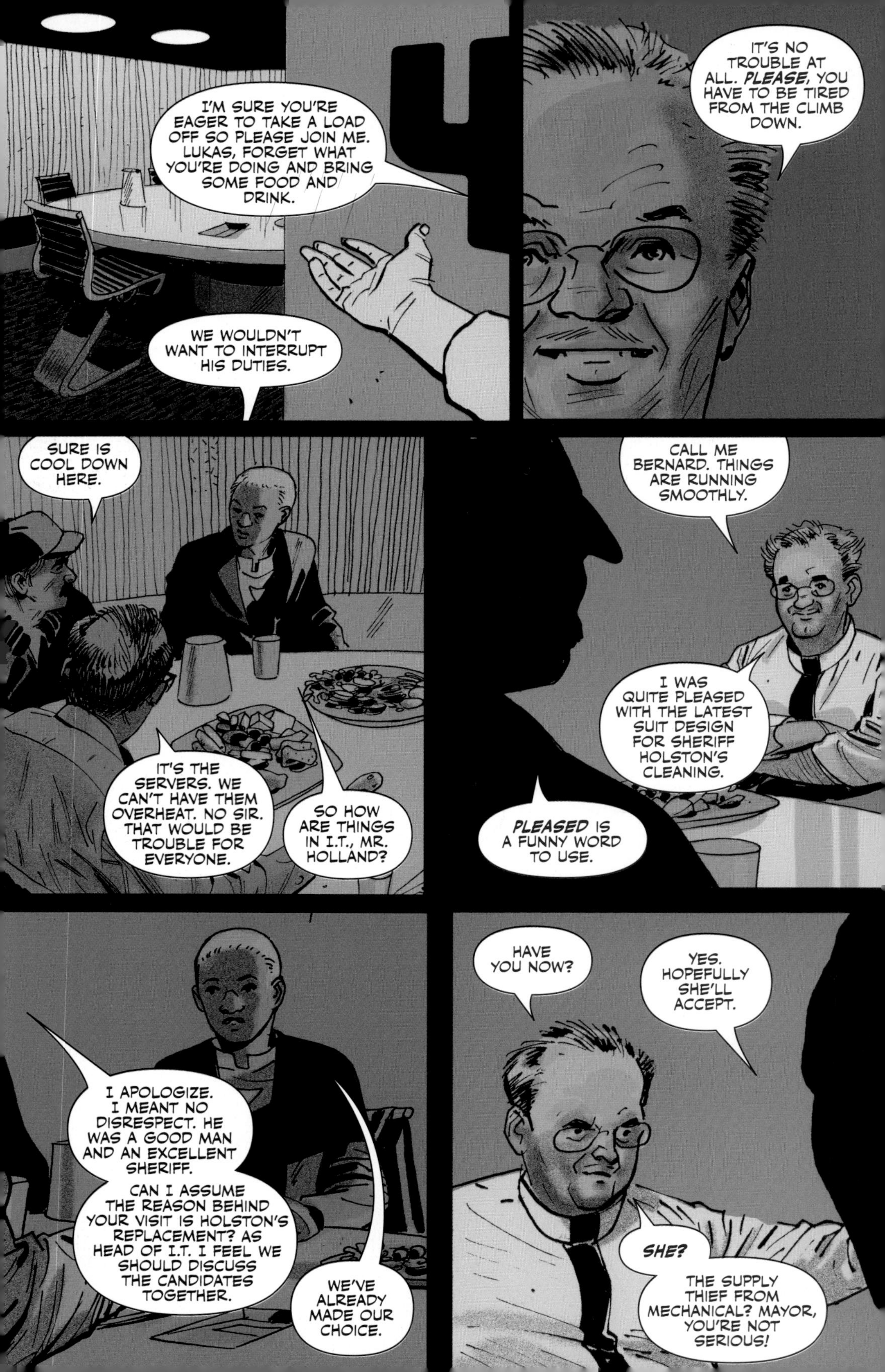
I'M SURE YOU'RE EAGER TO TAKE A LOAD OFF SO PLEASE JOIN ME. LUKAS, FORGET WHAT YOU'RE DOING AND BRING SOME FOOD AND DRINK.
WE WOULDN'T WANT TO INTERRUPT HIS DUTIES.
IT'S NO TROUBLE AT ALL. *PLEASE,* YOU HAVE TO BE TIRED FROM THE CLIMB DOWN.
SURE IS COOL DOWN HERE.
IT'S THE SERVERS. WE CAN'T HAVE THEM OVERHEAT. NO SIR. THAT WOULD BE TROUBLE FOR EVERYONE.
SO HOW ARE THINGS IN I.T., MR. HOLLAND?
CALL ME BERNARD. THINGS ARE RUNNING SMOOTHLY.
I WAS QUITE PLEASED WITH THE LATEST SUIT DESIGN FOR SHERIFF HOLSTON'S CLEANING.
PLEASED IS A FUNNY WORD TO USE.
I APOLOGIZE. I MEANT NO DISRESPECT. HE WAS A GOOD MAN AND AN EXCELLENT SHERIFF.
CAN I ASSUME THE REASON BEHIND YOUR VISIT IS HOLSTON'S REPLACEMENT? AS HEAD OF I.T. I FEEL WE SHOULD DISCUSS THE CANDIDATES TOGETHER.
WE'VE ALREADY MADE OUR CHOICE.
HAVE YOU NOW?
YES. HOPEFULLY SHE'LL ACCEPT.
SHE?
THE SUPPLY THIEF FROM MECHANICAL? MAYOR, YOU'RE NOT SERIOUS!

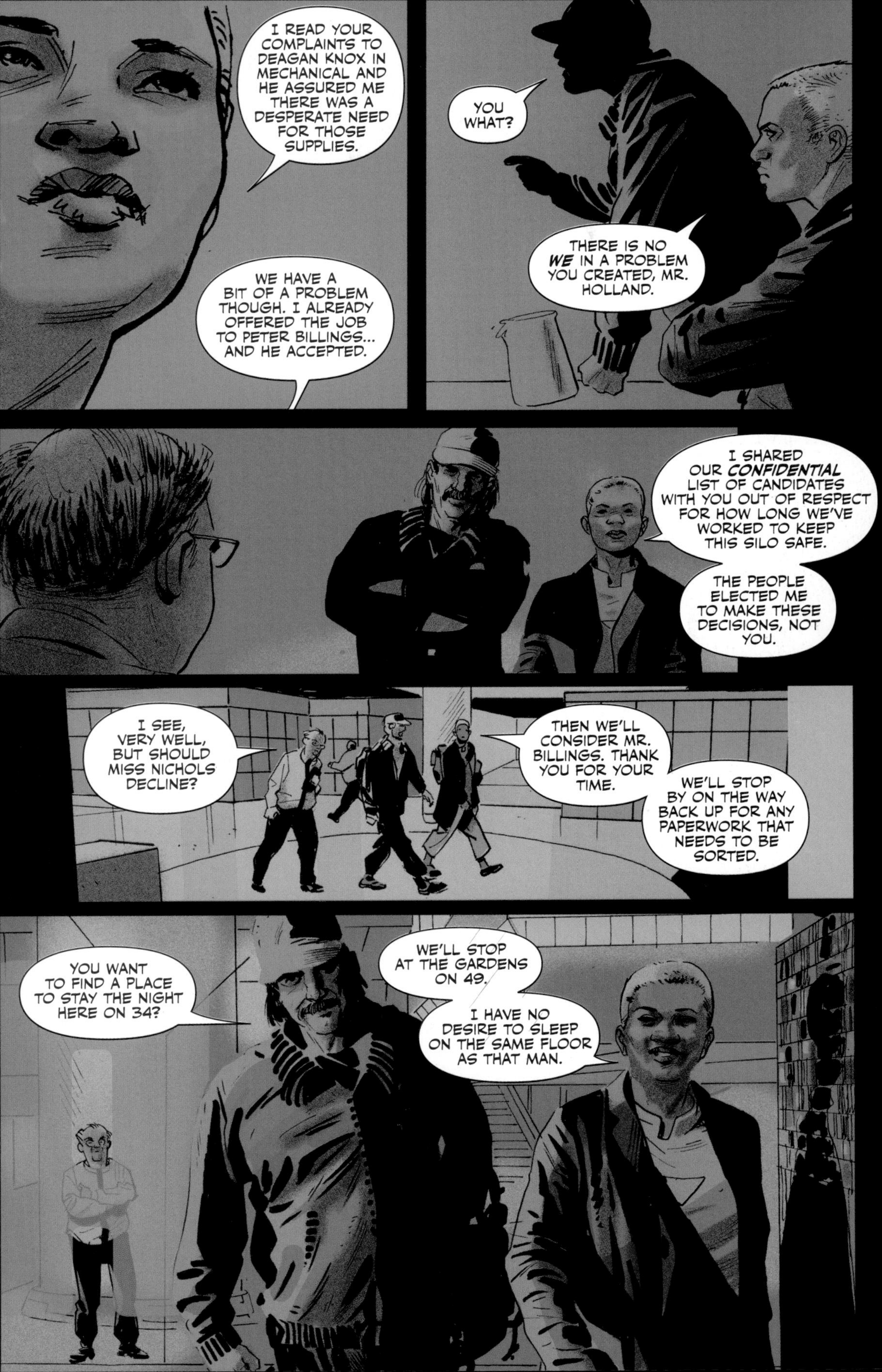
I READ YOUR COMPLAINTS TO DEAGAN KNOX IN MECHANICAL AND HE ASSURED ME THERE WAS A DESPERATE NEED FOR THOSE SUPPLIES.
WE HAVE A BIT OF A PROBLEM THOUGH. I ALREADY OFFERED THE JOB TO PETER BILLINGS... AND HE ACCEPTED.
YOU WHAT?
THERE IS NO *WE* IN A PROBLEM YOU CREATED, MR. HOLLAND.
I SHARED OUR ***CONFIDENTIAL*** LIST OF CANDIDATES WITH YOU OUT OF RESPECT FOR HOW LONG WE'VE WORKED TO KEEP THIS SILO SAFE.
THE PEOPLE ELECTED ME TO MAKE THESE DECISIONS, NOT YOU.
I SEE, VERY WELL, BUT SHOULD MISS NICHOLS DECLINE?
THEN WE'LL CONSIDER MR. BILLINGS. THANK YOU FOR YOUR TIME.
WE'LL STOP BY ON THE WAY BACK UP FOR ANY PAPERWORK THAT NEEDS TO BE SORTED.
YOU WANT TO FIND A PLACE TO STAY THE NIGHT HERE ON 34?
WE'LL STOP AT THE GARDENS ON 49.
I HAVE NO DESIRE TO SLEEP ON THE SAME FLOOR AS THAT MAN.

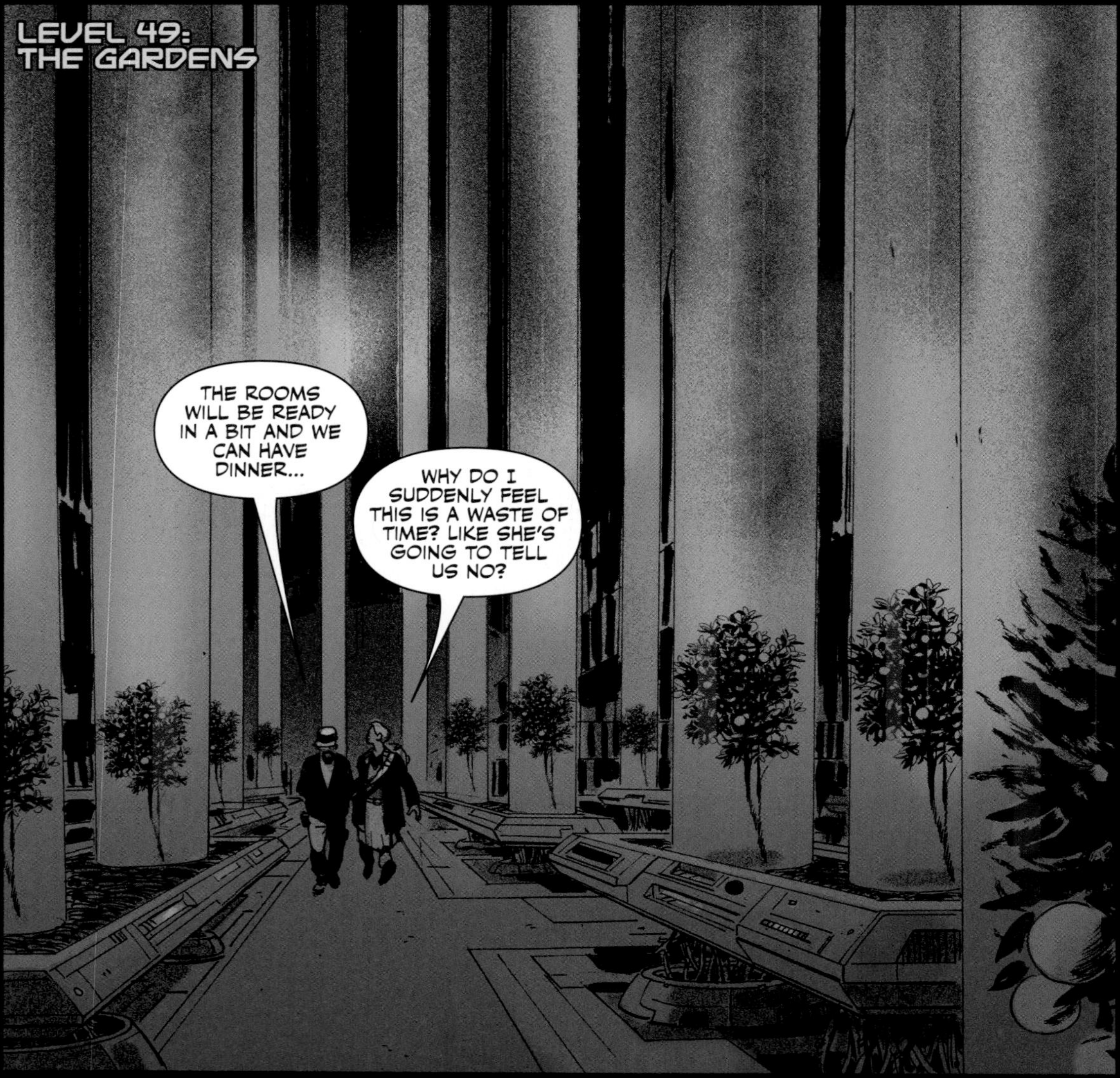
LEVEL 49:
THE GARDENS
THE ROOMS WILL BE READY IN A BIT AND WE CAN HAVE DINNER...
WHY DO I SUDDENLY FEEL THIS IS A WASTE OF TIME? LIKE SHE'S GOING TO TELL US NO?

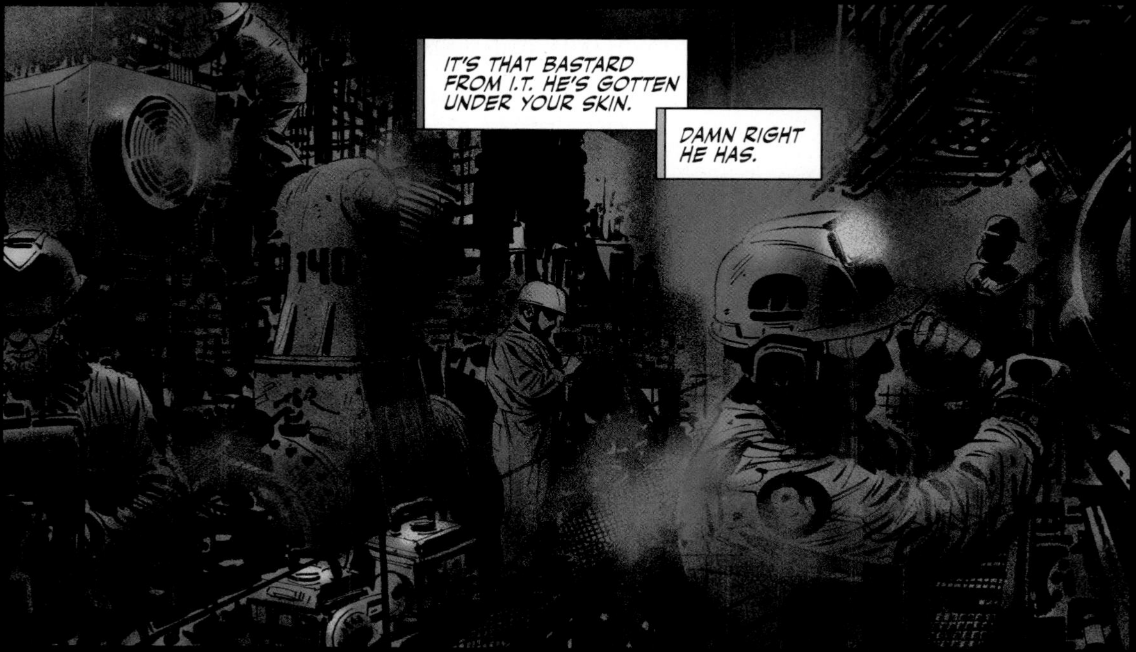
IT'S THAT BASTARD FROM I.T. HE'S GOTTEN UNDER YOUR SKIN.
DAMN RIGHT HE HAS.

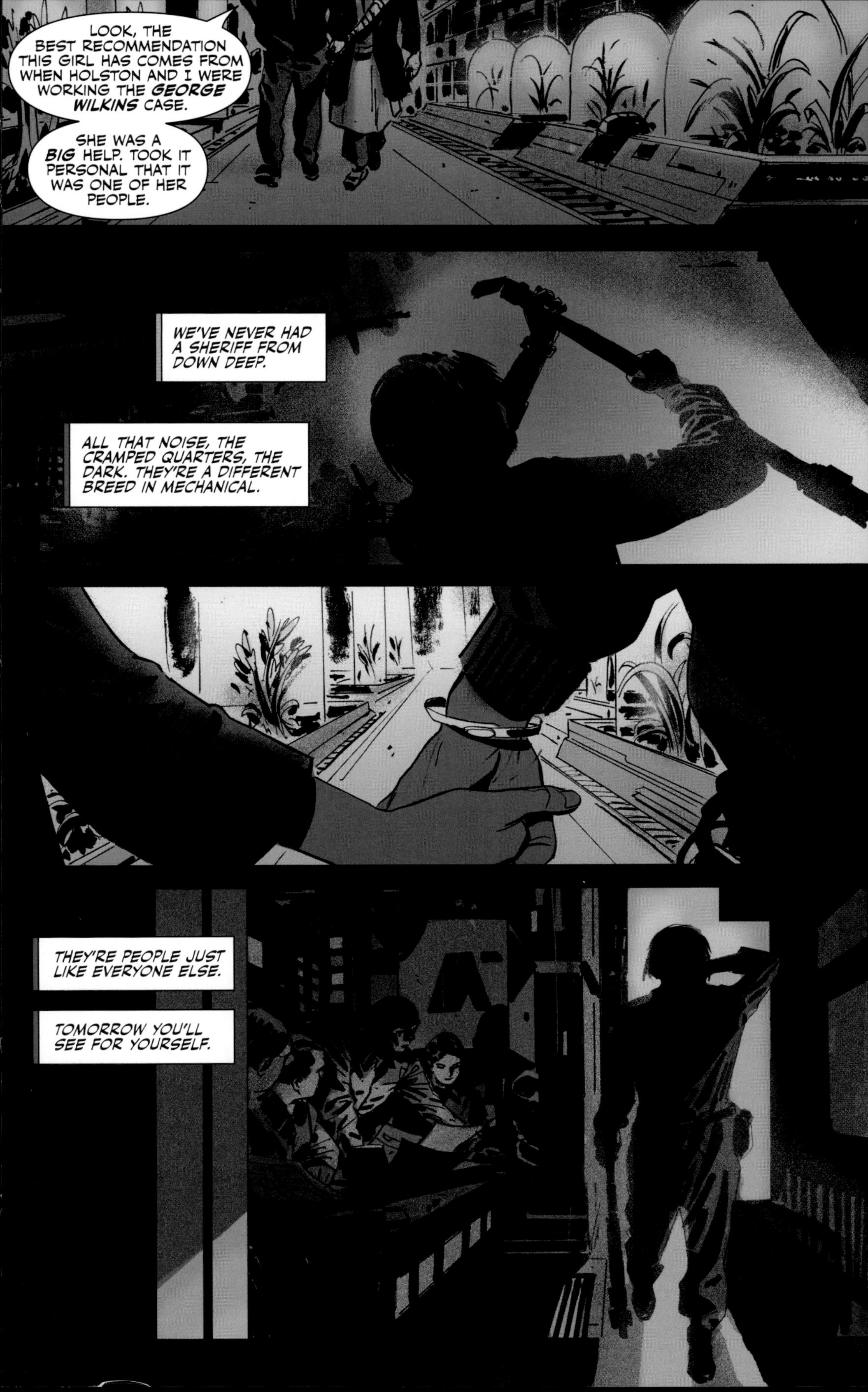

LOOK, THE BEST RECOMMENDATION THIS GIRL HAS COMES FROM WHEN HOLSTON AND I WERE WORKING THE *GEORGE WILKINS* CASE.
SHE WAS A *BIG* HELP. TOOK IT PERSONAL THAT IT WAS ONE OF HER PEOPLE.
WE'VE NEVER HAD A SHERIFF FROM DOWN DEEP.
ALL THAT NOISE, THE CRAMPED QUARTERS, THE DARK. THEY'RE A DIFFERENT BREED IN MECHANICAL.
THEY'RE PEOPLE JUST LIKE EVERYONE ELSE.
TOMORROW YOU'LL SEE FOR YOURSELF.

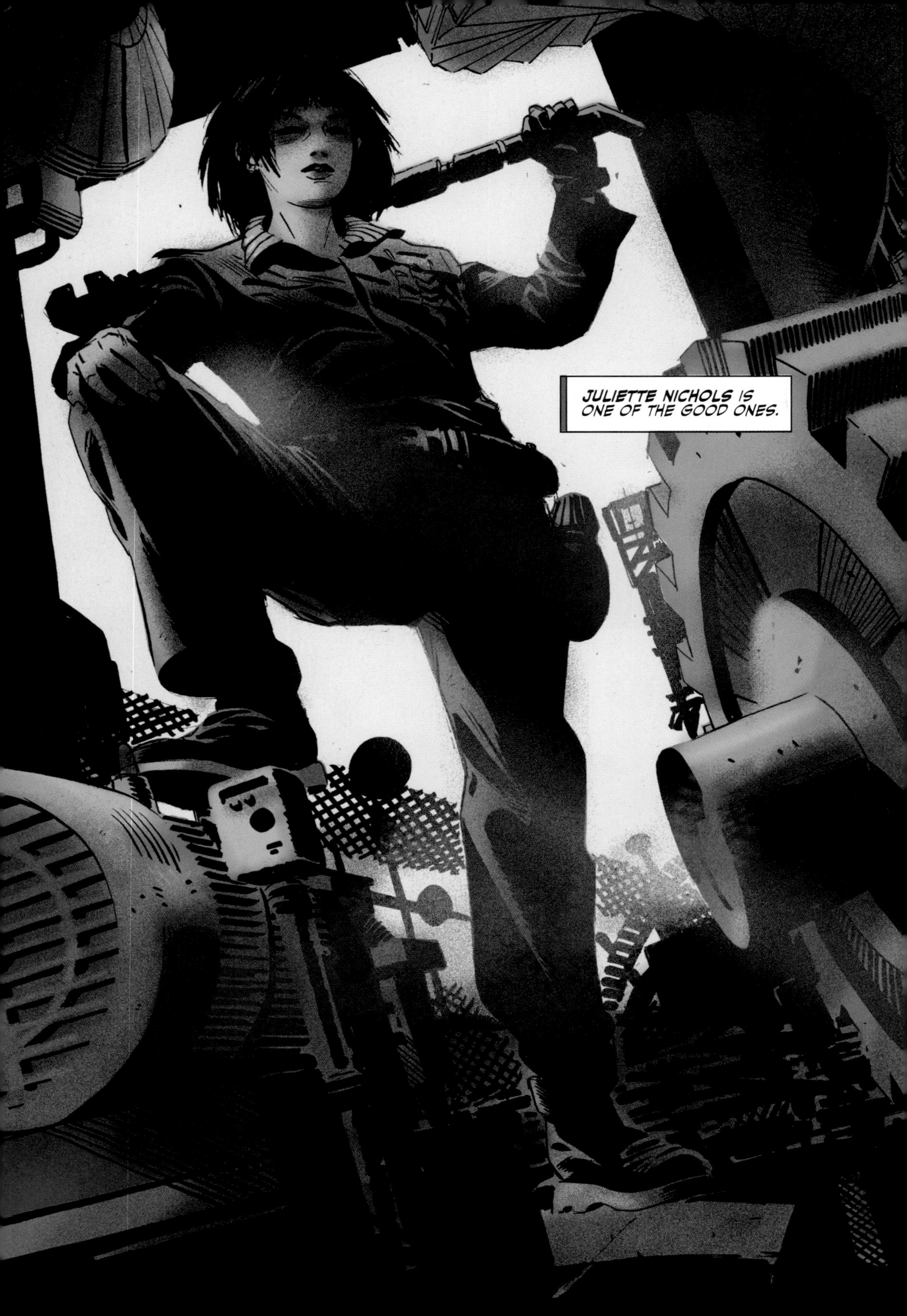
JULIETTE NICHOLS IS ONE OF THE GOOD ONES.

TO BE CONTINUED IN THE NEXT ISSUE.

END ISSUE 1

ISSUE 2

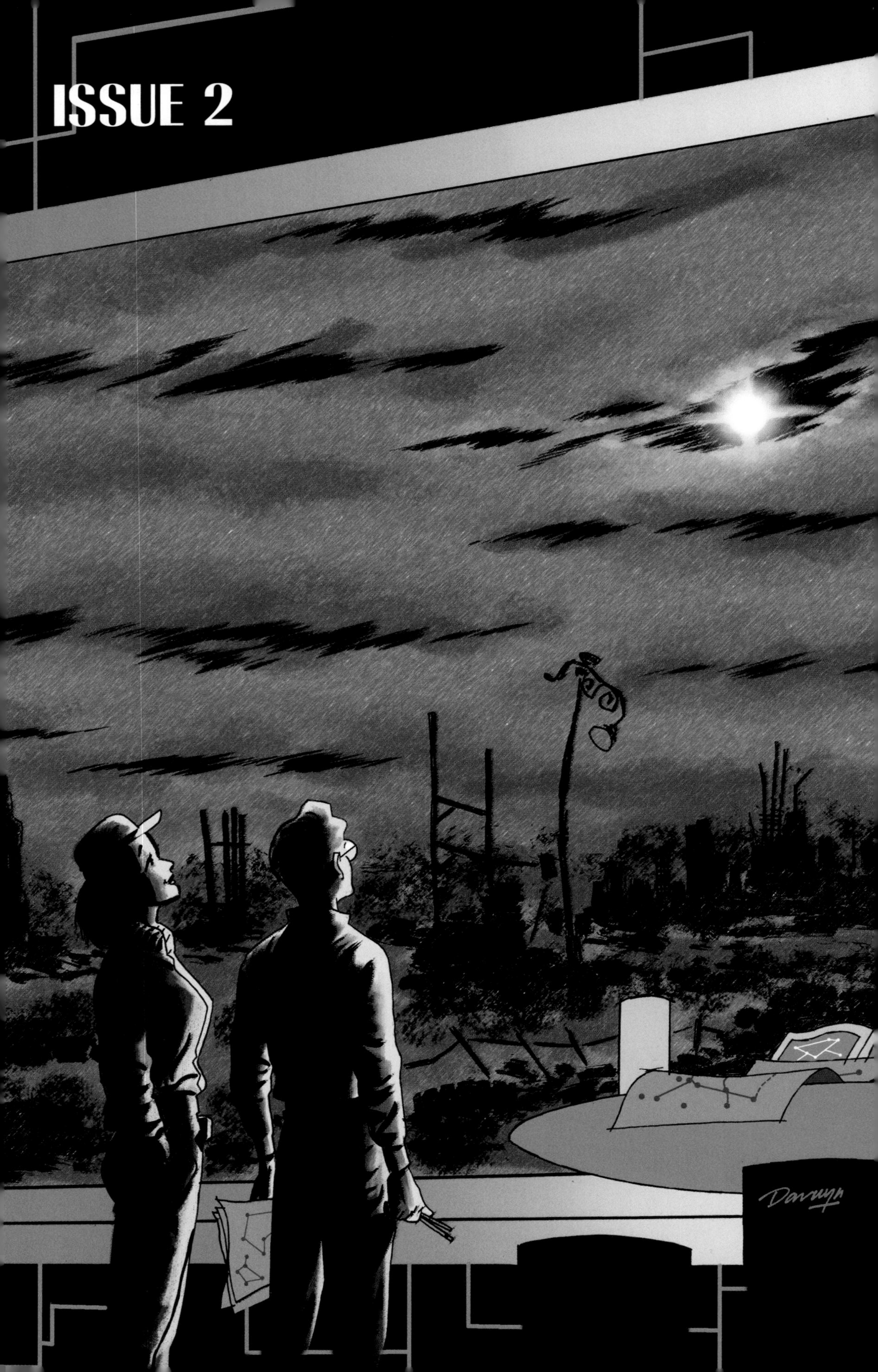

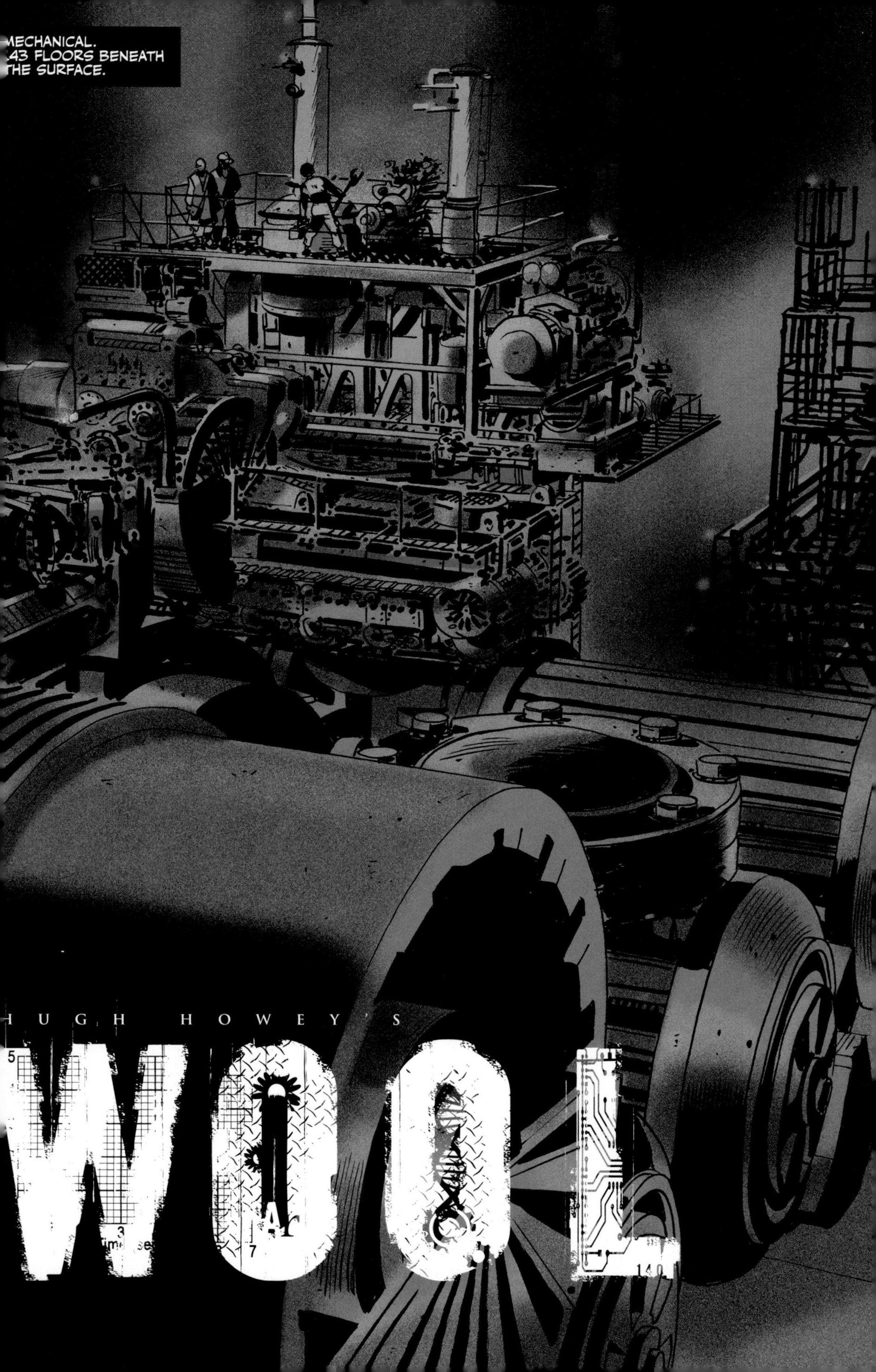
MECHANICAL.
143 FLOORS BENEATH
THE SURFACE.
HUGH HOWEY'S
WOOL

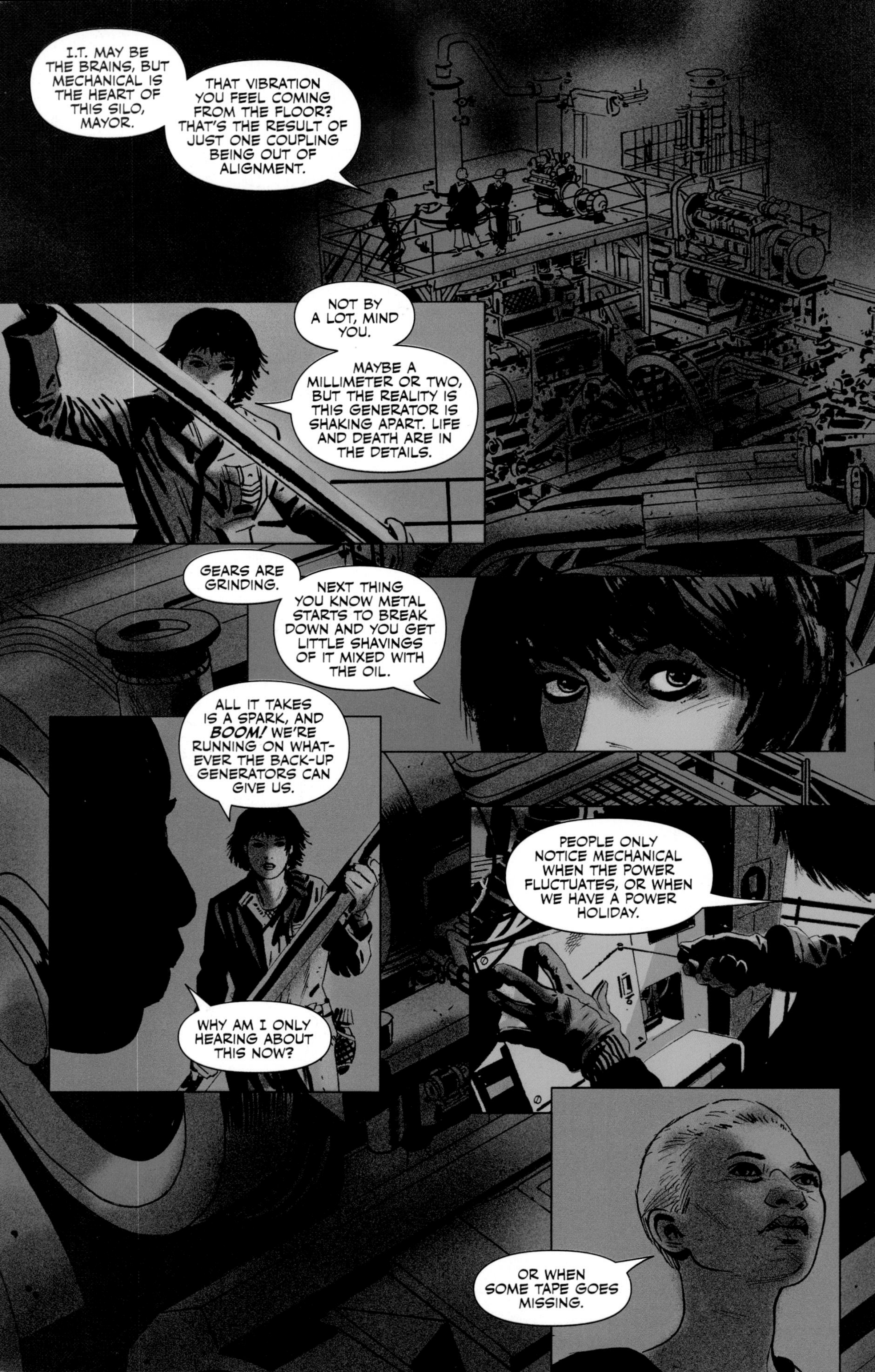
I.T. MAY BE THE BRAINS, BUT MECHANICAL IS THE HEART OF THIS SILO, MAYOR.
THAT VIBRATION YOU FEEL COMING FROM THE FLOOR? THAT'S THE RESULT OF JUST ONE COUPLING BEING OUT OF ALIGNMENT.
NOT BY A LOT, MIND YOU.
MAYBE A MILLIMETER OR TWO, BUT THE REALITY IS THIS GENERATOR IS SHAKING APART. LIFE AND DEATH ARE IN THE DETAILS.
GEARS ARE GRINDING.
NEXT THING YOU KNOW METAL STARTS TO BREAK DOWN AND YOU GET LITTLE SHAVINGS OF IT MIXED WITH THE OIL.
ALL IT TAKES IS A SPARK, AND ***BOOM!*** WE'RE RUNNING ON WHATEVER THE BACK-UP GENERATORS CAN GIVE US.
WHY AM I ONLY HEARING ABOUT THIS NOW?
PEOPLE ONLY NOTICE MECHANICAL WHEN THE POWER FLUCTUATES, OR WHEN WE HAVE A POWER HOLIDAY.
OR WHEN SOME TAPE GOES MISSING.

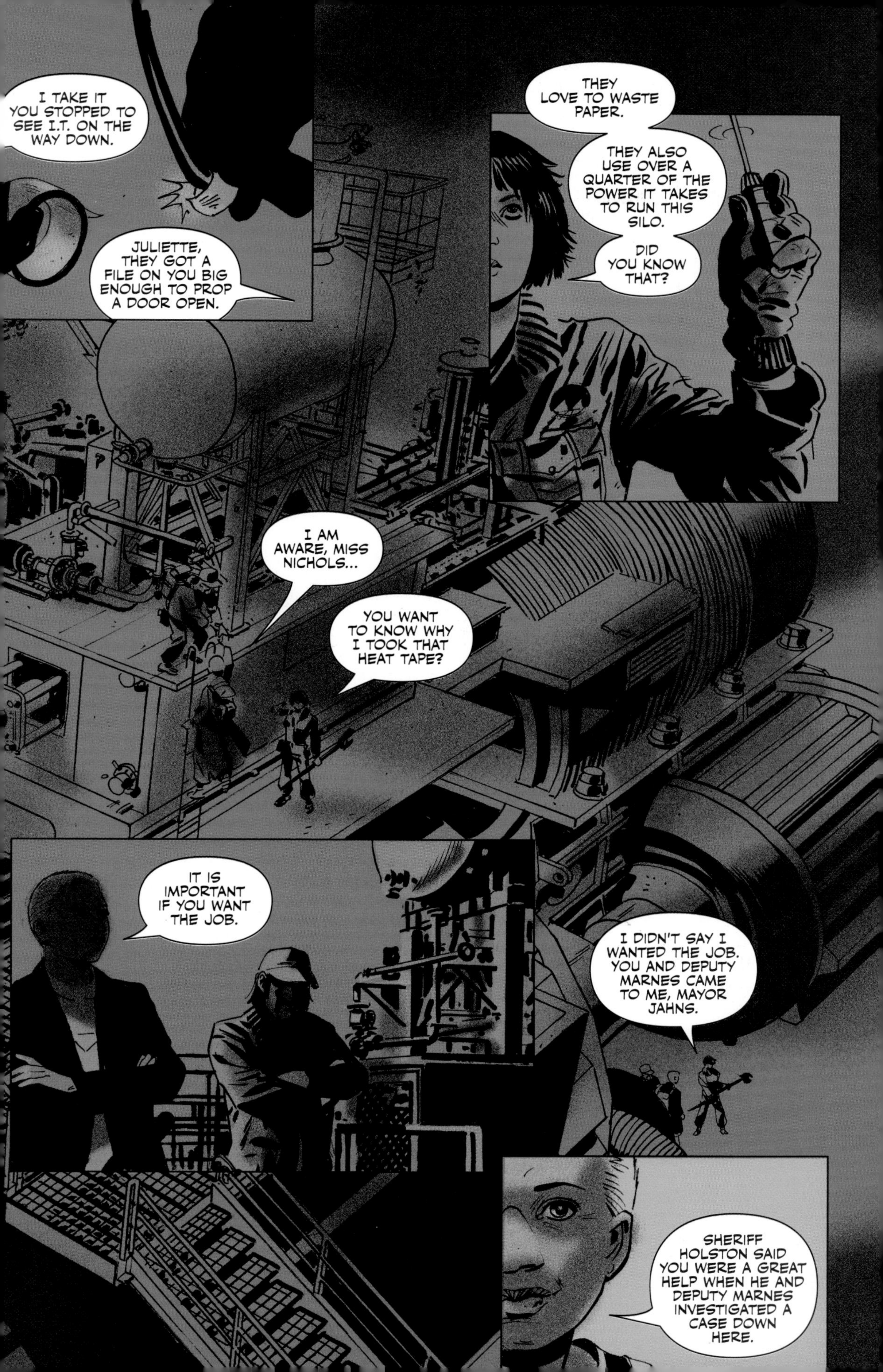
I TAKE IT YOU STOPPED TO SEE I.T. ON THE WAY DOWN.
JULIETTE, THEY GOT A FILE ON YOU BIG ENOUGH TO PROP A DOOR OPEN.
THEY LOVE TO WASTE PAPER.
THEY ALSO USE OVER A QUARTER OF THE POWER IT TAKES TO RUN THIS SILO.
DID YOU KNOW THAT?
I AM AWARE, MISS NICHOLS...
YOU WANT TO KNOW WHY I TOOK THAT HEAT TAPE?
IT IS IMPORTANT IF YOU WANT THE JOB.
I DIDN'T SAY I WANTED THE JOB. YOU AND DEPUTY MARNES CAME TO ME, MAYOR JAHNS.
SHERIFF HOLSTON SAID YOU WERE A GREAT HELP WHEN HE AND DEPUTY MARNES INVESTIGATED A CASE DOWN HERE.

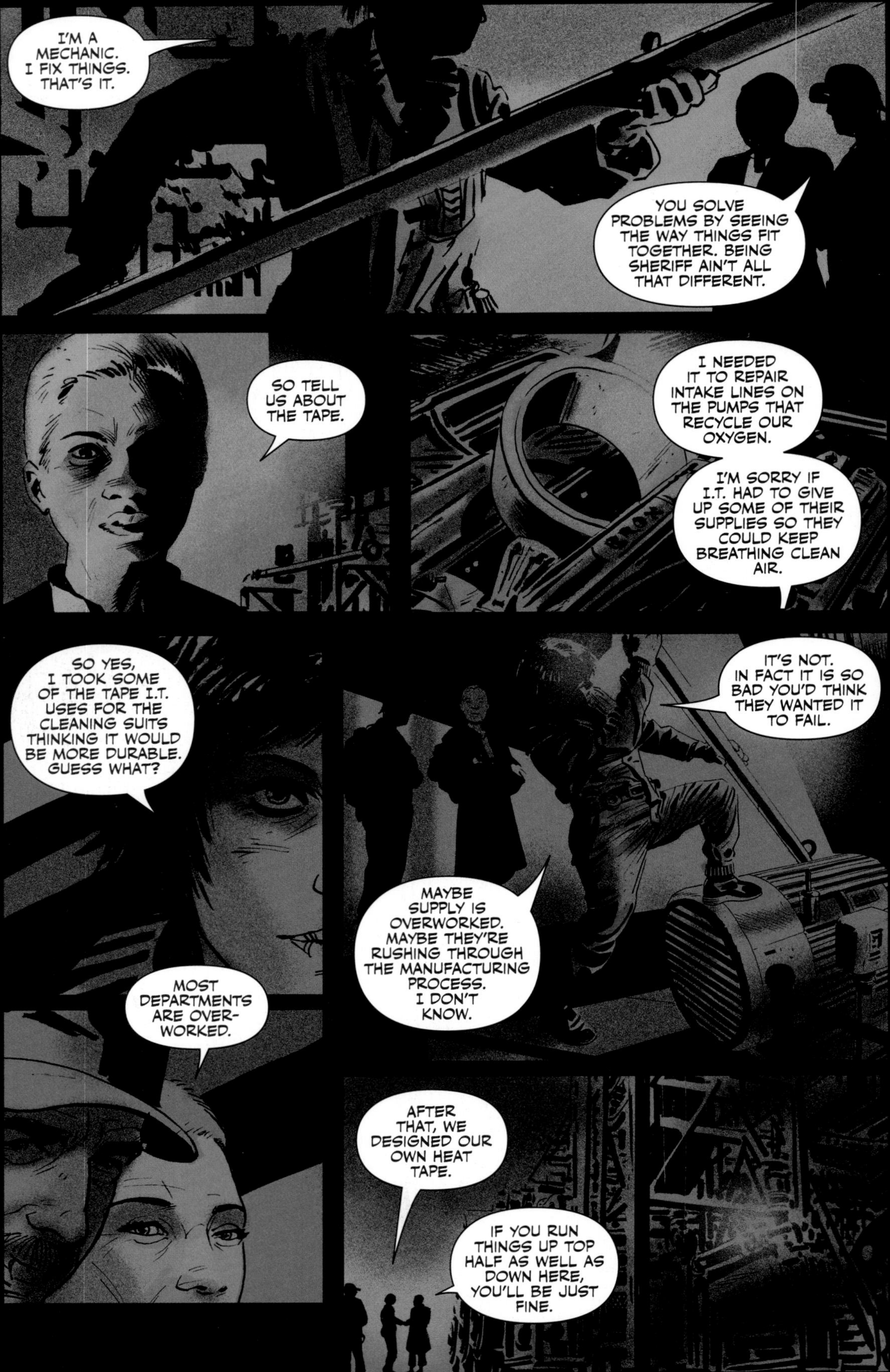
I'M A MECHANIC. I FIX THINGS. THAT'S IT.
YOU SOLVE PROBLEMS BY SEEING THE WAY THINGS FIT TOGETHER. BEING SHERIFF AIN'T ALL THAT DIFFERENT.
SO TELL US ABOUT THE TAPE.
I NEEDED IT TO REPAIR INTAKE LINES ON THE PUMPS THAT RECYCLE OUR OXYGEN.
I'M SORRY IF I.T. HAD TO GIVE UP SOME OF THEIR SUPPLIES SO THEY COULD KEEP BREATHING CLEAN AIR.
SO YES, I TOOK SOME OF THE TAPE I.T. USES FOR THE CLEANING SUITS THINKING IT WOULD BE MORE DURABLE. GUESS WHAT?
IT'S NOT. IN FACT IT IS SO BAD YOU'D THINK THEY WANTED IT TO FAIL.
MAYBE SUPPLY IS OVERWORKED. MAYBE THEY'RE RUSHING THROUGH THE MANUFACTURING PROCESS. I DON'T KNOW.
MOST DEPARTMENTS ARE OVER-WORKED.
AFTER THAT, WE DESIGNED OUR OWN HEAT TAPE.
IF YOU RUN THINGS UP TOP HALF AS WELL AS DOWN HERE, YOU'LL BE JUST FINE.

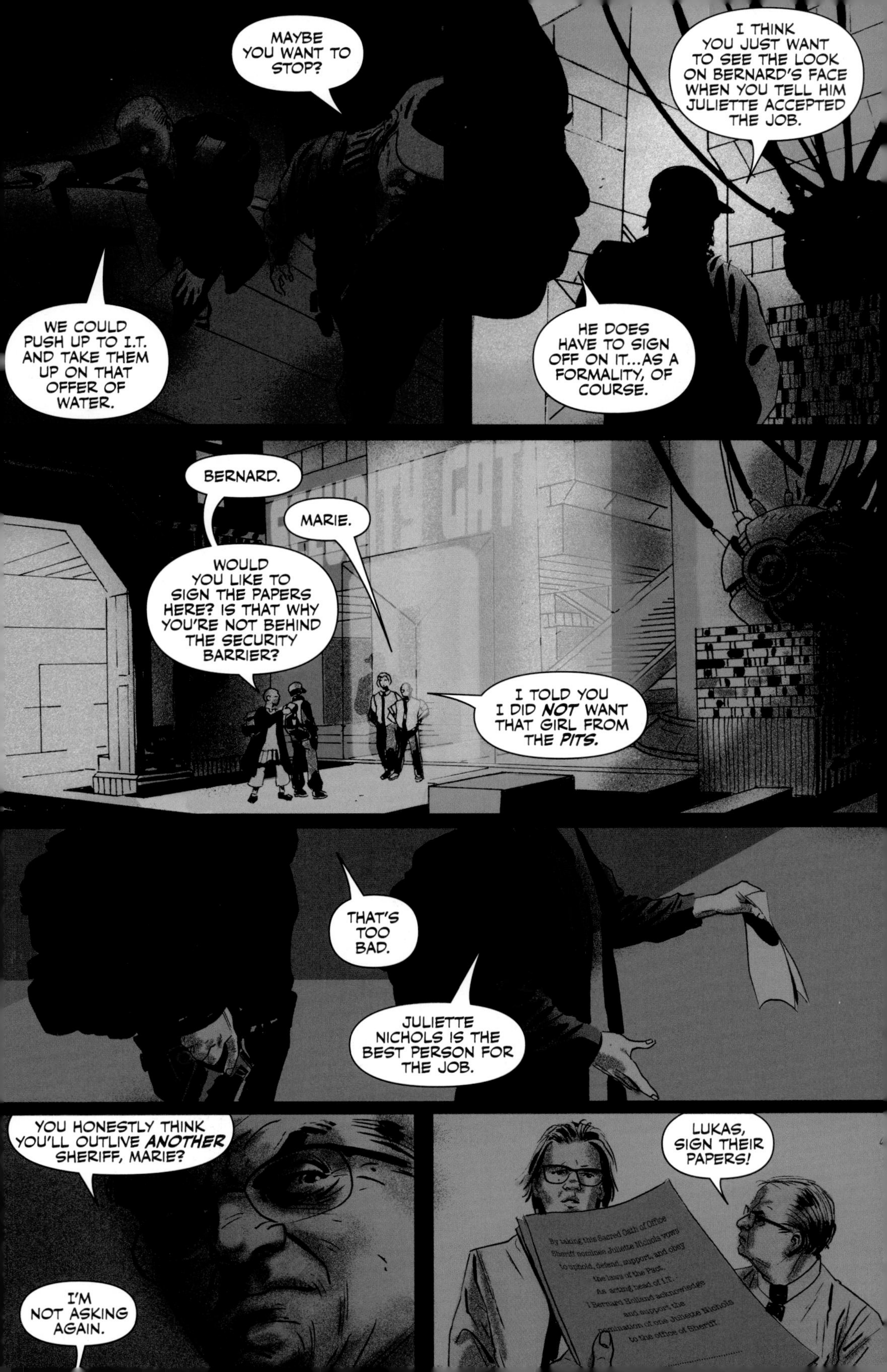
MAYBE YOU WANT TO STOP?
WE COULD PUSH UP TO I.T. AND TAKE THEM UP ON THAT OFFER OF WATER.
I THINK YOU JUST WANT TO SEE THE LOOK ON BERNARD'S FACE WHEN YOU TELL HIM JULIETTE ACCEPTED THE JOB.
HE DOES HAVE TO SIGN OFF ON IT...AS A FORMALITY, OF COURSE.
BERNARD.
MARIE.
WOULD YOU LIKE TO SIGN THE PAPERS HERE? IS THAT WHY YOU'RE NOT BEHIND THE SECURITY BARRIER?
I TOLD YOU I DID *NOT* WANT THAT GIRL FROM THE *PITS.*
THAT'S TOO BAD.
JULIETTE NICHOLS IS THE BEST PERSON FOR THE JOB.
YOU HONESTLY THINK YOU'LL OUTLIVE *ANOTHER* SHERIFF, MARIE?
I'M NOT ASKING AGAIN.
LUKAS, SIGN THEIR PAPERS!
By taking this Sacred Oath of Office Sheriff nominee Juliette Nichols vows to uphold, defend, support, and obey the laws of the Pact.
As acting head of I.T. I Bernard Holland acknowledge and support the nomination of one Juliette Nichols to the office of Sheriff.

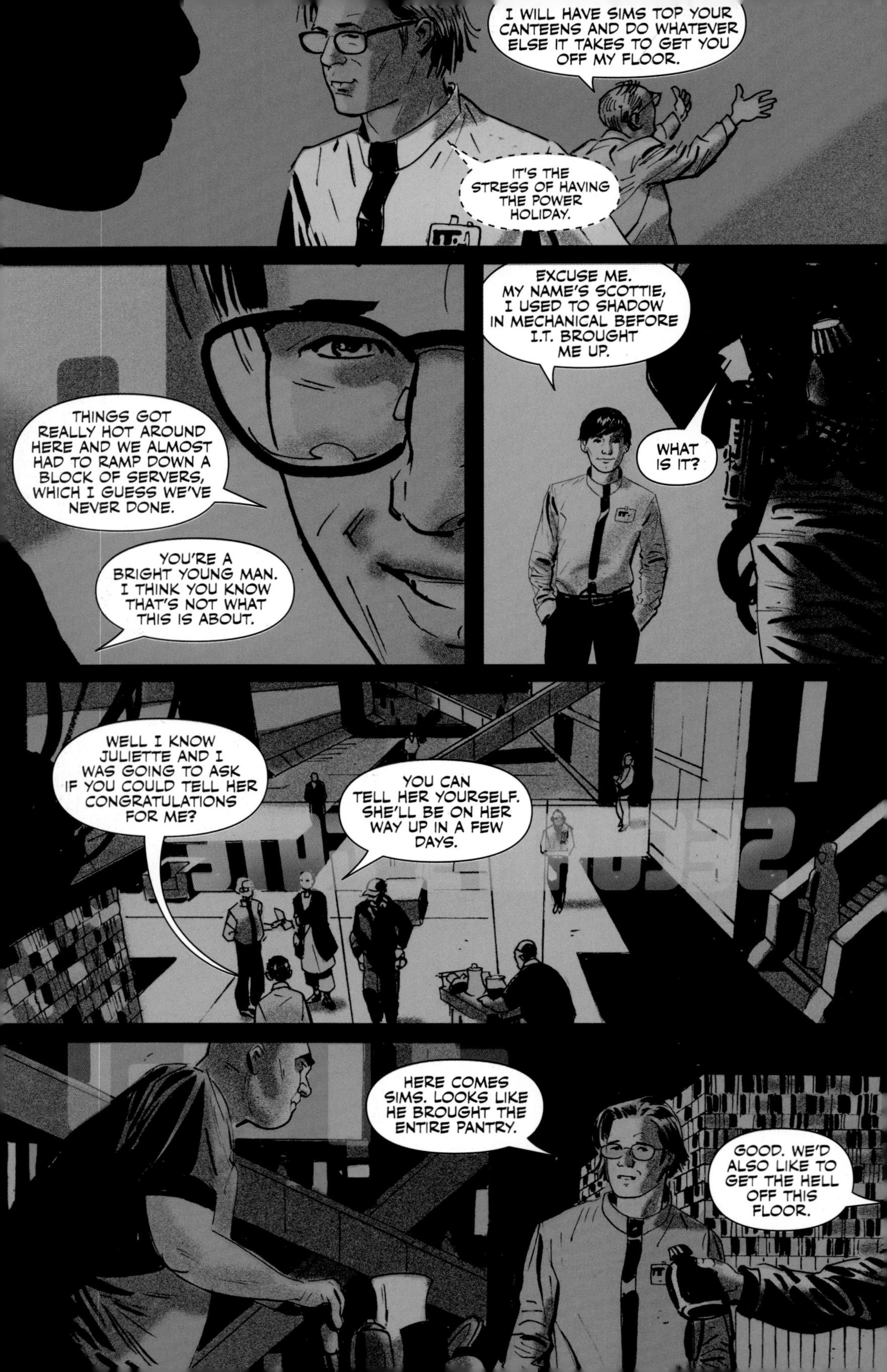
I WILL HAVE SIMS TOP YOUR CANTEENS AND DO WHATEVER ELSE IT TAKES TO GET YOU OFF MY FLOOR.
IT'S THE STRESS OF HAVING THE POWER HOLIDAY.
THINGS GOT REALLY HOT AROUND HERE AND WE ALMOST HAD TO RAMP DOWN A BLOCK OF SERVERS, WHICH I GUESS WE'VE NEVER DONE.
YOU'RE A BRIGHT YOUNG MAN. I THINK YOU KNOW THAT'S NOT WHAT THIS IS ABOUT.
EXCUSE ME. MY NAME'S SCOTTIE, I USED TO SHADOW IN MECHANICAL BEFORE I.T. BROUGHT ME UP.
WHAT IS IT?
WELL I KNOW JULIETTE AND I WAS GOING TO ASK IF YOU COULD TELL HER CONGRATULATIONS FOR ME?
YOU CAN TELL HER YOURSELF. SHE'LL BE ON HER WAY UP IN A FEW DAYS.
HERE COMES SIMS. LOOKS LIKE HE BROUGHT THE ENTIRE PANTRY.
GOOD. WE'D ALSO LIKE TO GET THE HELL OFF THIS FLOOR.

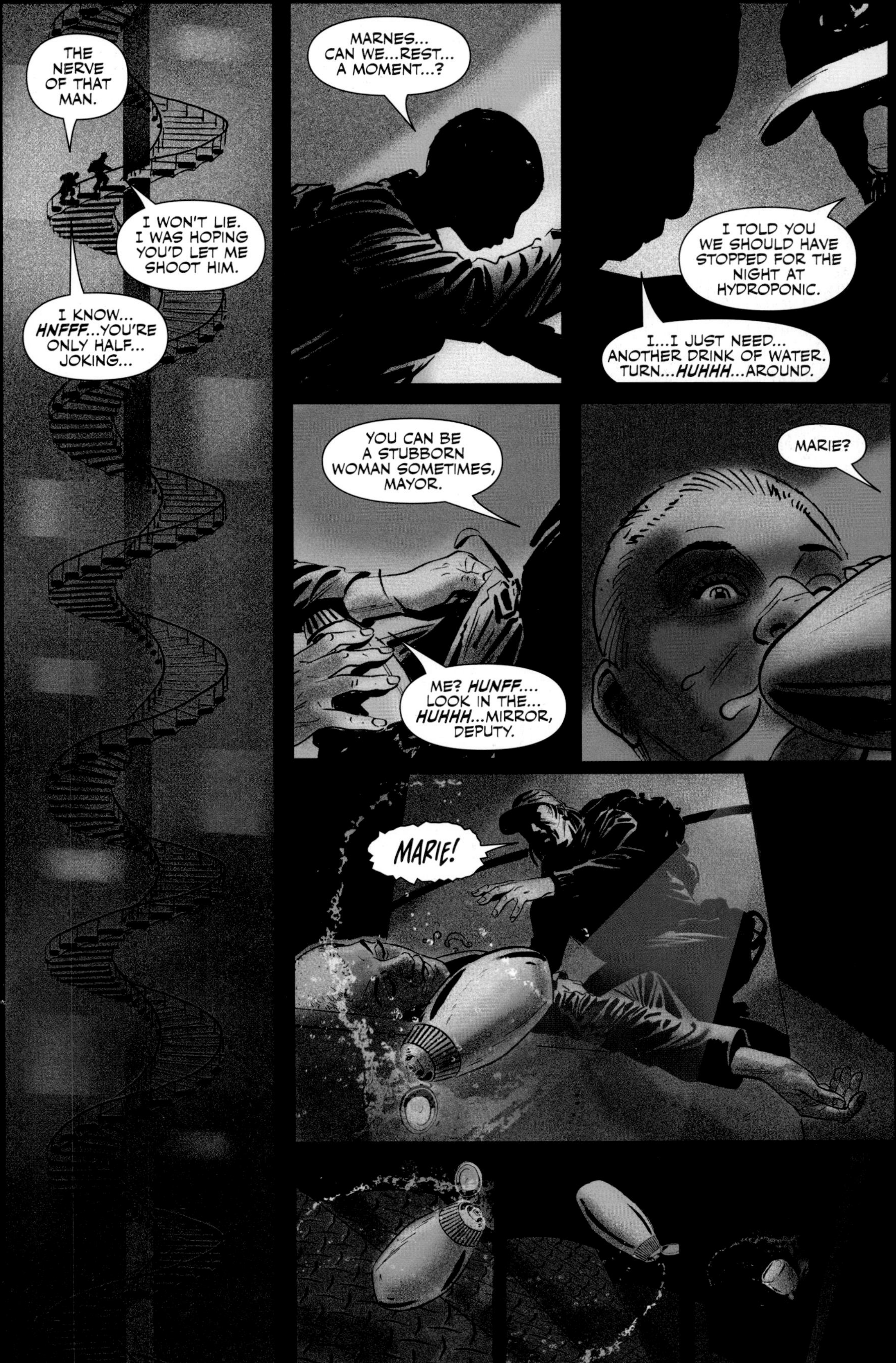
THE NERVE OF THAT MAN.
I WON'T LIE. I WAS HOPING YOU'D LET ME SHOOT HIM.
I KNOW... HNFFF...YOU'RE ONLY HALF... JOKING...
MARNES... CAN WE...REST... A MOMENT...?
I TOLD YOU WE SHOULD HAVE STOPPED FOR THE NIGHT AT HYDROPONIC.
I...I JUST NEED... ANOTHER DRINK OF WATER. TURN...HUHHH...AROUND.
YOU CAN BE A STUBBORN WOMAN SOMETIMES, MAYOR.
ME? HUNFF.... LOOK IN THE... HUHHH...MIRROR, DEPUTY.
MARIE?
MARIE!

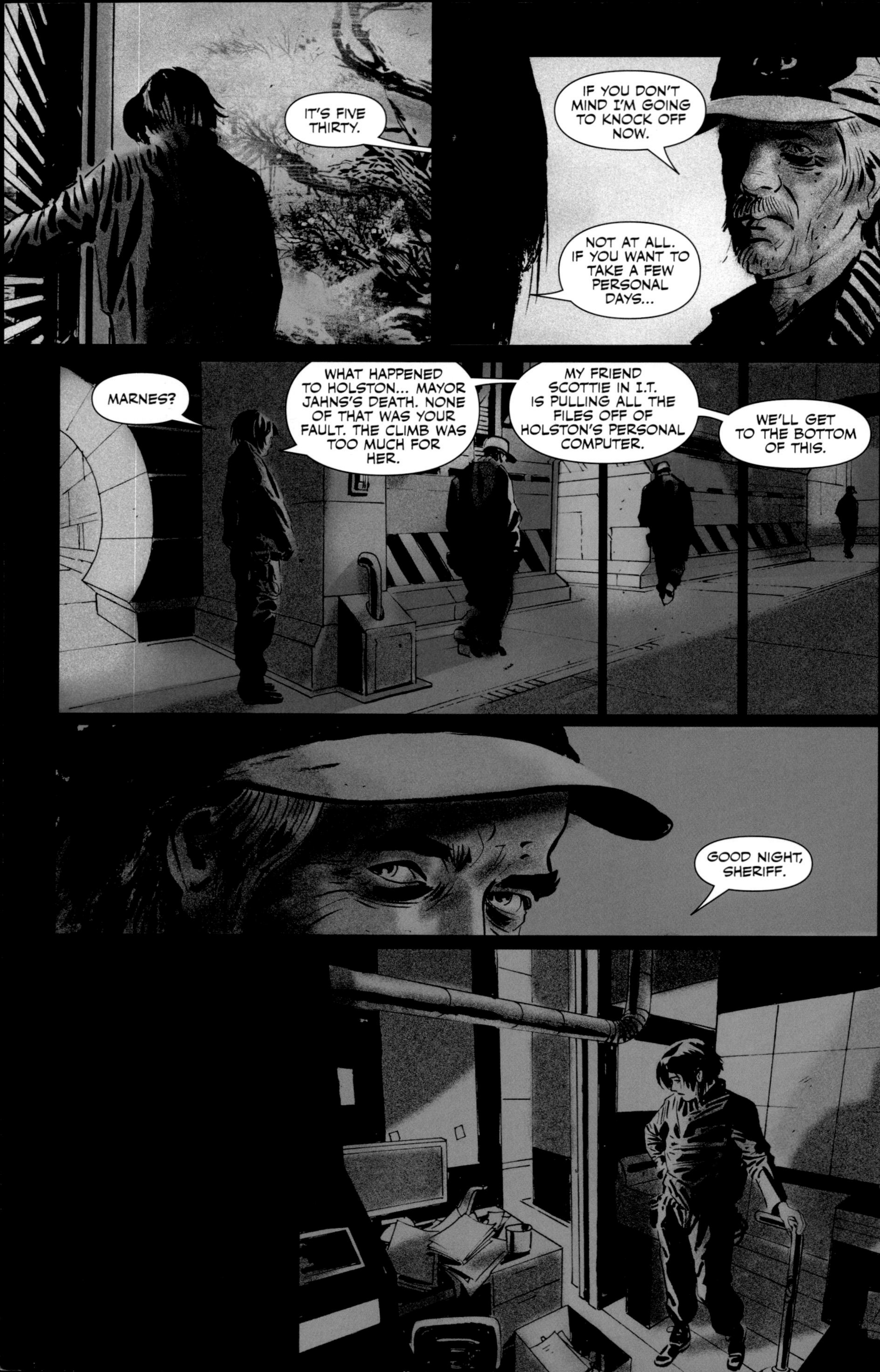
IT'S FIVE THIRTY.
IF YOU DON'T MIND I'M GOING TO KNOCK OFF NOW.
NOT AT ALL. IF YOU WANT TO TAKE A FEW PERSONAL DAYS...
MARNES?
WHAT HAPPENED TO HOLSTON... MAYOR JAHNS'S DEATH. NONE OF THAT WAS YOUR FAULT. THE CLIMB WAS TOO MUCH FOR HER.
MY FRIEND SCOTTIE IN I.T. IS PULLING ALL THE FILES OFF OF HOLSTON'S PERSONAL COMPUTER.
WE'LL GET TO THE BOTTOM OF THIS.
GOOD NIGHT, SHERIFF.

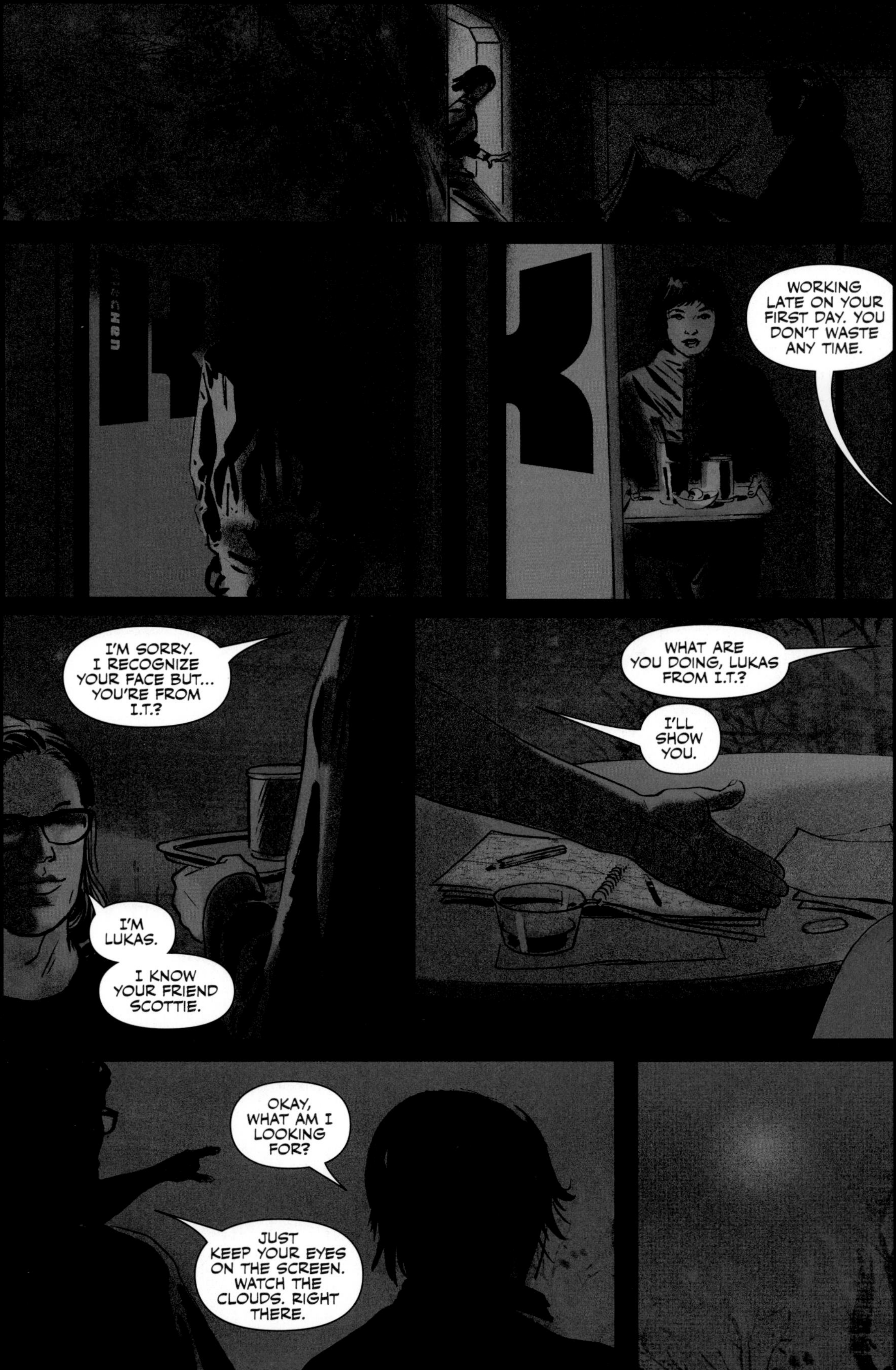
WORKING LATE ON YOUR FIRST DAY. YOU DON'T WASTE ANY TIME.
I'M SORRY. I RECOGNIZE YOUR FACE BUT... YOU'RE FROM I.T.?
I'M LUKAS.
I KNOW YOUR FRIEND SCOTTIE.
WHAT ARE YOU DOING, LUKAS FROM I.T.?
I'LL SHOW YOU.
OKAY, WHAT AM I LOOKING FOR?
JUST KEEP YOUR EYES ON THE SCREEN. WATCH THE CLOUDS. RIGHT THERE.

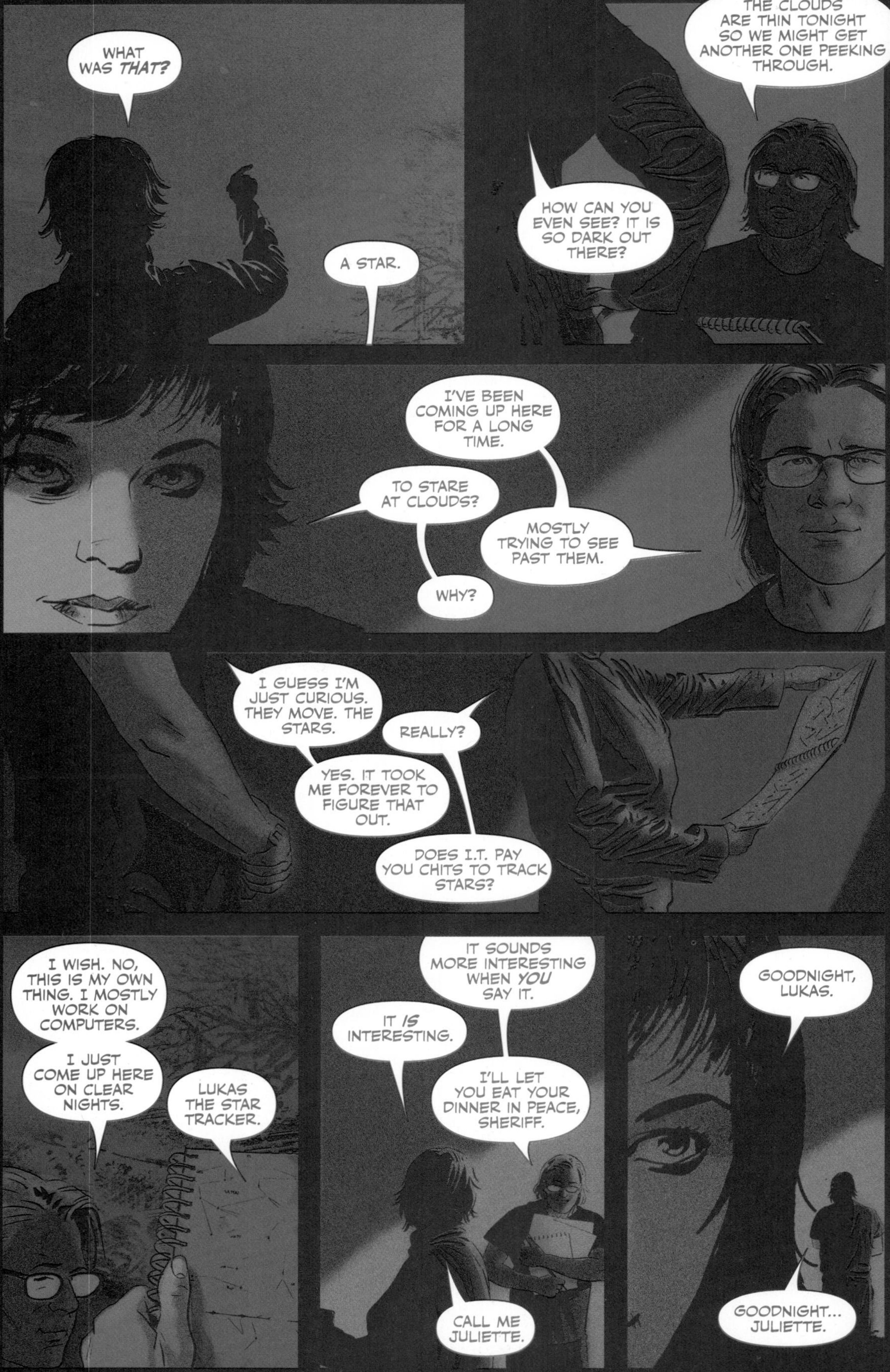
WHAT WAS *THAT?*
A STAR.
THE CLOUDS ARE THIN TONIGHT SO WE MIGHT GET ANOTHER ONE PEEKING THROUGH.
HOW CAN YOU EVEN SEE? IT IS SO DARK OUT THERE?
I'VE BEEN COMING UP HERE FOR A LONG TIME.
TO STARE AT CLOUDS?
MOSTLY TRYING TO SEE PAST THEM.
WHY?
I GUESS I'M JUST CURIOUS. THEY MOVE. THE STARS.
REALLY?
YES. IT TOOK ME FOREVER TO FIGURE THAT OUT.
DOES I.T. PAY YOU CHITS TO TRACK STARS?
I WISH. NO, THIS IS MY OWN THING. I MOSTLY WORK ON COMPUTERS.
I JUST COME UP HERE ON CLEAR NIGHTS.
LUKAS THE STAR TRACKER.
IT SOUNDS MORE INTERESTING WHEN *YOU* SAY IT.
IT *IS* INTERESTING.
I'LL LET YOU EAT YOUR DINNER IN PEACE, SHERIFF.
CALL ME JULIETTE.
GOODNIGHT, LUKAS.
GOODNIGHT... JULIETTE.

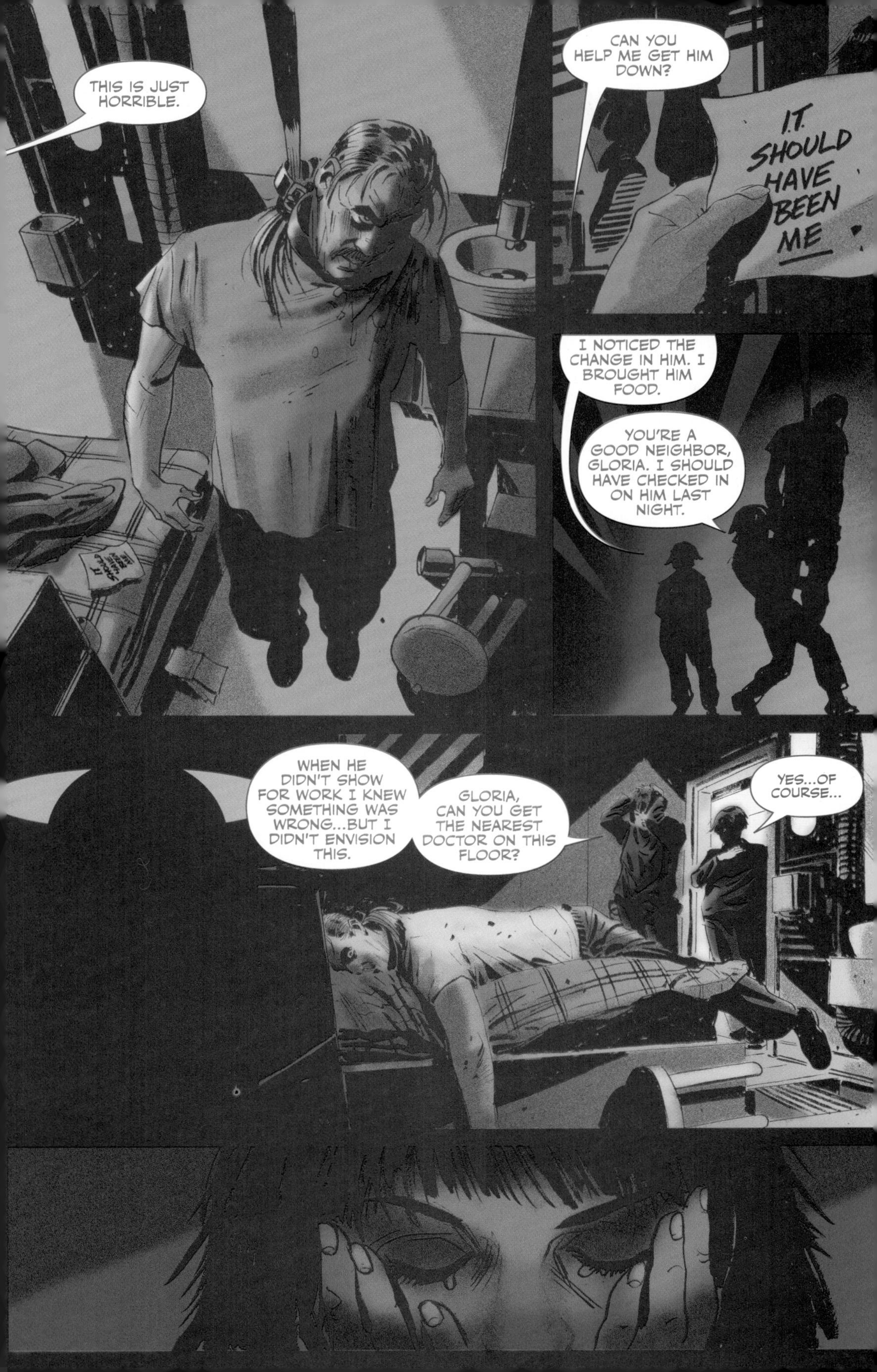
THIS IS JUST HORRIBLE.
CAN YOU HELP ME GET HIM DOWN?
I.T. SHOULD HAVE BEEN ME
I NOTICED THE CHANGE IN HIM. I BROUGHT HIM FOOD.
YOU'RE A GOOD NEIGHBOR, GLORIA. I SHOULD HAVE CHECKED IN ON HIM LAST NIGHT.
WHEN HE DIDN'T SHOW FOR WORK I KNEW SOMETHING WAS WRONG...BUT I DIDN'T ENVISION THIS.
GLORIA, CAN YOU GET THE NEAREST DOCTOR ON THIS FLOOR?
YES...OF COURSE...

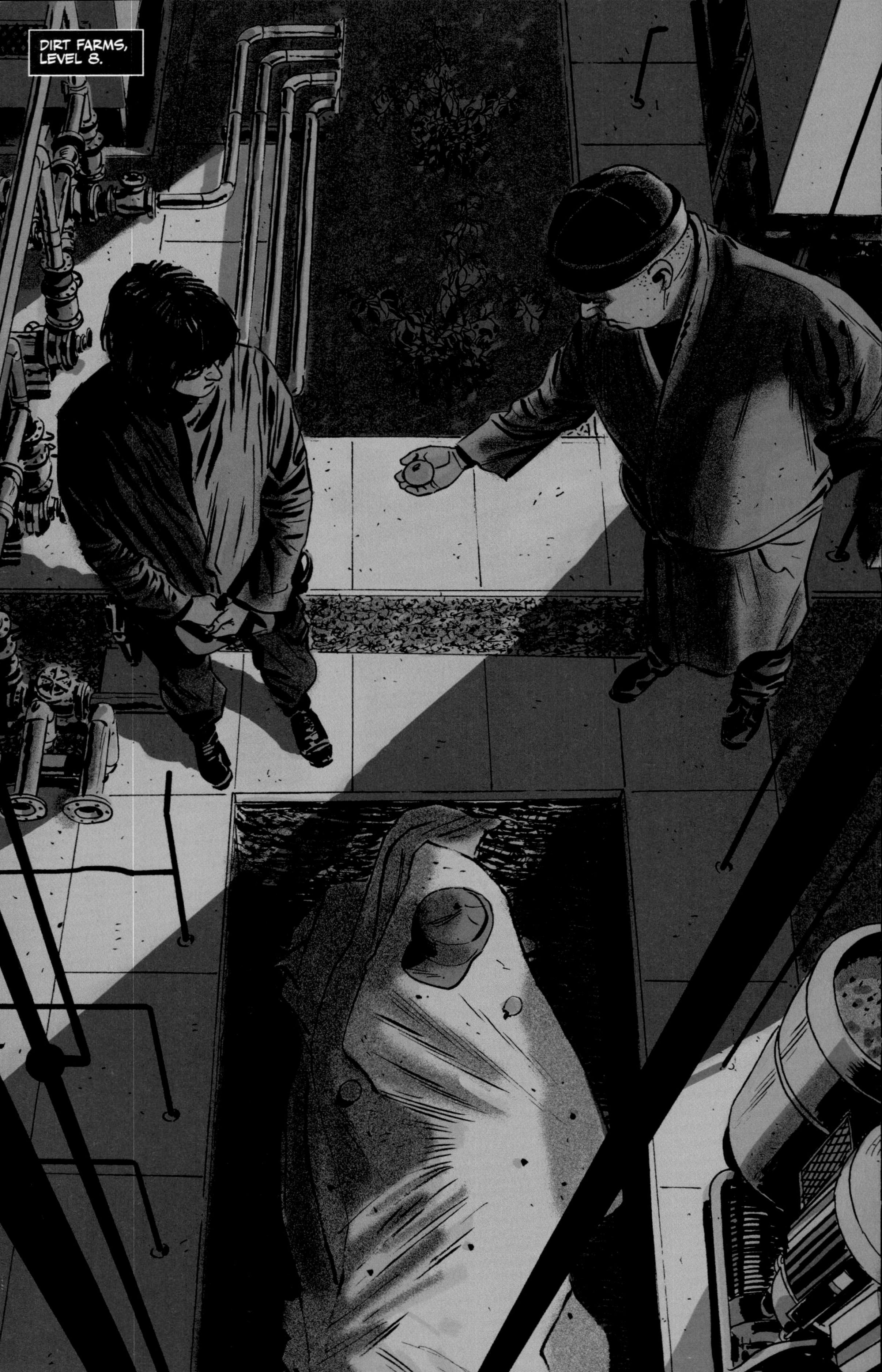
DIRT FARMS,
LEVEL 8.

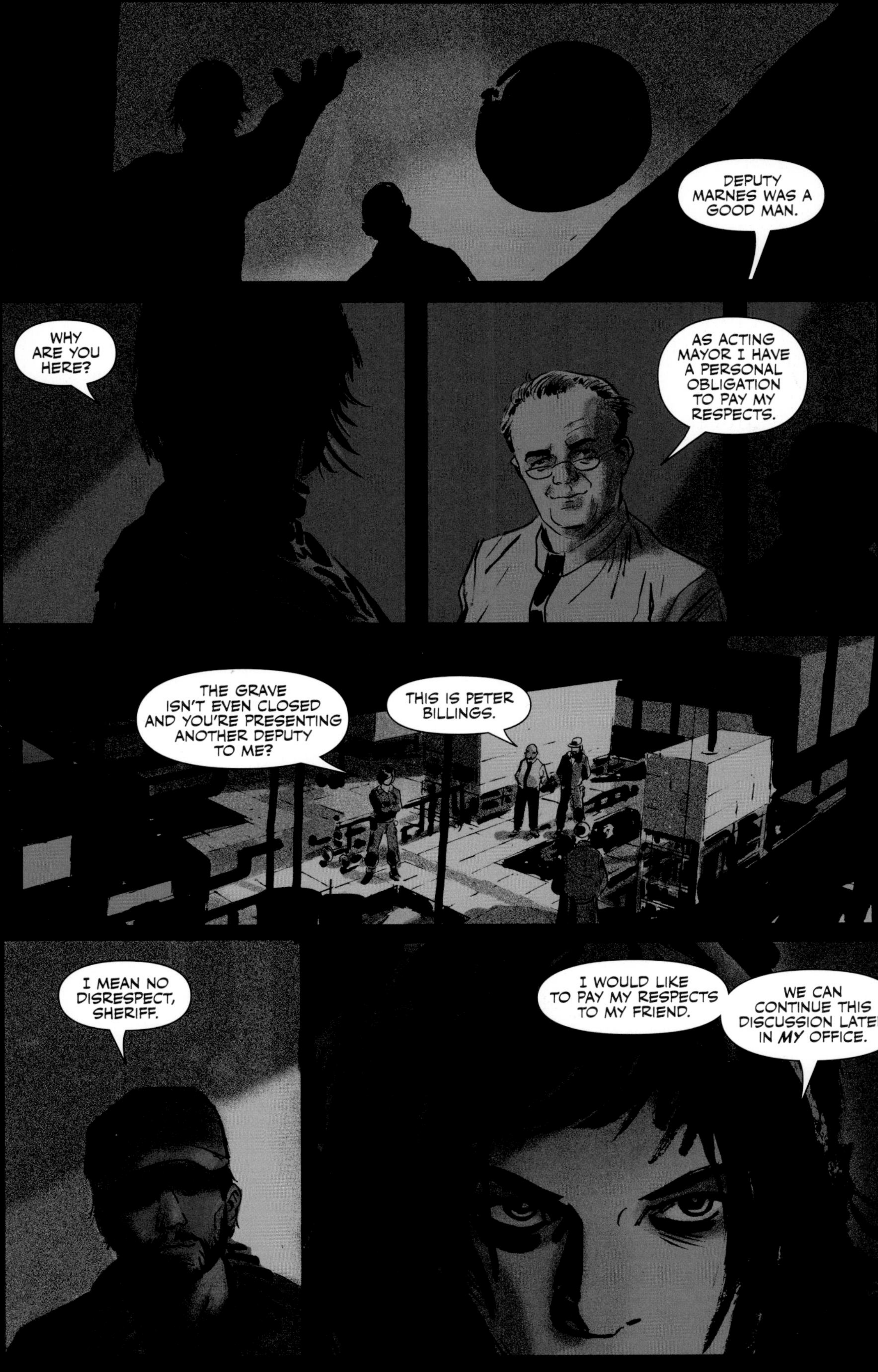
DEPUTY MARNES WAS A GOOD MAN.
WHY ARE YOU HERE?
AS ACTING MAYOR I HAVE A PERSONAL OBLIGATION TO PAY MY RESPECTS.
THE GRAVE ISN'T EVEN CLOSED AND YOU'RE PRESENTING ANOTHER DEPUTY TO ME?
THIS IS PETER BILLINGS.
I MEAN NO DISRESPECT, SHERIFF.
I WOULD LIKE TO PAY MY RESPECTS TO MY FRIEND.
WE CAN CONTINUE THIS DISCUSSION LATER IN *MY* OFFICE.

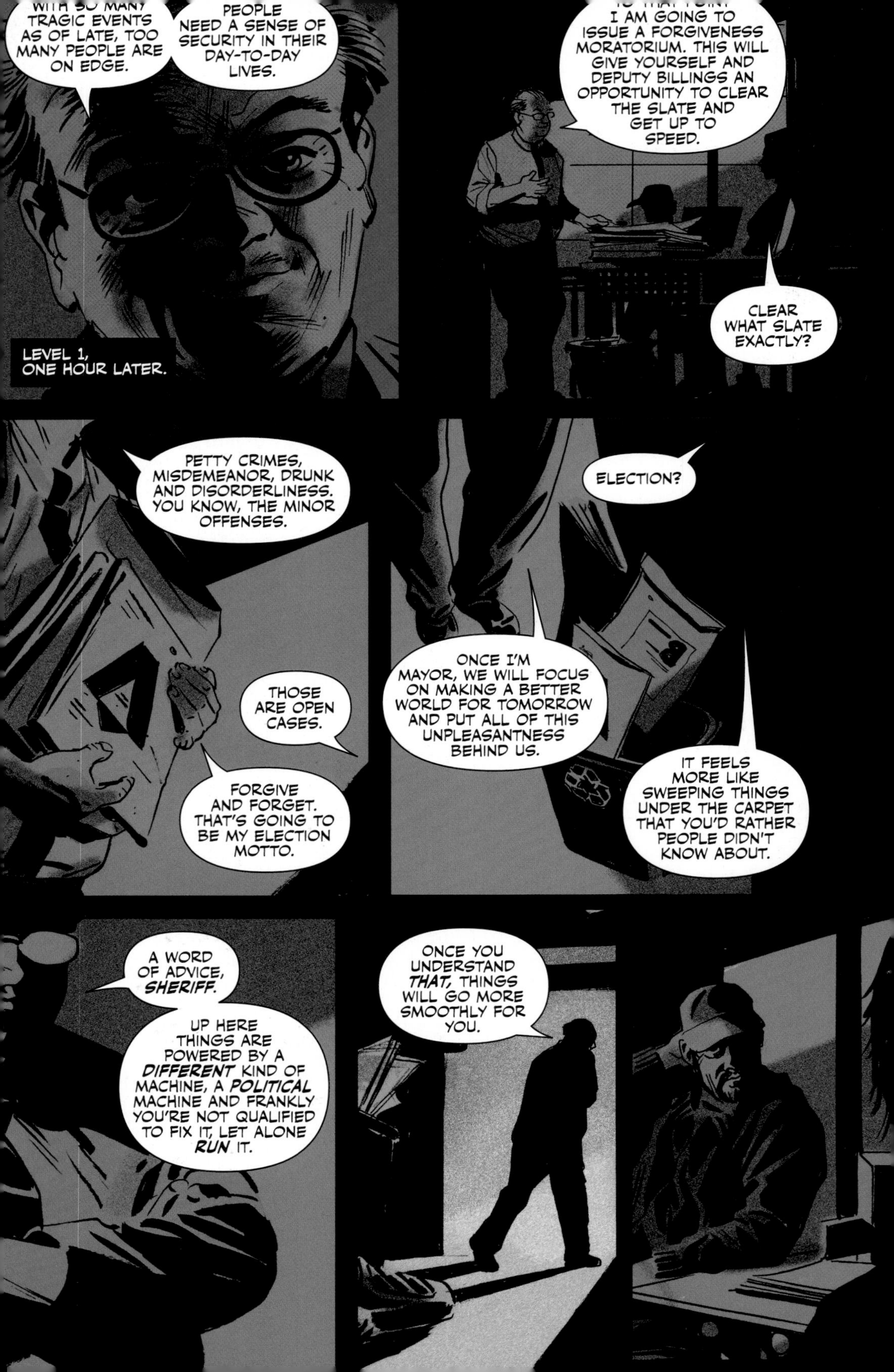
WITH SO MANY TRAGIC EVENTS AS OF LATE, TOO MANY PEOPLE ARE ON EDGE.
PEOPLE NEED A SENSE OF SECURITY IN THEIR DAY-TO-DAY LIVES.
LEVEL 1, ONE HOUR LATER.
I AM GOING TO ISSUE A FORGIVENESS MORATORIUM. THIS WILL GIVE YOURSELF AND DEPUTY BILLINGS AN OPPORTUNITY TO CLEAR THE SLATE AND GET UP TO SPEED.
CLEAR WHAT SLATE EXACTLY?
PETTY CRIMES, MISDEMEANOR, DRUNK AND DISORDERLINESS. YOU KNOW, THE MINOR OFFENSES.
THOSE ARE OPEN CASES.
FORGIVE AND FORGET. THAT'S GOING TO BE MY ELECTION MOTTO.
ELECTION?
ONCE I'M MAYOR, WE WILL FOCUS ON MAKING A BETTER WORLD FOR TOMORROW AND PUT ALL OF THIS UNPLEASANTNESS BEHIND US.
IT FEELS MORE LIKE SWEEPING THINGS UNDER THE CARPET THAT YOU'D RATHER PEOPLE DIDN'T KNOW ABOUT.
A WORD OF ADVICE, ***SHERIFF.***
UP HERE THINGS ARE POWERED BY A ***DIFFERENT*** KIND OF MACHINE, A ***POLITICAL*** MACHINE AND FRANKLY YOU'RE NOT QUALIFIED TO FIX IT, LET ALONE ***RUN*** IT.
ONCE YOU UNDERSTAND ***THAT,*** THINGS WILL GO MORE SMOOTHLY FOR YOU.

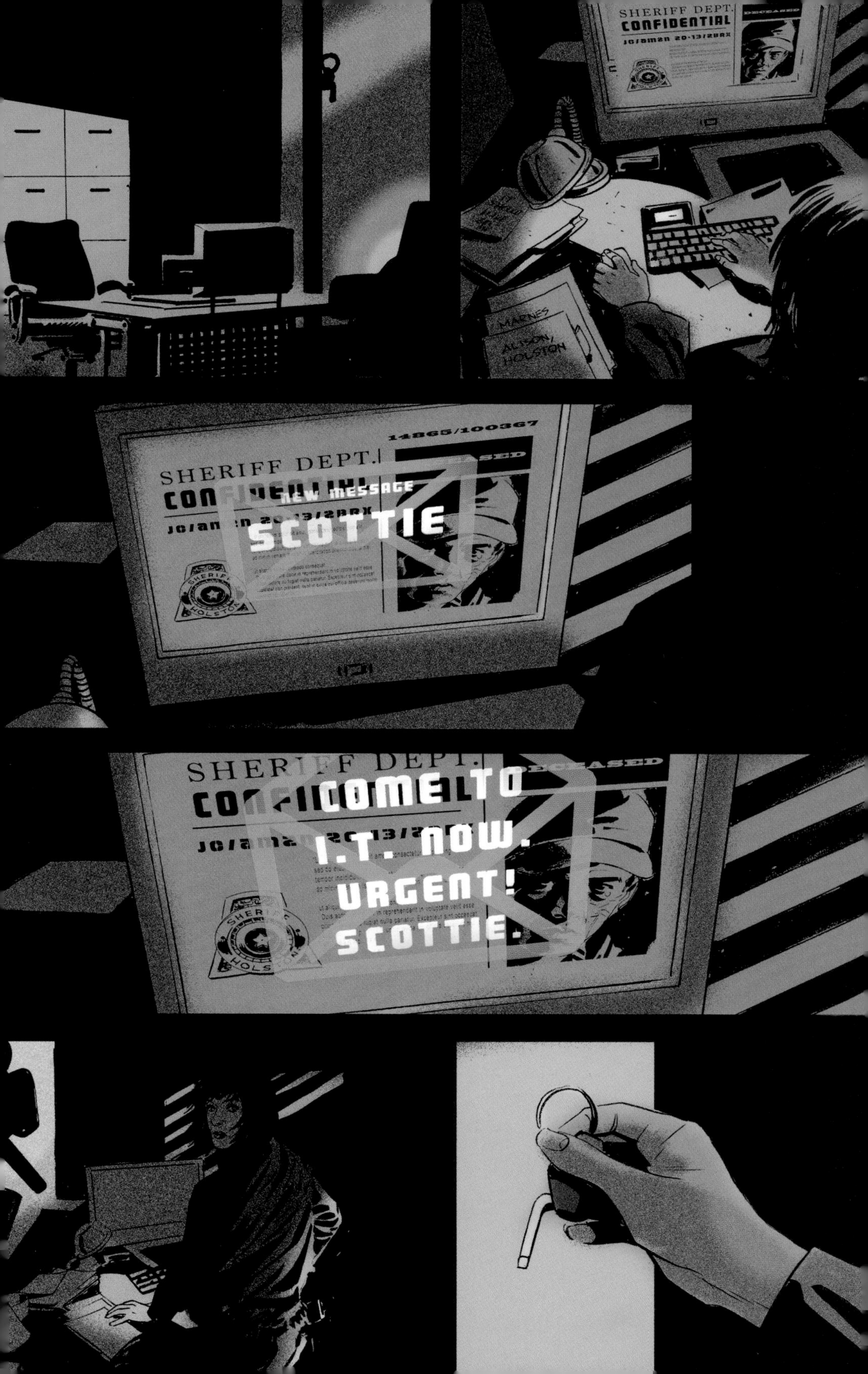
SHERIFF DEPT.
CONFIDENTIAL
DECEASED
MARNES
ALISON, HOLSTON
14865/100367
SHERIFF DEPT.
NEW MESSAGE
SCOTTIE
SHERIFF DEPT.
DECEASED
COME TO I.T. NOW. URGENT! SCOTTIE.

CAN I HELP YOU?

SHERIFF NICHOLS, I'M HERE TO SEE SCOTTIE. HE'S ONE OF YOUR TECHS.

DO YOU HAVE AN APPOINTMENT?

I'M THE SHERIFF. I DON'T NEED AN APPOINTMENT.

ACTUALLY YOU DO.

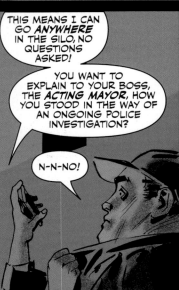

THIS MEANS I CAN GO ANYWHERE IN THE SILO, NO QUESTIONS ASKED!

YOU WANT TO EXPLAIN TO YOUR BOSS, THE ACTING MAYOR, HOW YOU STOOD IN THE WAY OF AN ONGOING POLICE INVESTIGATION?

N-N-NO!

WHERE'S HIS OFFICE?

SECOND HALL. LAST DOOR ON THE LEFT.

WHO'S THERE?

JULIETTE. OPEN THE DOOR.

DID ANYONE SEE YOU?

THERE ARE PEOPLE EVERY-WHERE.

YEAH, WHAT ABOUT THEM? WHAT IS THIS?

THE FILES FROM HOLSTON'S COMPUTER, THE FILES HIS WIFE WAS WORKING ON, THE ONES YOU ASKED ME TO SEND?

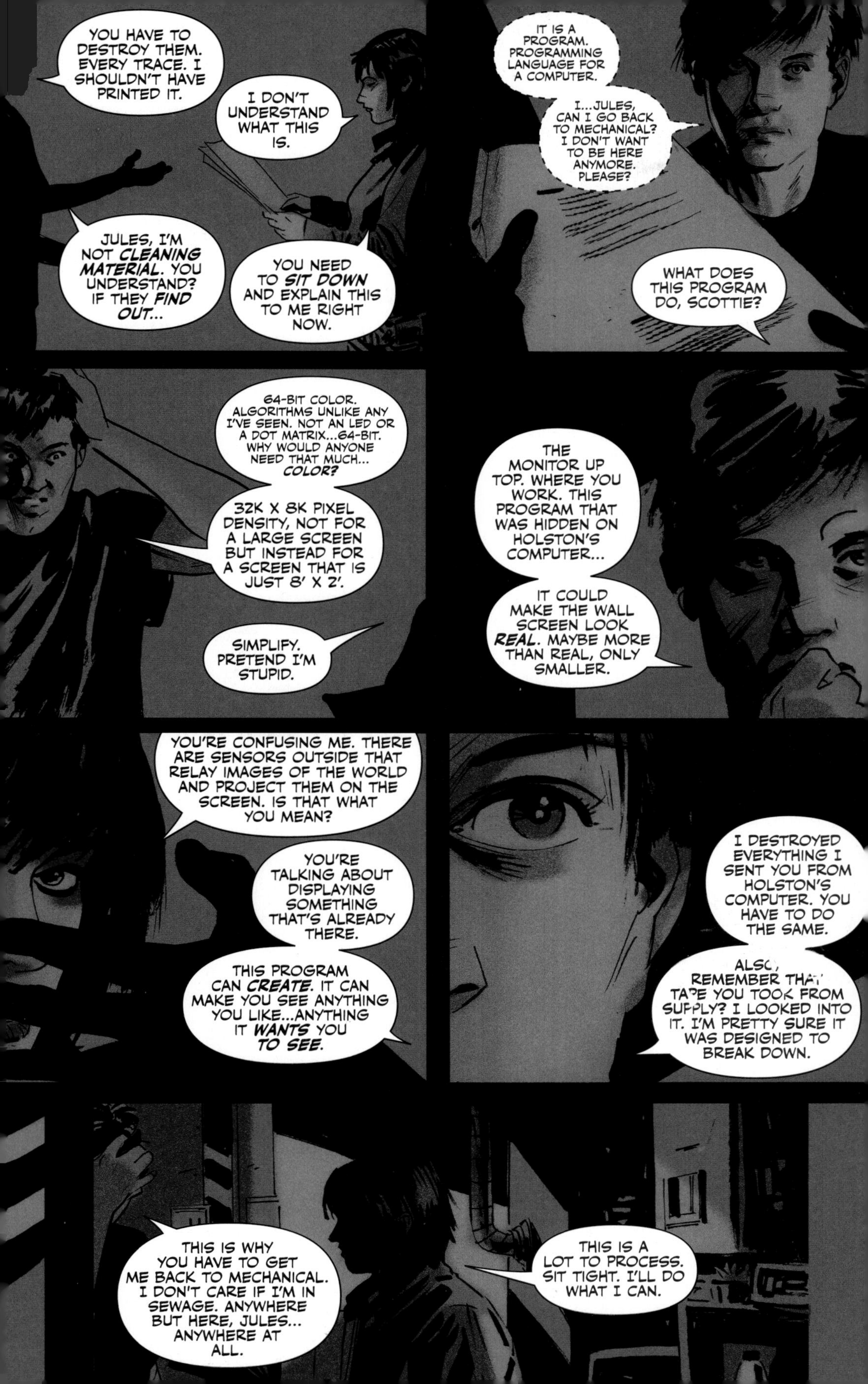
YOU HAVE TO DESTROY THEM. EVERY TRACE. I SHOULDN'T HAVE PRINTED IT.
I DON'T UNDERSTAND WHAT THIS IS.
JULES, I'M NOT *CLEANING MATERIAL*. YOU UNDERSTAND? IF THEY *FIND OUT*...
YOU NEED TO ***SIT DOWN*** AND EXPLAIN THIS TO ME RIGHT NOW.
IT IS A PROGRAM. PROGRAMMING LANGUAGE FOR A COMPUTER.
I...JULES, CAN I GO BACK TO MECHANICAL? I DON'T WANT TO BE HERE ANYMORE. PLEASE?
WHAT DOES THIS PROGRAM DO, SCOTTIE?
64-BIT COLOR. ALGORITHMS UNLIKE ANY I'VE SEEN. NOT AN LED OR A DOT MATRIX...64-BIT. WHY WOULD ANYONE NEED THAT MUCH... ***COLOR?***
32K X 8K PIXEL DENSITY, NOT FOR A LARGE SCREEN BUT INSTEAD FOR A SCREEN THAT IS JUST 8' X 2'.
SIMPLIFY. PRETEND I'M STUPID.
THE MONITOR UP TOP. WHERE YOU WORK. THIS PROGRAM THAT WAS HIDDEN ON HOLSTON'S COMPUTER...
IT COULD MAKE THE WALL SCREEN LOOK ***REAL***. MAYBE MORE THAN REAL, ONLY SMALLER.
YOU'RE CONFUSING ME. THERE ARE SENSORS OUTSIDE THAT RELAY IMAGES OF THE WORLD AND PROJECT THEM ON THE SCREEN. IS THAT WHAT YOU MEAN?
YOU'RE TALKING ABOUT DISPLAYING SOMETHING THAT'S ALREADY THERE.
THIS PROGRAM CAN ***CREATE***. IT CAN MAKE YOU SEE ANYTHING YOU LIKE...ANYTHING IT ***WANTS*** YOU ***TO SEE***.
I DESTROYED EVERYTHING I SENT YOU FROM HOLSTON'S COMPUTER. YOU HAVE TO DO THE SAME.
ALSO, REMEMBER THAT TAPE YOU TOOK FROM SUPPLY? I LOOKED INTO IT. I'M PRETTY SURE IT WAS DESIGNED TO BREAK DOWN.
THIS IS WHY YOU HAVE TO GET ME BACK TO MECHANICAL. I DON'T CARE IF I'M IN SEWAGE. ANYWHERE BUT HERE, JULES... ANYWHERE AT ALL.
THIS IS A LOT TO PROCESS. SIT TIGHT. I'LL DO WHAT I CAN.

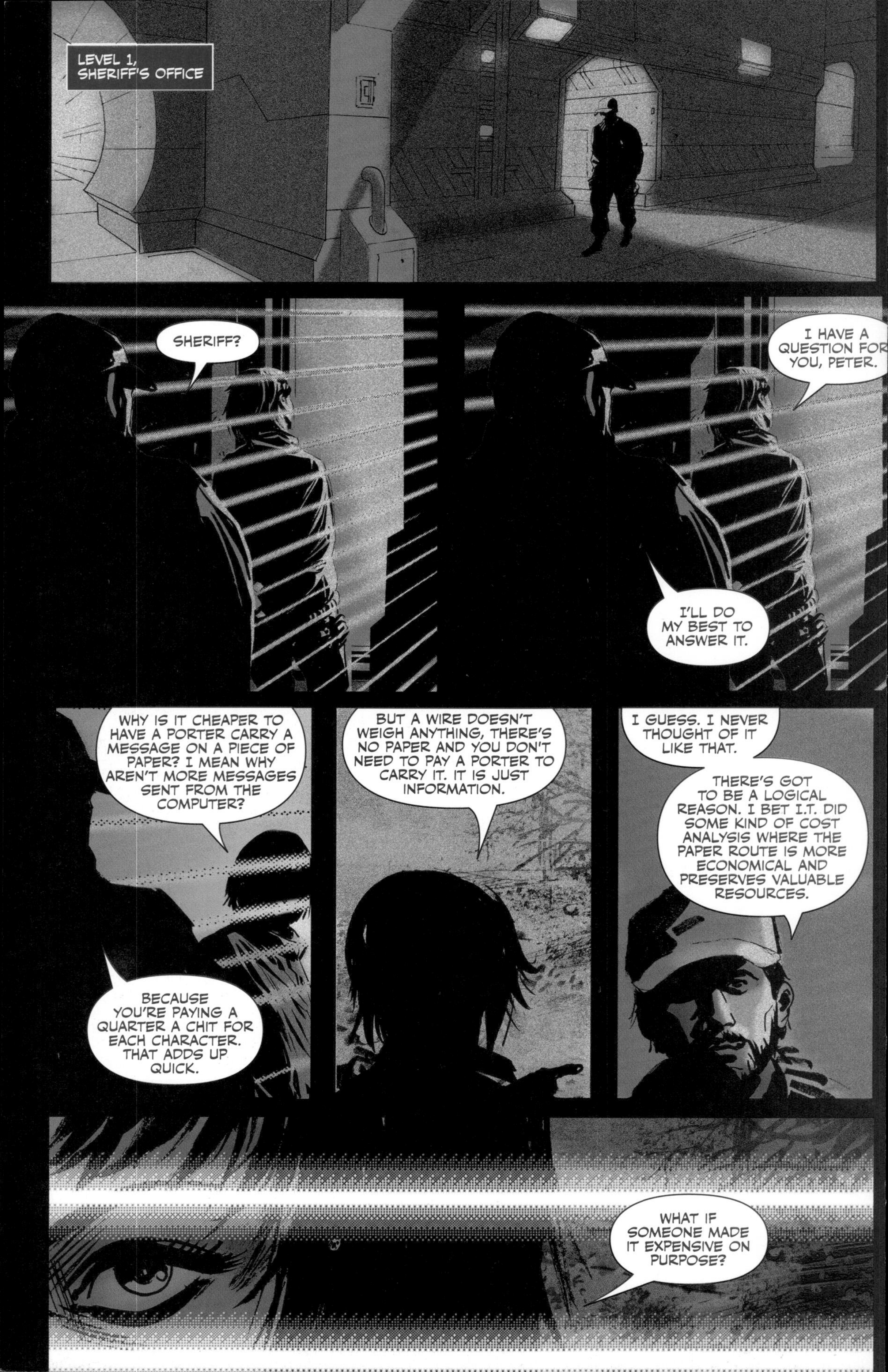
LEVEL 1, SHERIFF'S OFFICE
SHERIFF?
I HAVE A QUESTION FOR YOU, PETER.
I'LL DO MY BEST TO ANSWER IT.
WHY IS IT CHEAPER TO HAVE A PORTER CARRY A MESSAGE ON A PIECE OF PAPER? I MEAN WHY AREN'T MORE MESSAGES SENT FROM THE COMPUTER?
BECAUSE YOU'RE PAYING A QUARTER A CHIT FOR EACH CHARACTER. THAT ADDS UP QUICK.
BUT A WIRE DOESN'T WEIGH ANYTHING, THERE'S NO PAPER AND YOU DON'T NEED TO PAY A PORTER TO CARRY IT. IT IS JUST INFORMATION.
I GUESS. I NEVER THOUGHT OF IT LIKE THAT.
THERE'S GOT TO BE A LOGICAL REASON. I BET I.T. DID SOME KIND OF COST ANALYSIS WHERE THE PAPER ROUTE IS MORE ECONOMICAL AND PRESERVES VALUABLE RESOURCES.
WHAT IF SOMEONE MADE IT EXPENSIVE ON PURPOSE?

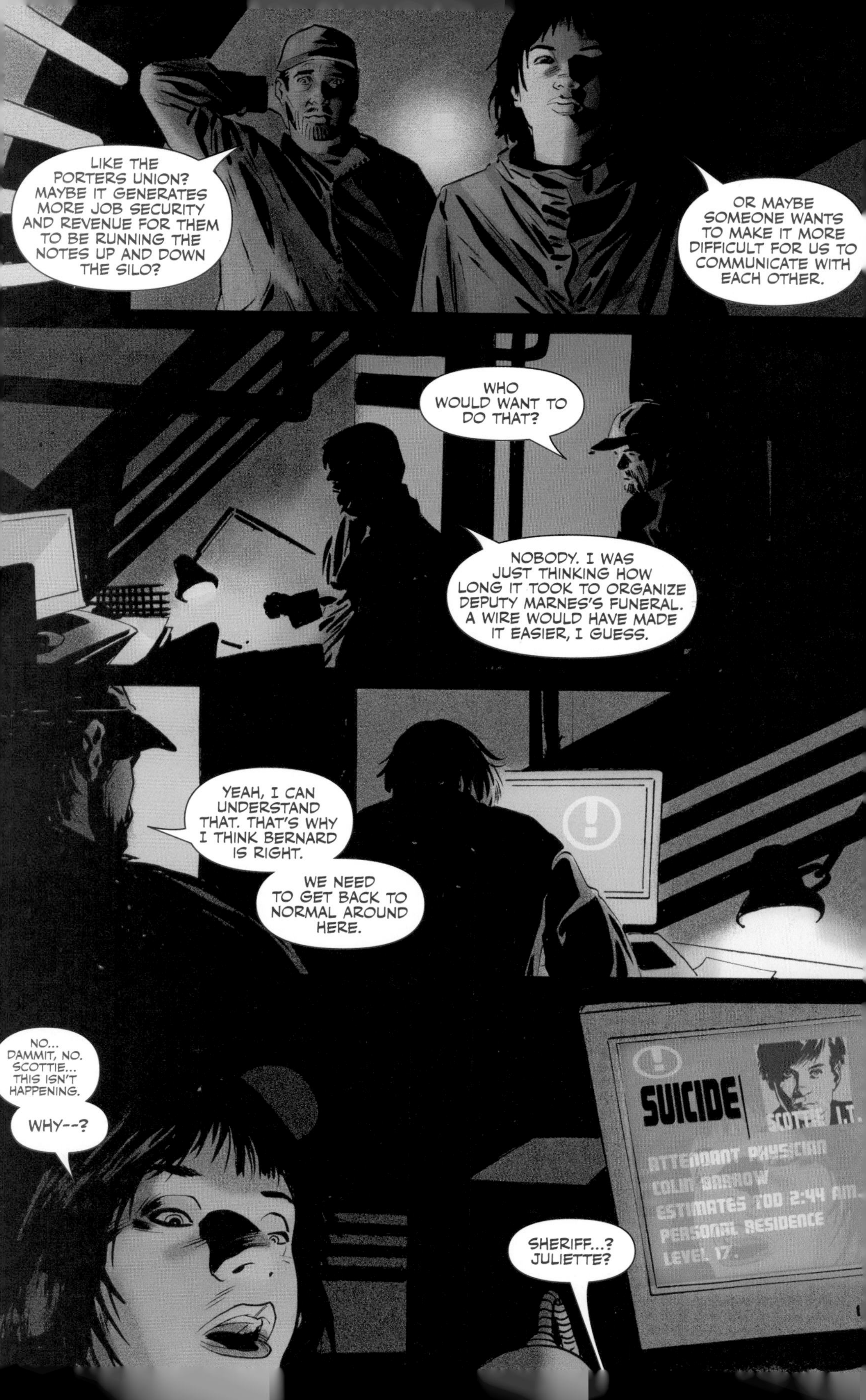
LIKE THE PORTERS UNION? MAYBE IT GENERATES MORE JOB SECURITY AND REVENUE FOR THEM TO BE RUNNING THE NOTES UP AND DOWN THE SILO?
OR MAYBE SOMEONE WANTS TO MAKE IT MORE DIFFICULT FOR US TO COMMUNICATE WITH EACH OTHER.
WHO WOULD WANT TO DO THAT?
NOBODY. I WAS JUST THINKING HOW LONG IT TOOK TO ORGANIZE DEPUTY MARNES'S FUNERAL. A WIRE WOULD HAVE MADE IT EASIER, I GUESS.
YEAH, I CAN UNDERSTAND THAT. THAT'S WHY I THINK BERNARD IS RIGHT.
WE NEED TO GET BACK TO NORMAL AROUND HERE.
NO... DAMMIT, NO. SCOTTIE... THIS ISN'T HAPPENING.
WHY--?
SUICIDE
SCOTTIE I.T.
ATTENDANT PHYSICIAN
COLIN BARROW
ESTIMATES TOD 2:44 AM.
PERSONAL RESIDENCE
LEVEL 17.
SHERIFF...? JULIETTE?

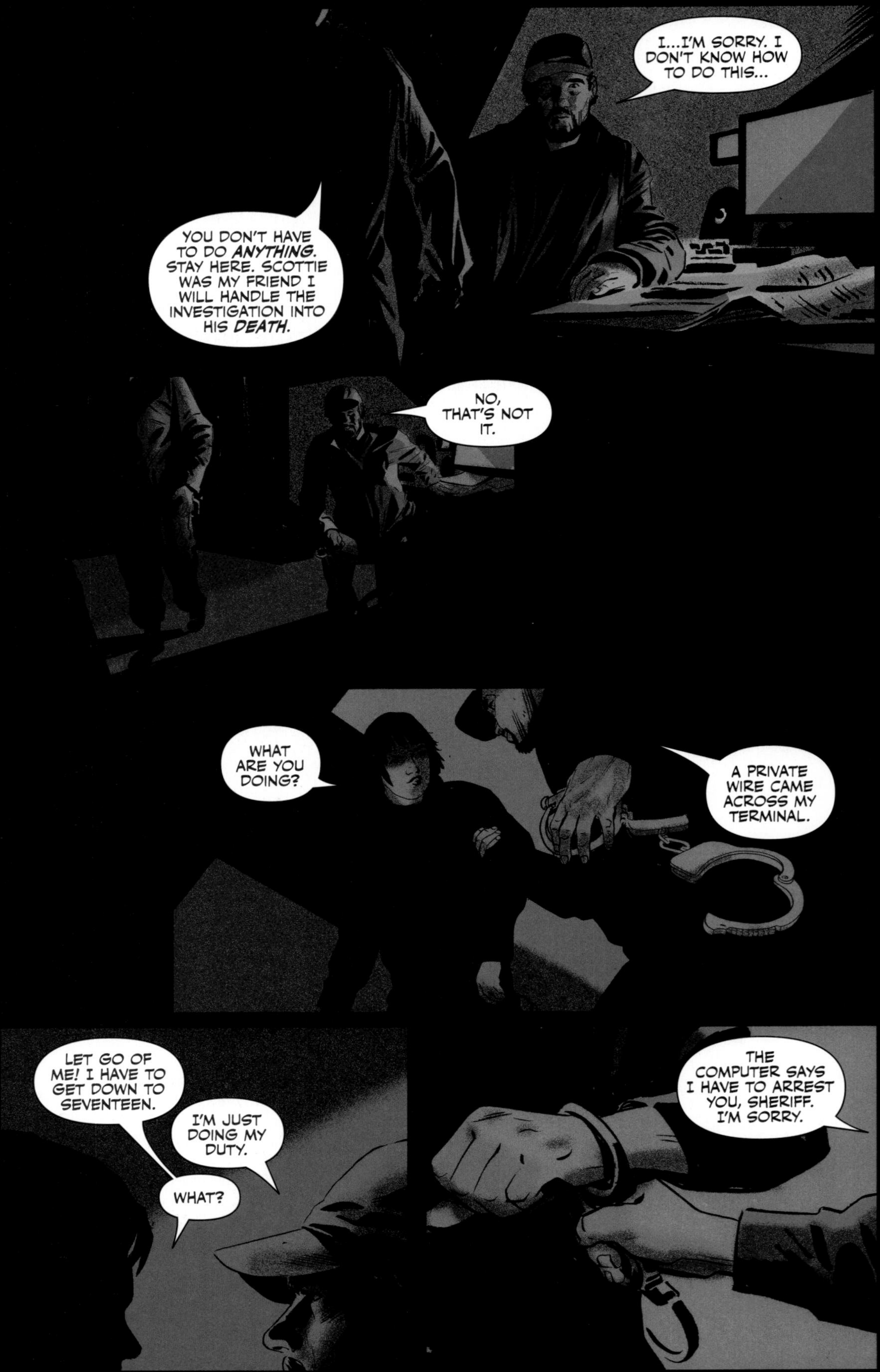
I...I'M SORRY. I DON'T KNOW HOW TO DO THIS...
YOU DON'T HAVE TO DO *ANYTHING*. STAY HERE. SCOTTIE WAS MY FRIEND I WILL HANDLE THE INVESTIGATION INTO HIS *DEATH*.
NO, THAT'S NOT IT.
WHAT ARE YOU DOING?
A PRIVATE WIRE CAME ACROSS MY TERMINAL.
LET GO OF ME! I HAVE TO GET DOWN TO SEVENTEEN.
I'M JUST DOING MY DUTY.
WHAT?
THE COMPUTER SAYS I HAVE TO ARREST YOU, SHERIFF. I'M SORRY.

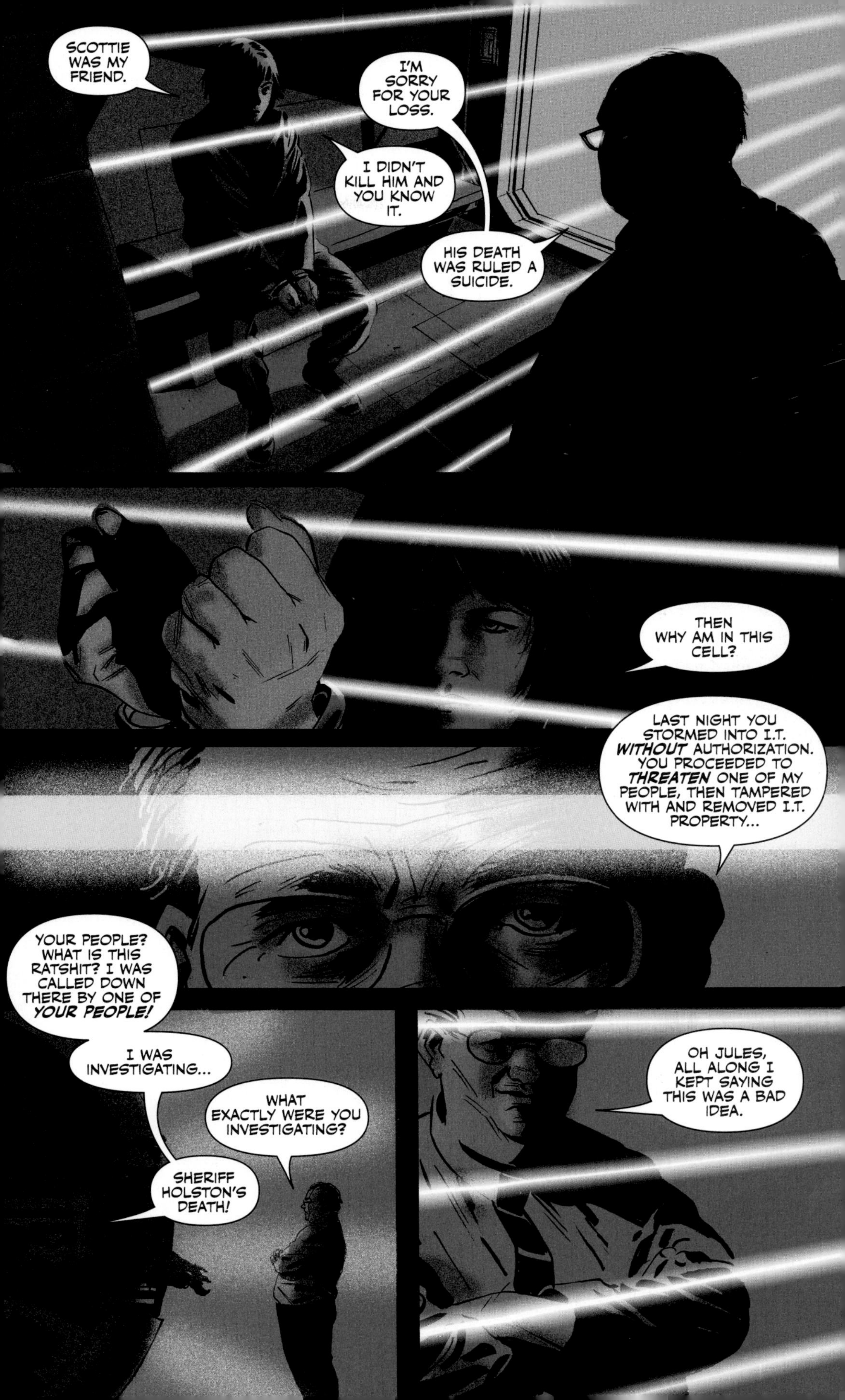
SCOTTIE WAS MY FRIEND.
I'M SORRY FOR YOUR LOSS.
I DIDN'T KILL HIM AND YOU KNOW IT.
HIS DEATH WAS RULED A SUICIDE.
THEN WHY AM IN THIS CELL?
LAST NIGHT YOU STORMED INTO I.T. *WITHOUT* AUTHORIZATION. YOU PROCEEDED TO *THREATEN* ONE OF MY PEOPLE, THEN TAMPERED WITH AND REMOVED I.T. PROPERTY...
YOUR PEOPLE? WHAT IS THIS RATSHIT? I WAS CALLED DOWN THERE BY ONE OF *YOUR PEOPLE!*
I WAS INVESTIGATING...
WHAT EXACTLY WERE YOU INVESTIGATING?
SHERIFF HOLSTON'S DEATH!
OH JULES, ALL ALONG I KEPT SAYING THIS WAS A BAD IDEA.

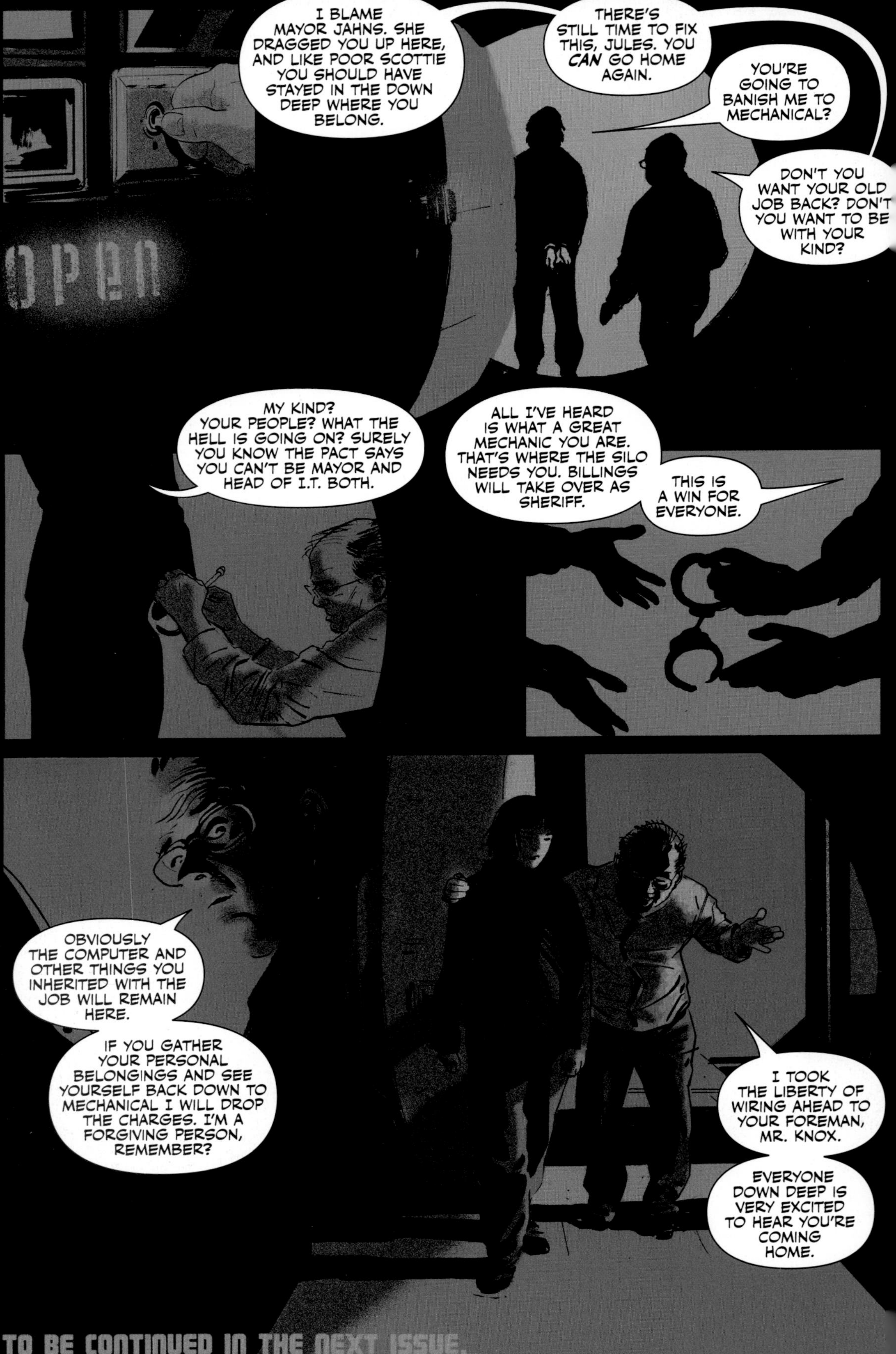

OPEN
I BLAME MAYOR JAHNS. SHE DRAGGED YOU UP HERE, AND LIKE POOR SCOTTIE YOU SHOULD HAVE STAYED IN THE DOWN DEEP WHERE YOU BELONG.
THERE'S STILL TIME TO FIX THIS, JULES. YOU *CAN* GO HOME AGAIN.
YOU'RE GOING TO BANISH ME TO MECHANICAL?
DON'T YOU WANT YOUR OLD JOB BACK? DON'T YOU WANT TO BE WITH YOUR KIND?
MY KIND? YOUR PEOPLE? WHAT THE HELL IS GOING ON? SURELY YOU KNOW THE PACT SAYS YOU CAN'T BE MAYOR AND HEAD OF I.T. BOTH.
ALL I'VE HEARD IS WHAT A GREAT MECHANIC YOU ARE. THAT'S WHERE THE SILO NEEDS YOU. BILLINGS WILL TAKE OVER AS SHERIFF.
THIS IS A WIN FOR EVERYONE.
OBVIOUSLY THE COMPUTER AND OTHER THINGS YOU INHERITED WITH THE JOB WILL REMAIN HERE.
IF YOU GATHER YOUR PERSONAL BELONGINGS AND SEE YOURSELF BACK DOWN TO MECHANICAL I WILL DROP THE CHARGES. I'M A FORGIVING PERSON, REMEMBER?
I TOOK THE LIBERTY OF WIRING AHEAD TO YOUR FOREMAN, MR. KNOX.
EVERYONE DOWN DEEP IS VERY EXCITED TO HEAR YOU'RE COMING HOME.

TO BE CONTINUED IN THE NEXT ISSUE.

END ISSUE 2

ISSUE 3

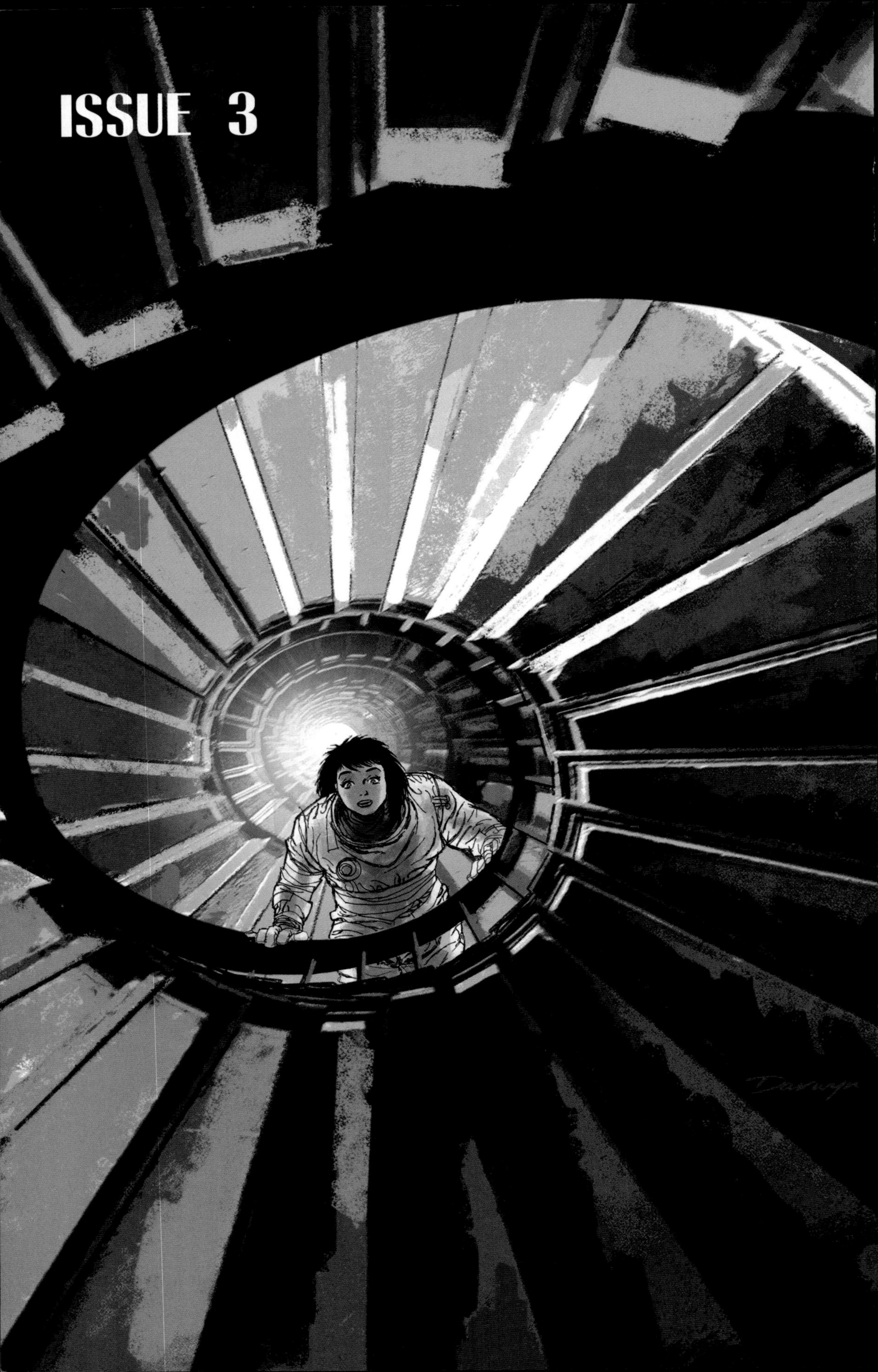

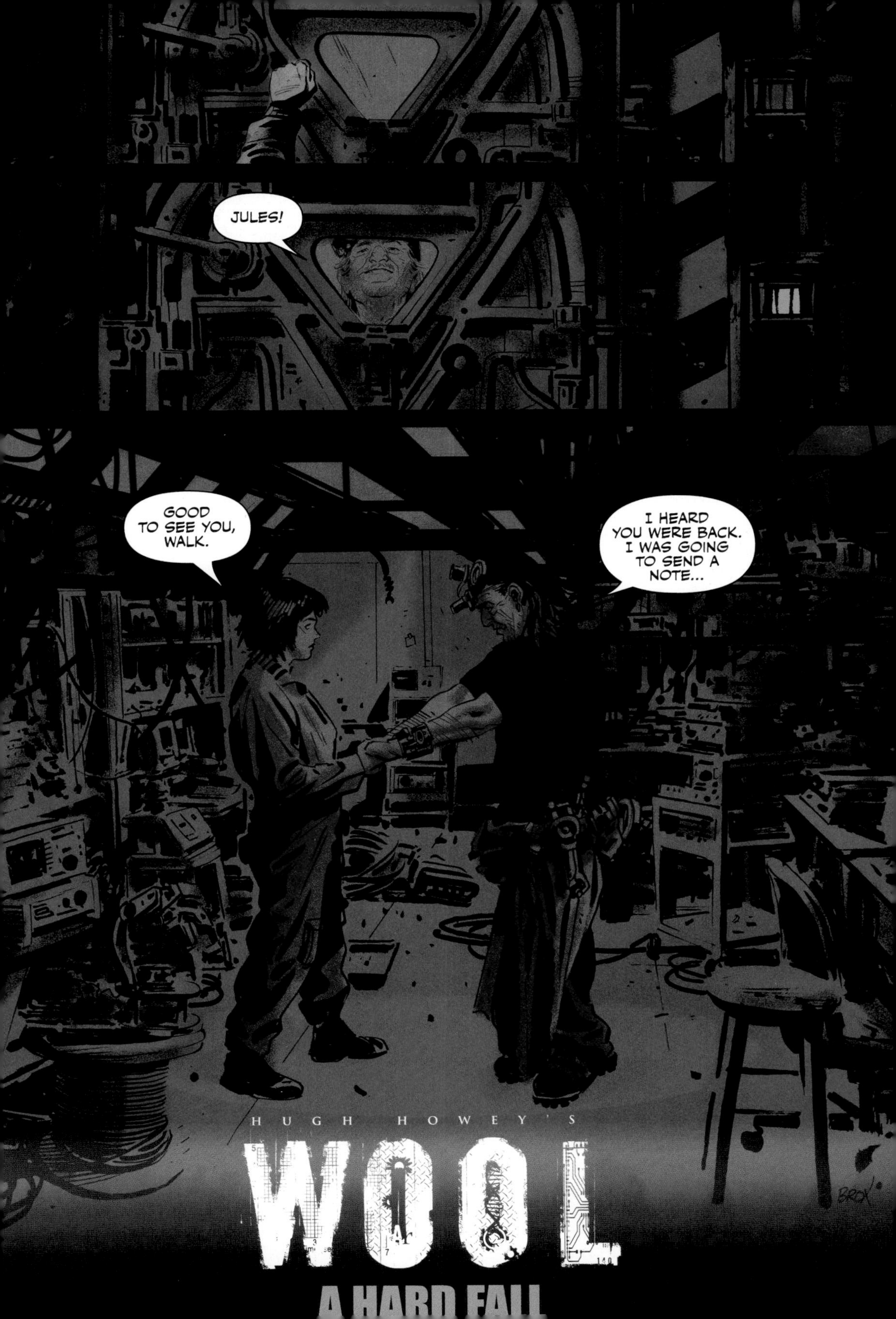
JULES!
GOOD TO SEE YOU, WALK.
I HEARD YOU WERE BACK. I WAS GOING TO SEND A NOTE...
HUGH HOWEY'S
WOOL
A HARD FALL
BROX

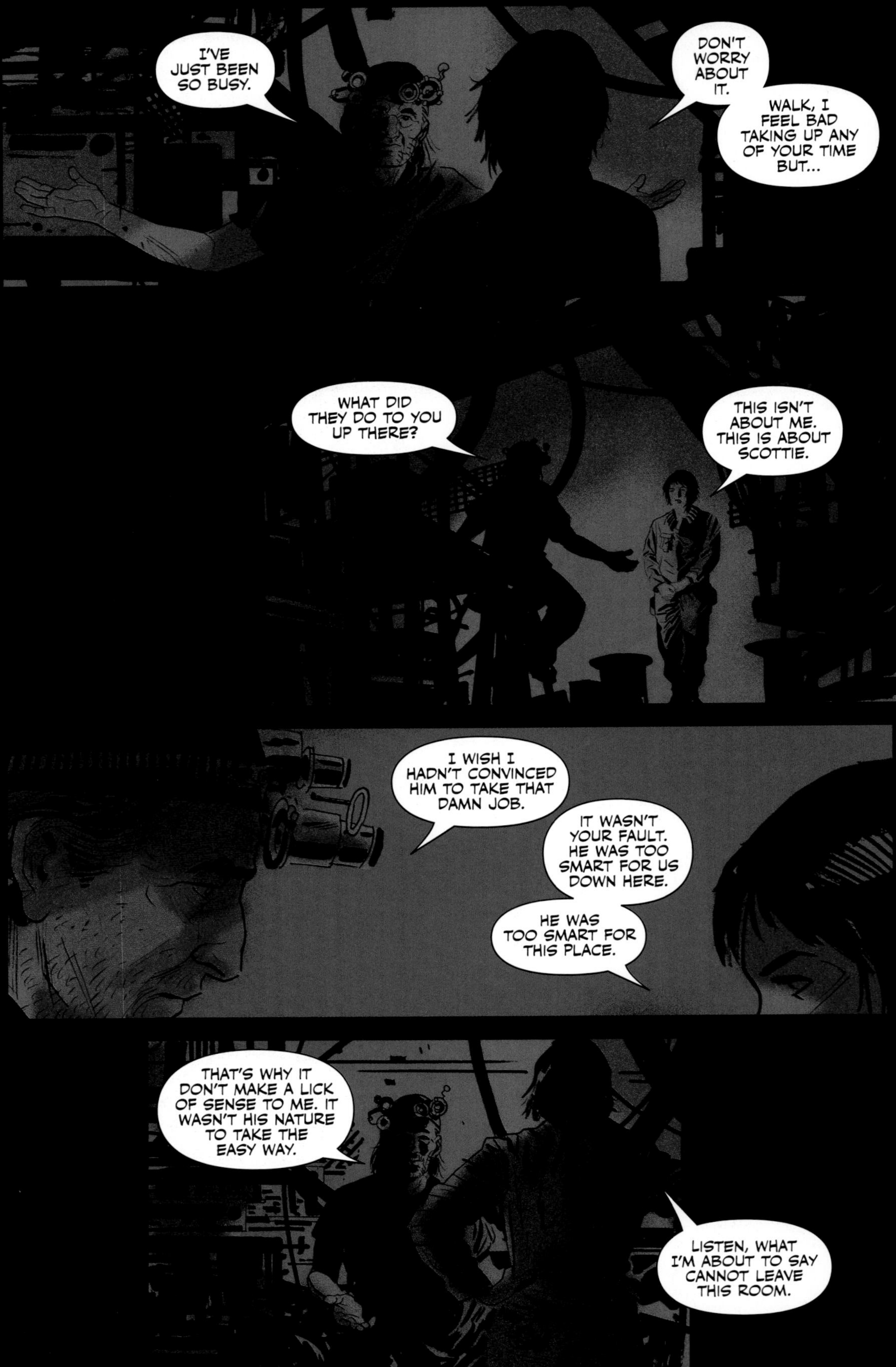
I'VE JUST BEEN SO BUSY.
DON'T WORRY ABOUT IT.
WALK, I FEEL BAD TAKING UP ANY OF YOUR TIME BUT...
WHAT DID THEY DO TO YOU UP THERE?
THIS ISN'T ABOUT ME. THIS IS ABOUT SCOTTIE.
I WISH I HADN'T CONVINCED HIM TO TAKE THAT DAMN JOB.
IT WASN'T YOUR FAULT. HE WAS TOO SMART FOR US DOWN HERE.
HE WAS TOO SMART FOR THIS PLACE.
THAT'S WHY IT DON'T MAKE A LICK OF SENSE TO ME. IT WASN'T HIS NATURE TO TAKE THE EASY WAY.
LISTEN, WHAT I'M ABOUT TO SAY CANNOT LEAVE THIS ROOM.

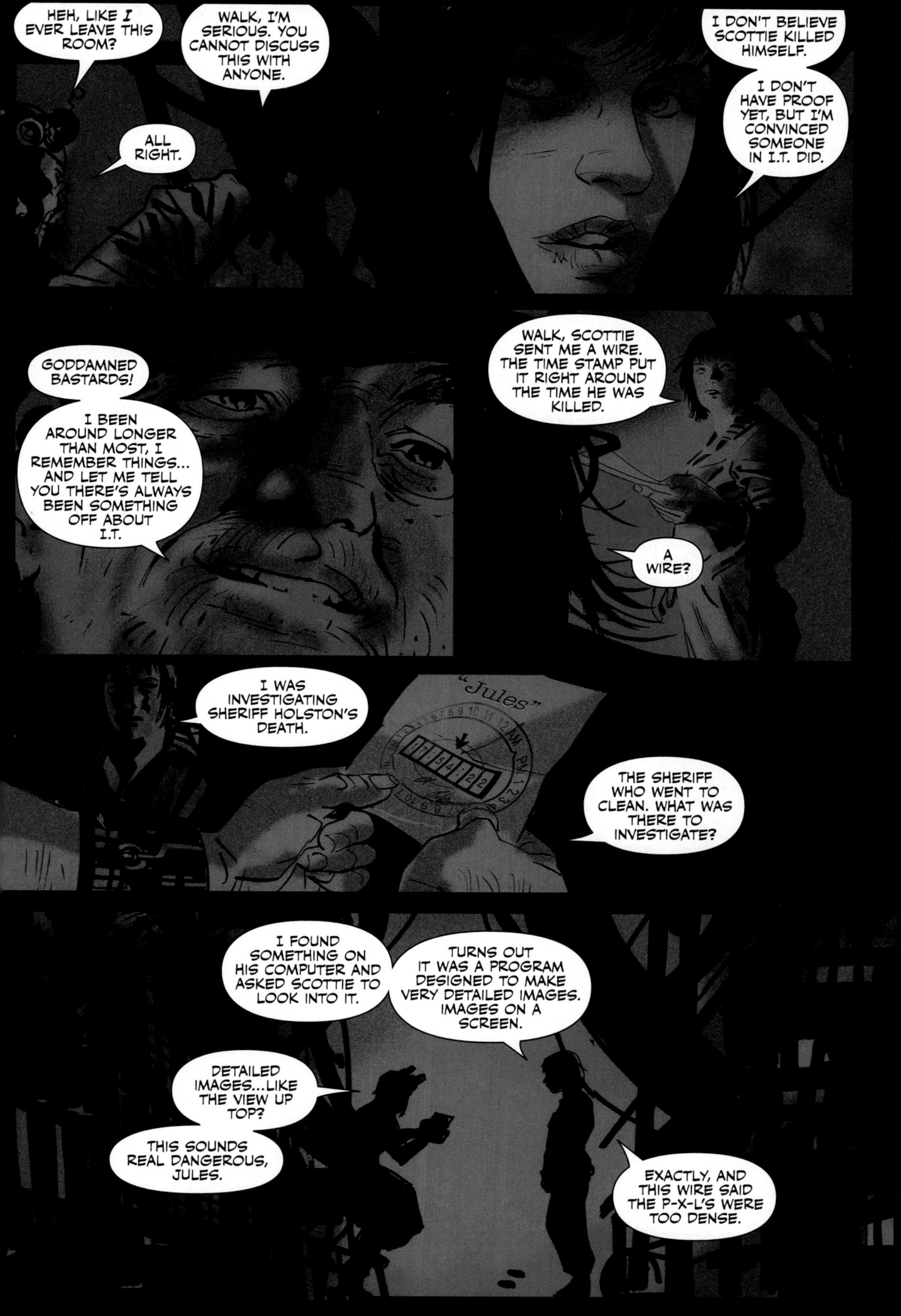
HEH, LIKE *I* EVER LEAVE THIS ROOM?
WALK, I'M SERIOUS. YOU CANNOT DISCUSS THIS WITH ANYONE.
ALL RIGHT.
I DON'T BELIEVE SCOTTIE KILLED HIMSELF.
I DON'T HAVE PROOF YET, BUT I'M CONVINCED SOMEONE IN I.T. DID.
GODDAMNED BASTARDS!
I BEEN AROUND LONGER THAN MOST, I REMEMBER THINGS... AND LET ME TELL YOU THERE'S ALWAYS BEEN SOMETHING OFF ABOUT I.T.
WALK, SCOTTIE SENT ME A WIRE. THE TIME STAMP PUT IT RIGHT AROUND THE TIME HE WAS KILLED.
A WIRE?
I WAS INVESTIGATING SHERIFF HOLSTON'S DEATH.
"Jules"
THE SHERIFF WHO WENT TO CLEAN. WHAT WAS THERE TO INVESTIGATE?
I FOUND SOMETHING ON HIS COMPUTER AND ASKED SCOTTIE TO LOOK INTO IT.
TURNS OUT IT WAS A PROGRAM DESIGNED TO MAKE VERY DETAILED IMAGES. IMAGES ON A SCREEN.
DETAILED IMAGES...LIKE THE VIEW UP TOP?
THIS SOUNDS REAL DANGEROUS, JULES.
EXACTLY, AND THIS WIRE SAID THE P-X-L'S WERE TOO DENSE.

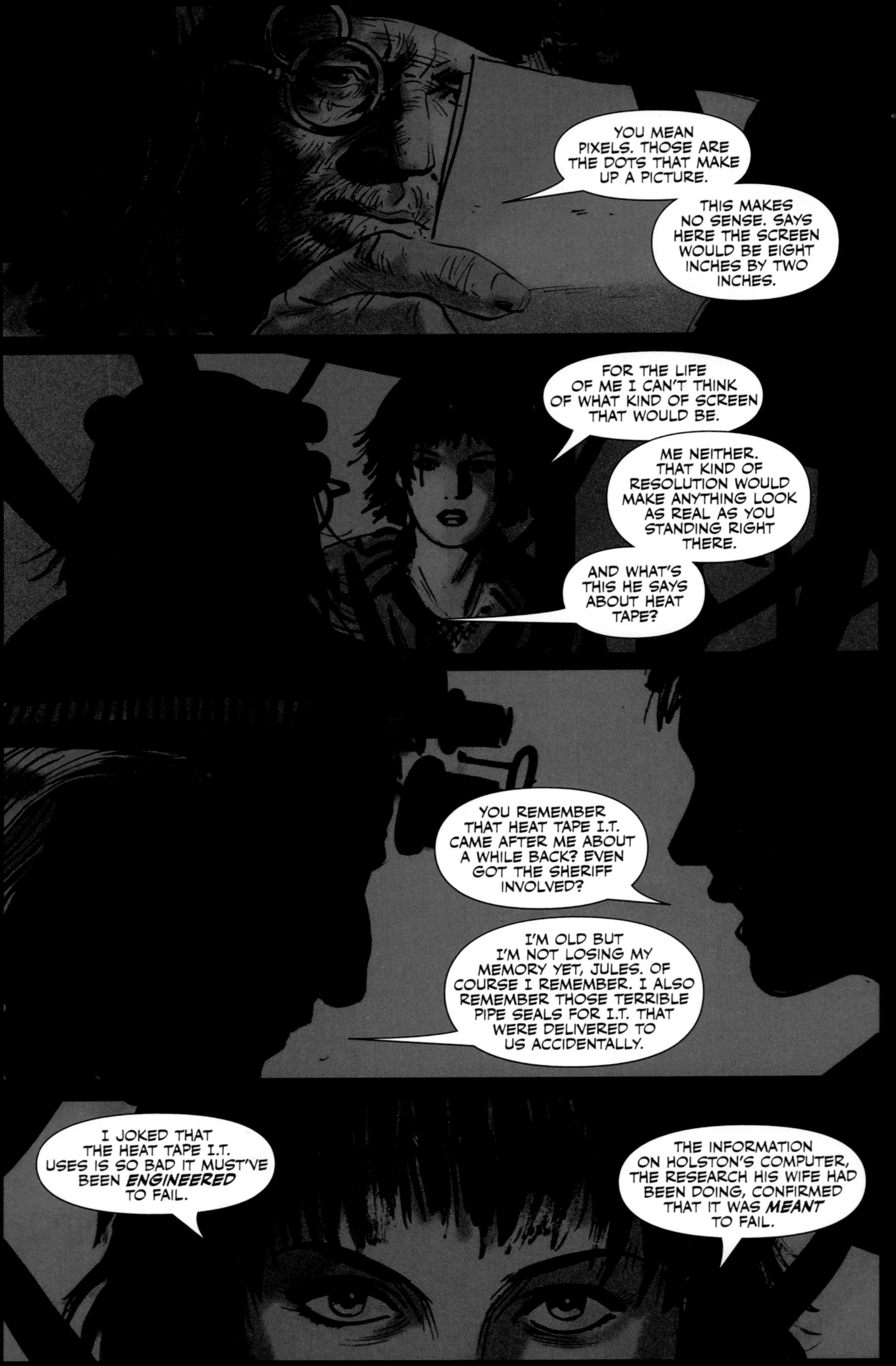

YOU MEAN PIXELS. THOSE ARE THE DOTS THAT MAKE UP A PICTURE.
THIS MAKES NO SENSE. SAYS HERE THE SCREEN WOULD BE EIGHT INCHES BY TWO INCHES.
FOR THE LIFE OF ME I CAN'T THINK OF WHAT KIND OF SCREEN THAT WOULD BE.
ME NEITHER. THAT KIND OF RESOLUTION WOULD MAKE ANYTHING LOOK AS REAL AS YOU STANDING RIGHT THERE.
AND WHAT'S THIS HE SAYS ABOUT HEAT TAPE?
YOU REMEMBER THAT HEAT TAPE I.T. CAME AFTER ME ABOUT A WHILE BACK? EVEN GOT THE SHERIFF INVOLVED?
I'M OLD BUT I'M NOT LOSING MY MEMORY YET, JULES. OF COURSE I REMEMBER. I ALSO REMEMBER THOSE TERRIBLE PIPE SEALS FOR I.T. THAT WERE DELIVERED TO US ACCIDENTALLY.
I JOKED THAT THE HEAT TAPE I.T. USES IS SO BAD IT MUST'VE BEEN *ENGINEERED* TO FAIL.
THE INFORMATION ON HOLSTON'S COMPUTER, THE RESEARCH HIS WIFE HAD BEEN DOING, CONFIRMED THAT IT WAS *MEANT* TO FAIL.

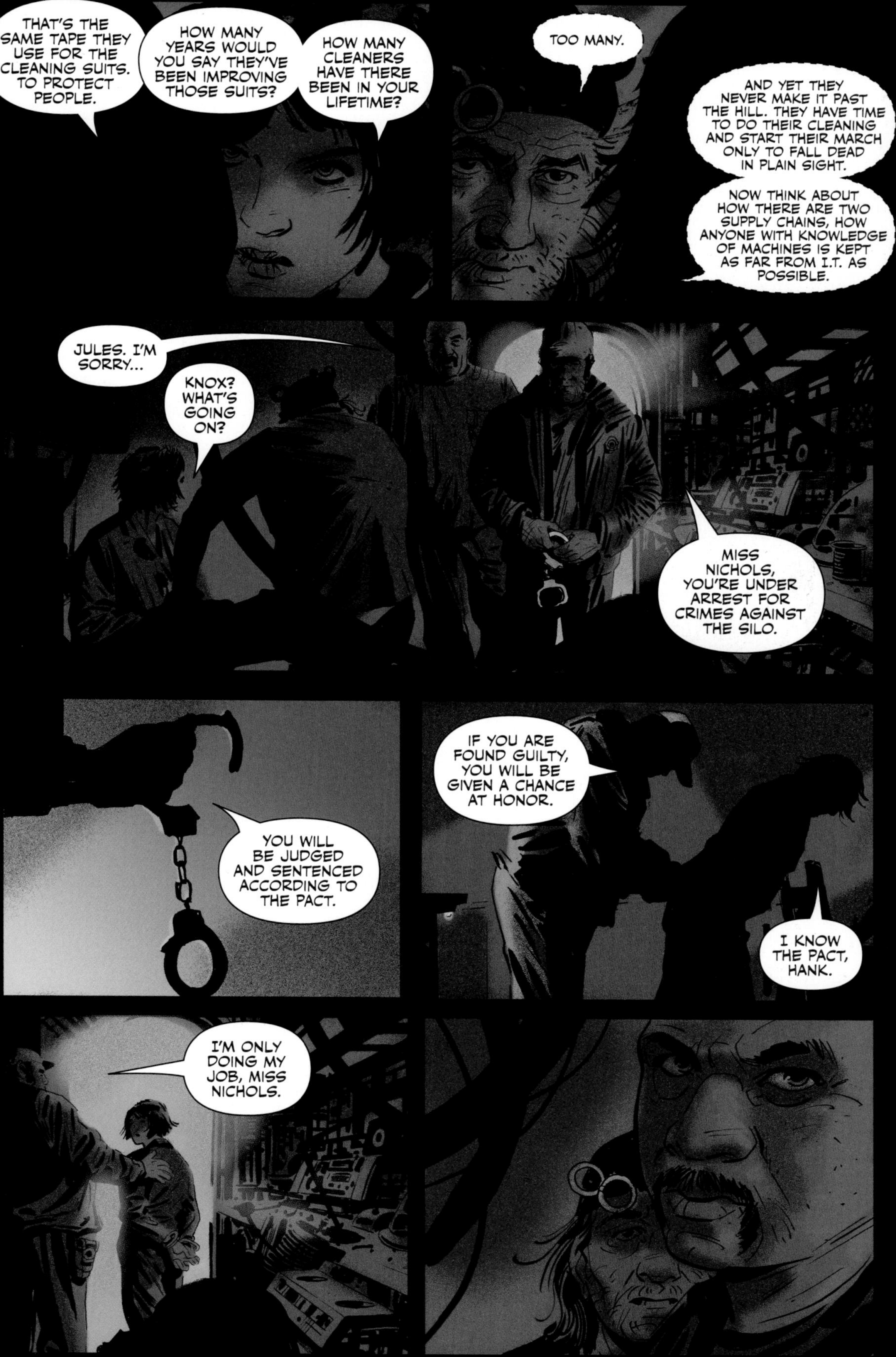
THAT'S THE SAME TAPE THEY USE FOR THE CLEANING SUITS. TO PROTECT PEOPLE.
HOW MANY YEARS WOULD YOU SAY THEY'VE BEEN IMPROVING THOSE SUITS?
HOW MANY CLEANERS HAVE THERE BEEN IN YOUR LIFETIME?
TOO MANY.
AND YET THEY NEVER MAKE IT PAST THE HILL. THEY HAVE TIME TO DO THEIR CLEANING AND START THEIR MARCH ONLY TO FALL DEAD IN PLAIN SIGHT.
NOW THINK ABOUT HOW THERE ARE TWO SUPPLY CHAINS, HOW ANYONE WITH KNOWLEDGE OF MACHINES IS KEPT AS FAR FROM I.T. AS POSSIBLE.
JULES. I'M SORRY...
KNOX? WHAT'S GOING ON?
MISS NICHOLS, YOU'RE UNDER ARREST FOR CRIMES AGAINST THE SILO.
YOU WILL BE JUDGED AND SENTENCED ACCORDING TO THE PACT.
IF YOU ARE FOUND GUILTY, YOU WILL BE GIVEN A CHANCE AT HONOR.
I KNOW THE PACT, HANK.
I'M ONLY DOING MY JOB, MISS NICHOLS.

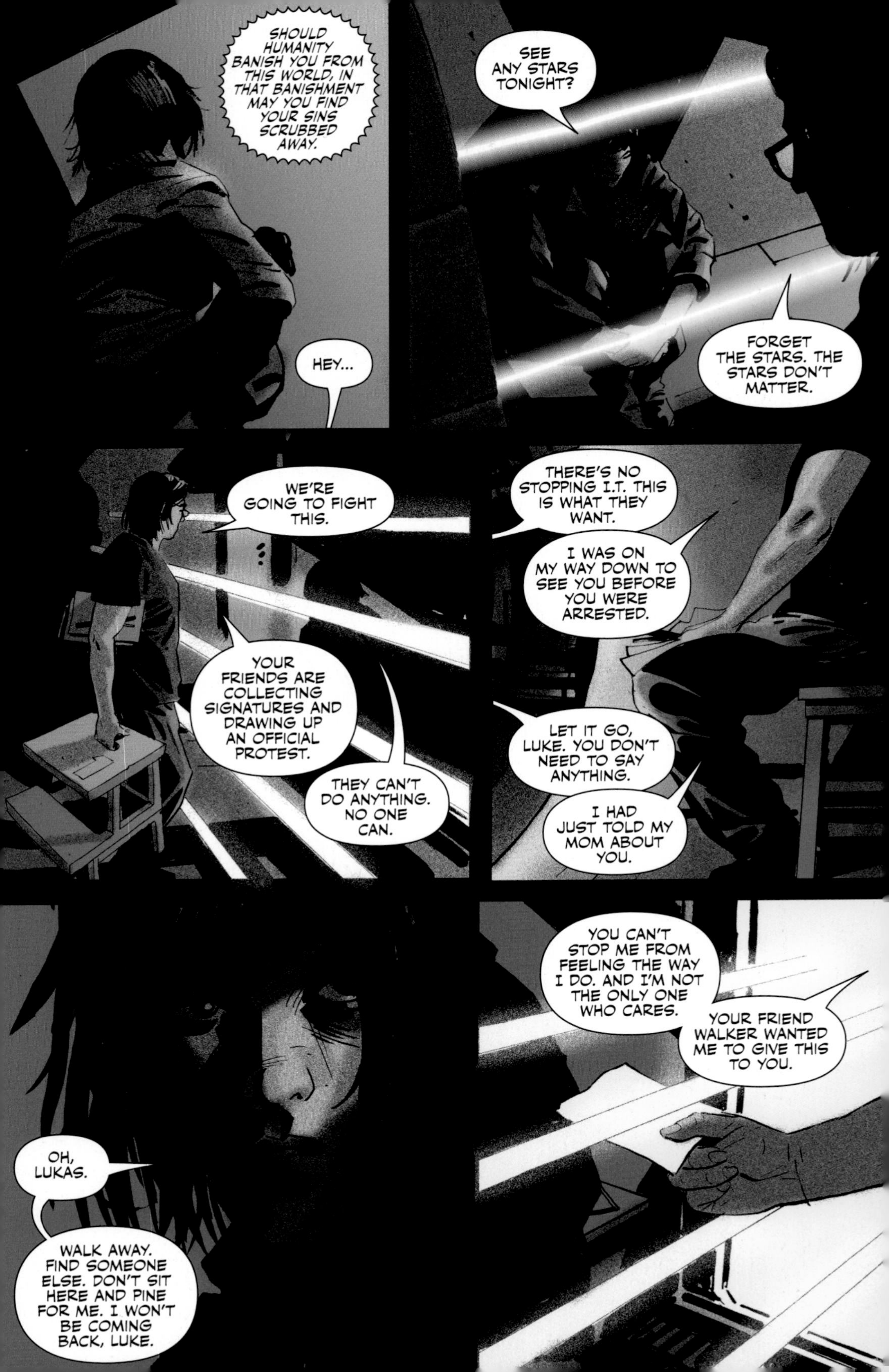
SHOULD HUMANITY BANISH YOU FROM THIS WORLD, IN THAT BANISHMENT MAY YOU FIND YOUR SINS SCRUBBED AWAY.
HEY...
SEE ANY STARS TONIGHT?
FORGET THE STARS. THE STARS DON'T MATTER.
WE'RE GOING TO FIGHT THIS.
YOUR FRIENDS ARE COLLECTING SIGNATURES AND DRAWING UP AN OFFICIAL PROTEST.
THEY CAN'T DO ANYTHING. NO ONE CAN.
THERE'S NO STOPPING I.T. THIS IS WHAT THEY WANT.
I WAS ON MY WAY DOWN TO SEE YOU BEFORE YOU WERE ARRESTED.
LET IT GO, LUKE. YOU DON'T NEED TO SAY ANYTHING.
I HAD JUST TOLD MY MOM ABOUT YOU.
OH, LUKAS.
WALK AWAY. FIND SOMEONE ELSE. DON'T SIT HERE AND PINE FOR ME. I WON'T BE COMING BACK, LUKE.
YOU CAN'T STOP ME FROM FEELING THE WAY I DO. AND I'M NOT THE ONLY ONE WHO CARES.
YOUR FRIEND WALKER WANTED ME TO GIVE THIS TO YOU.

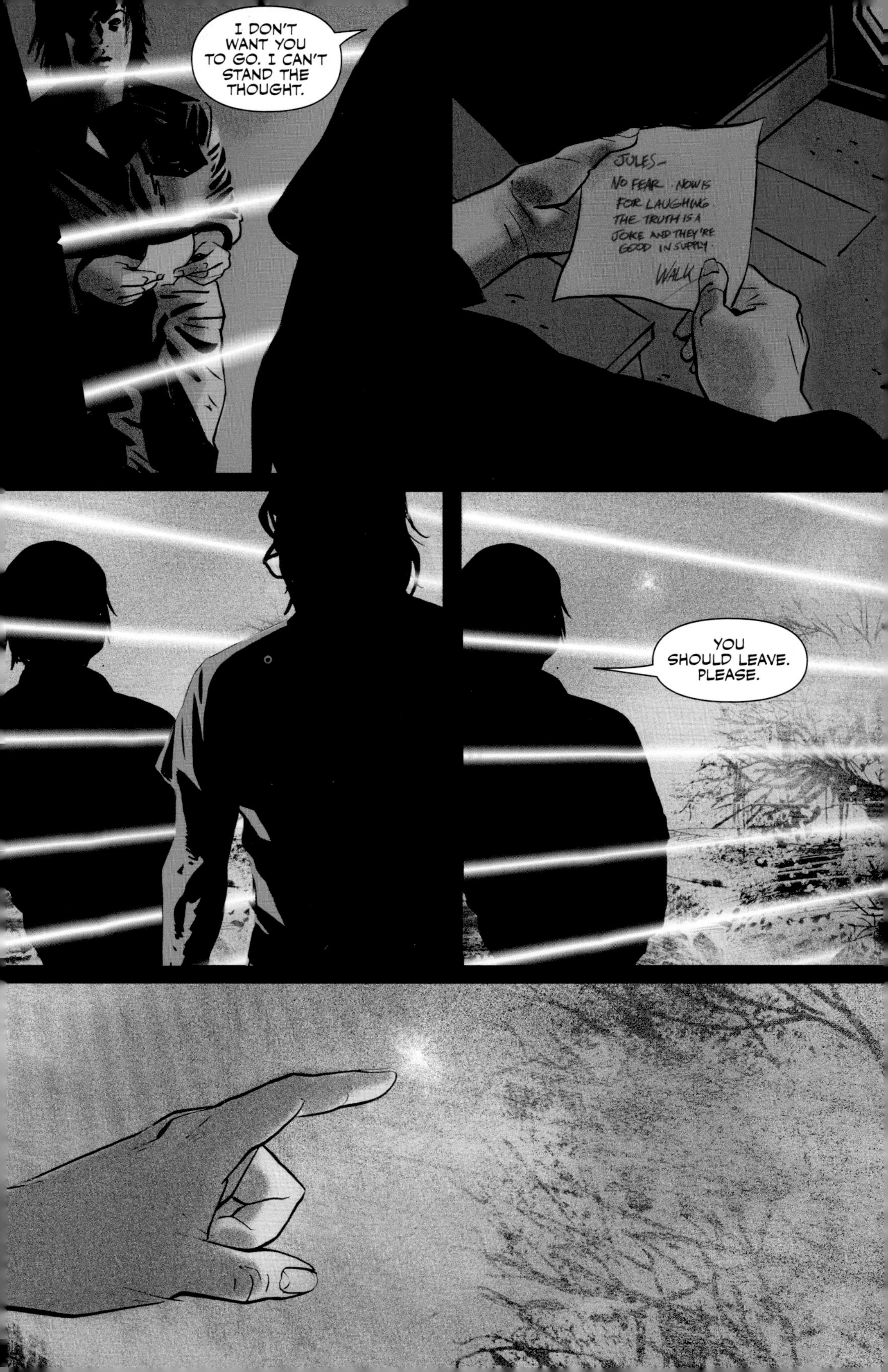
I DON'T WANT YOU TO GO. I CAN'T STAND THE THOUGHT.
JULES—
NO FEAR. NOW IS FOR LAUGHING. THE TRUTH IS A JOKE AND THEY'RE GOOD IN SUPPLY.
WALK
YOU SHOULD LEAVE. PLEASE.

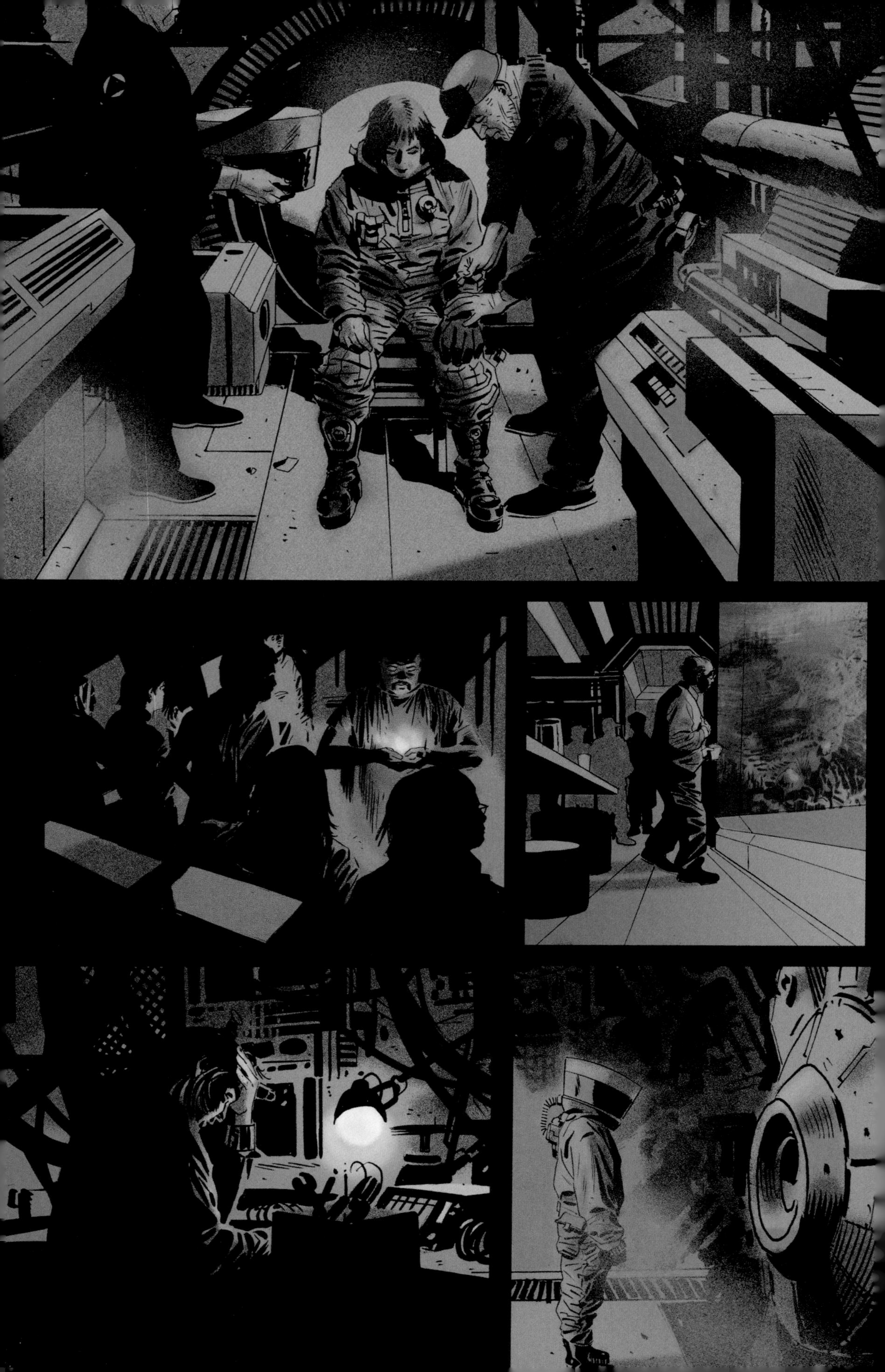

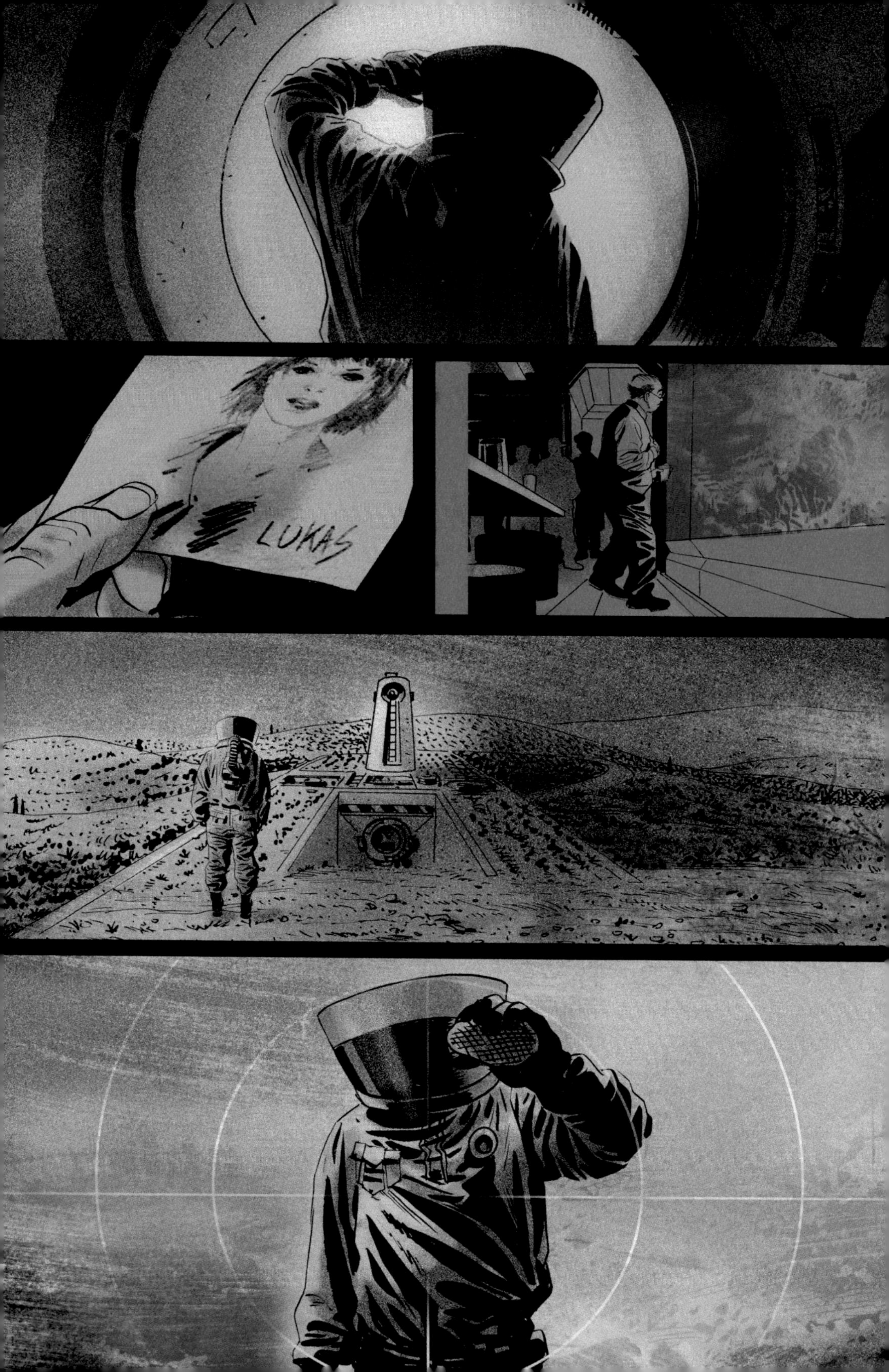
LUKAS

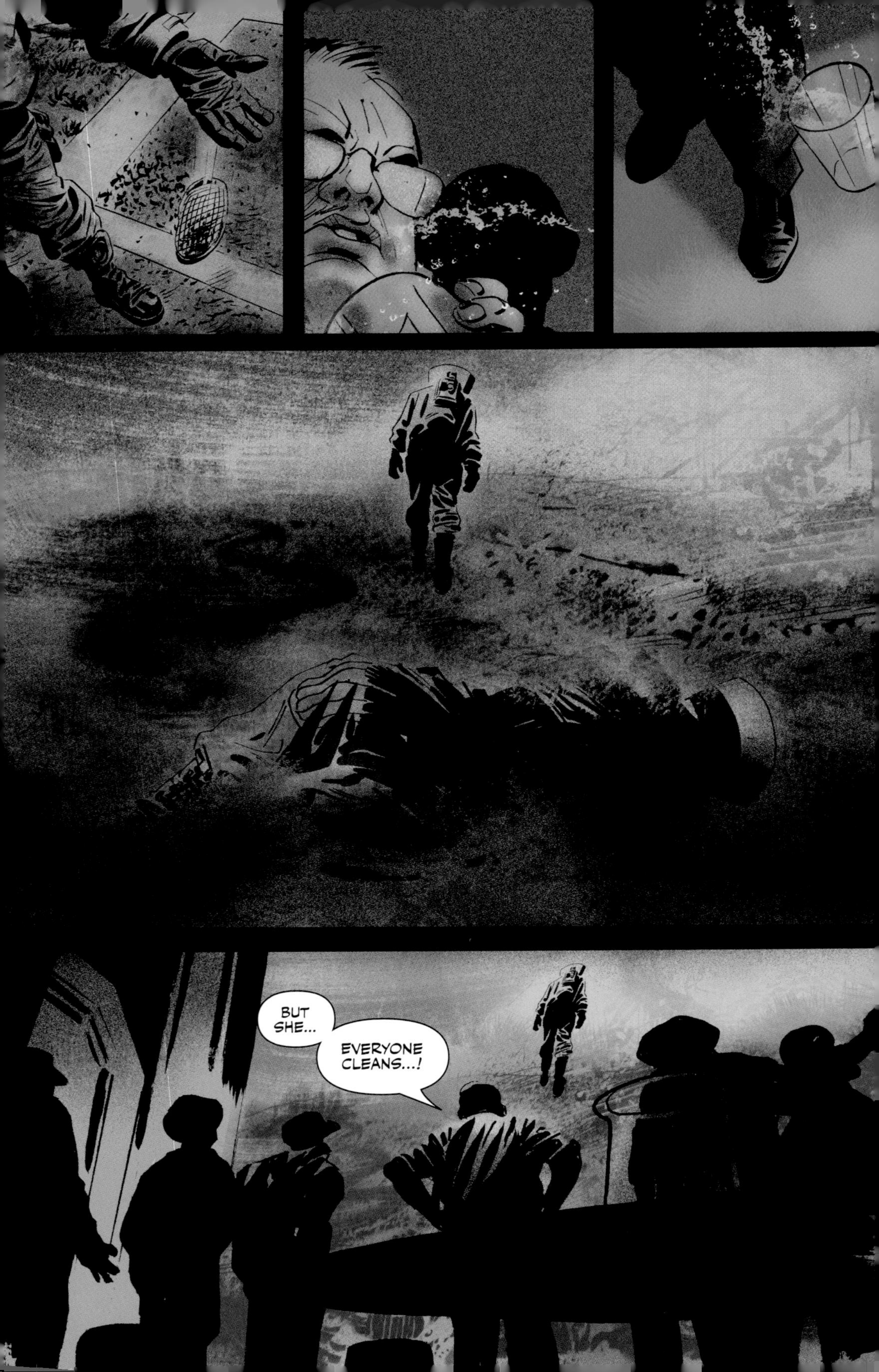
BUT SHE...
EVERYONE CLEANS...!

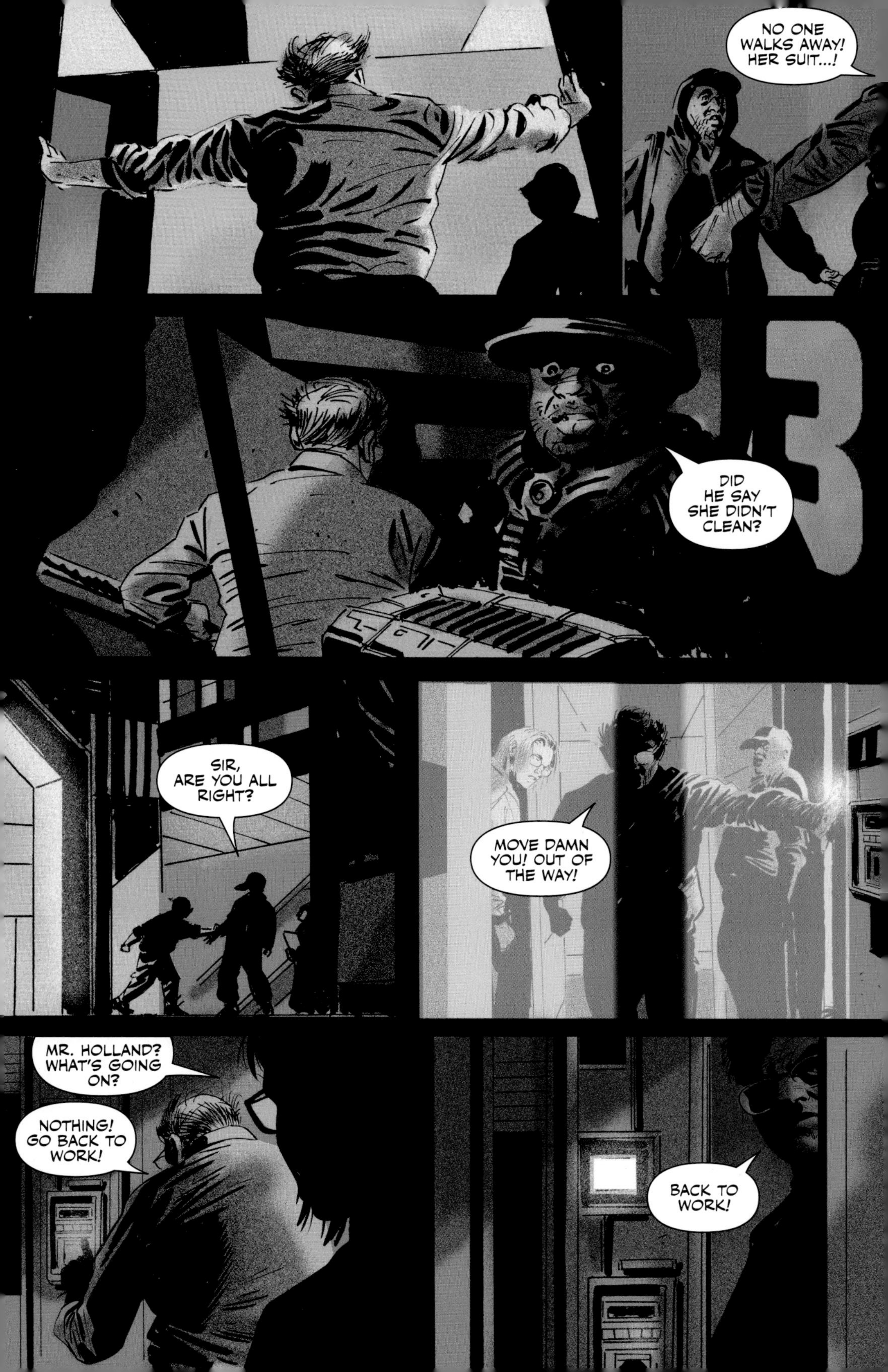
NO ONE WALKS AWAY! HER SUIT...!
DID HE SAY SHE DIDN'T CLEAN?
SIR, ARE YOU ALL RIGHT?
MOVE DAMN YOU! OUT OF THE WAY!
MR. HOLLAND? WHAT'S GOING ON?
NOTHING! GO BACK TO WORK!
BACK TO WORK!

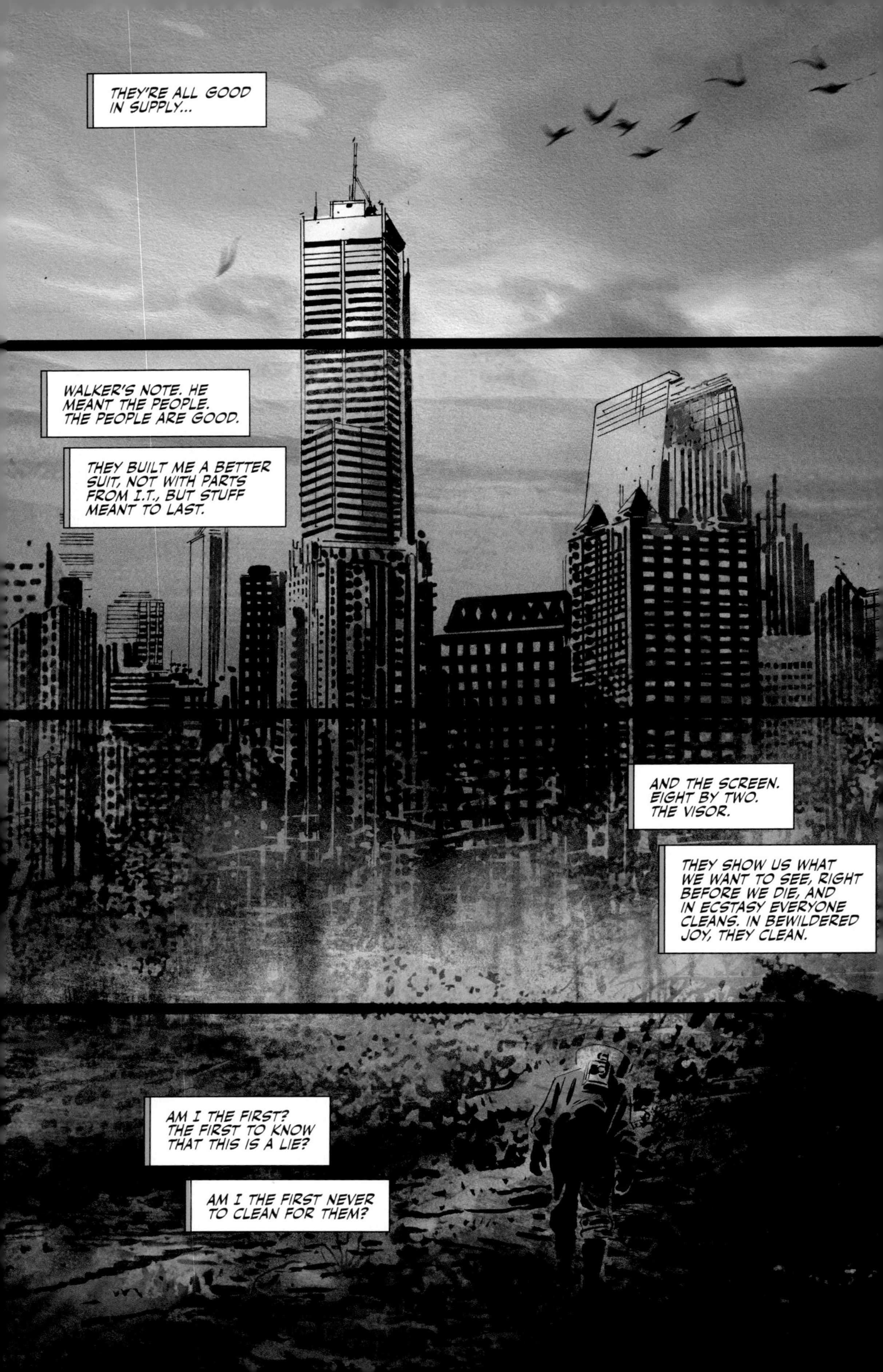
THEY'RE ALL GOOD IN SUPPLY...
WALKER'S NOTE. HE MEANT THE PEOPLE. THE PEOPLE ARE GOOD.
THEY BUILT ME A BETTER SUIT, NOT WITH PARTS FROM I.T., BUT STUFF MEANT TO LAST.
AND THE SCREEN. EIGHT BY TWO. THE VISOR.
THEY SHOW US WHAT WE WANT TO SEE, RIGHT BEFORE WE DIE, AND IN ECSTASY EVERYONE CLEANS. IN BEWILDERED JOY, THEY CLEAN.
AM I THE FIRST? THE FIRST TO KNOW THAT THIS IS A LIE?
AM I THE FIRST NEVER TO CLEAN FOR THEM?

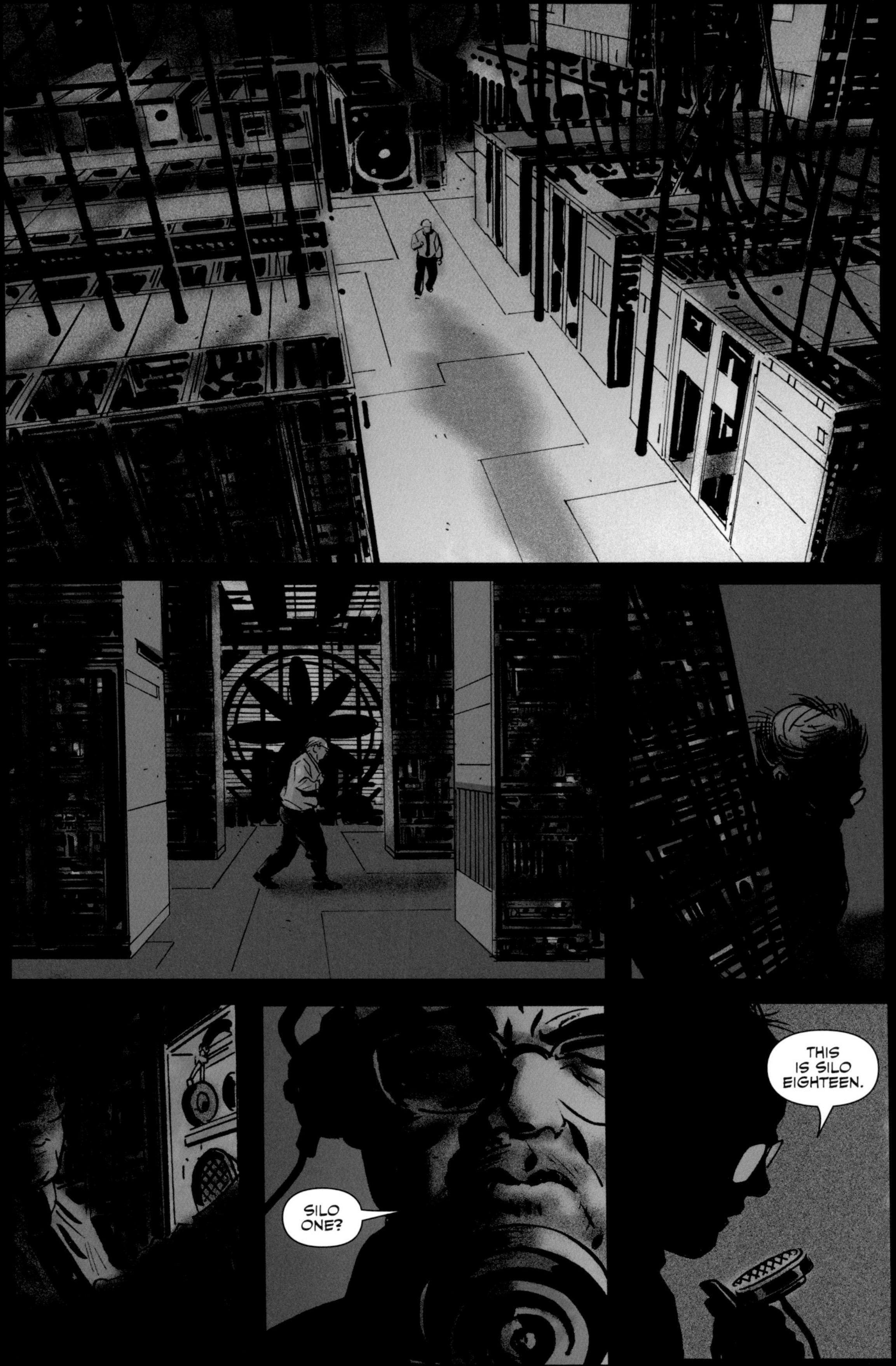
SILO ONE?
THIS IS SILO EIGHTEEN.

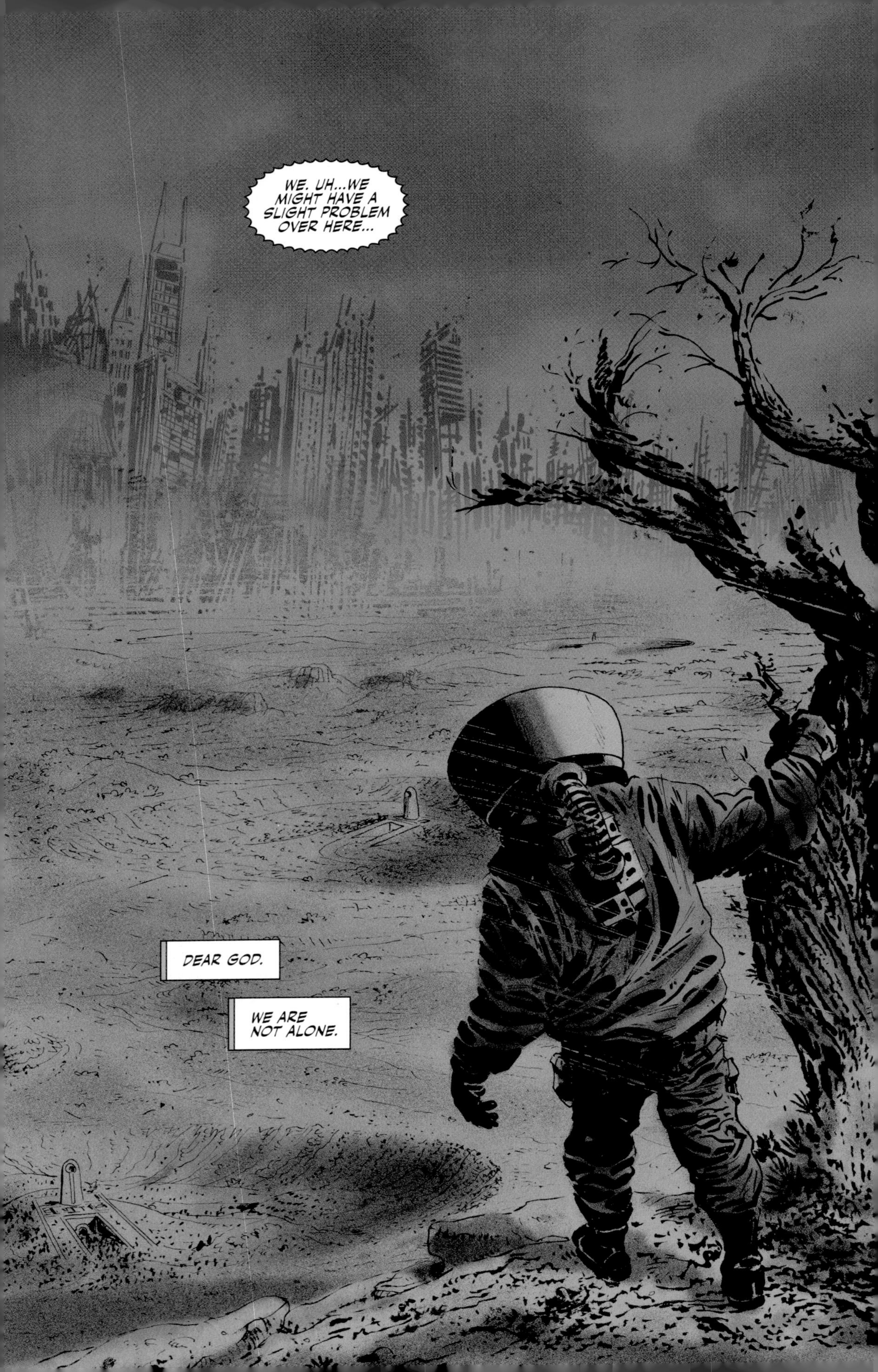

WE. UH...WE MIGHT HAVE A SLIGHT PROBLEM OVER HERE...
DEAR GOD.
WE ARE NOT ALONE.

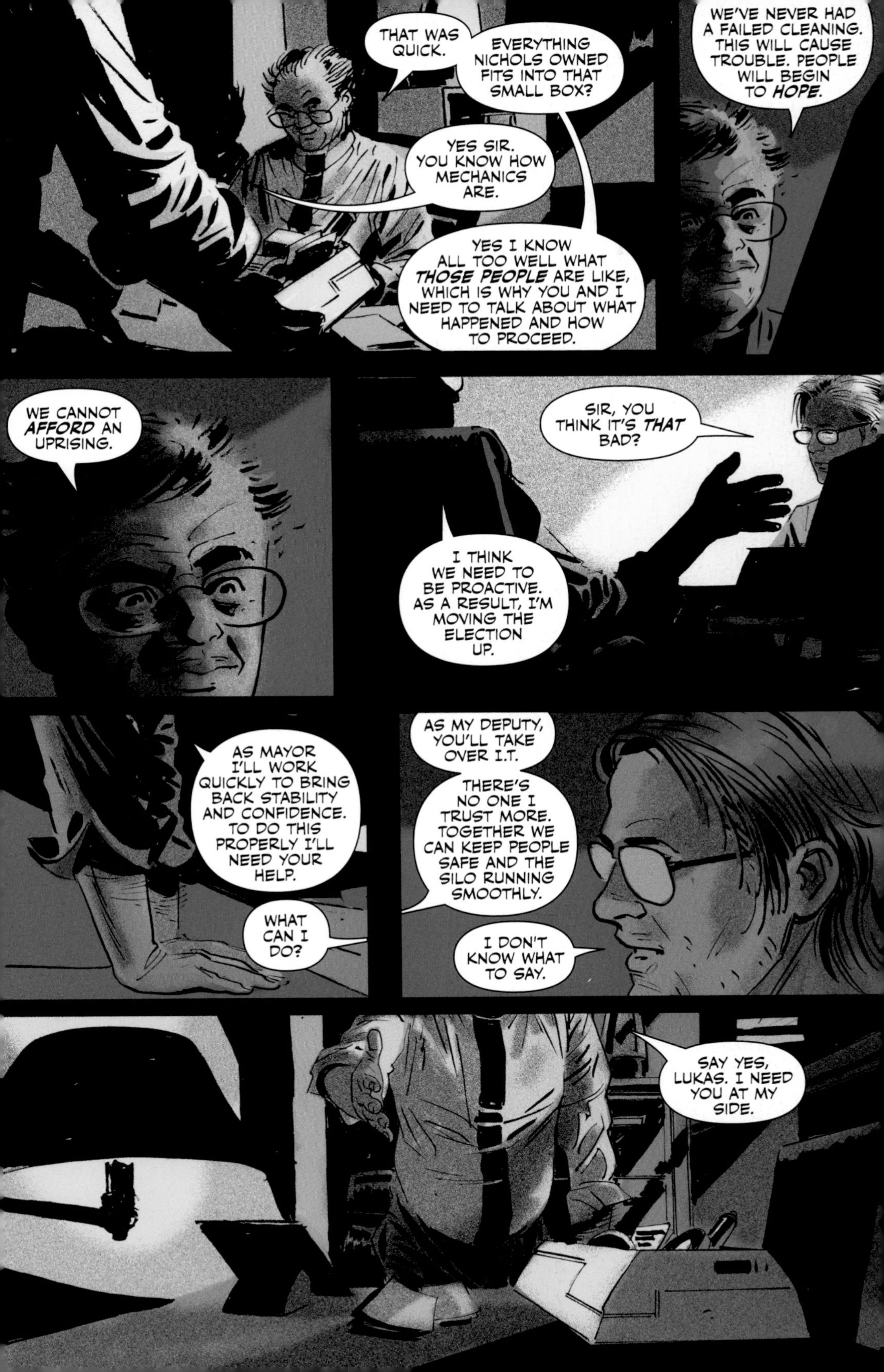
THAT WAS QUICK.
EVERYTHING NICHOLS OWNED FITS INTO THAT SMALL BOX?
YES SIR. YOU KNOW HOW MECHANICS ARE.
YES I KNOW ALL TOO WELL WHAT *THOSE PEOPLE* ARE LIKE, WHICH IS WHY YOU AND I NEED TO TALK ABOUT WHAT HAPPENED AND HOW TO PROCEED.
WE'VE NEVER HAD A FAILED CLEANING. THIS WILL CAUSE TROUBLE. PEOPLE WILL BEGIN TO *HOPE*.
WE CANNOT *AFFORD* AN UPRISING.
SIR, YOU THINK IT'S *THAT* BAD?
I THINK WE NEED TO BE PROACTIVE. AS A RESULT, I'M MOVING THE ELECTION UP.
AS MAYOR I'LL WORK QUICKLY TO BRING BACK STABILITY AND CONFIDENCE. TO DO THIS PROPERLY I'LL NEED YOUR HELP.
WHAT CAN I DO?
AS MY DEPUTY, YOU'LL TAKE OVER I.T.
THERE'S NO ONE I TRUST MORE. TOGETHER WE CAN KEEP PEOPLE SAFE AND THE SILO RUNNING SMOOTHLY.
I DON'T KNOW WHAT TO SAY.
SAY YES, LUKAS. I NEED YOU AT MY SIDE.

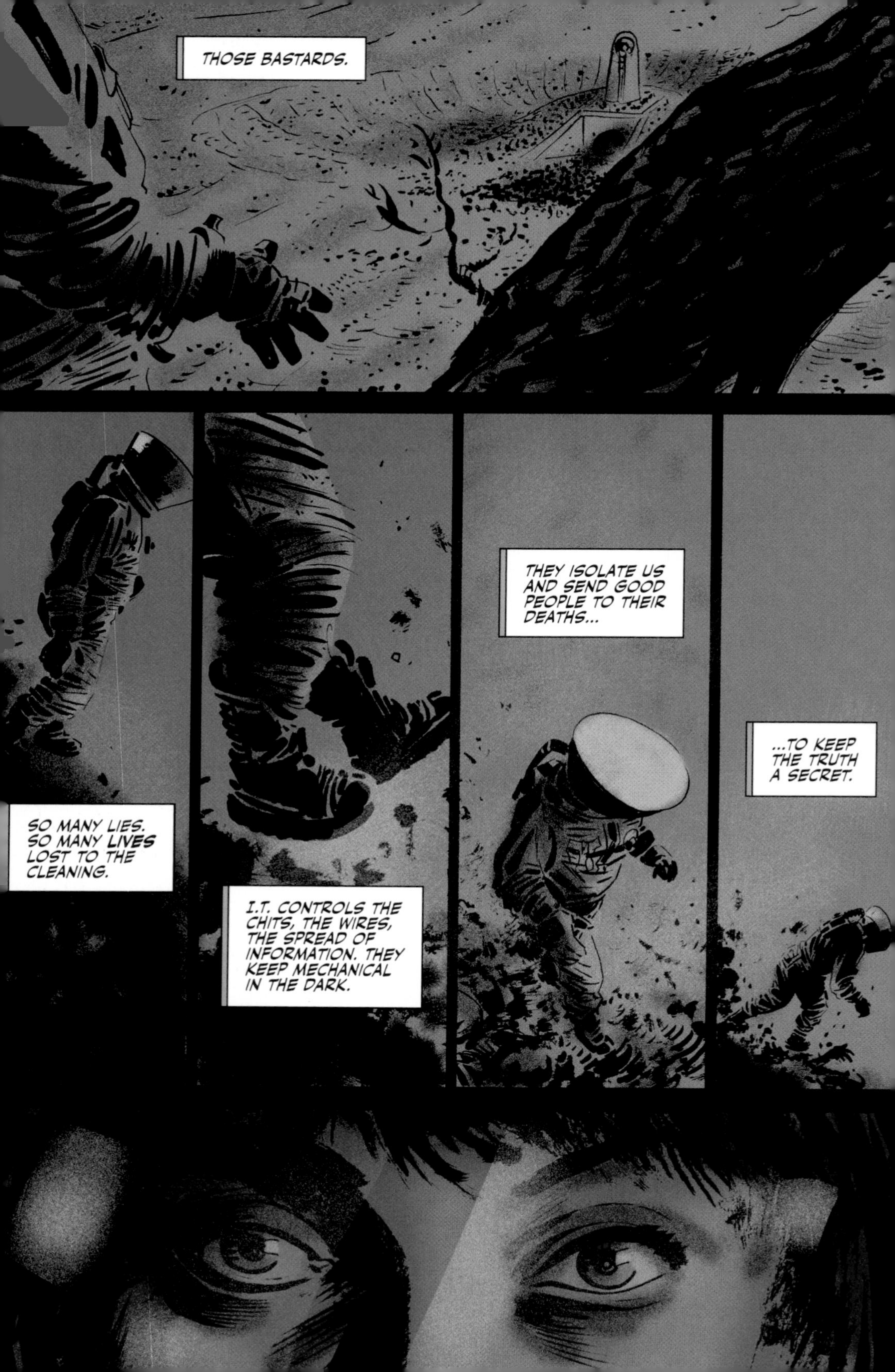
THOSE BASTARDS.
SO MANY LIES. SO MANY LIVES LOST TO THE CLEANING.
I.T. CONTROLS THE CHITS, THE WIRES, THE SPREAD OF INFORMATION. THEY KEEP MECHANICAL IN THE DARK.
THEY ISOLATE US AND SEND GOOD PEOPLE TO THEIR DEATHS...
...TO KEEP THE TRUTH A SECRET.

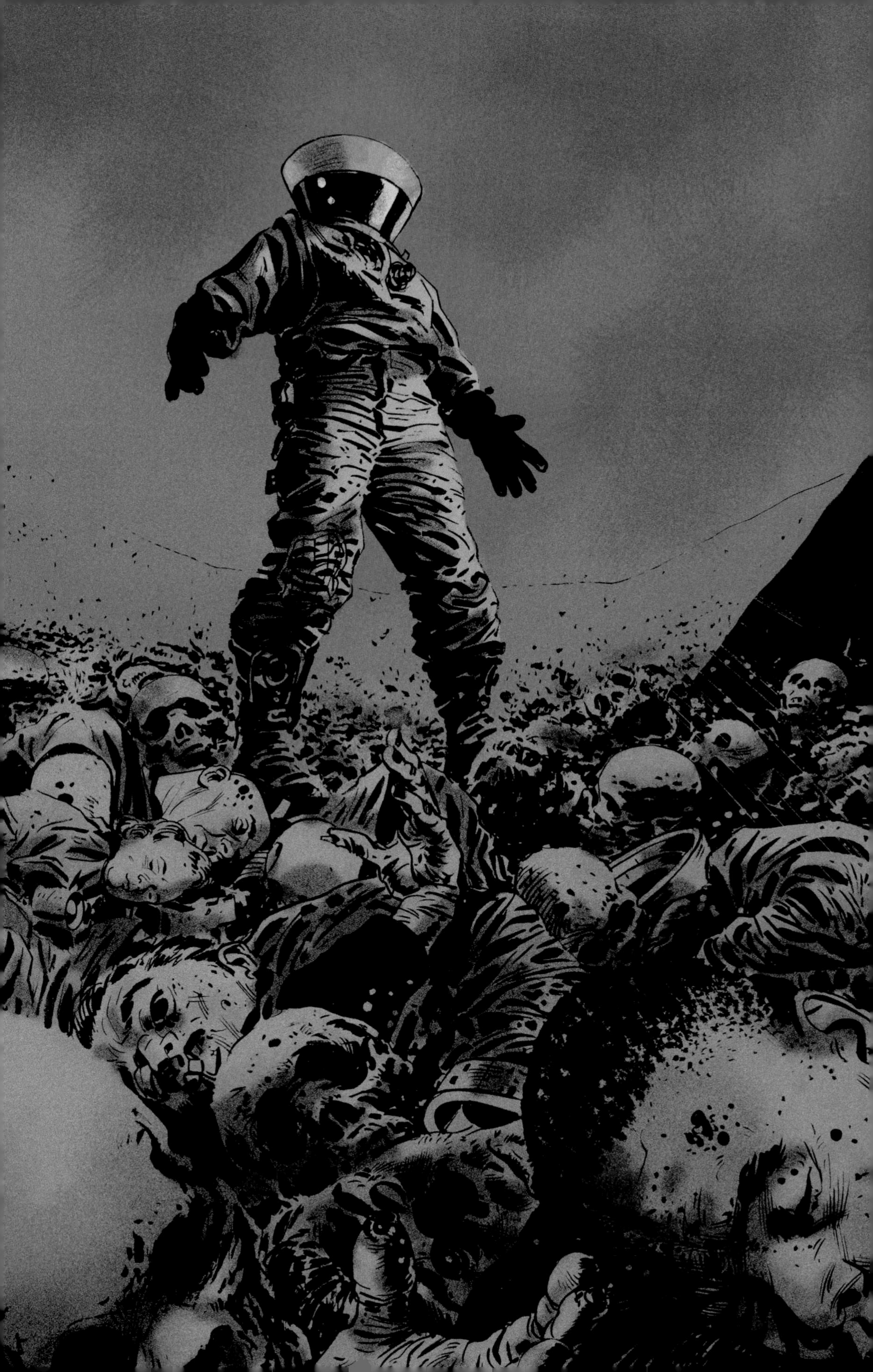

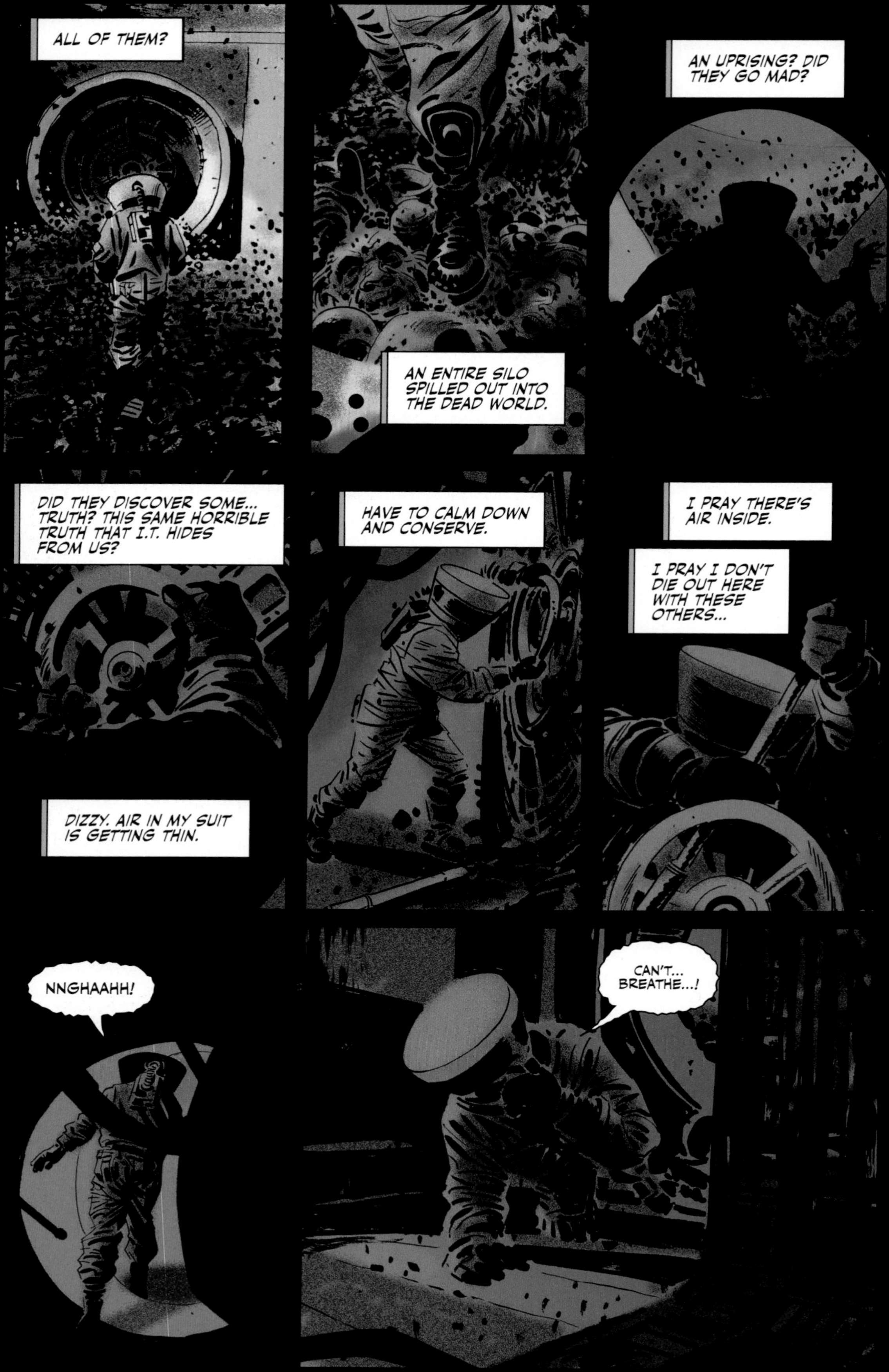
ALL OF THEM?
AN ENTIRE SILO SPILLED OUT INTO THE DEAD WORLD.
AN UPRISING? DID THEY GO MAD?
DID THEY DISCOVER SOME... TRUTH? THIS SAME HORRIBLE TRUTH THAT I.T. HIDES FROM US?
DIZZY. AIR IN MY SUIT IS GETTING THIN.
HAVE TO CALM DOWN AND CONSERVE.
I PRAY THERE'S AIR INSIDE.
I PRAY I DON'T DIE OUT HERE WITH THESE OTHERS...
NNGHAAHH!
CAN'T... BREATHE...!

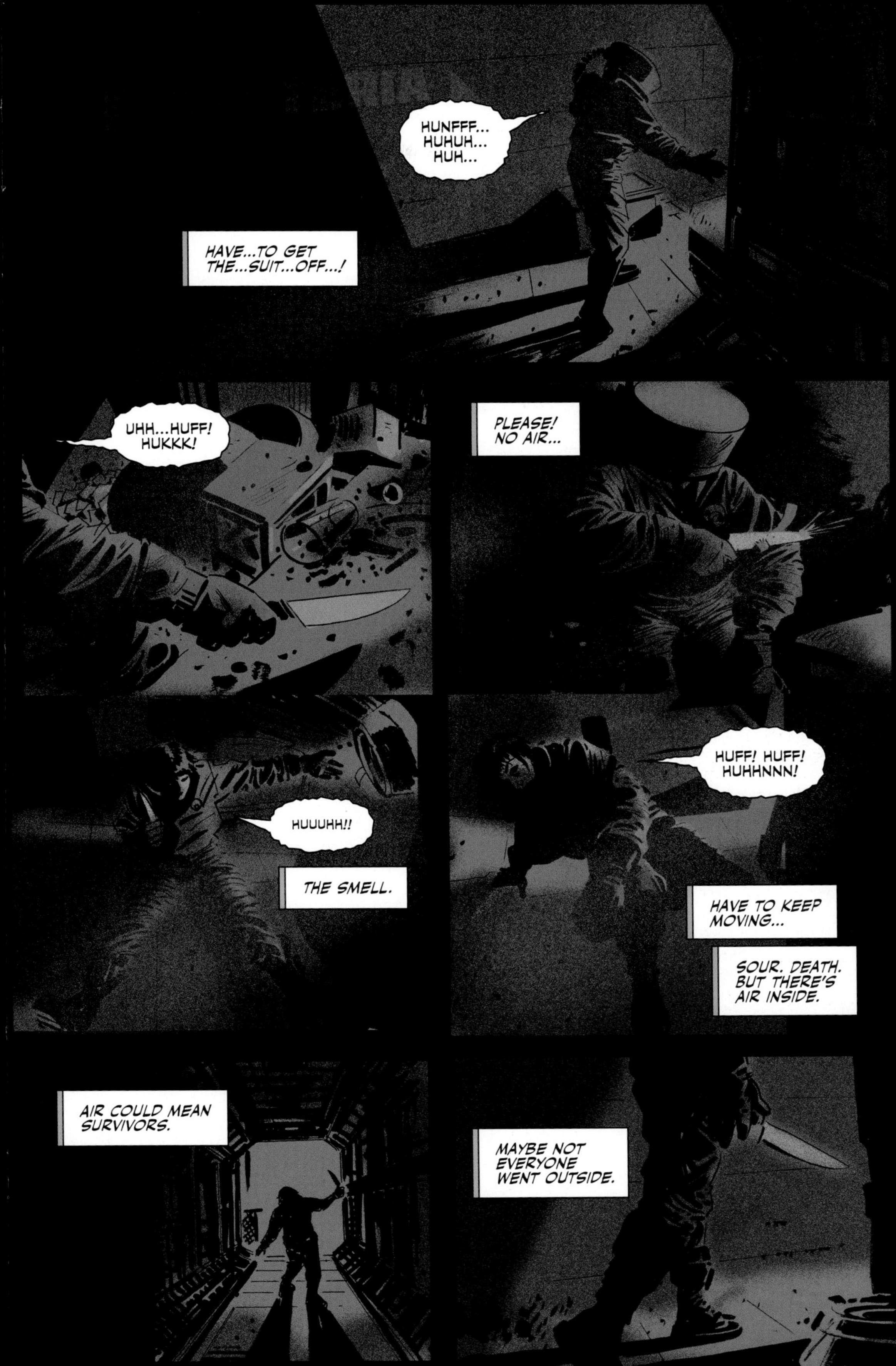
HUNFFF... HUHUH... HUH...
HAVE...TO GET THE...SUIT...OFF...!
UHH...HUFF! HUKKK!
PLEASE! NO AIR...
HUUUHH!!
THE SMELL.
HUFF! HUFF! HUHHNNN!
HAVE TO KEEP MOVING...
SOUR. DEATH. BUT THERE'S AIR INSIDE.
AIR COULD MEAN SURVIVORS.
MAYBE NOT EVERYONE WENT OUTSIDE.

A LIGHT. THERE'S STILL POWER HERE. HOW FAR DOWN...?
32...33... 34.
I.T.
TO BE CONTINUED IN THE NEXT ISSUE.

END ISSUE 3

ISSUE 4

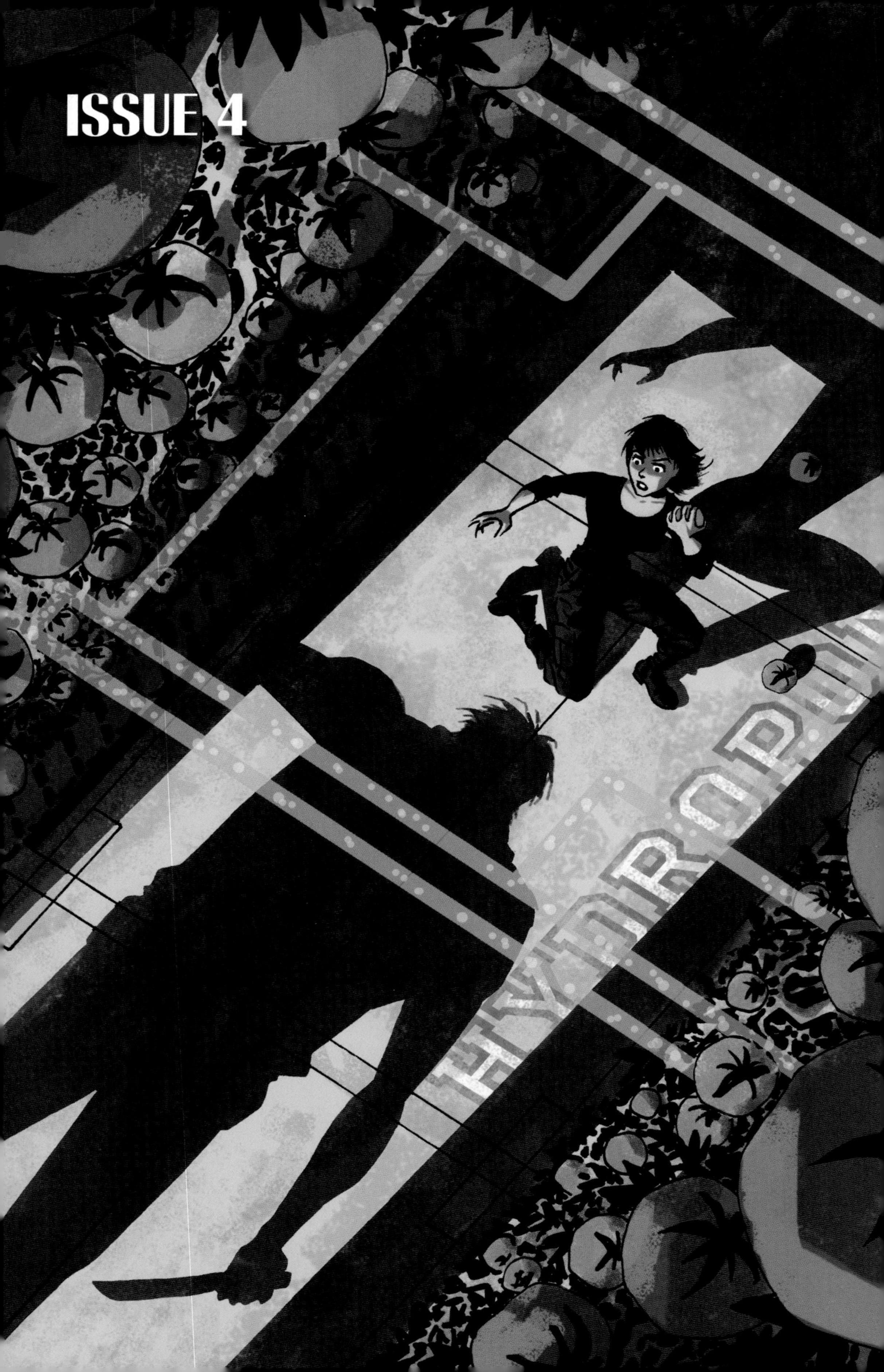

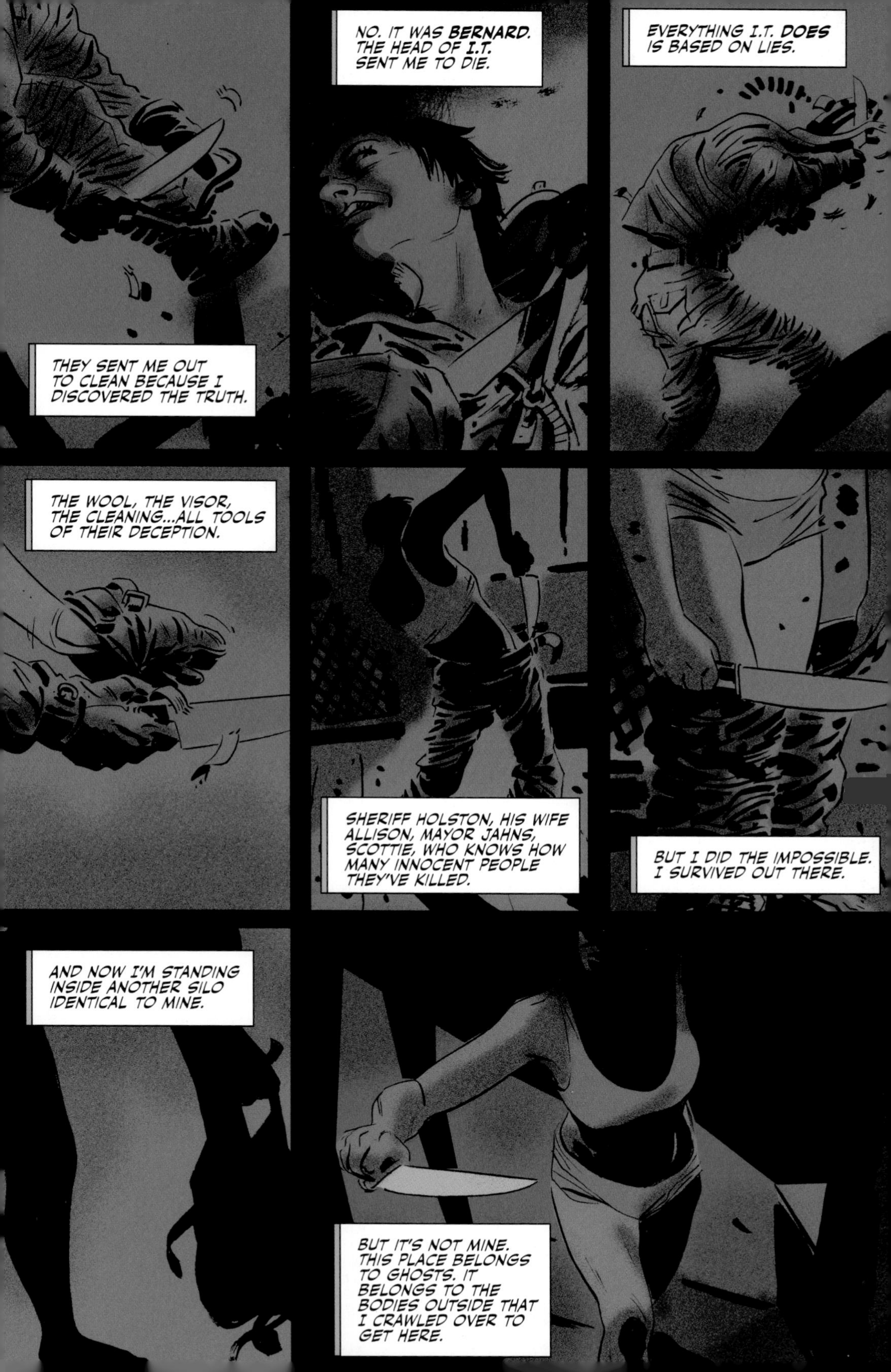
THEY SENT ME OUT TO CLEAN BECAUSE I DISCOVERED THE TRUTH.
NO. IT WAS BERNARD. THE HEAD OF I.T. SENT ME TO DIE.
EVERYTHING I.T. DOES IS BASED ON LIES.
THE WOOL, THE VISOR, THE CLEANING...ALL TOOLS OF THEIR DECEPTION.
SHERIFF HOLSTON, HIS WIFE ALLISON, MAYOR JAHNS, SCOTTIE, WHO KNOWS HOW MANY INNOCENT PEOPLE THEY'VE KILLED.
BUT I DID THE IMPOSSIBLE. I SURVIVED OUT THERE.
AND NOW I'M STANDING INSIDE ANOTHER SILO IDENTICAL TO MINE.
BUT IT'S NOT MINE. THIS PLACE BELONGS TO GHOSTS. IT BELONGS TO THE BODIES OUTSIDE THAT I CRAWLED OVER TO GET HERE.

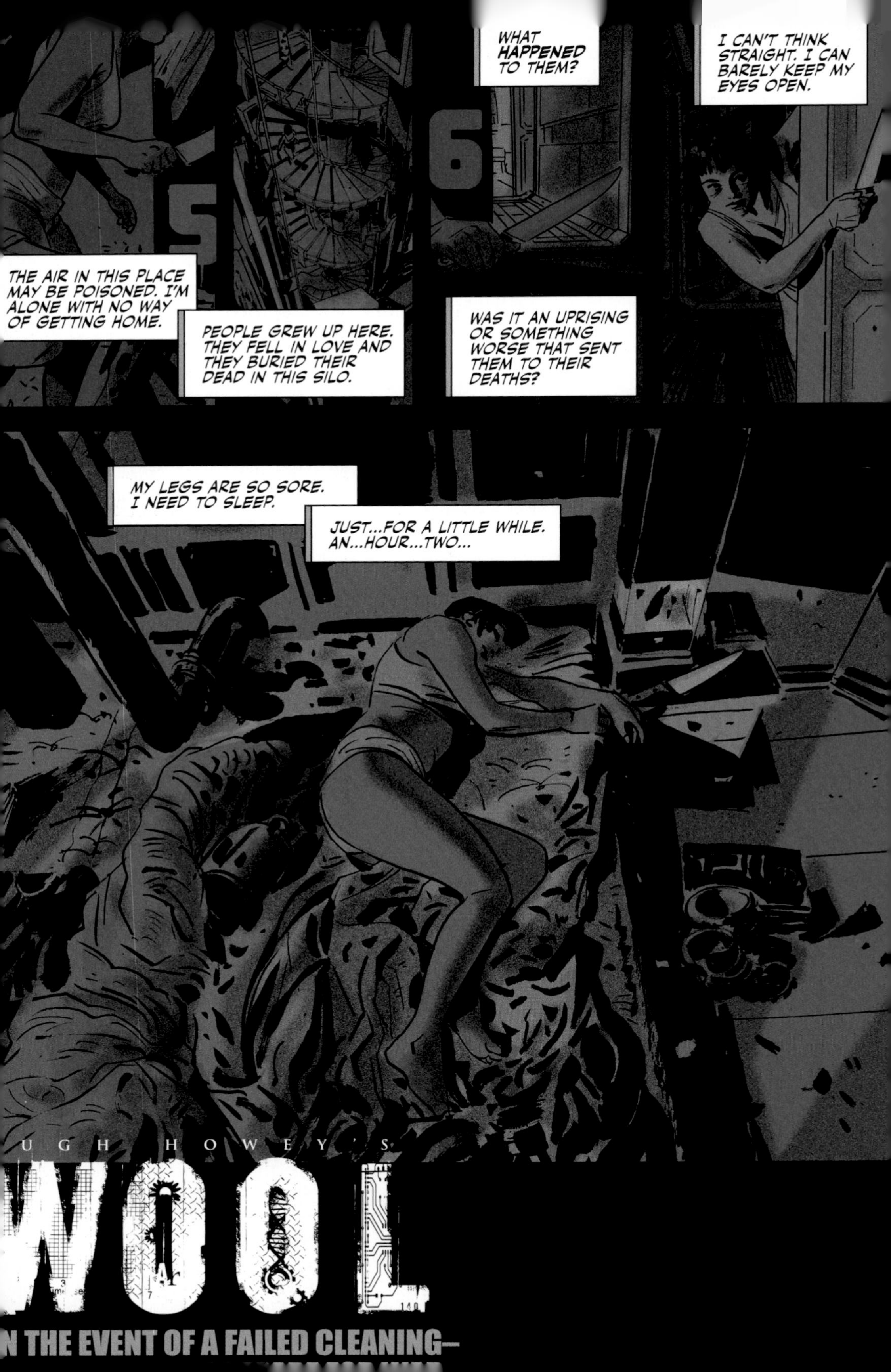
THE AIR IN THIS PLACE MAY BE POISONED. I'M ALONE WITH NO WAY OF GETTING HOME.
PEOPLE GREW UP HERE. THEY FELL IN LOVE AND THEY BURIED THEIR DEAD IN THIS SILO.
5
6
WHAT HAPPENED TO THEM?
WAS IT AN UPRISING OR SOMETHING WORSE THAT SENT THEM TO THEIR DEATHS?
I CAN'T THINK STRAIGHT. I CAN BARELY KEEP MY EYES OPEN.
MY LEGS ARE SO SORE. I NEED TO SLEEP.
JUST...FOR A LITTLE WHILE. AN...HOUR...TWO...
UGH HOWEY'S
WOOL
N THE EVENT OF A FAILED CLEANING–

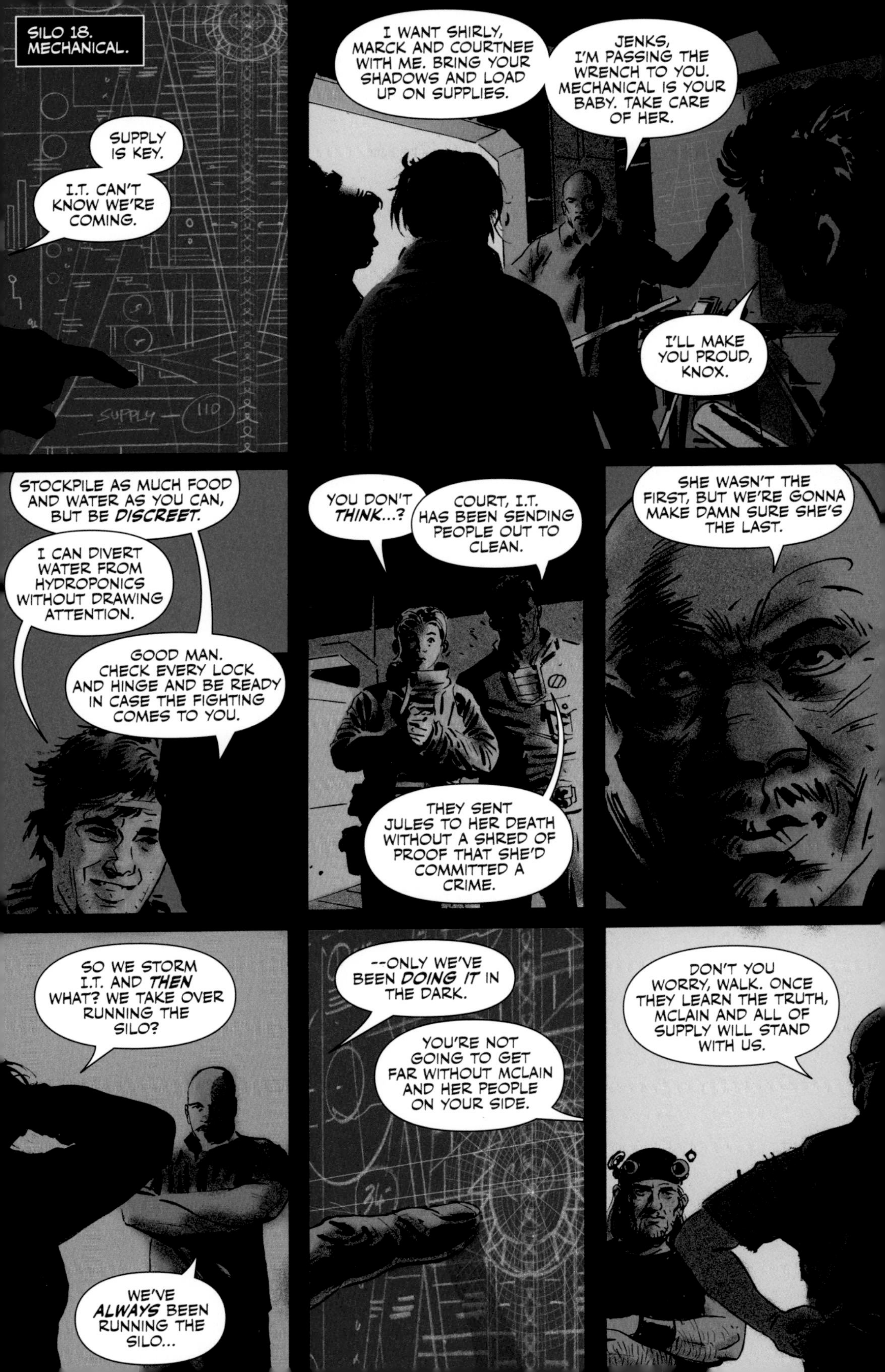
SILO 18. MECHANICAL.
SUPPLY IS KEY.
I.T. CAN'T KNOW WE'RE COMING.
SUPPLY
110
I WANT SHIRLY, MARCK AND COURTNEE WITH ME. BRING YOUR SHADOWS AND LOAD UP ON SUPPLIES.
JENKS, I'M PASSING THE WRENCH TO YOU. MECHANICAL IS YOUR BABY. TAKE CARE OF HER.
I'LL MAKE YOU PROUD, KNOX.
STOCKPILE AS MUCH FOOD AND WATER AS YOU CAN, BUT BE *DISCREET*.
I CAN DIVERT WATER FROM HYDROPONICS WITHOUT DRAWING ATTENTION.
GOOD MAN. CHECK EVERY LOCK AND HINGE AND BE READY IN CASE THE FIGHTING COMES TO YOU.
YOU DON'T *THINK*...?
COURT, I.T. HAS BEEN SENDING PEOPLE OUT TO CLEAN.
THEY SENT JULES TO HER DEATH WITHOUT A SHRED OF PROOF THAT SHE'D COMMITTED A CRIME.
SHE WASN'T THE FIRST, BUT WE'RE GONNA MAKE DAMN SURE SHE'S THE LAST.
SO WE STORM I.T. AND *THEN* WHAT? WE TAKE OVER RUNNING THE SILO?
WE'VE *ALWAYS* BEEN RUNNING THE SILO...
--ONLY WE'VE BEEN *DOING IT* IN THE DARK.
YOU'RE NOT GOING TO GET FAR WITHOUT MCLAIN AND HER PEOPLE ON YOUR SIDE.
DON'T YOU WORRY, WALK. ONCE THEY LEARN THE TRUTH, MCLAIN AND ALL OF SUPPLY WILL STAND WITH US.

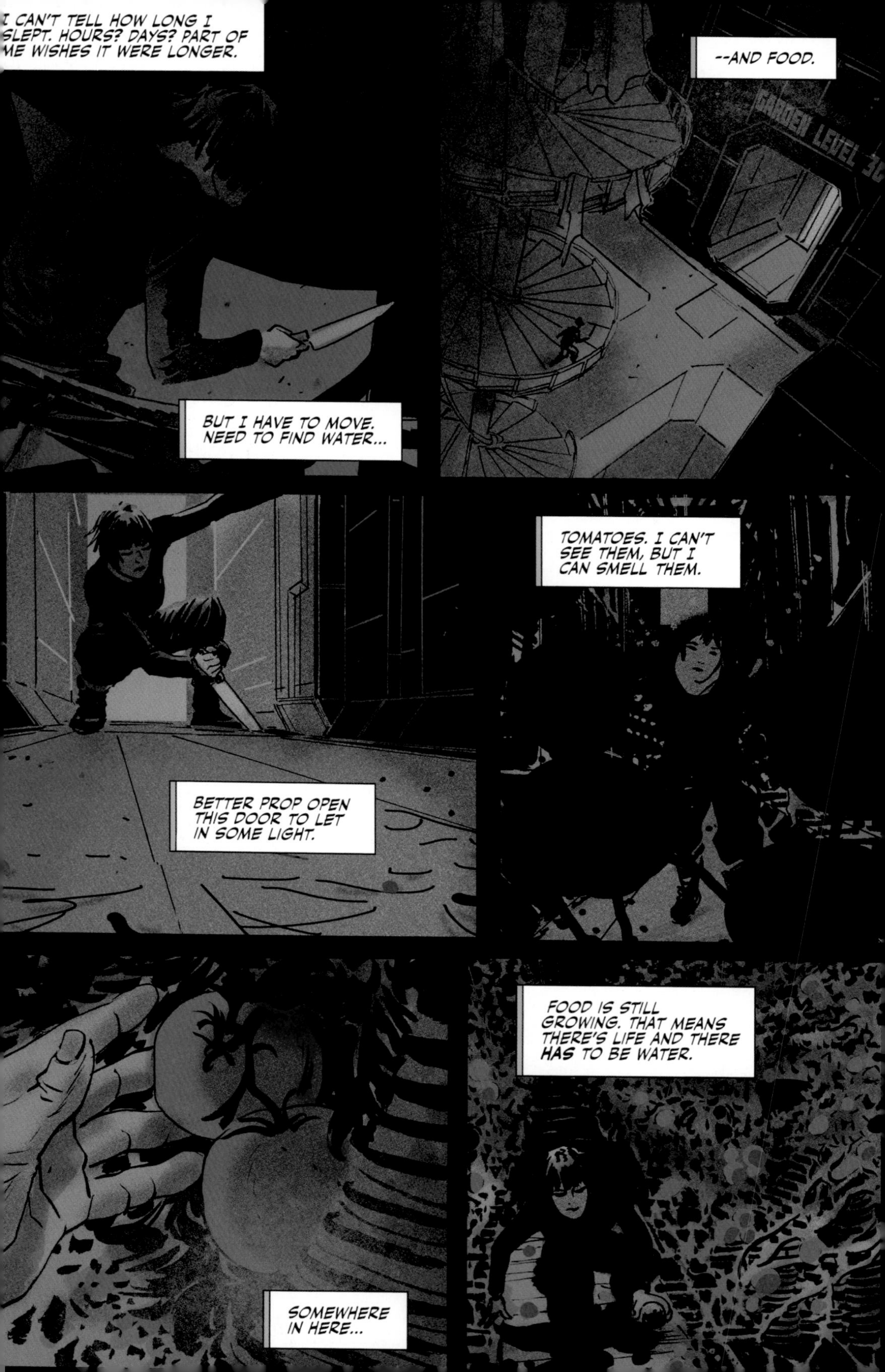
I CAN'T TELL HOW LONG I SLEPT. HOURS? DAYS? PART OF ME WISHES IT WERE LONGER.
BUT I HAVE TO MOVE. NEED TO FIND WATER...
--AND FOOD.
GARDEN LEVEL 3
BETTER PROP OPEN THIS DOOR TO LET IN SOME LIGHT.
TOMATOES. I CAN'T SEE THEM, BUT I CAN SMELL THEM.
SOMEWHERE IN HERE...
FOOD IS STILL GROWING. THAT MEANS THERE'S LIFE AND THERE HAS TO BE WATER.

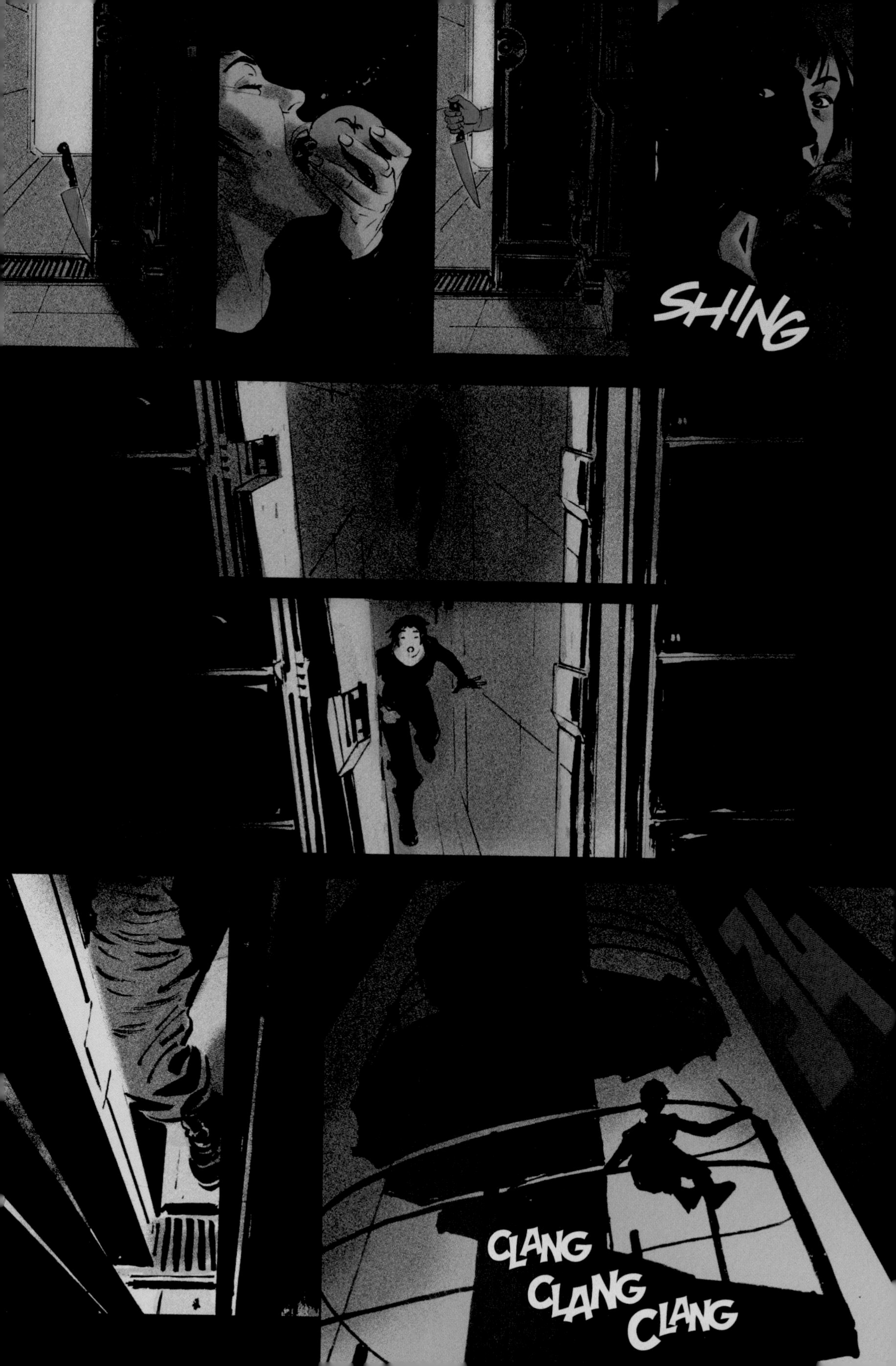
SHING
CLANG
CLANG
CLANG

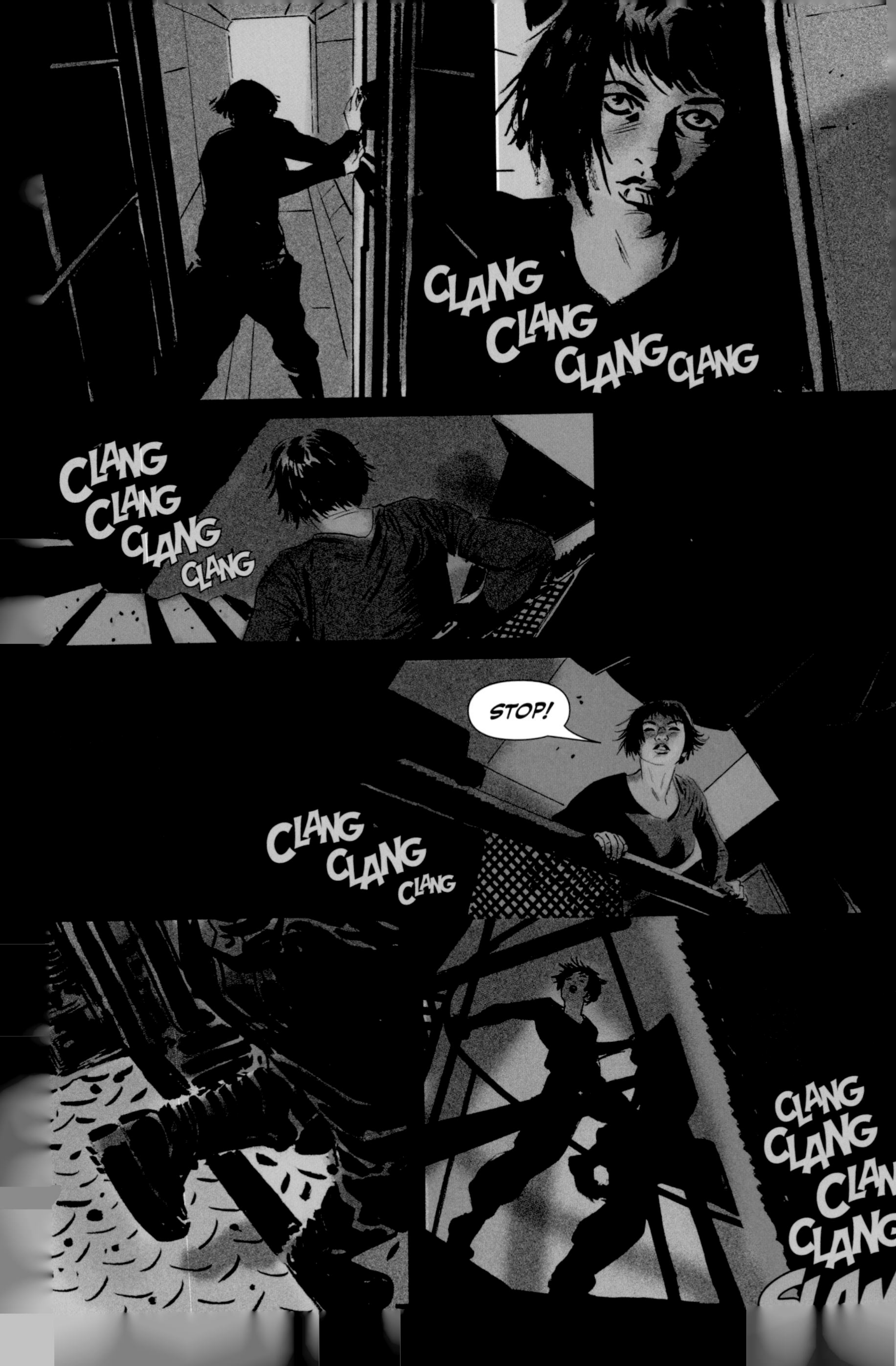
CLANG
CLANG
CLANG CLANG
CLANG
CLANG
CLANG
CLANG
STOP!
CLANG
CLANG
CLANG
CLANG
CLANG
CLAN
CLANG

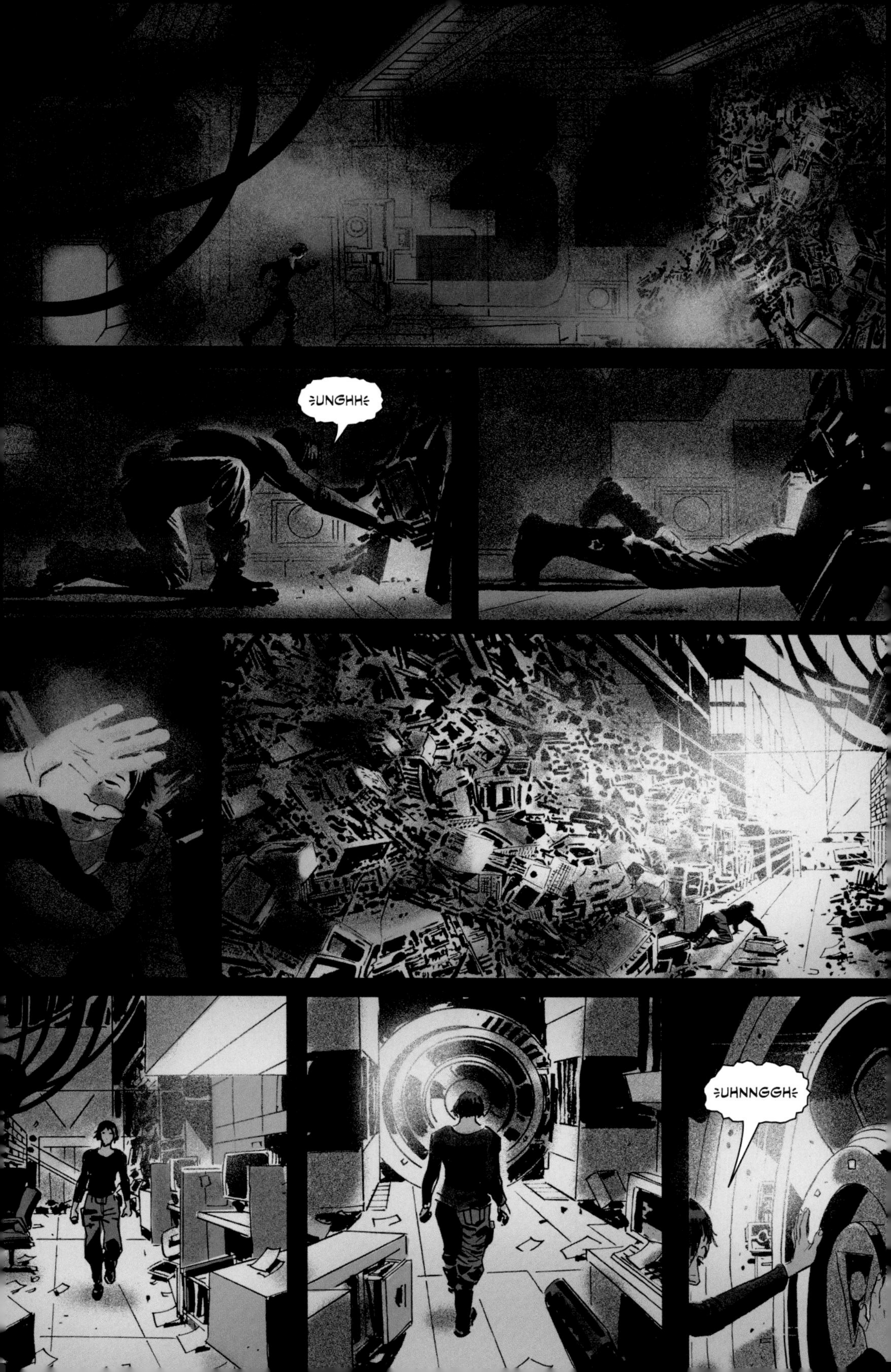
UNGHH
UHNNGGH

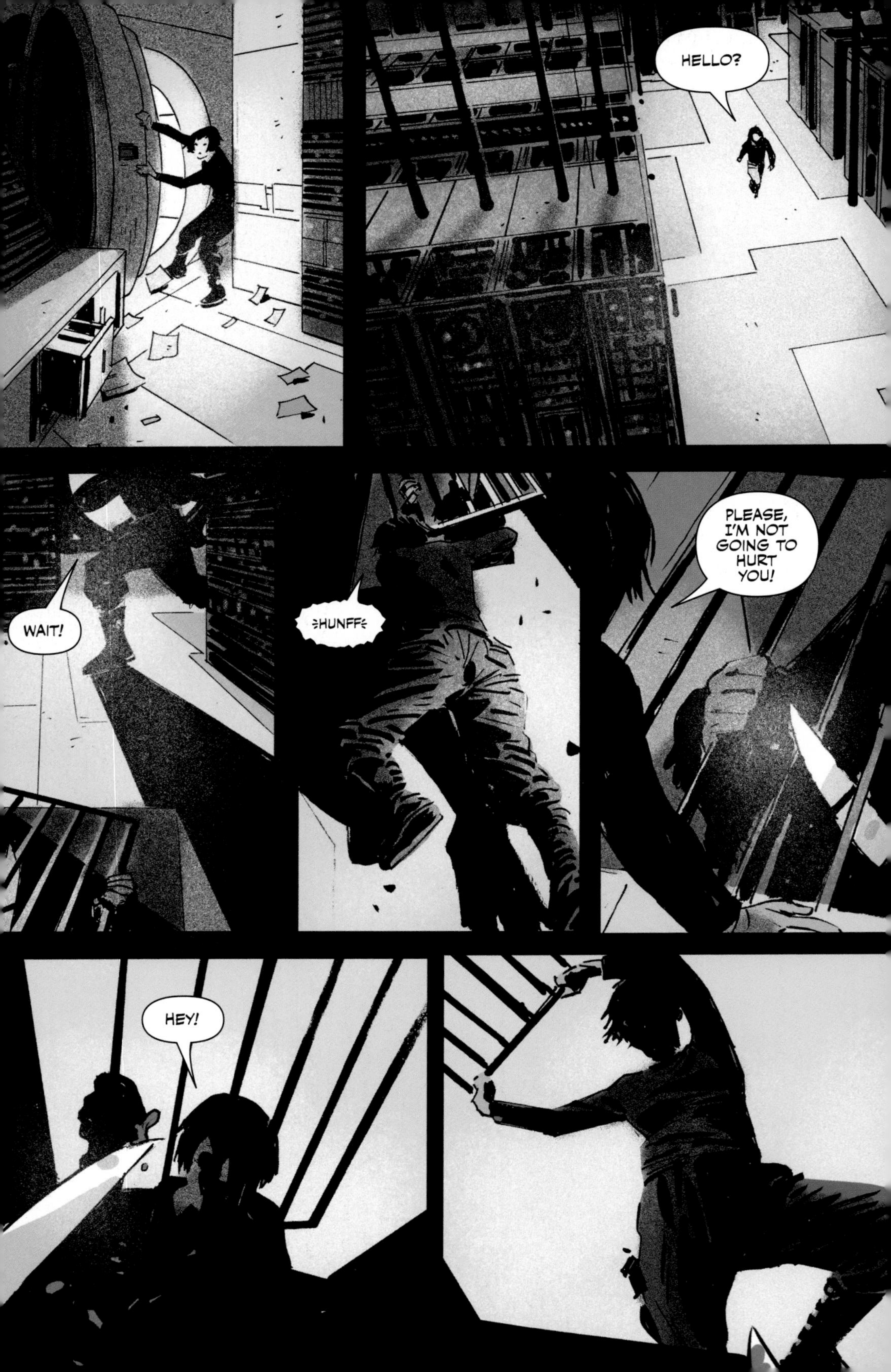
HELLO?
WAIT!
HUNFF
PLEASE, I'M NOT GOING TO HURT YOU!
HEY!

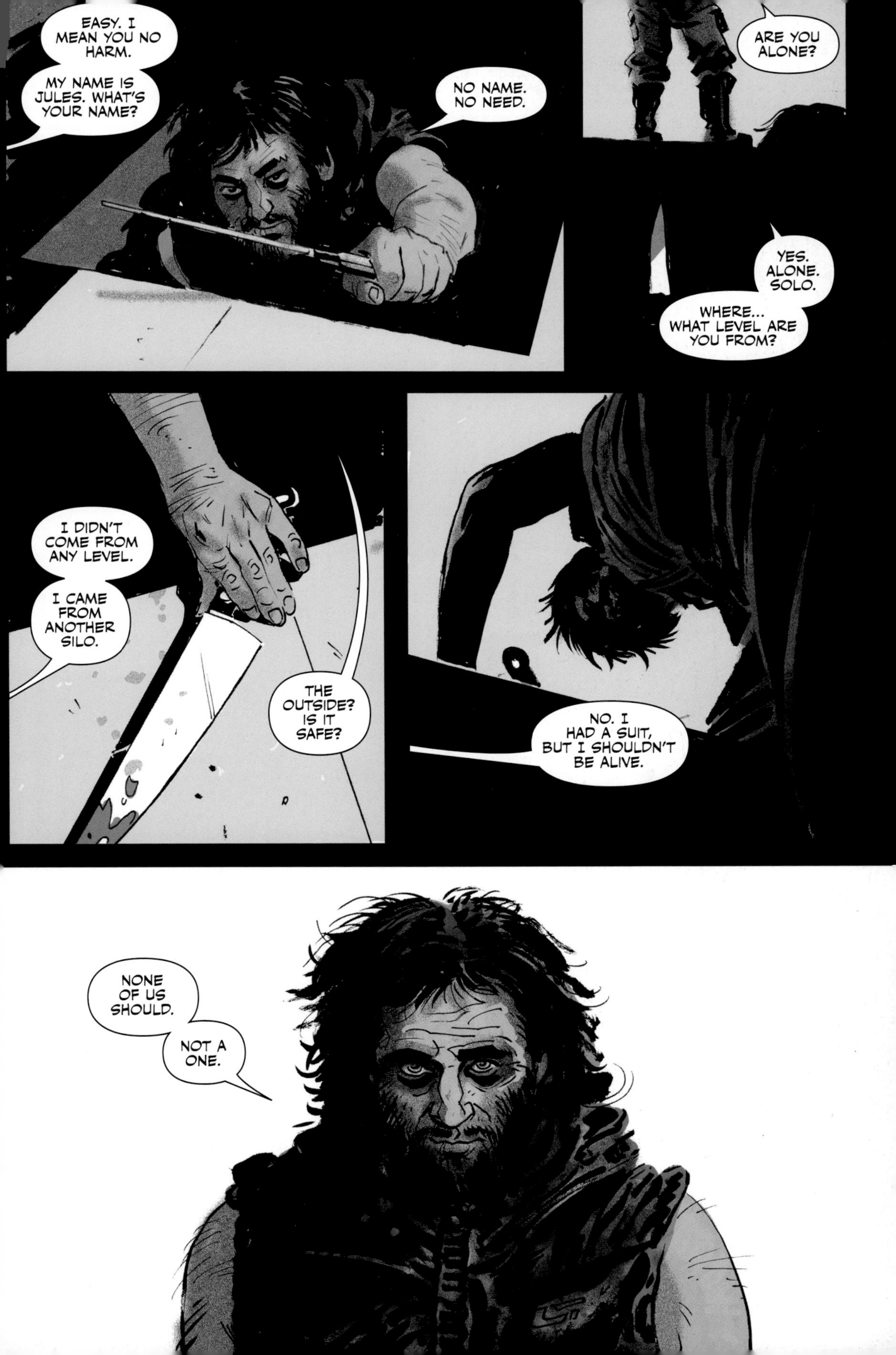
EASY. I MEAN YOU NO HARM.
MY NAME IS JULES. WHAT'S YOUR NAME?
NO NAME. NO NEED.
ARE YOU ALONE?
YES. ALONE. SOLO.
WHERE... WHAT LEVEL ARE YOU FROM?
I DIDN'T COME FROM ANY LEVEL.
I CAME FROM ANOTHER SILO.
THE OUTSIDE? IS IT SAFE?
NO. I HAD A SUIT, BUT I SHOULDN'T BE ALIVE.
NONE OF US SHOULD.
NOT A ONE.

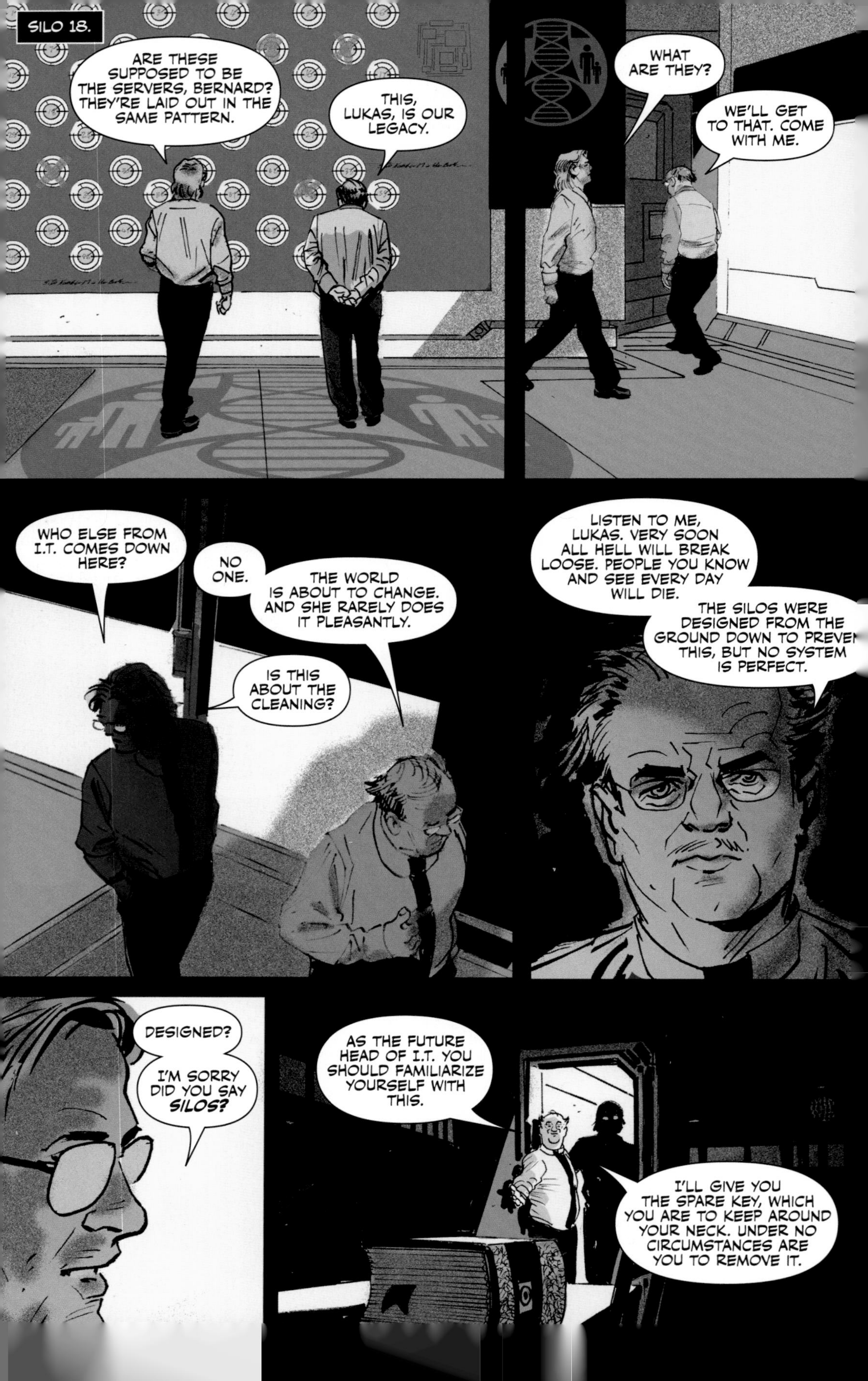
SILO 18.
ARE THESE SUPPOSED TO BE THE SERVERS, BERNARD? THEY'RE LAID OUT IN THE SAME PATTERN.
THIS, LUKAS, IS OUR LEGACY.
WHAT ARE THEY?
WE'LL GET TO THAT. COME WITH ME.
WHO ELSE FROM I.T. COMES DOWN HERE?
NO ONE.
THE WORLD IS ABOUT TO CHANGE. AND SHE RARELY DOES IT PLEASANTLY.
IS THIS ABOUT THE CLEANING?
LISTEN TO ME, LUKAS. VERY SOON ALL HELL WILL BREAK LOOSE. PEOPLE YOU KNOW AND SEE EVERY DAY WILL DIE.
THE SILOS WERE DESIGNED FROM THE GROUND DOWN TO PREVEN THIS, BUT NO SYSTEM IS PERFECT.
DESIGNED?
I'M SORRY DID YOU SAY *SILOS?*
AS THE FUTURE HEAD OF I.T. YOU SHOULD FAMILIARIZE YOURSELF WITH THIS.
I'LL GIVE YOU THE SPARE KEY, WHICH YOU ARE TO KEEP AROUND YOUR NECK. UNDER NO CIRCUMSTANCES ARE YOU TO REMOVE IT.

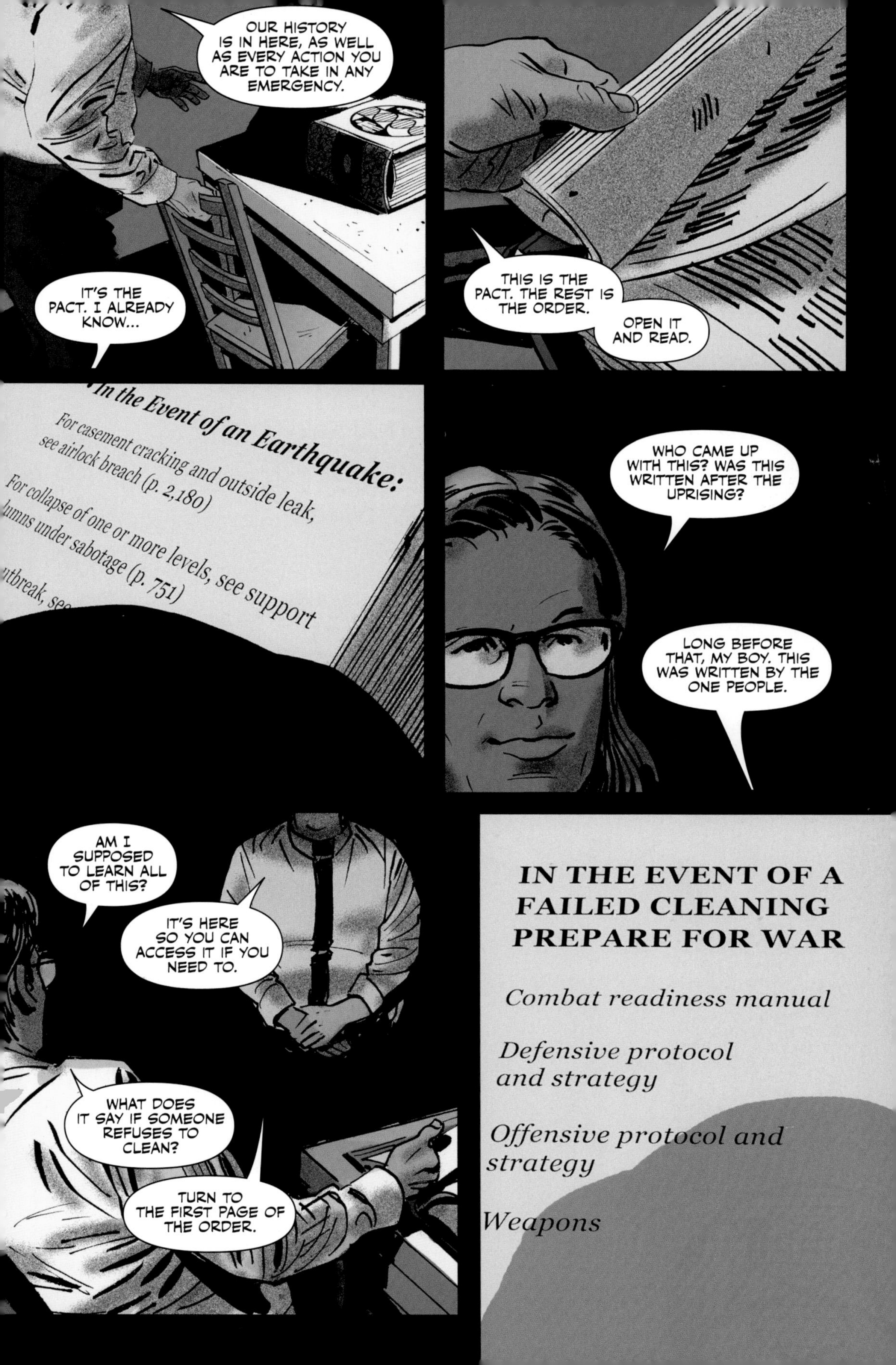
OUR HISTORY IS IN HERE, AS WELL AS EVERY ACTION YOU ARE TO TAKE IN ANY EMERGENCY.
IT'S THE PACT. I ALREADY KNOW...
THIS IS THE PACT. THE REST IS THE ORDER.
OPEN IT AND READ.
In the Event of an Earthquake:
For casement cracking and outside leak, see airlock breach (p. 2,180)
For collapse of one or more levels, see support lumns under sabotage (p. 751)
utbreak, se
WHO CAME UP WITH THIS? WAS THIS WRITTEN AFTER THE UPRISING?
LONG BEFORE THAT, MY BOY. THIS WAS WRITTEN BY THE ONE PEOPLE.
AM I SUPPOSED TO LEARN ALL OF THIS?
IT'S HERE SO YOU CAN ACCESS IT IF YOU NEED TO.
WHAT DOES IT SAY IF SOMEONE REFUSES TO CLEAN?
TURN TO THE FIRST PAGE OF THE ORDER.
IN THE EVENT OF A FAILED CLEANING PREPARE FOR WAR
Combat readiness manual
Defensive protocol and strategy
Offensive protocol and strategy
Weapons

YOU LIVE HERE?

IT ISN'T MUCH, BUT IT IS MY HOME.

IS THERE NO ONE ELSE IN THE SILO? MAYBE FARTHER DOWN?

I DON'T THINK SO. A TOMATO GOES MISSING NOW AND THEN, BUT I FIGURE IT'S THE RATS...

SOMETIMES I HEAR THINGS AND I THINK THERE MIGHT BE OTHERS. NEVER SEE ANYONE THOUGH.

HOW MANY YEARS HAS IT BEEN?

THIRTY-FOUR.

YOU'VE BEEN ALONE FOR THIRTY-FOUR *YEARS*?

HOW *OLD* ARE YOU?

NEXT MONTH I'LL BE FIFTY. I THINK.

THIS IS FUN, TALKING. I TALK TO THINGS SOMETIMES. I ALSO WHISTLE.

I'M A GOOD WHISTLER.

YOU WOULD'VE BEEN SIXTEEN. WHAT HAPPENED HERE?

SAME THING THAT ALWAYS HAPPENS. PEOPLE GO CRAZY.

HOW DID YOU SURVIVE?

MY DAD'S CASTER WAS THE HEAD OF I.T.

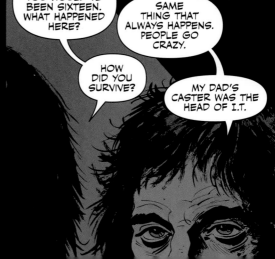

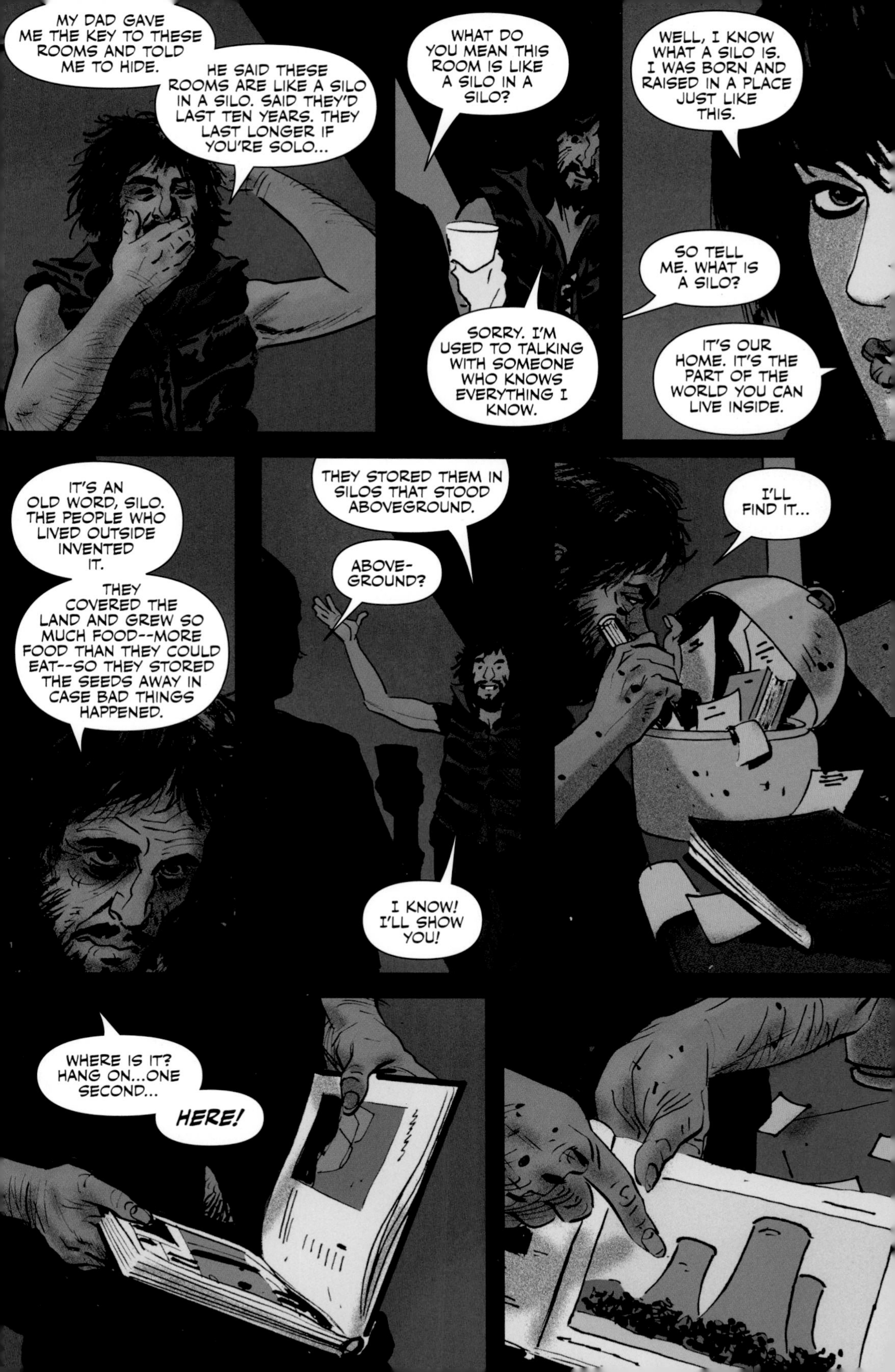
MY DAD GAVE ME THE KEY TO THESE ROOMS AND TOLD ME TO HIDE.
HE SAID THESE ROOMS ARE LIKE A SILO IN A SILO. SAID THEY'D LAST TEN YEARS. THEY LAST LONGER IF YOU'RE SOLO...
WHAT DO YOU MEAN THIS ROOM IS LIKE A SILO IN A SILO?
SORRY. I'M USED TO TALKING WITH SOMEONE WHO KNOWS EVERYTHING I KNOW.
WELL, I KNOW WHAT A SILO IS. I WAS BORN AND RAISED IN A PLACE JUST LIKE THIS.
SO TELL ME. WHAT IS A SILO?
IT'S OUR HOME. IT'S THE PART OF THE WORLD YOU CAN LIVE INSIDE.
IT'S AN OLD WORD, SILO. THE PEOPLE WHO LIVED OUTSIDE INVENTED IT.
THEY COVERED THE LAND AND GREW SO MUCH FOOD--MORE FOOD THAN THEY COULD EAT--SO THEY STORED THE SEEDS AWAY IN CASE BAD THINGS HAPPENED.
THEY STORED THEM IN SILOS THAT STOOD ABOVEGROUND.
ABOVE-GROUND?
I KNOW! I'LL SHOW YOU!
I'LL FIND IT...
WHERE IS IT? HANG ON...ONE SECOND...
HERE!

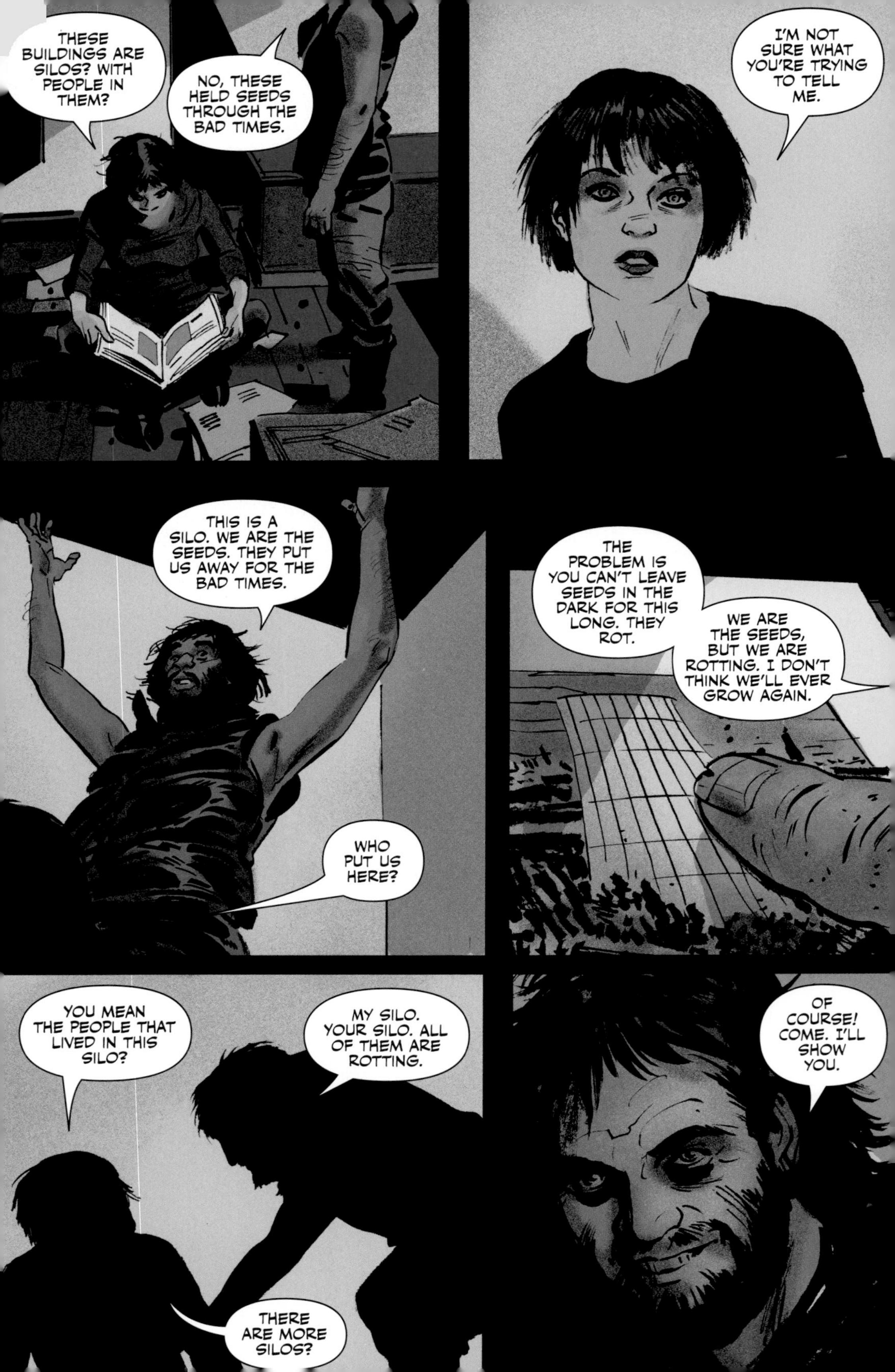
THESE BUILDINGS ARE SILOS? WITH PEOPLE IN THEM?
NO, THESE HELD SEEDS THROUGH THE BAD TIMES.
I'M NOT SURE WHAT YOU'RE TRYING TO TELL ME.
THIS IS A SILO. WE ARE THE SEEDS. THEY PUT US AWAY FOR THE BAD TIMES.
WHO PUT US HERE?
THE PROBLEM IS YOU CAN'T LEAVE SEEDS IN THE DARK FOR THIS LONG. THEY ROT.
WE ARE THE SEEDS, BUT WE ARE ROTTING. I DON'T THINK WE'LL EVER GROW AGAIN.
YOU MEAN THE PEOPLE THAT LIVED IN THIS SILO?
MY SILO. YOUR SILO. ALL OF THEM ARE ROTTING.
THERE ARE MORE SILOS?
OF COURSE! COME. I'LL SHOW YOU.

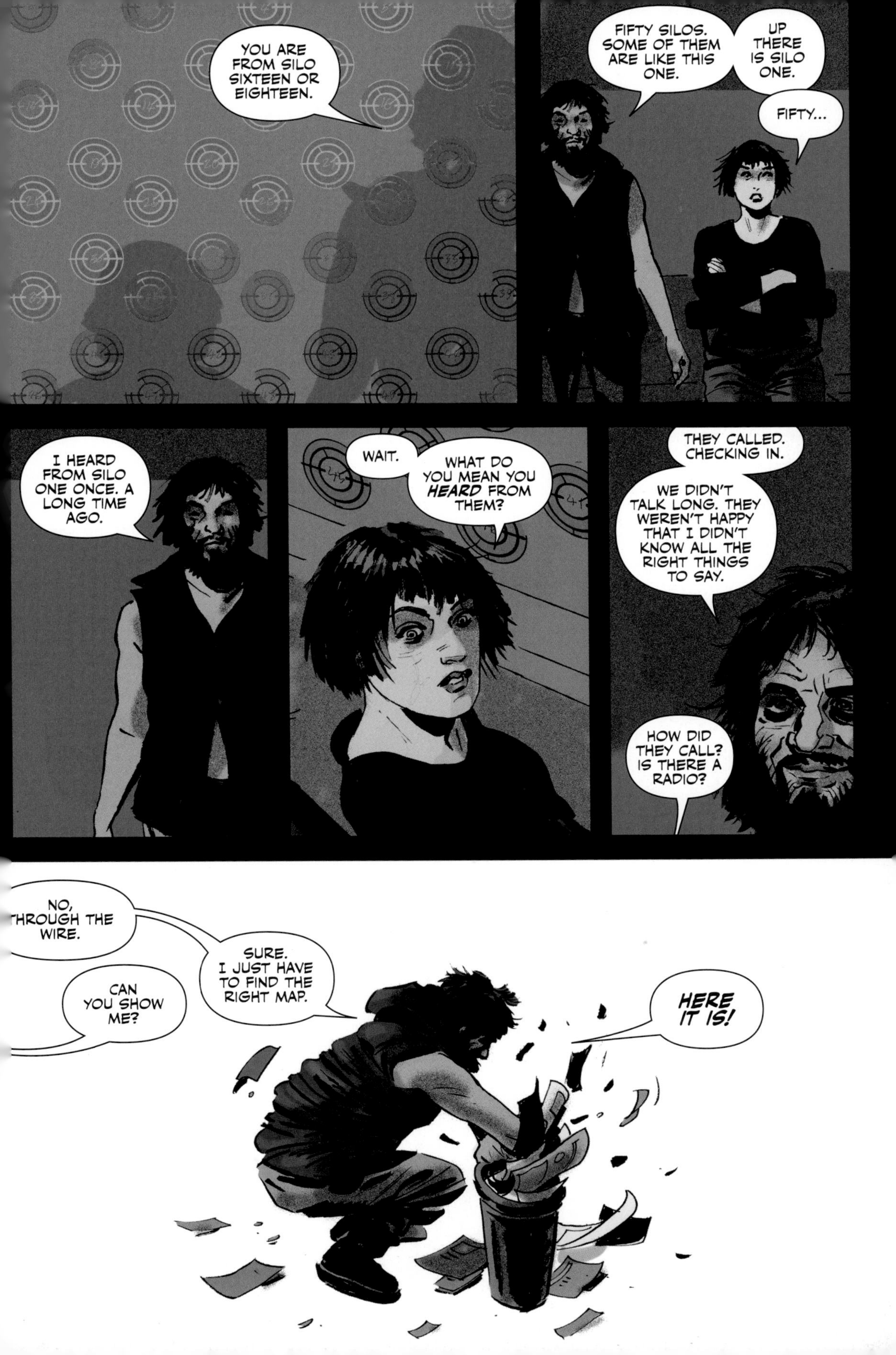
YOU ARE FROM SILO SIXTEEN OR EIGHTEEN.
FIFTY SILOS. SOME OF THEM ARE LIKE THIS ONE.
UP THERE IS SILO ONE.
FIFTY...
I HEARD FROM SILO ONE ONCE. A LONG TIME AGO.
WAIT.
WHAT DO YOU MEAN YOU *HEARD* FROM THEM?
THEY CALLED. CHECKING IN.
WE DIDN'T TALK LONG. THEY WEREN'T HAPPY THAT I DIDN'T KNOW ALL THE RIGHT THINGS TO SAY.
HOW DID THEY CALL? IS THERE A RADIO?
NO, THROUGH THE WIRE.
CAN YOU SHOW ME?
SURE. I JUST HAVE TO FIND THE RIGHT MAP.
HERE IT IS!

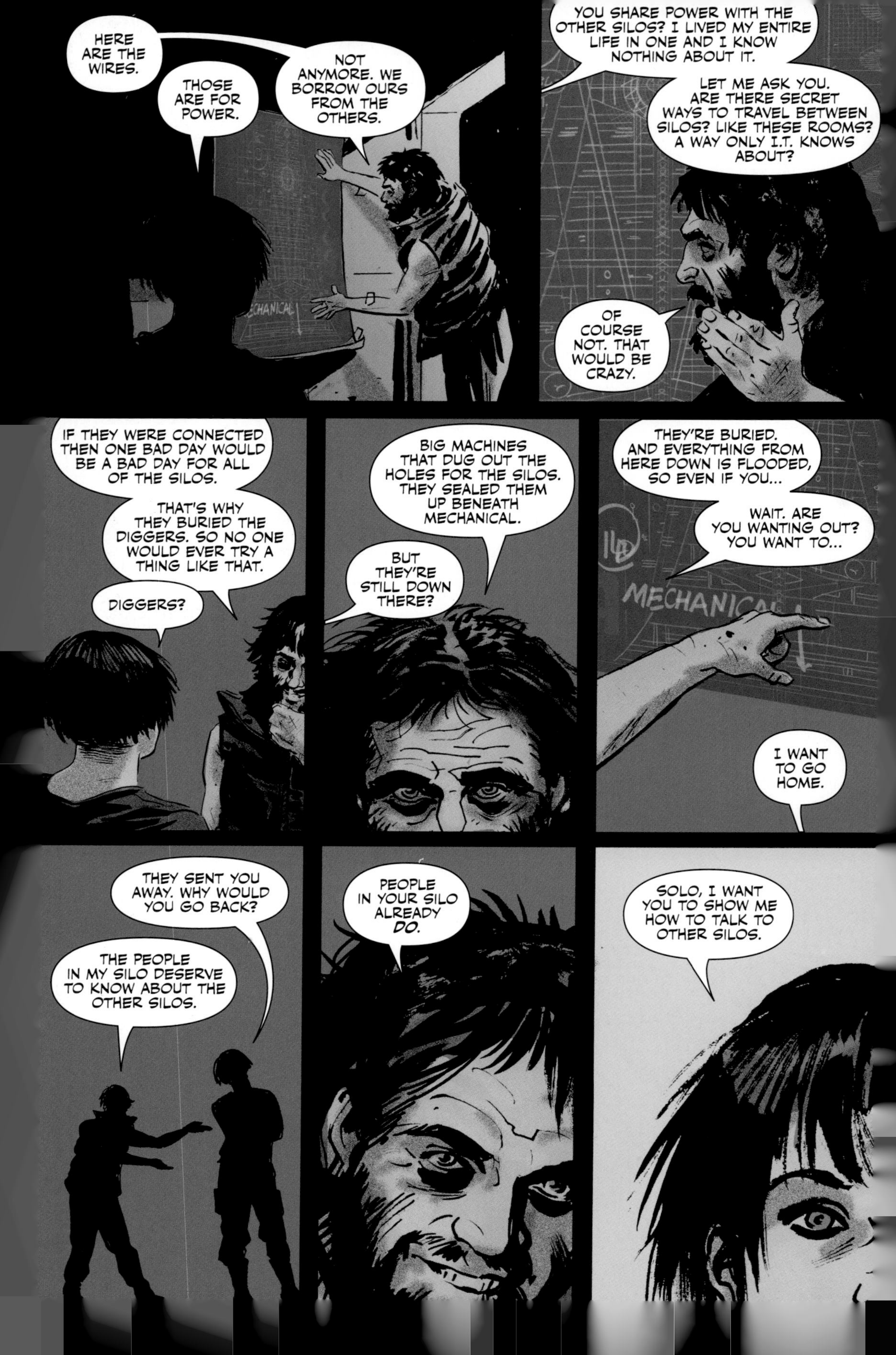
HERE ARE THE WIRES.
THOSE ARE FOR POWER.
NOT ANYMORE. WE BORROW OURS FROM THE OTHERS.
MECHANICAL
YOU SHARE POWER WITH THE OTHER SILOS? I LIVED MY ENTIRE LIFE IN ONE AND I KNOW NOTHING ABOUT IT.
LET ME ASK YOU. ARE THERE SECRET WAYS TO TRAVEL BETWEEN SILOS? LIKE THESE ROOMS? A WAY ONLY I.T. KNOWS ABOUT?
OF COURSE NOT. THAT WOULD BE CRAZY.
IF THEY WERE CONNECTED THEN ONE BAD DAY WOULD BE A BAD DAY FOR ALL OF THE SILOS.
THAT'S WHY THEY BURIED THE DIGGERS. SO NO ONE WOULD EVER TRY A THING LIKE THAT.
DIGGERS?
BIG MACHINES THAT DUG OUT THE HOLES FOR THE SILOS. THEY SEALED THEM UP BENEATH MECHANICAL.
BUT THEY'RE STILL DOWN THERE?
THEY'RE BURIED. AND EVERYTHING FROM HERE DOWN IS FLOODED, SO EVEN IF YOU...
WAIT. ARE YOU WANTING OUT? YOU WANT TO...
MECHANICAL
I WANT TO GO HOME.
THEY SENT YOU AWAY. WHY WOULD YOU GO BACK?
THE PEOPLE IN MY SILO DESERVE TO KNOW ABOUT THE OTHER SILOS.
PEOPLE IN YOUR SILO ALREADY *DO*.
SOLO, I WANT YOU TO SHOW ME HOW TO TALK TO OTHER SILOS.

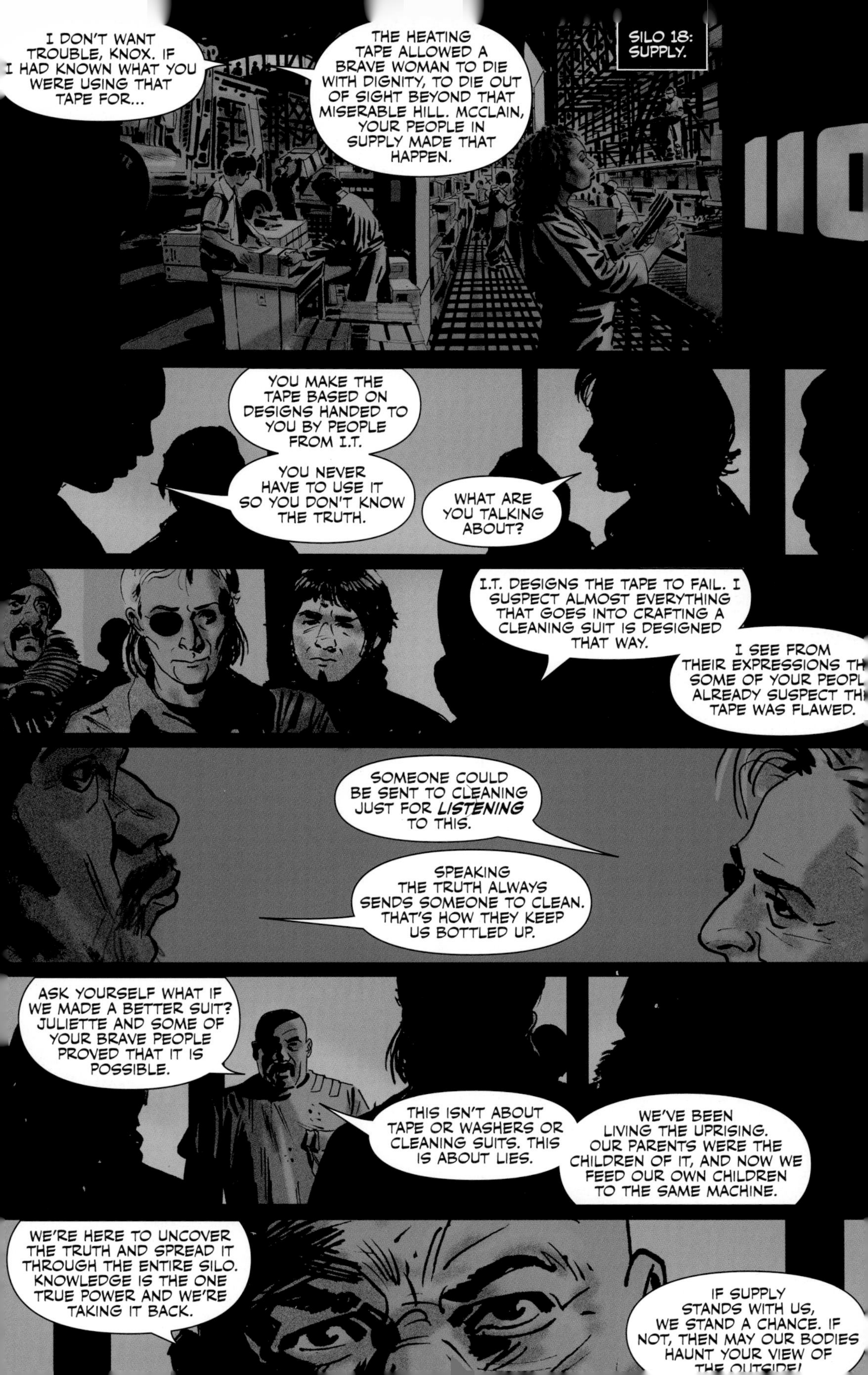
SILO 18: SUPPLY.
I DON'T WANT TROUBLE, KNOX. IF I HAD KNOWN WHAT YOU WERE USING THAT TAPE FOR...
THE HEATING TAPE ALLOWED A BRAVE WOMAN TO DIE WITH DIGNITY, TO DIE OUT OF SIGHT BEYOND THAT MISERABLE HILL. MCCLAIN, YOUR PEOPLE IN SUPPLY MADE THAT HAPPEN.
110
YOU MAKE THE TAPE BASED ON DESIGNS HANDED TO YOU BY PEOPLE FROM I.T.
YOU NEVER HAVE TO USE IT SO YOU DON'T KNOW THE TRUTH.
WHAT ARE YOU TALKING ABOUT?
I.T. DESIGNS THE TAPE TO FAIL. I SUSPECT ALMOST EVERYTHING THAT GOES INTO CRAFTING A CLEANING SUIT IS DESIGNED THAT WAY.
I SEE FROM THEIR EXPRESSIONS TH SOME OF YOUR PEOPL ALREADY SUSPECT TH TAPE WAS FLAWED.
SOMEONE COULD BE SENT TO CLEANING JUST FOR *LISTENING* TO THIS.
SPEAKING THE TRUTH ALWAYS SENDS SOMEONE TO CLEAN. THAT'S HOW THEY KEEP US BOTTLED UP.
ASK YOURSELF WHAT IF WE MADE A BETTER SUIT? JULIETTE AND SOME OF YOUR BRAVE PEOPLE PROVED THAT IT IS POSSIBLE.
THIS ISN'T ABOUT TAPE OR WASHERS OR CLEANING SUITS. THIS IS ABOUT LIES.
WE'VE BEEN LIVING THE UPRISING. OUR PARENTS WERE THE CHILDREN OF IT, AND NOW WE FEED OUR OWN CHILDREN TO THE SAME MACHINE.
WE'RE HERE TO UNCOVER THE TRUTH AND SPREAD IT THROUGH THE ENTIRE SILO. KNOWLEDGE IS THE ONE TRUE POWER AND WE'RE TAKING IT BACK.
IF SUPPLY STANDS WITH US, WE STAND A CHANCE. IF NOT, THEN MAY OUR BODIES HAUNT YOUR VIEW OF

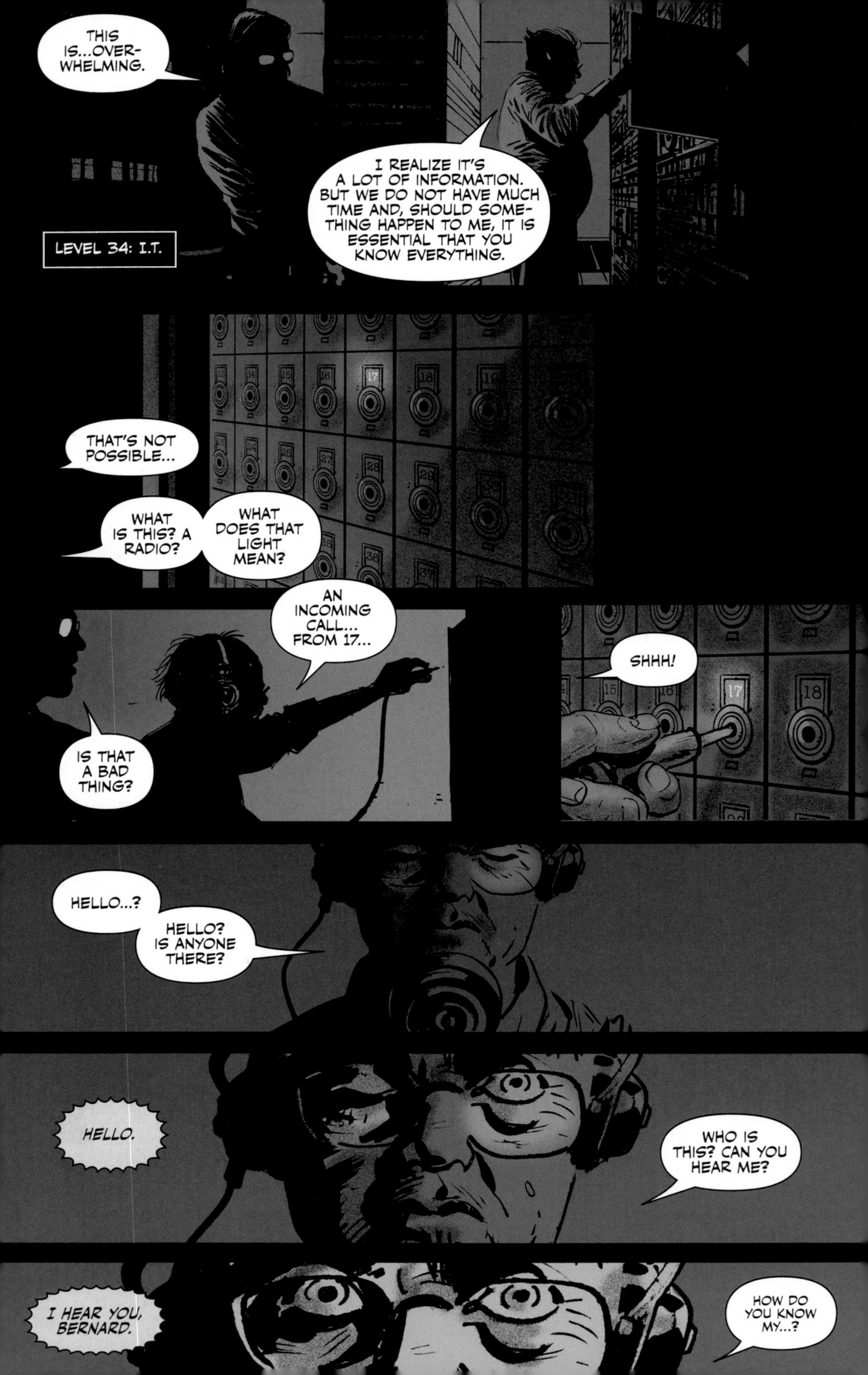
THIS IS...OVER-WHELMING.
I REALIZE IT'S A LOT OF INFORMATION. BUT WE DO NOT HAVE MUCH TIME AND, SHOULD SOME-THING HAPPEN TO ME, IT IS ESSENTIAL THAT YOU KNOW EVERYTHING.
LEVEL 34: I.T.
THAT'S NOT POSSIBLE...
WHAT IS THIS? A RADIO?
WHAT DOES THAT LIGHT MEAN?
AN INCOMING CALL... FROM 17...
IS THAT A BAD THING?
SHHH!
HELLO...?
HELLO? IS ANYONE THERE?
HELLO.
WHO IS THIS? CAN YOU HEAR ME?
I HEAR YOU, BERNARD.
HOW DO YOU KNOW MY...?

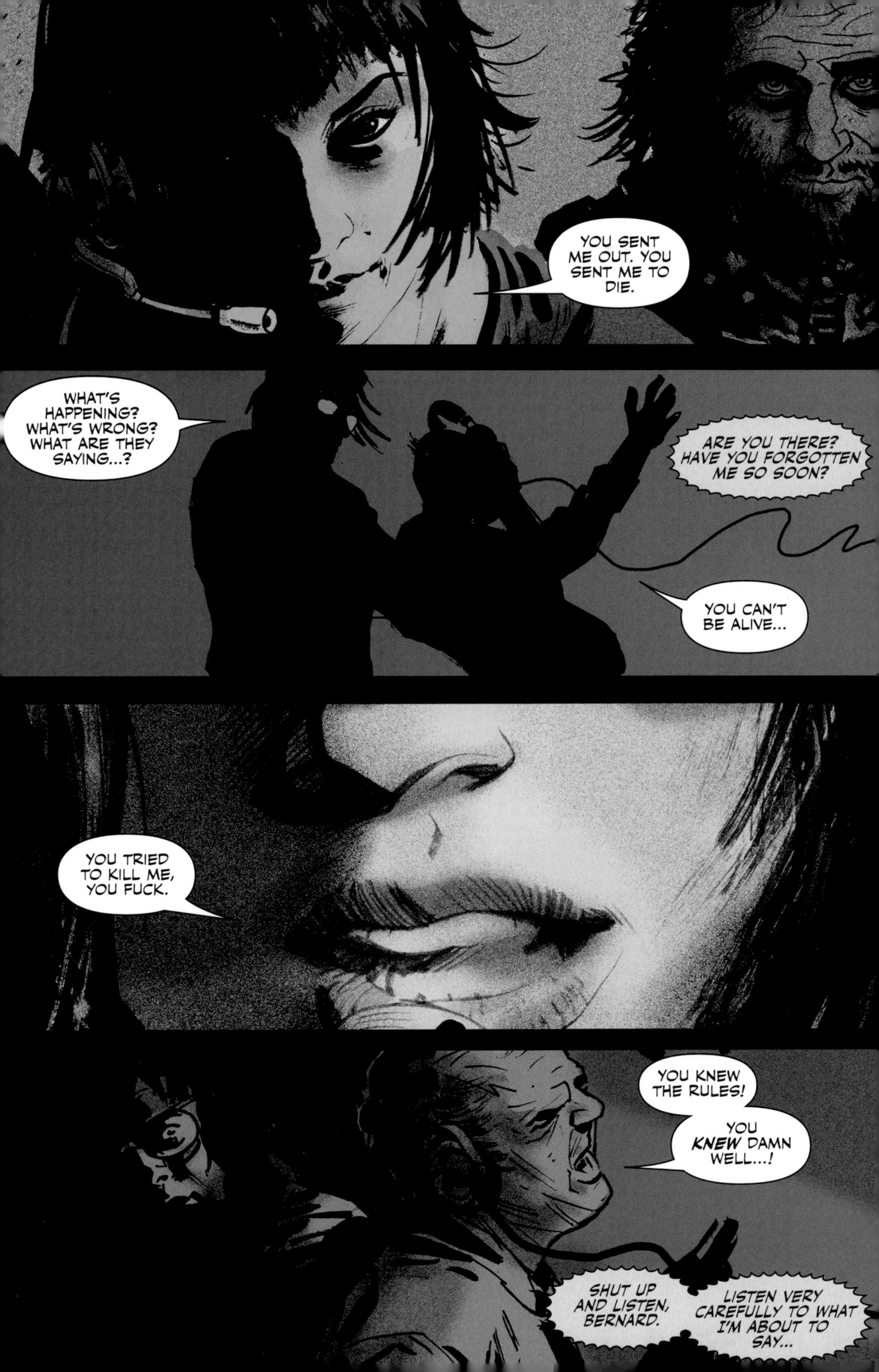
YOU SENT ME OUT. YOU SENT ME TO DIE.
WHAT'S HAPPENING? WHAT'S WRONG? WHAT ARE THEY SAYING...?
ARE YOU THERE? HAVE YOU FORGOTTEN ME SO SOON?
YOU CAN'T BE ALIVE...
YOU TRIED TO KILL ME, YOU FUCK.
YOU KNEW THE RULES!
YOU *KNEW* DAMN WELL...!
SHUT UP AND LISTEN, BERNARD.
LISTEN VERY CAREFULLY TO WHAT I'M ABOUT TO SAY...

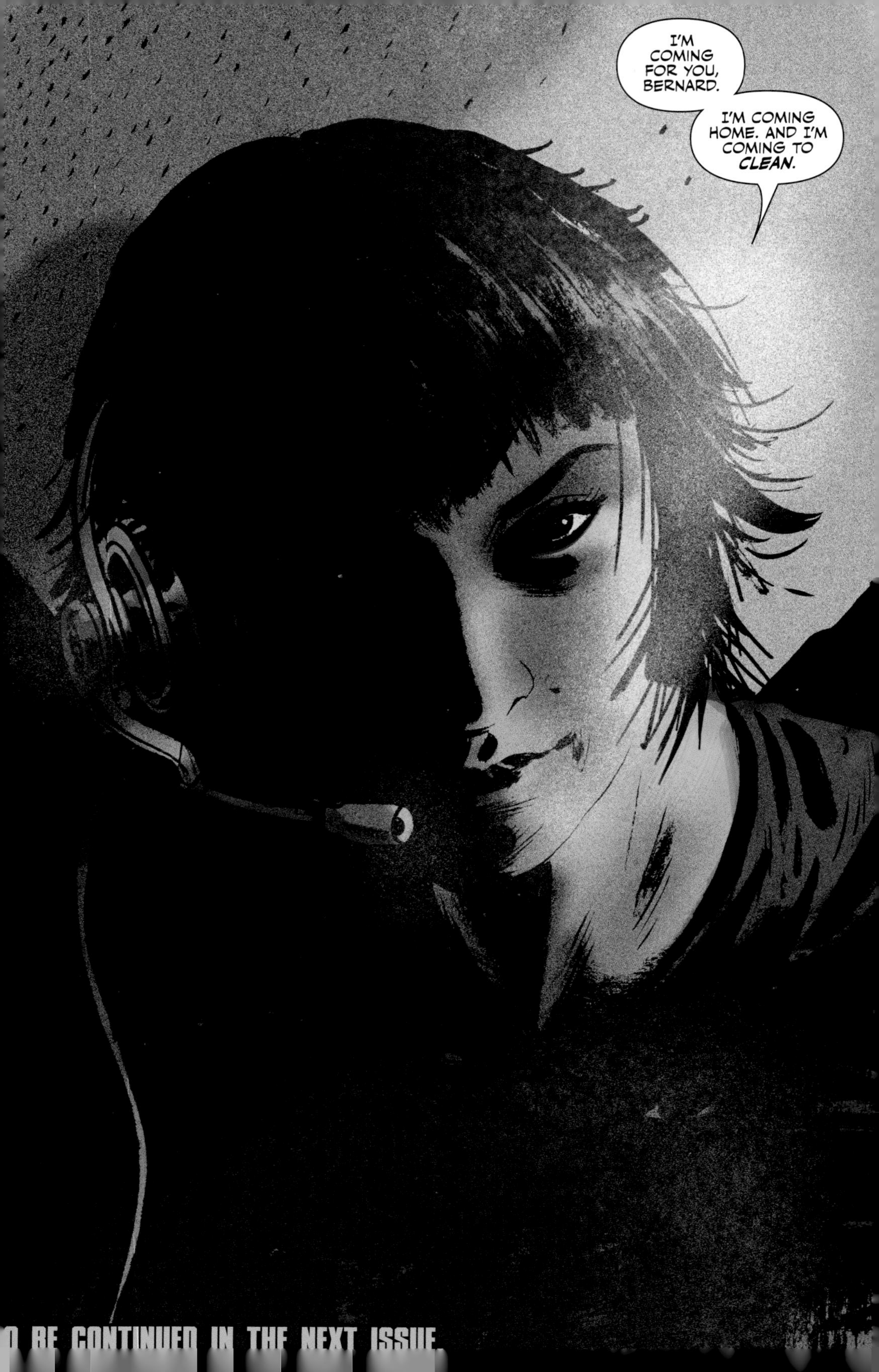
I'M COMING FOR YOU, BERNARD.
I'M COMING HOME. AND I'M COMING TO *CLEAN*.
O BE CONTINUED IN THE NEXT ISSUE

END ISSUE 4

ISSUE 5

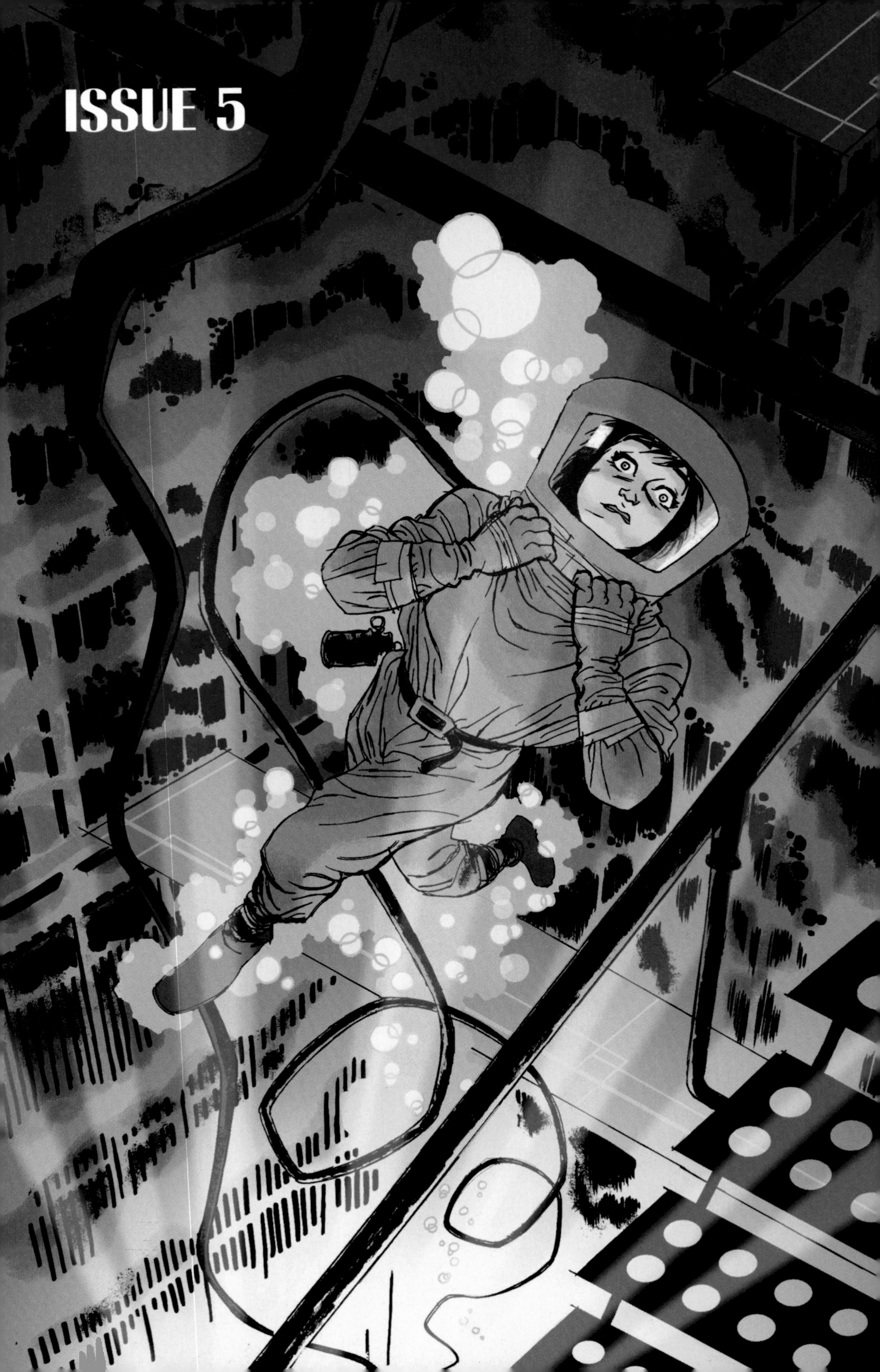

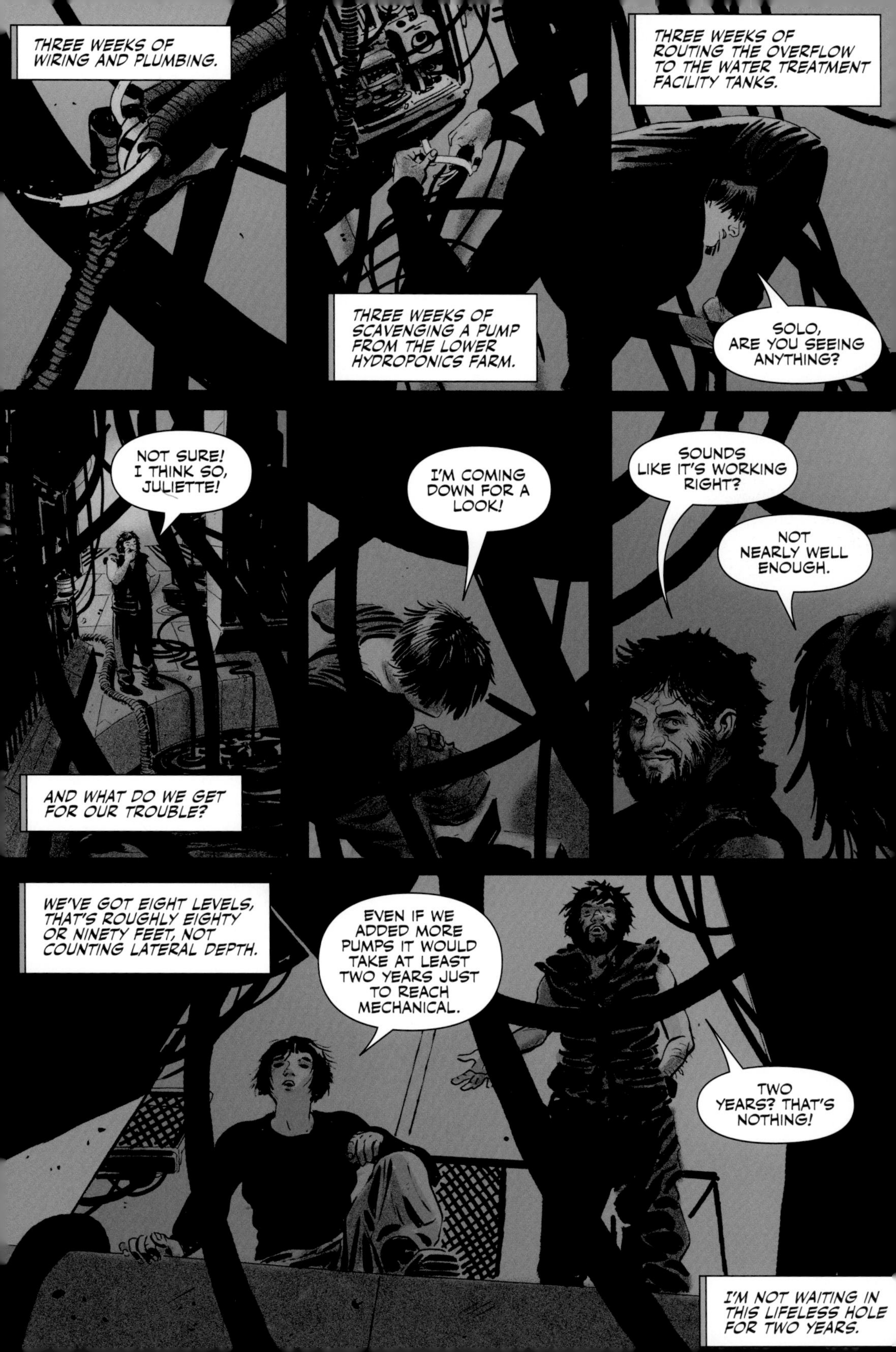
THREE WEEKS OF WIRING AND PLUMBING.
THREE WEEKS OF SCAVENGING A PUMP FROM THE LOWER HYDROPONICS FARM.
THREE WEEKS OF ROUTING THE OVERFLOW TO THE WATER TREATMENT FACILITY TANKS.
SOLO, ARE YOU SEEING ANYTHING?
NOT SURE! I THINK SO, JULIETTE!
AND WHAT DO WE GET FOR OUR TROUBLE?
I'M COMING DOWN FOR A LOOK!
SOUNDS LIKE IT'S WORKING RIGHT?
NOT NEARLY WELL ENOUGH.
WE'VE GOT EIGHT LEVELS, THAT'S ROUGHLY EIGHTY OR NINETY FEET, NOT COUNTING LATERAL DEPTH.
EVEN IF WE ADDED MORE PUMPS IT WOULD TAKE AT LEAST TWO YEARS JUST TO REACH MECHANICAL.
TWO YEARS? THAT'S NOTHING!
I'M NOT WAITING IN THIS LIFELESS HOLE FOR TWO YEARS.

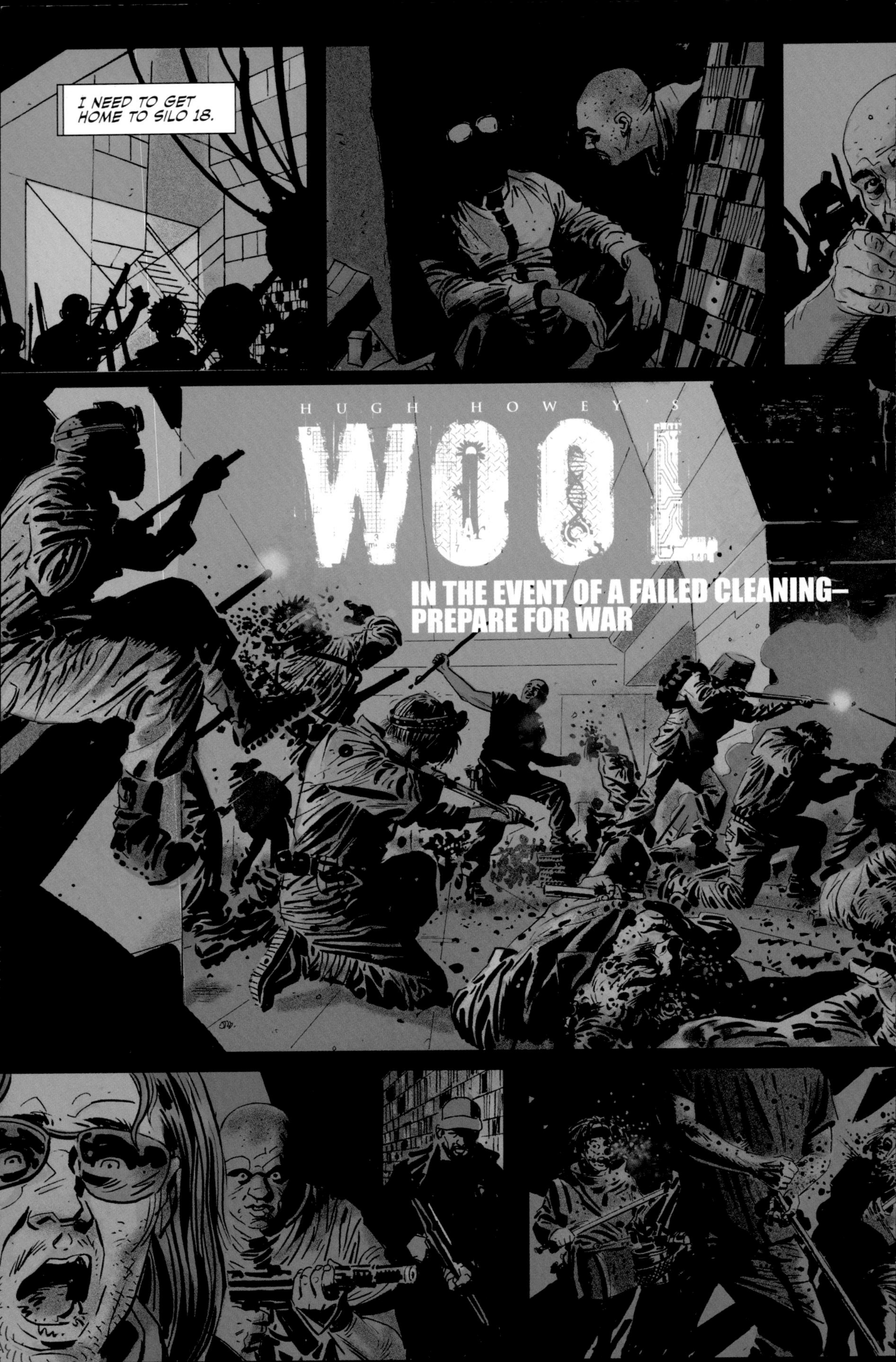

I NEED TO GET HOME TO SILO 18.
HUGH HOWEY'S
WOOL
IN THE EVENT OF A FAILED CLEANING–
PREPARE FOR WAR

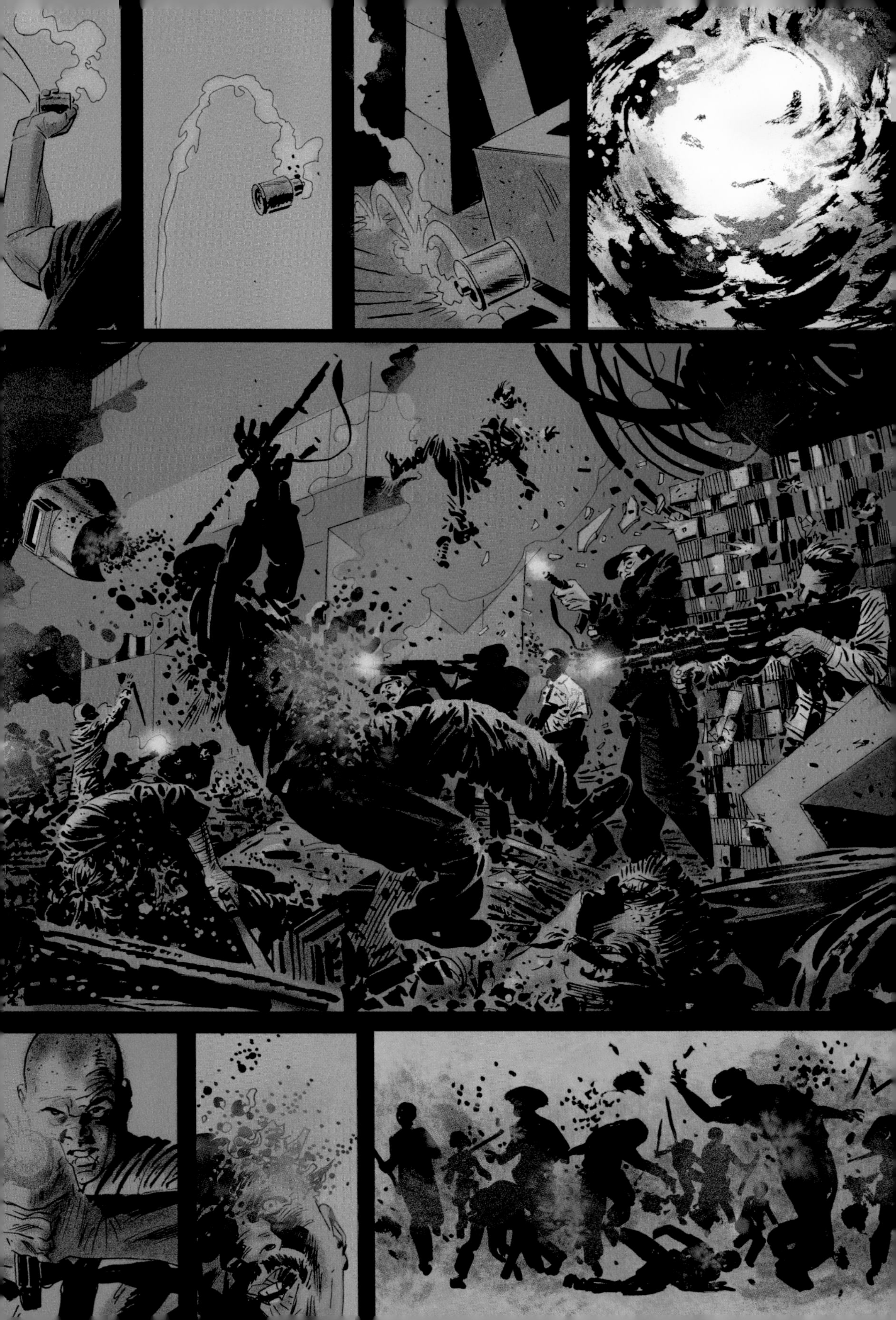

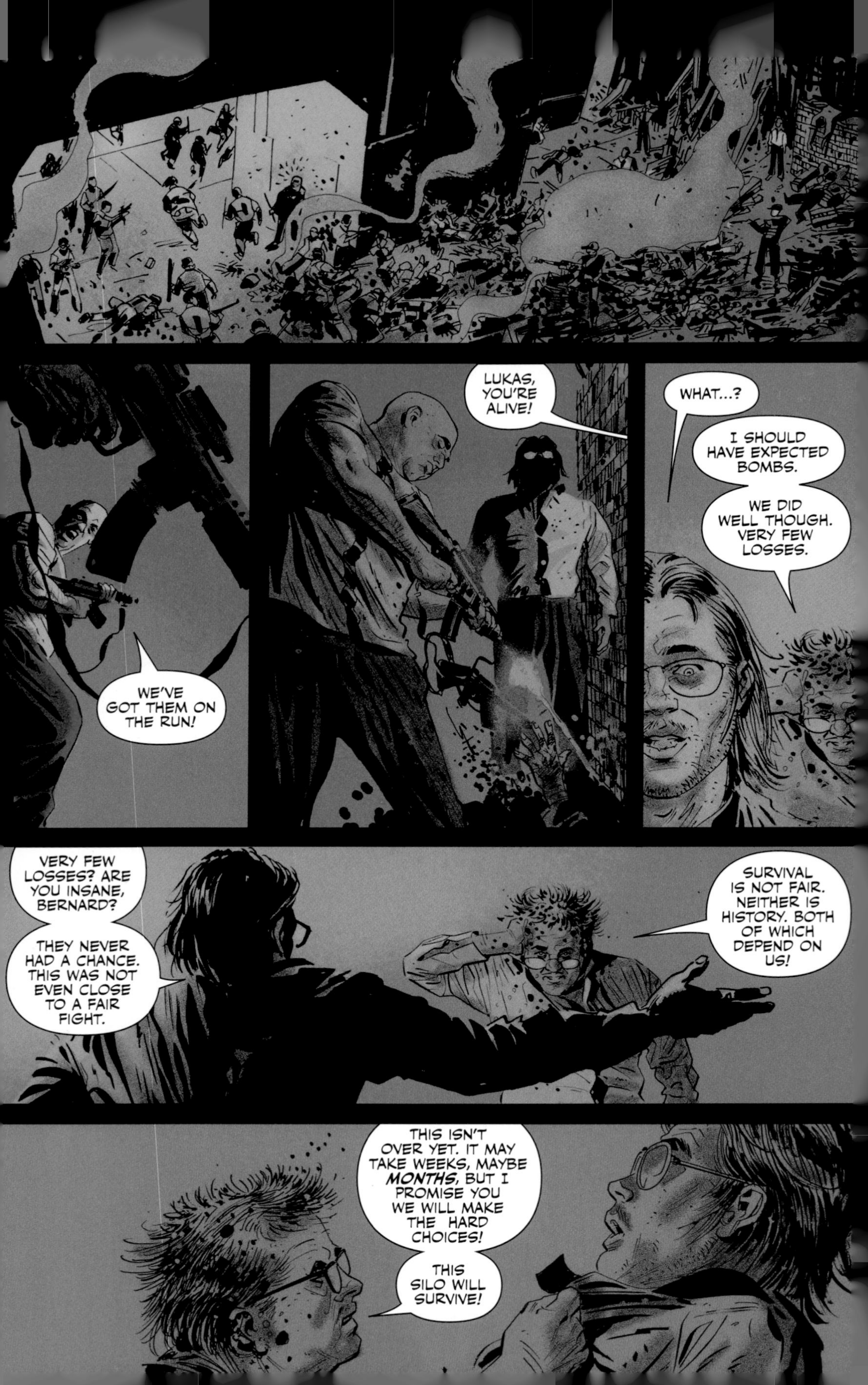

WE'VE GOT THEM ON THE RUN!
LUKAS, YOU'RE ALIVE!
WHAT...?
I SHOULD HAVE EXPECTED BOMBS.
WE DID WELL THOUGH. VERY FEW LOSSES.
VERY FEW LOSSES? ARE YOU INSANE, BERNARD?
THEY NEVER HAD A CHANCE. THIS WAS NOT EVEN CLOSE TO A FAIR FIGHT.
SURVIVAL IS NOT FAIR. NEITHER IS HISTORY. BOTH OF WHICH DEPEND ON US!
THIS ISN'T OVER YET. IT MAY TAKE WEEKS, MAYBE MONTHS, BUT I PROMISE YOU WE WILL MAKE THE HARD CHOICES!
THIS SILO WILL SURVIVE!

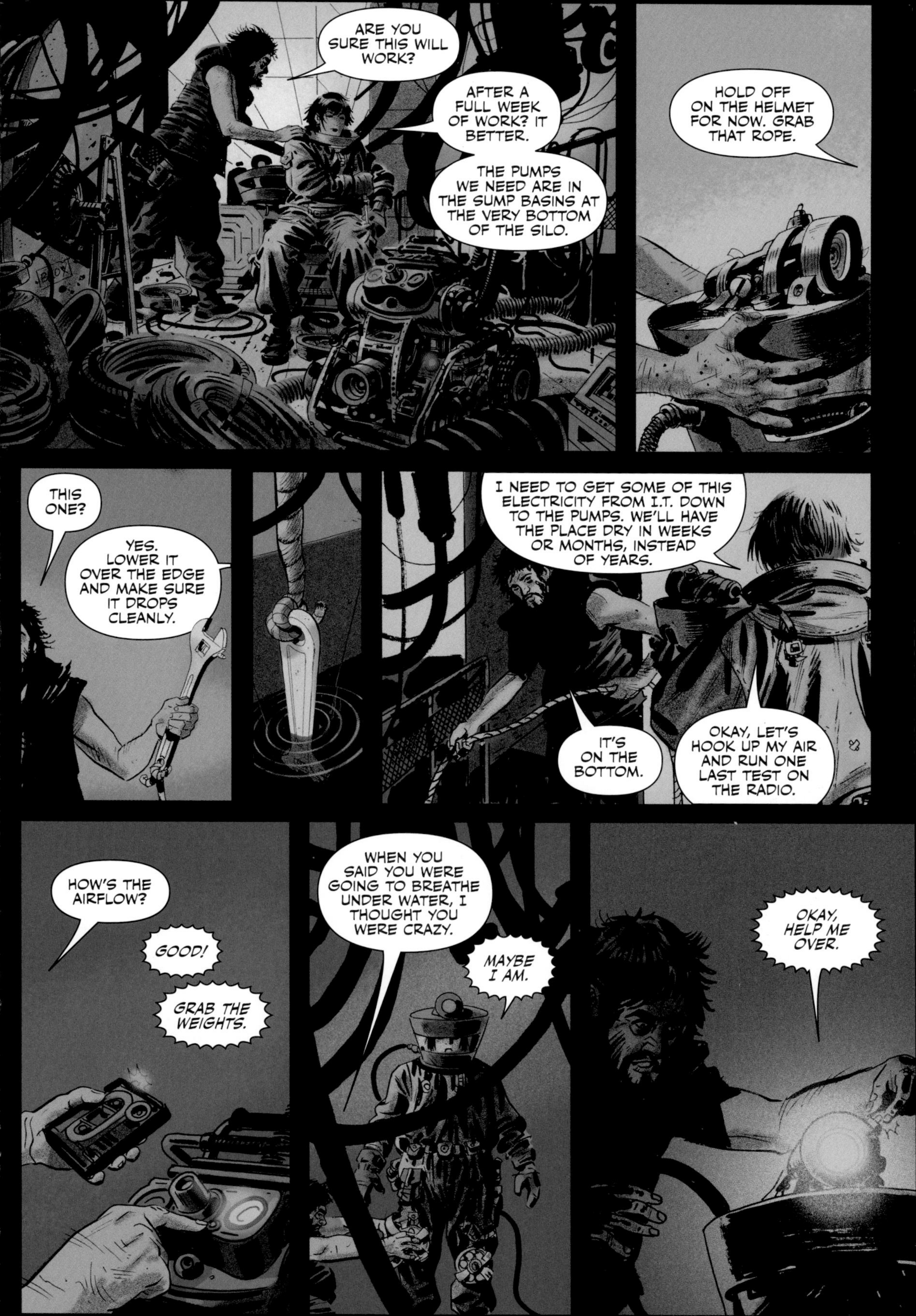

ARE YOU SURE THIS WILL WORK?
AFTER A FULL WEEK OF WORK? IT BETTER.
THE PUMPS WE NEED ARE IN THE SUMP BASINS AT THE VERY BOTTOM OF THE SILO.
HOLD OFF ON THE HELMET FOR NOW. GRAB THAT ROPE.
THIS ONE?
YES. LOWER IT OVER THE EDGE AND MAKE SURE IT DROPS CLEANLY.
I NEED TO GET SOME OF THIS ELECTRICITY FROM I.T. DOWN TO THE PUMPS. WE'LL HAVE THE PLACE DRY IN WEEKS OR MONTHS, INSTEAD OF YEARS.
IT'S ON THE BOTTOM.
OKAY, LET'S HOOK UP MY AIR AND RUN ONE LAST TEST ON THE RADIO.
HOW'S THE AIRFLOW?
GOOD!
GRAB THE WEIGHTS.
WHEN YOU SAID YOU WERE GOING TO BREATHE UNDER WATER, I THOUGHT YOU WERE CRAZY.
MAYBE I AM.
OKAY, HELP ME OVER.

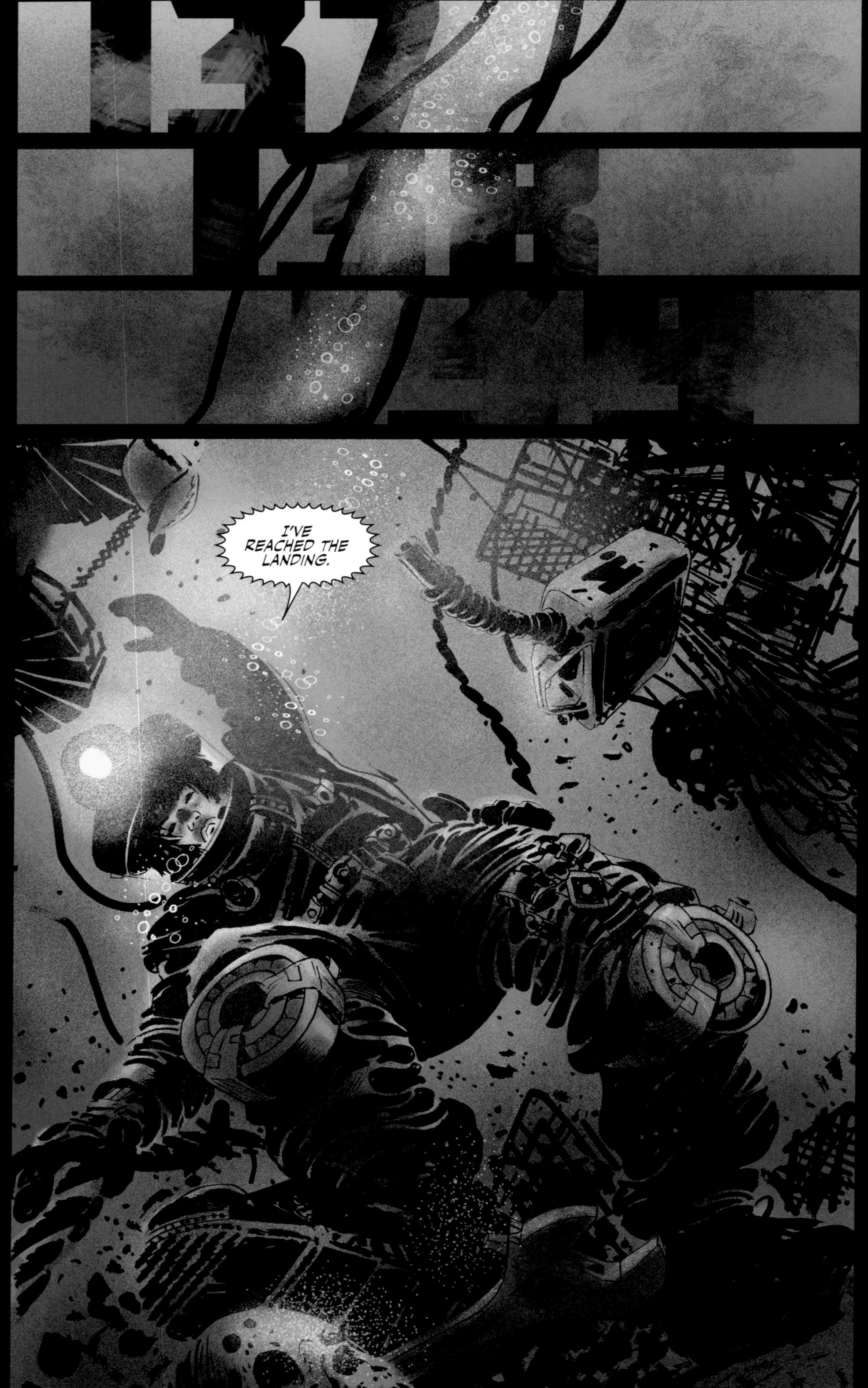
I'VE REACHED THE LANDING.

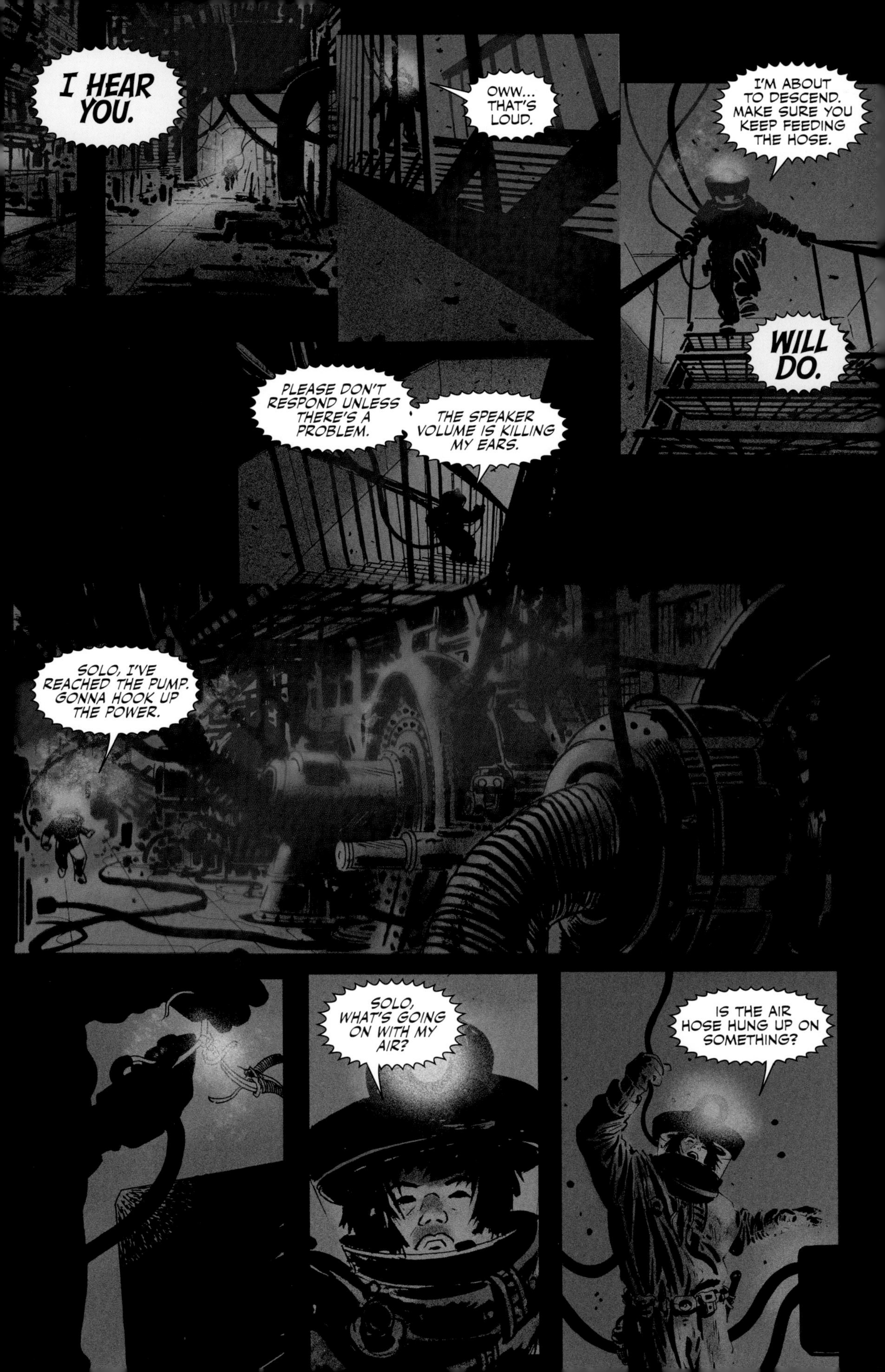
I HEAR YOU.
OWW... THAT'S LOUD.
I'M ABOUT TO DESCEND. MAKE SURE YOU KEEP FEEDING THE HOSE.
WILL DO.
PLEASE DON'T RESPOND UNLESS THERE'S A PROBLEM.
THE SPEAKER VOLUME IS KILLING MY EARS.
SOLO, I'VE REACHED THE PUMP. GONNA HOOK UP THE POWER.
SOLO, WHAT'S GOING ON WITH MY AIR?
IS THE AIR HOSE HUNG UP ON SOMETHING?

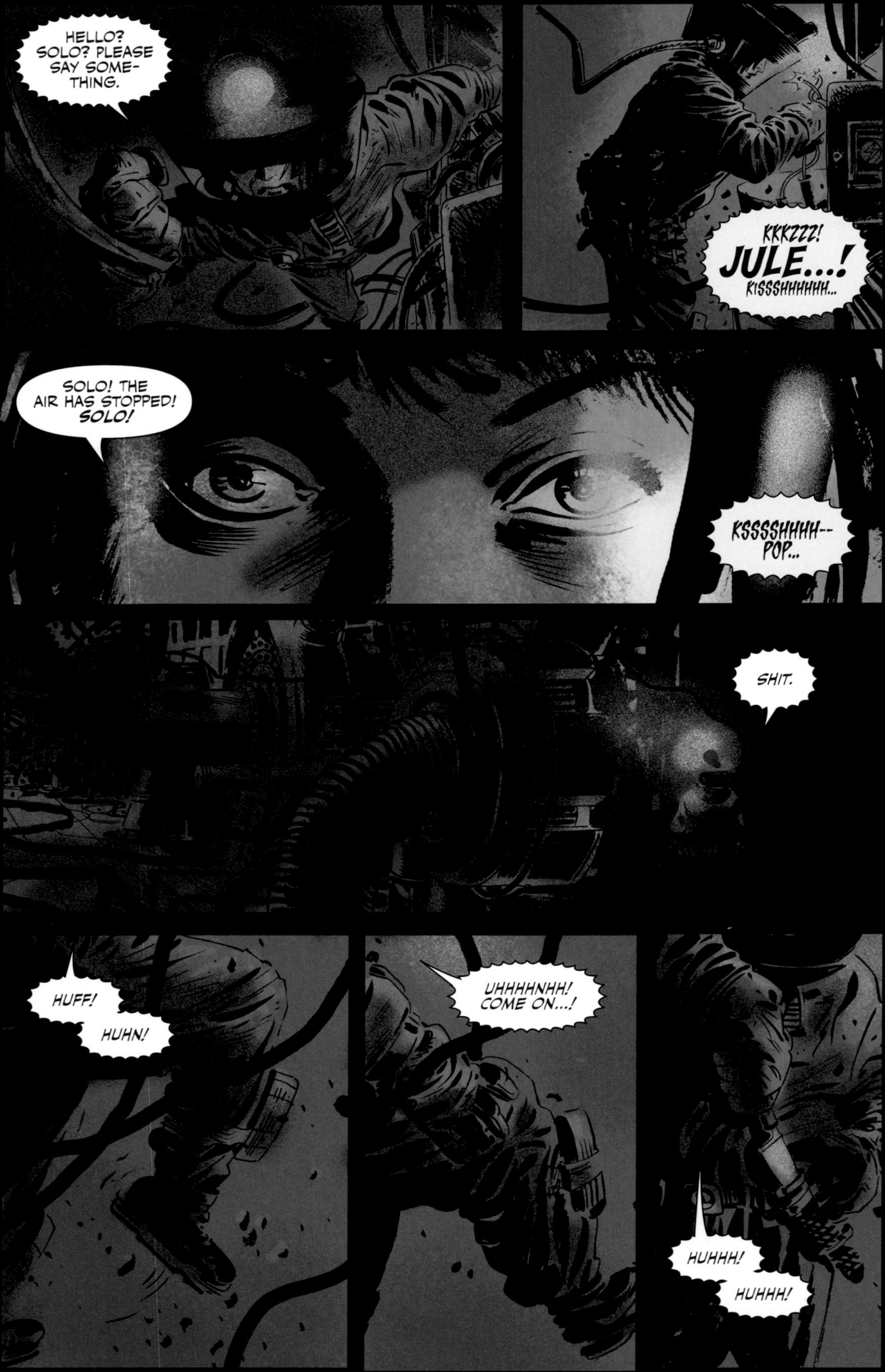
HELLO? SOLO? PLEASE SAY SOME- THING.
KKKZZZ! JULE...! KISSSHHHHHH...
SOLO! THE AIR HAS STOPPED! SOLO!
KSSSSHHHH-- POP...
SHIT.
HUFF!
HUHN!
UHHHHNHH! COME ON...!
HUHHH!
HUHHH!

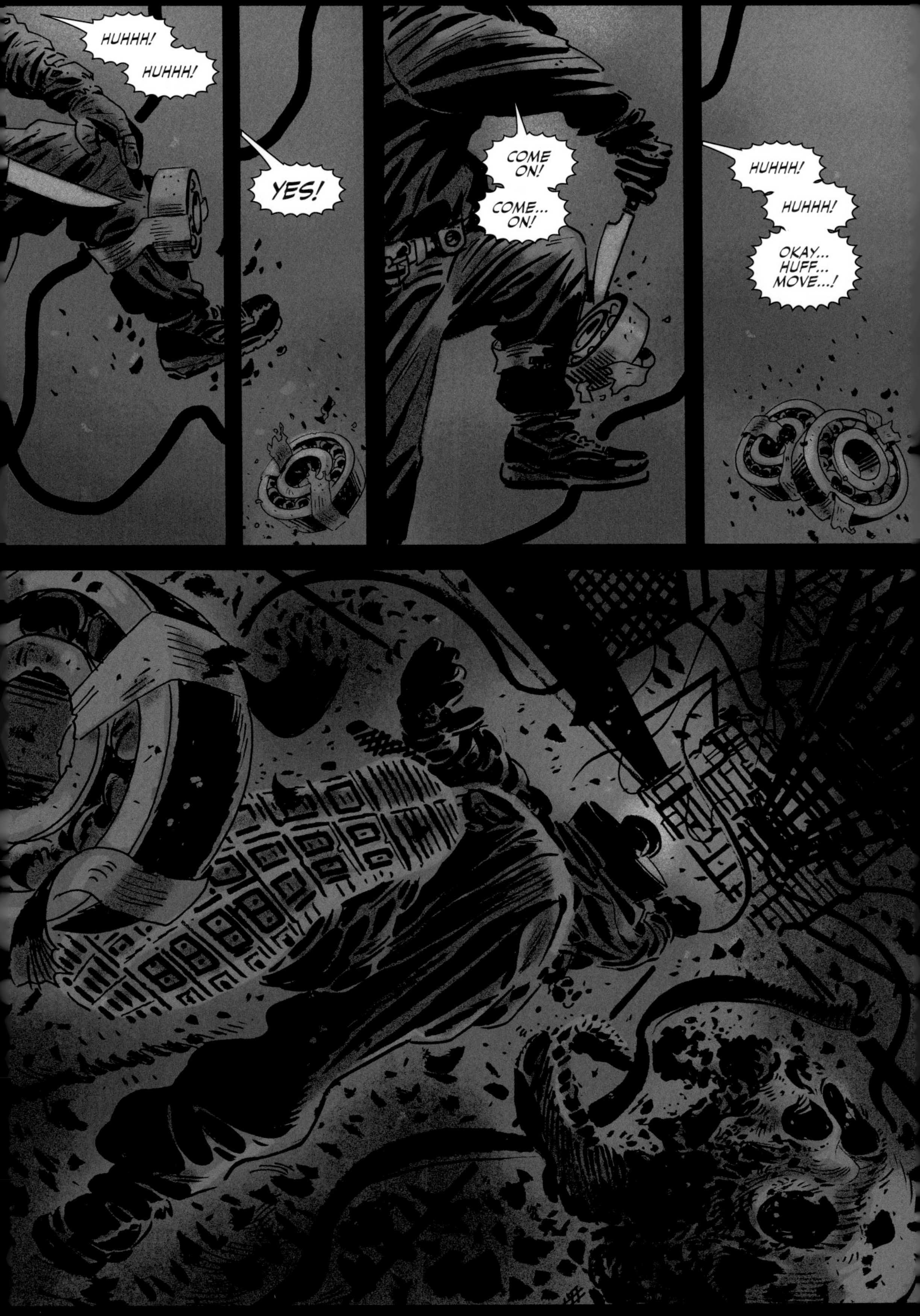
HUHHH!
HUHHH!
YES!
COME ON!
COME... ON!
HUHHH!
HUHHH!
OKAY... HUFF... MOVE...!

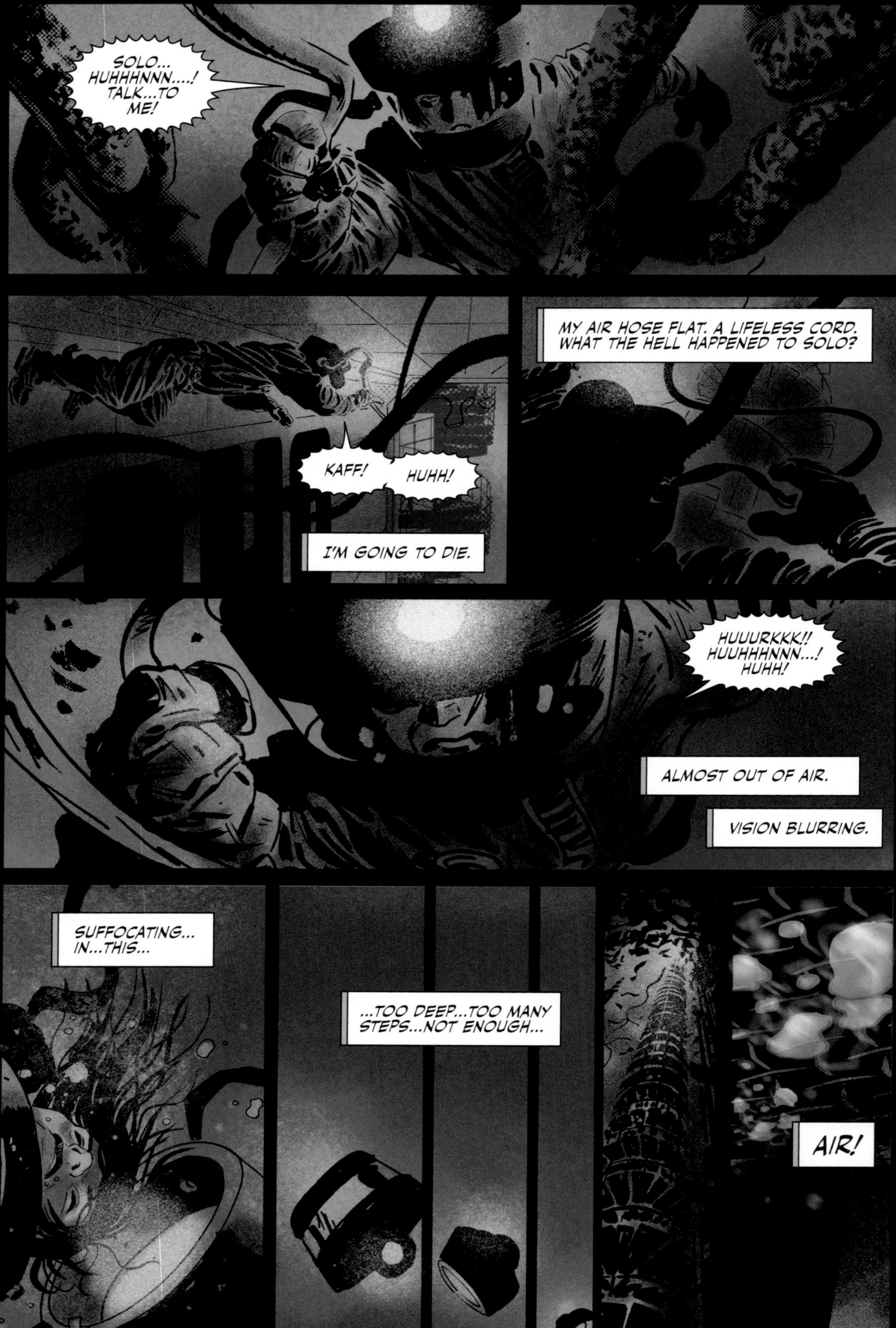
SOLO... HUHHHNNN....! TALK...TO ME!
KAFF!
HUHH!
I'M GOING TO DIE.
MY AIR HOSE FLAT. A LIFELESS CORD. WHAT THE HELL HAPPENED TO SOLO?
HUUURKKK!! HUUHHHNNN...! HUHH!
ALMOST OUT OF AIR.
VISION BLURRING.
SUFFOCATING... IN...THIS...
...TOO DEEP...TOO MANY STEPS...NOT ENOUGH...
AIR!

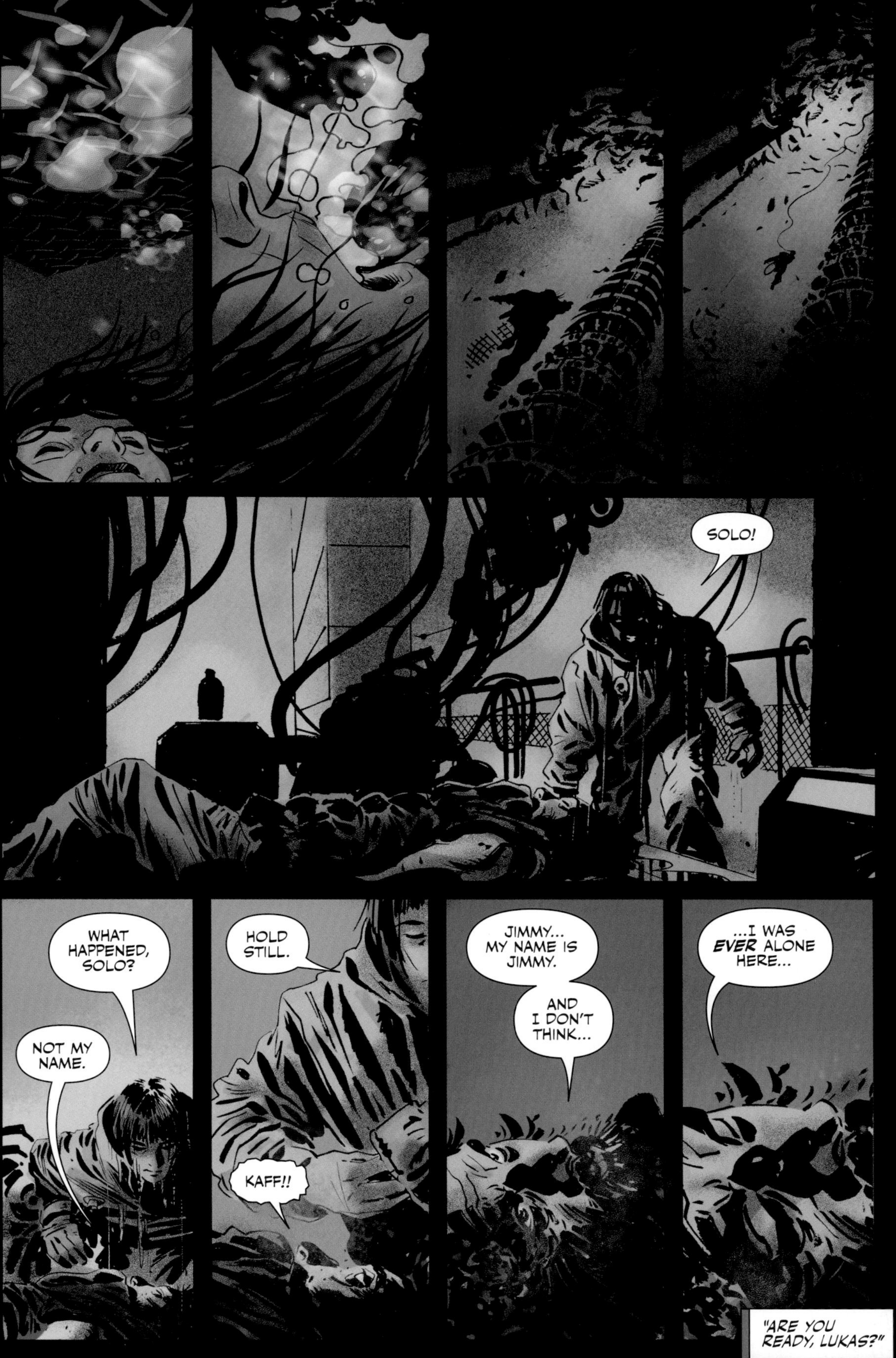
SOLO!
WHAT HAPPENED, SOLO?
NOT MY NAME.
HOLD STILL.
KAFF!!
JIMMY... MY NAME IS JIMMY.
AND I DON'T THINK...
...I WAS EVER ALONE HERE...
"ARE YOU READY, LUKAS?"

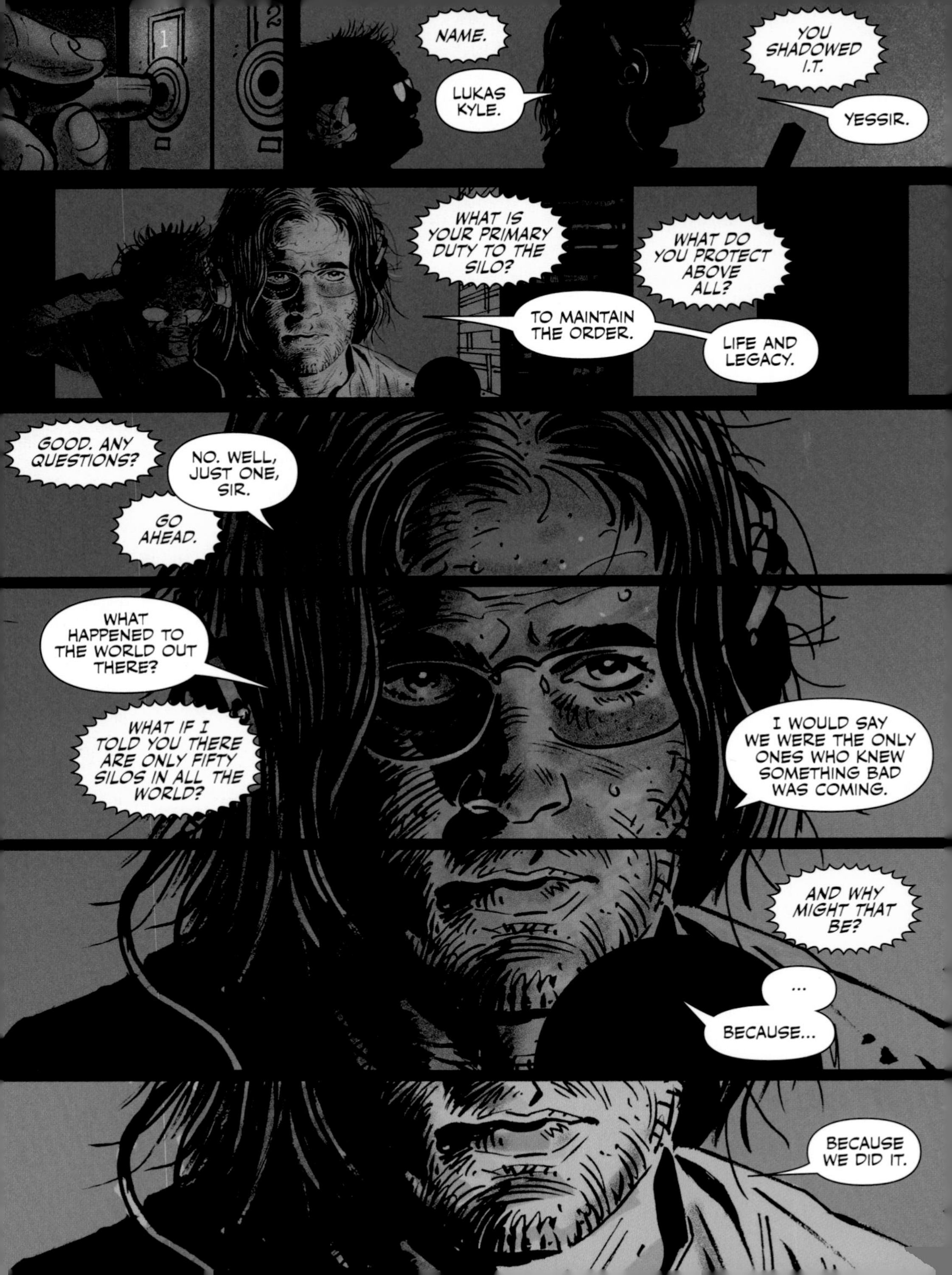

NAME.
LUKAS KYLE.
YOU SHADOWED I.T.
YESSIR.
WHAT IS YOUR PRIMARY DUTY TO THE SILO?
TO MAINTAIN THE ORDER.
WHAT DO YOU PROTECT ABOVE ALL?
LIFE AND LEGACY.
GOOD. ANY QUESTIONS?
NO. WELL, JUST ONE, SIR.
GO AHEAD.
WHAT HAPPENED TO THE WORLD OUT THERE?
WHAT IF I TOLD YOU THERE ARE ONLY FIFTY SILOS IN ALL THE WORLD?
I WOULD SAY WE WERE THE ONLY ONES WHO KNEW SOMETHING BAD WAS COMING.
AND WHY MIGHT THAT BE?
...
BECAUSE...
BECAUSE WE DID IT.

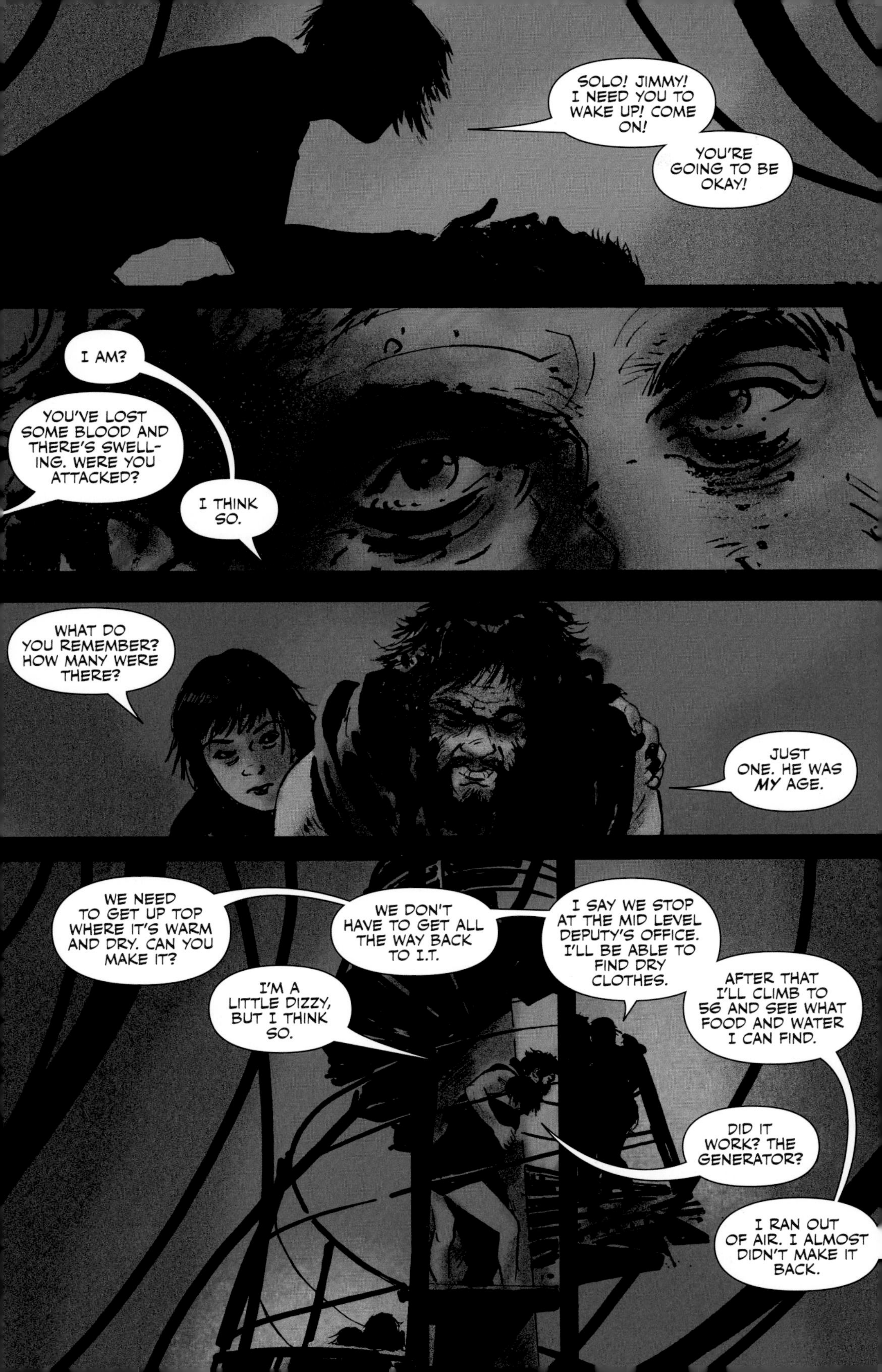
SOLO! JIMMY! I NEED YOU TO WAKE UP! COME ON!
YOU'RE GOING TO BE OKAY!
I AM?
YOU'VE LOST SOME BLOOD AND THERE'S SWELL-ING. WERE YOU ATTACKED?
I THINK SO.
WHAT DO YOU REMEMBER? HOW MANY WERE THERE?
JUST ONE. HE WAS MY AGE.
WE NEED TO GET UP TOP WHERE IT'S WARM AND DRY. CAN YOU MAKE IT?
I'M A LITTLE DIZZY, BUT I THINK SO.
WE DON'T HAVE TO GET ALL THE WAY BACK TO I.T.
I SAY WE STOP AT THE MID LEVEL DEPUTY'S OFFICE. I'LL BE ABLE TO FIND DRY CLOTHES.
AFTER THAT I'LL CLIMB TO 56 AND SEE WHAT FOOD AND WATER I CAN FIND.
DID IT WORK? THE GENERATOR?
I RAN OUT OF AIR. I ALMOST DIDN'T MAKE IT BACK.

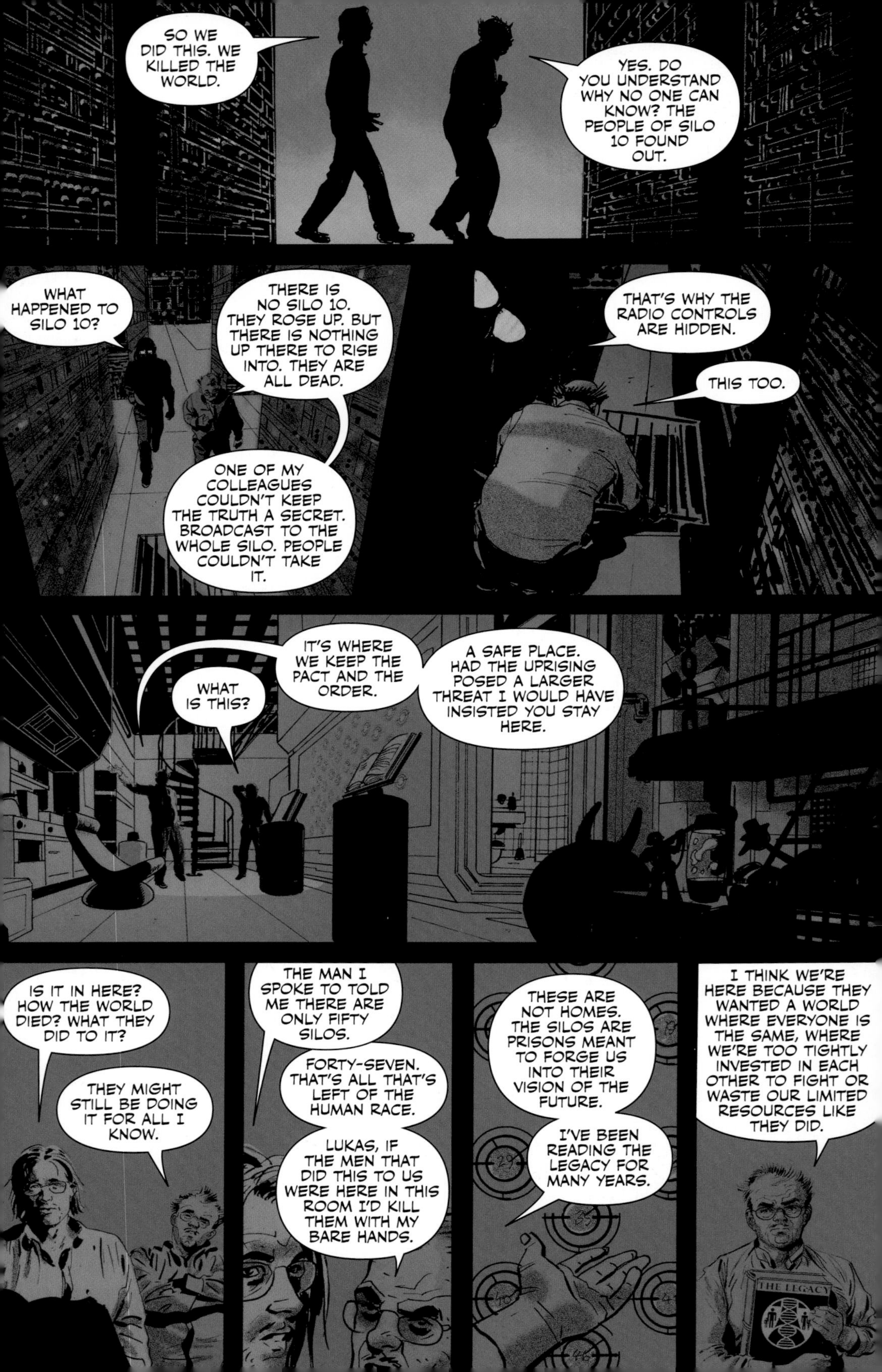
SO WE DID THIS. WE KILLED THE WORLD.
YES. DO YOU UNDERSTAND WHY NO ONE CAN KNOW? THE PEOPLE OF SILO 10 FOUND OUT.
WHAT HAPPENED TO SILO 10?
THERE IS NO SILO 10. THEY ROSE UP. BUT THERE IS NOTHING UP THERE TO RISE INTO. THEY ARE ALL DEAD.
ONE OF MY COLLEAGUES COULDN'T KEEP THE TRUTH A SECRET. BROADCAST TO THE WHOLE SILO. PEOPLE COULDN'T TAKE IT.
THAT'S WHY THE RADIO CONTROLS ARE HIDDEN.
THIS TOO.
WHAT IS THIS?
IT'S WHERE WE KEEP THE PACT AND THE ORDER.
A SAFE PLACE. HAD THE UPRISING POSED A LARGER THREAT I WOULD HAVE INSISTED YOU STAY HERE.
IS IT IN HERE? HOW THE WORLD DIED? WHAT THEY DID TO IT?
THEY MIGHT STILL BE DOING IT FOR ALL I KNOW.
THE MAN I SPOKE TO TOLD ME THERE ARE ONLY FIFTY SILOS.
FORTY-SEVEN. THAT'S ALL THAT'S LEFT OF THE HUMAN RACE.
LUKAS, IF THE MEN THAT DID THIS TO US WERE HERE IN THIS ROOM I'D KILL THEM WITH MY BARE HANDS.
THESE ARE NOT HOMES. THE SILOS ARE PRISONS MEANT TO FORGE US INTO THEIR VISION OF THE FUTURE.
I'VE BEEN READING THE LEGACY FOR MANY YEARS.
I THINK WE'RE HERE BECAUSE THEY WANTED A WORLD WHERE EVERYONE IS THE SAME, WHERE WE'RE TOO TIGHTLY INVESTED IN EACH OTHER TO FIGHT OR WASTE OUR LIMITED RESOURCES LIKE THEY DID.
THE LEGACY

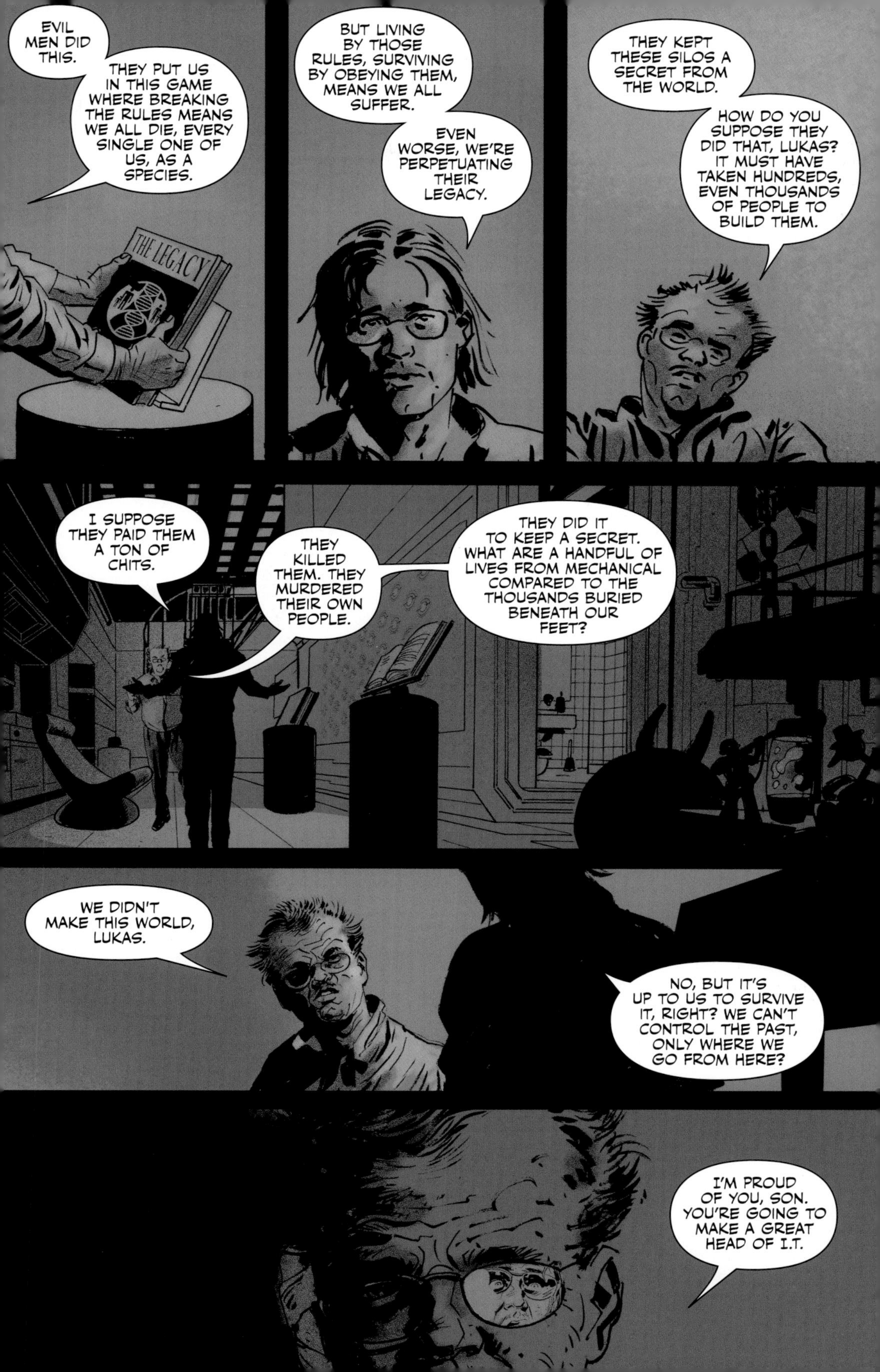
EVIL MEN DID THIS.
THEY PUT US IN THIS GAME WHERE BREAKING THE RULES MEANS WE ALL DIE, EVERY SINGLE ONE OF US, AS A SPECIES.
THE LEGACY
BUT LIVING BY THOSE RULES, SURVIVING BY OBEYING THEM, MEANS WE ALL SUFFER.
EVEN WORSE, WE'RE PERPETUATING THEIR LEGACY.
THEY KEPT THESE SILOS A SECRET FROM THE WORLD.
HOW DO YOU SUPPOSE THEY DID THAT, LUKAS? IT MUST HAVE TAKEN HUNDREDS, EVEN THOUSANDS OF PEOPLE TO BUILD THEM.
I SUPPOSE THEY PAID THEM A TON OF CHITS.
THEY KILLED THEM. THEY MURDERED THEIR OWN PEOPLE.
THEY DID IT TO KEEP A SECRET. WHAT ARE A HANDFUL OF LIVES FROM MECHANICAL COMPARED TO THE THOUSANDS BURIED BENEATH OUR FEET?
WE DIDN'T MAKE THIS WORLD, LUKAS.
NO, BUT IT'S UP TO US TO SURVIVE IT, RIGHT? WE CAN'T CONTROL THE PAST, ONLY WHERE WE GO FROM HERE?
I'M PROUD OF YOU, SON. YOU'RE GOING TO MAKE A GREAT HEAD OF I.T.

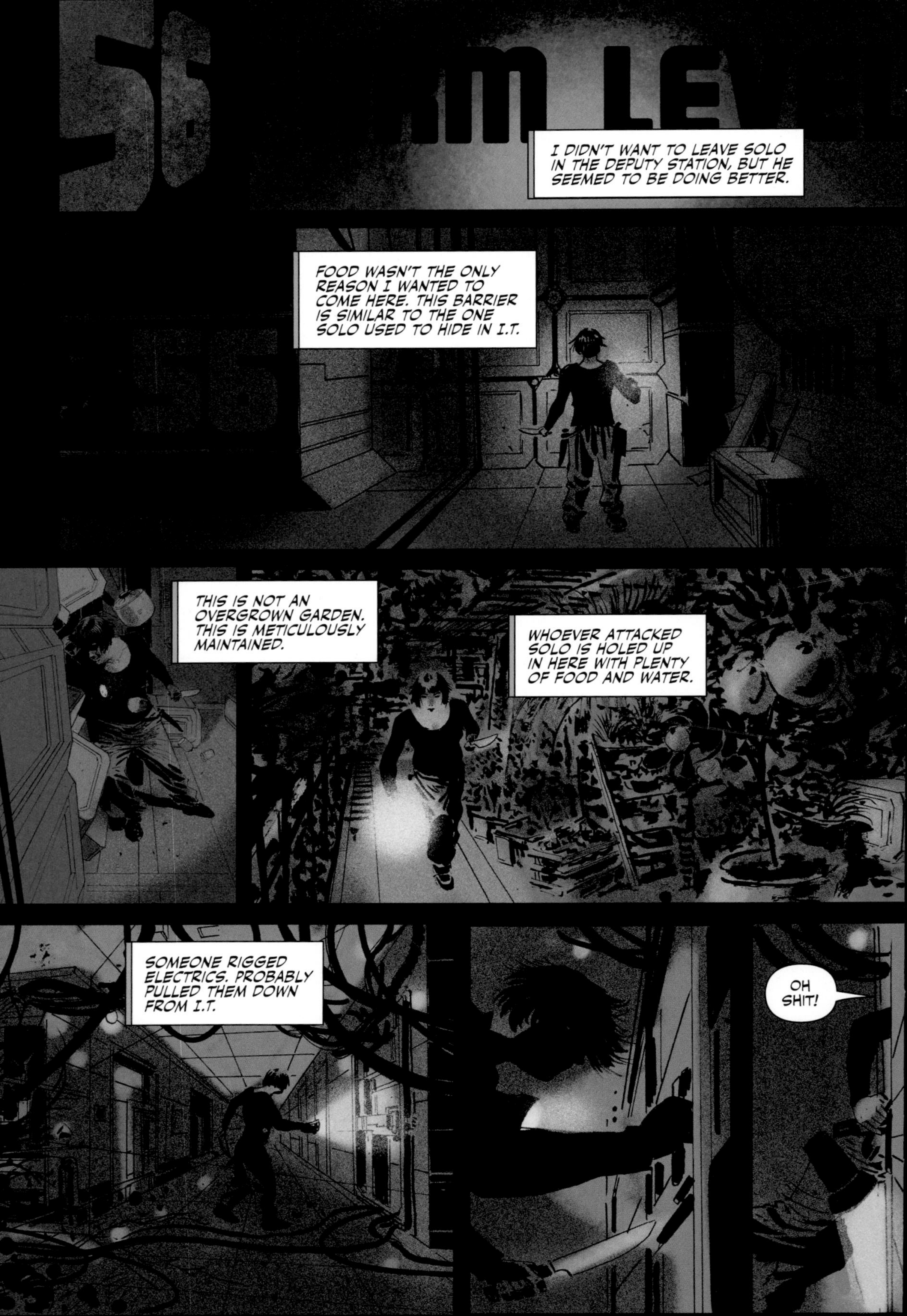
I DIDN'T WANT TO LEAVE SOLO IN THE DEPUTY STATION, BUT HE SEEMED TO BE DOING BETTER.
FOOD WASN'T THE ONLY REASON I WANTED TO COME HERE. THIS BARRIER IS SIMILAR TO THE ONE SOLO USED TO HIDE IN I.T.
THIS IS NOT AN OVERGROWN GARDEN. THIS IS METICULOUSLY MAINTAINED.
WHOEVER ATTACKED SOLO IS HOLED UP IN HERE WITH PLENTY OF FOOD AND WATER.
SOMEONE RIGGED ELECTRICS. PROBABLY PULLED THEM DOWN FROM I.T.
OH SHIT!

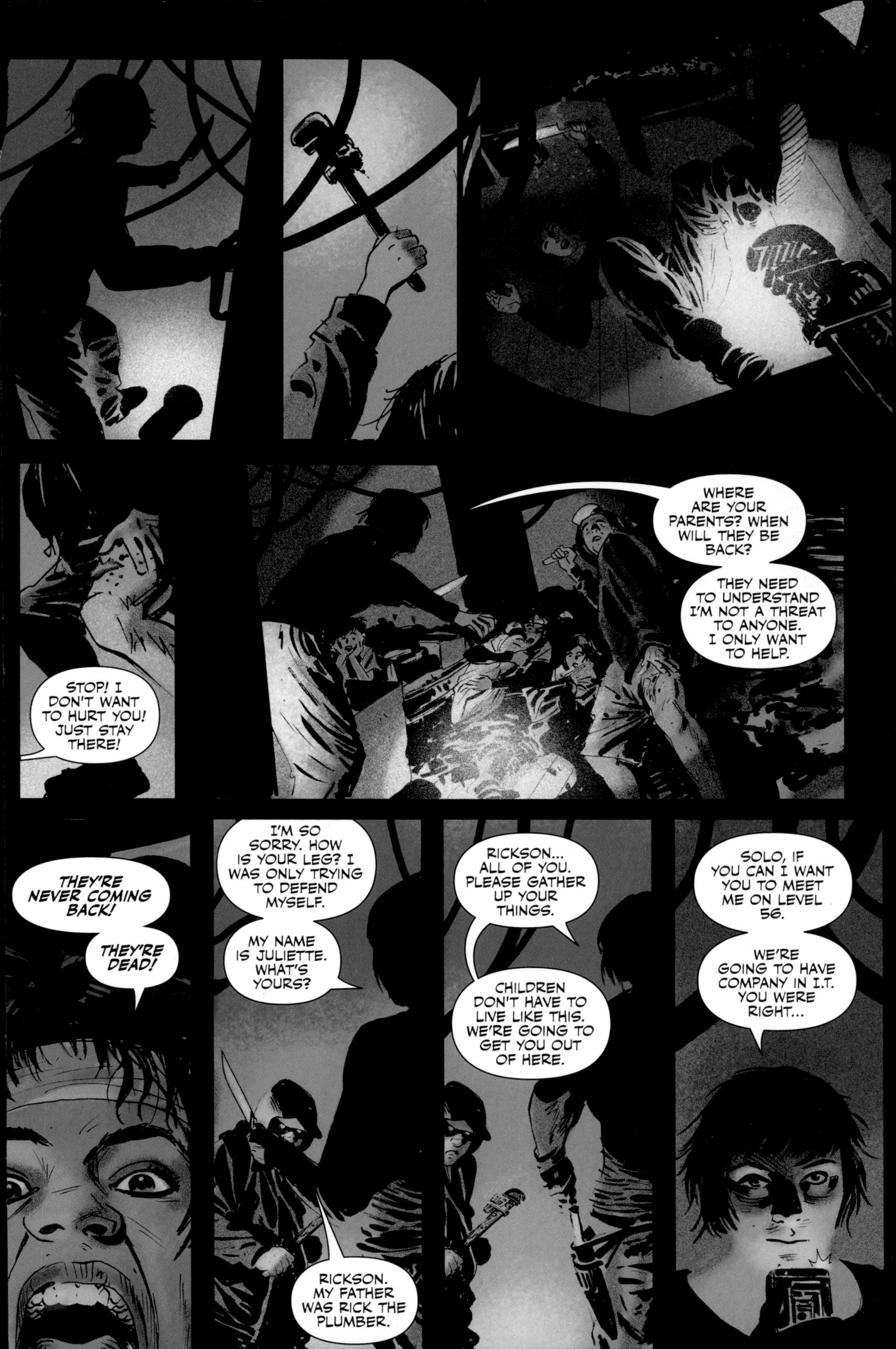
WHERE ARE YOUR PARENTS? WHEN WILL THEY BE BACK?
THEY NEED TO UNDERSTAND I'M NOT A THREAT TO ANYONE. I ONLY WANT TO HELP.
STOP! I DON'T WANT TO HURT YOU! JUST STAY THERE!
THEY'RE NEVER COMING BACK!
THEY'RE DEAD!
I'M SO SORRY. HOW IS YOUR LEG? I WAS ONLY TRYING TO DEFEND MYSELF.
MY NAME IS JULIETTE. WHAT'S YOURS?
RICKSON. MY FATHER WAS RICK THE PLUMBER.
RICKSON... ALL OF YOU. PLEASE GATHER UP YOUR THINGS.
CHILDREN DON'T HAVE TO LIVE LIKE THIS. WE'RE GOING TO GET YOU OUT OF HERE.
SOLO, IF YOU CAN I WANT YOU TO MEET ME ON LEVEL 56.
WE'RE GOING TO HAVE COMPANY IN I.T. YOU WERE RIGHT...

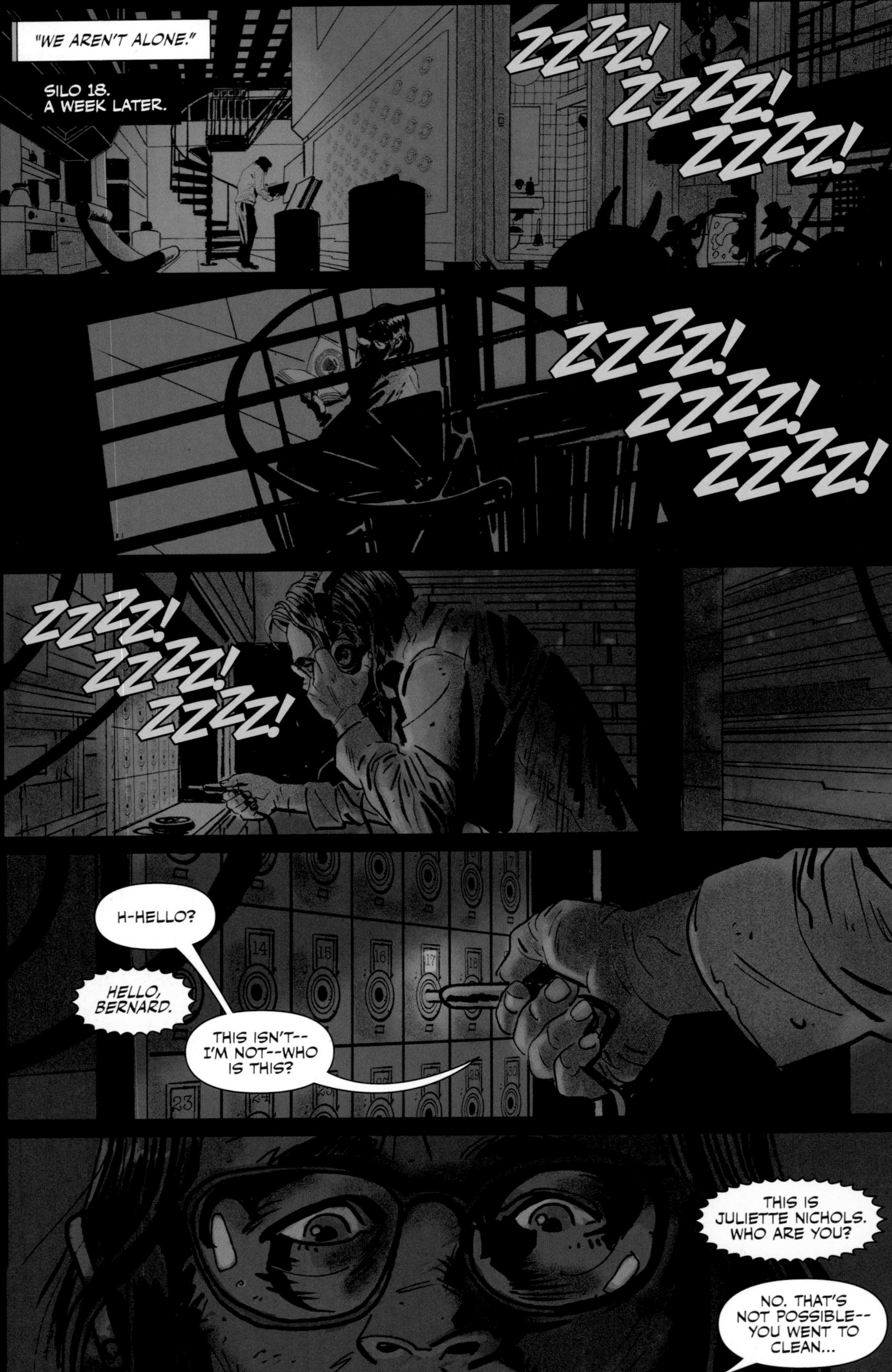
"WE AREN'T ALONE."
SILO 18. A WEEK LATER.
ZZZZZ! ZZZZZ! ZZZZZ!
ZZZZZ! ZZZZZ! ZZZZZ!
ZZZZZ! ZZZZZ! ZZZZZ!
H-HELLO?
HELLO, BERNARD.
THIS ISN'T-- I'M NOT--WHO IS THIS?
THIS IS JULIETTE NICHOLS. WHO ARE YOU?
NO. THAT'S NOT POSSIBLE-- YOU WENT TO CLEAN...

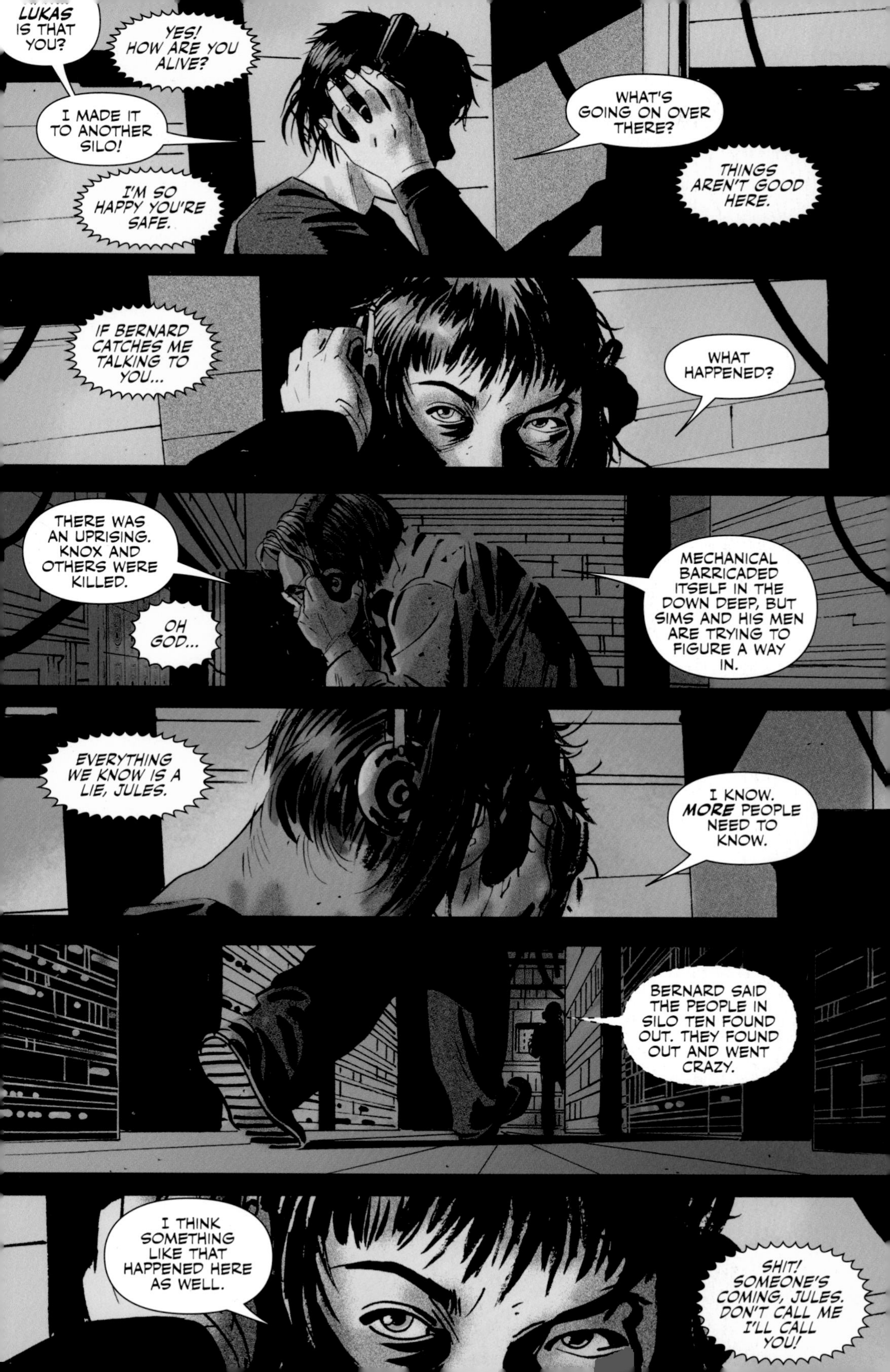
LUKAS IS THAT YOU?
YES! HOW ARE YOU ALIVE?
I MADE IT TO ANOTHER SILO!
I'M SO HAPPY YOU'RE SAFE.
WHAT'S GOING ON OVER THERE?
THINGS AREN'T GOOD HERE.
IF BERNARD CATCHES ME TALKING TO YOU...
WHAT HAPPENED?
THERE WAS AN UPRISING. KNOX AND OTHERS WERE KILLED.
OH GOD...
MECHANICAL BARRICADED ITSELF IN THE DOWN DEEP, BUT SIMS AND HIS MEN ARE TRYING TO FIGURE A WAY IN.
EVERYTHING WE KNOW IS A LIE, JULES.
I KNOW. MORE PEOPLE NEED TO KNOW.
BERNARD SAID THE PEOPLE IN SILO TEN FOUND OUT. THEY FOUND OUT AND WENT CRAZY.
I THINK SOMETHING LIKE THAT HAPPENED HERE AS WELL.
SHIT! SOMEONE'S COMING, JULES. DON'T CALL ME I'LL CALL YOU!

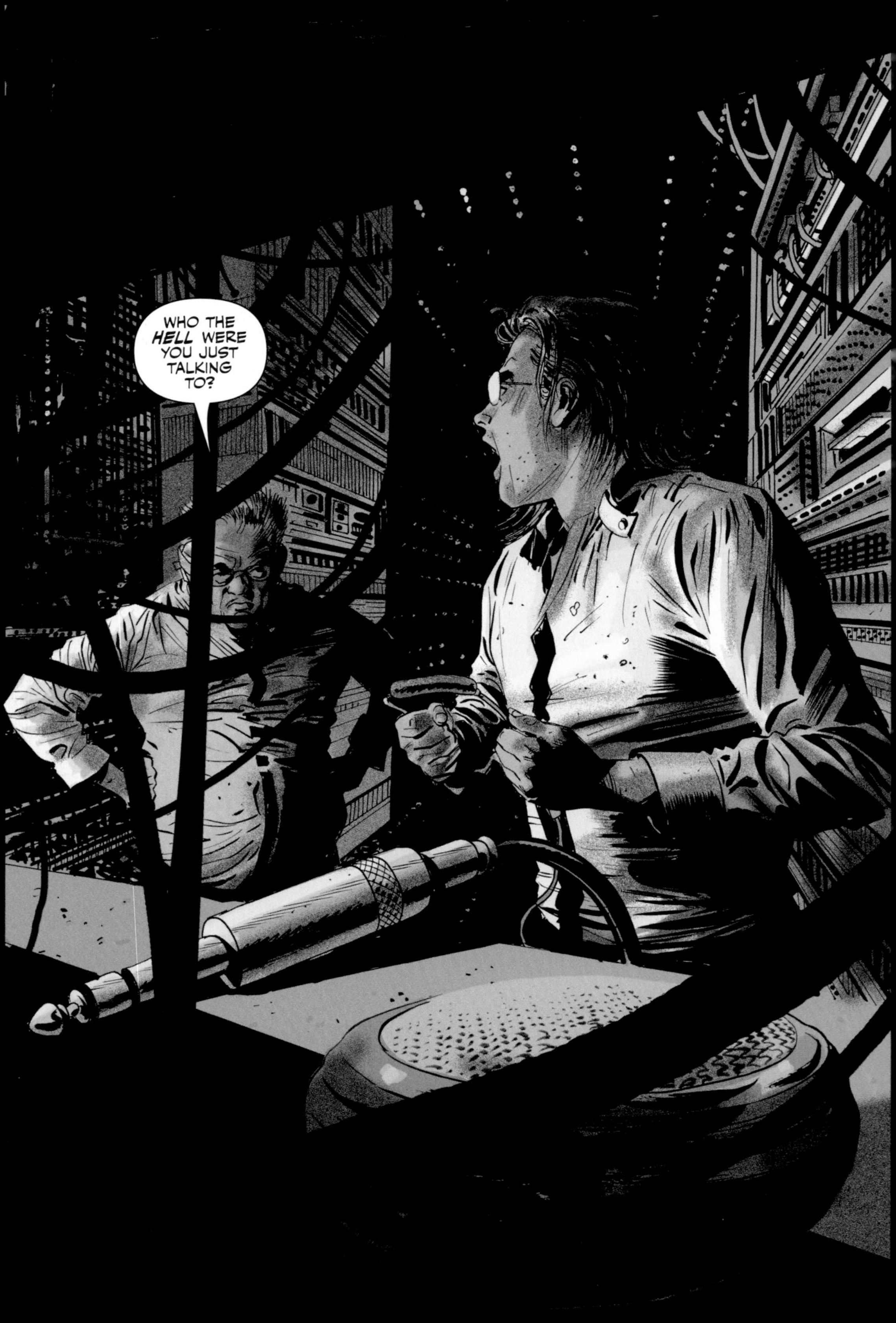
WHO THE *HELL* WERE YOU JUST TALKING TO?

TO BE CONTINUED IN THE NEXT ISSUE.

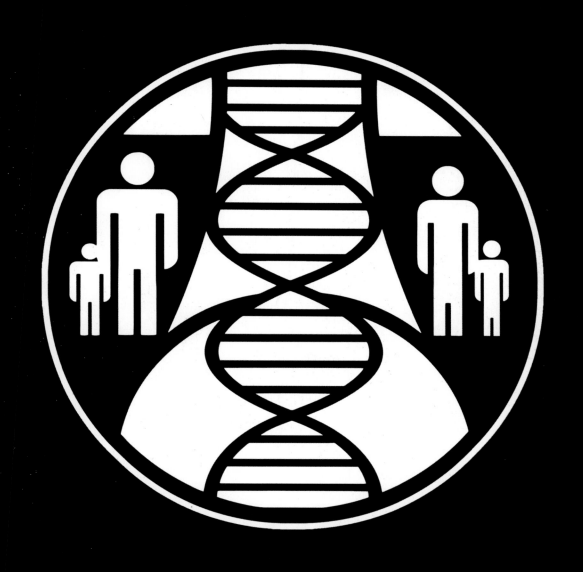

END ISSUE 5

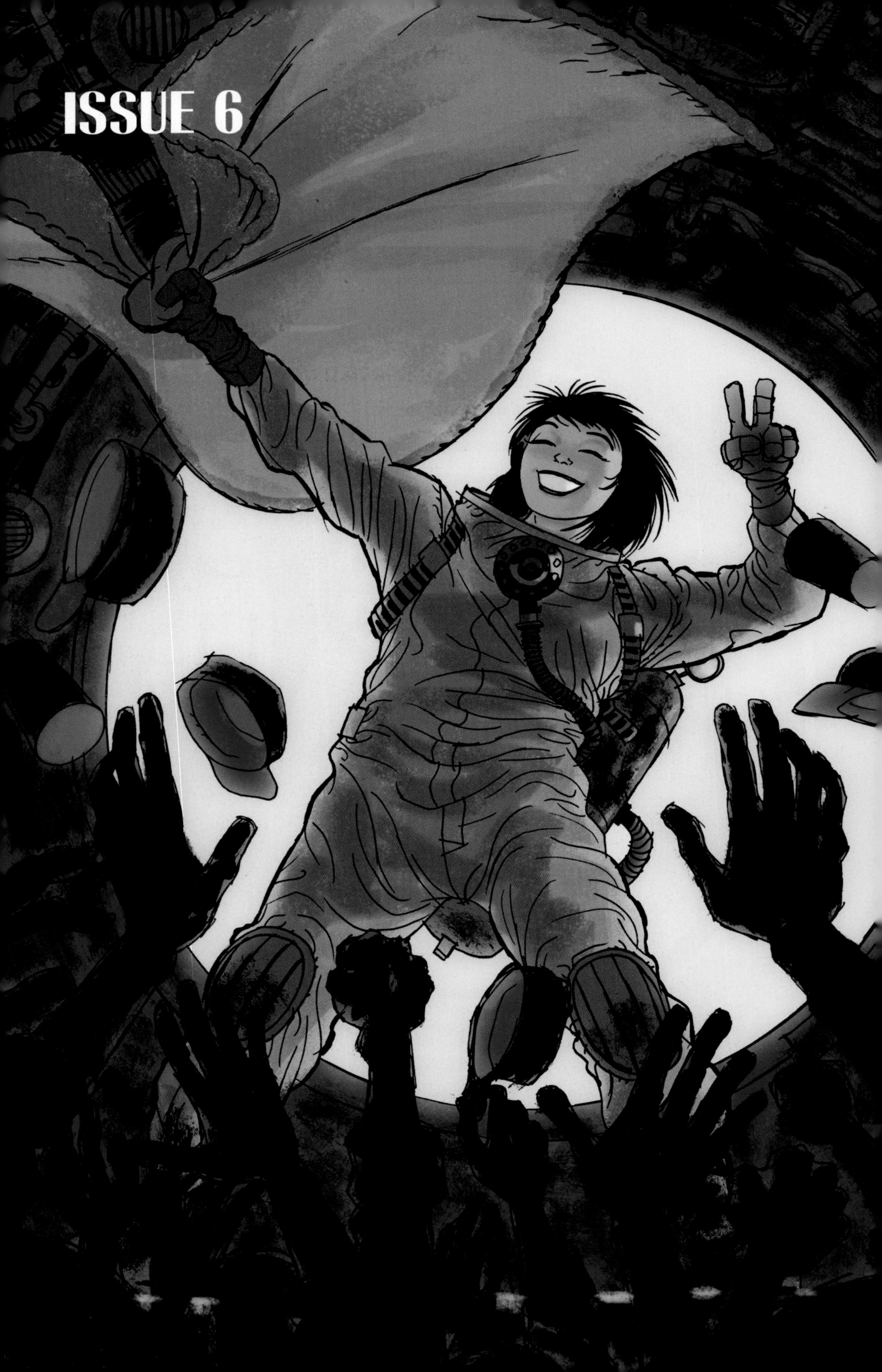
ISSUE 6

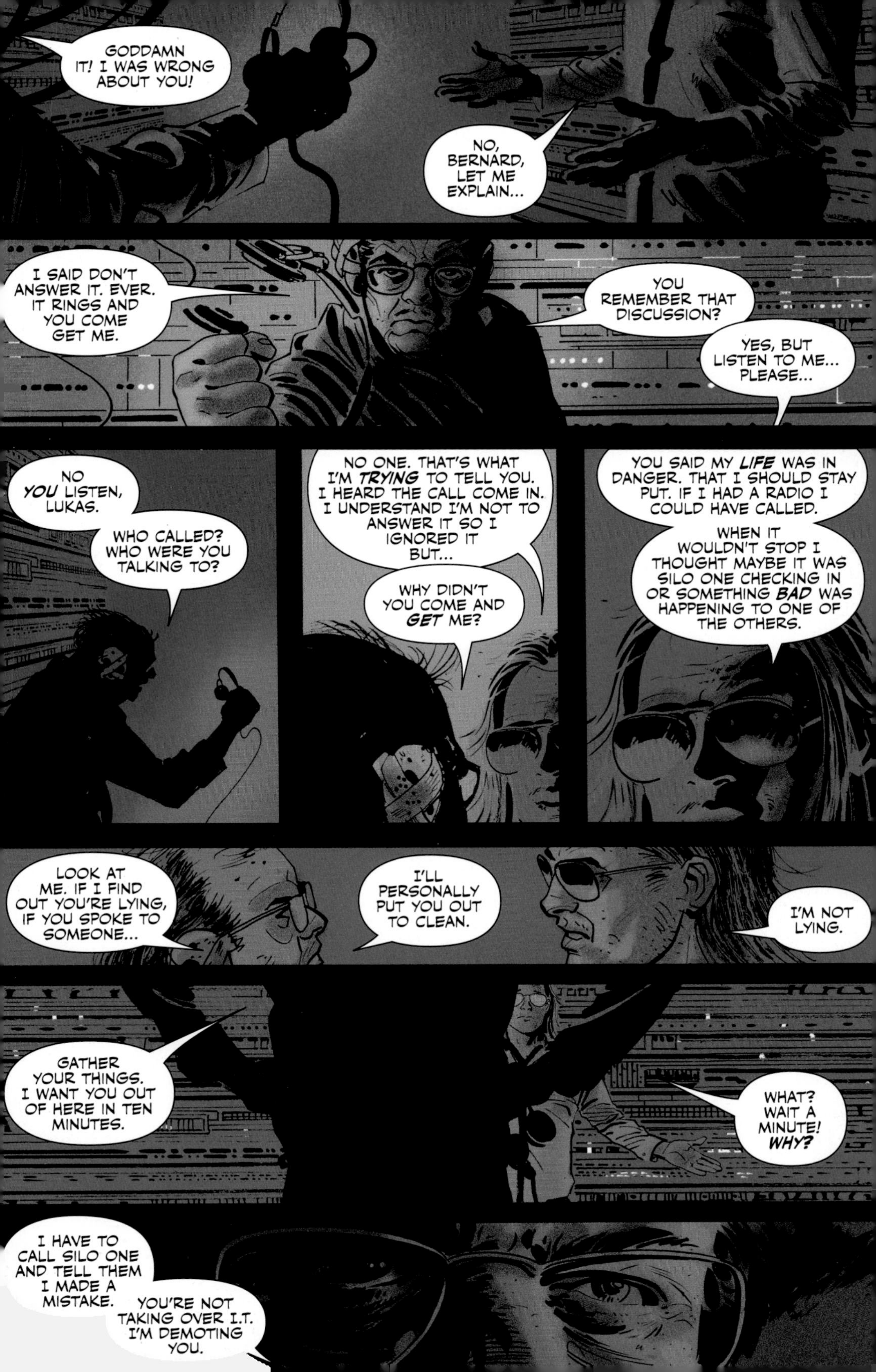
GODDAMN IT! I WAS WRONG ABOUT YOU!
NO, BERNARD, LET ME EXPLAIN...
I SAID DON'T ANSWER IT. EVER. IT RINGS AND YOU COME GET ME.
YOU REMEMBER THAT DISCUSSION?
YES, BUT LISTEN TO ME... PLEASE...
NO *YOU* LISTEN, LUKAS.
WHO CALLED? WHO WERE YOU TALKING TO?
NO ONE. THAT'S WHAT I'M *TRYING* TO TELL YOU. I HEARD THE CALL COME IN. I UNDERSTAND I'M NOT TO ANSWER IT SO I IGNORED IT BUT...
WHY DIDN'T YOU COME AND *GET* ME?
YOU SAID MY *LIFE* WAS IN DANGER. THAT I SHOULD STAY PUT. IF I HAD A RADIO I COULD HAVE CALLED.
WHEN IT WOULDN'T STOP I THOUGHT MAYBE IT WAS SILO ONE CHECKING IN OR SOMETHING *BAD* WAS HAPPENING TO ONE OF THE OTHERS.
LOOK AT ME. IF I FIND OUT YOU'RE LYING, IF YOU SPOKE TO SOMEONE...
I'LL PERSONALLY PUT YOU OUT TO CLEAN.
I'M NOT LYING.
GATHER YOUR THINGS. I WANT YOU OUT OF HERE IN TEN MINUTES.
WHAT? WAIT A MINUTE! *WHY?*
I HAVE TO CALL SILO ONE AND TELL THEM I MADE A MISTAKE.
YOU'RE NOT TAKING OVER I.T. I'M DEMOTING YOU.

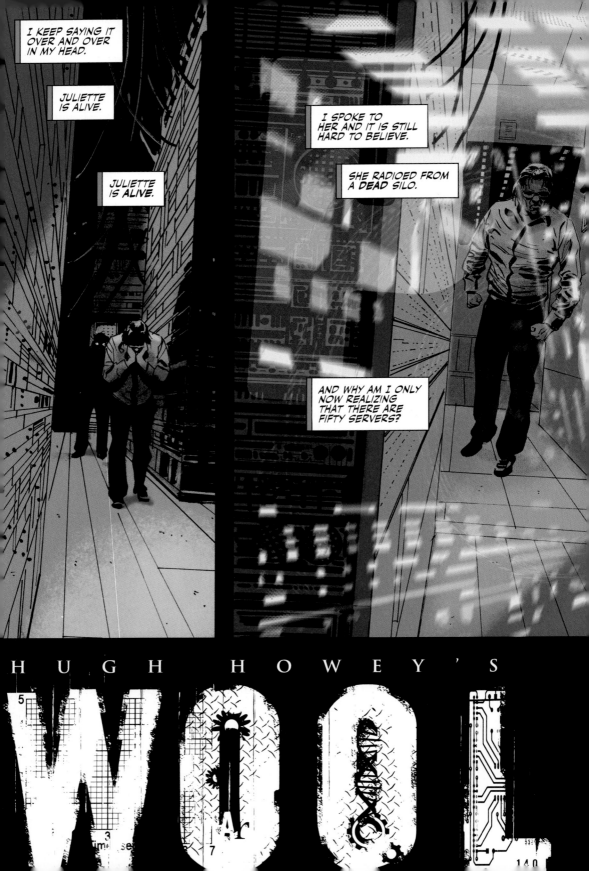

I KEEP SAYING IT OVER AND OVER IN MY HEAD.

JULIETTE IS ALIVE.

JULIETTE IS ALIVE.

I SPOKE TO HER AND IT IS STILL HARD TO BELIEVE.

SHE RADIOED FROM A DEAD SILO.

AND WHY AM I ONLY NOW REALIZING THAT THERE ARE FIFTY SERVERS?

HUGH HOWEY'S

WOOL

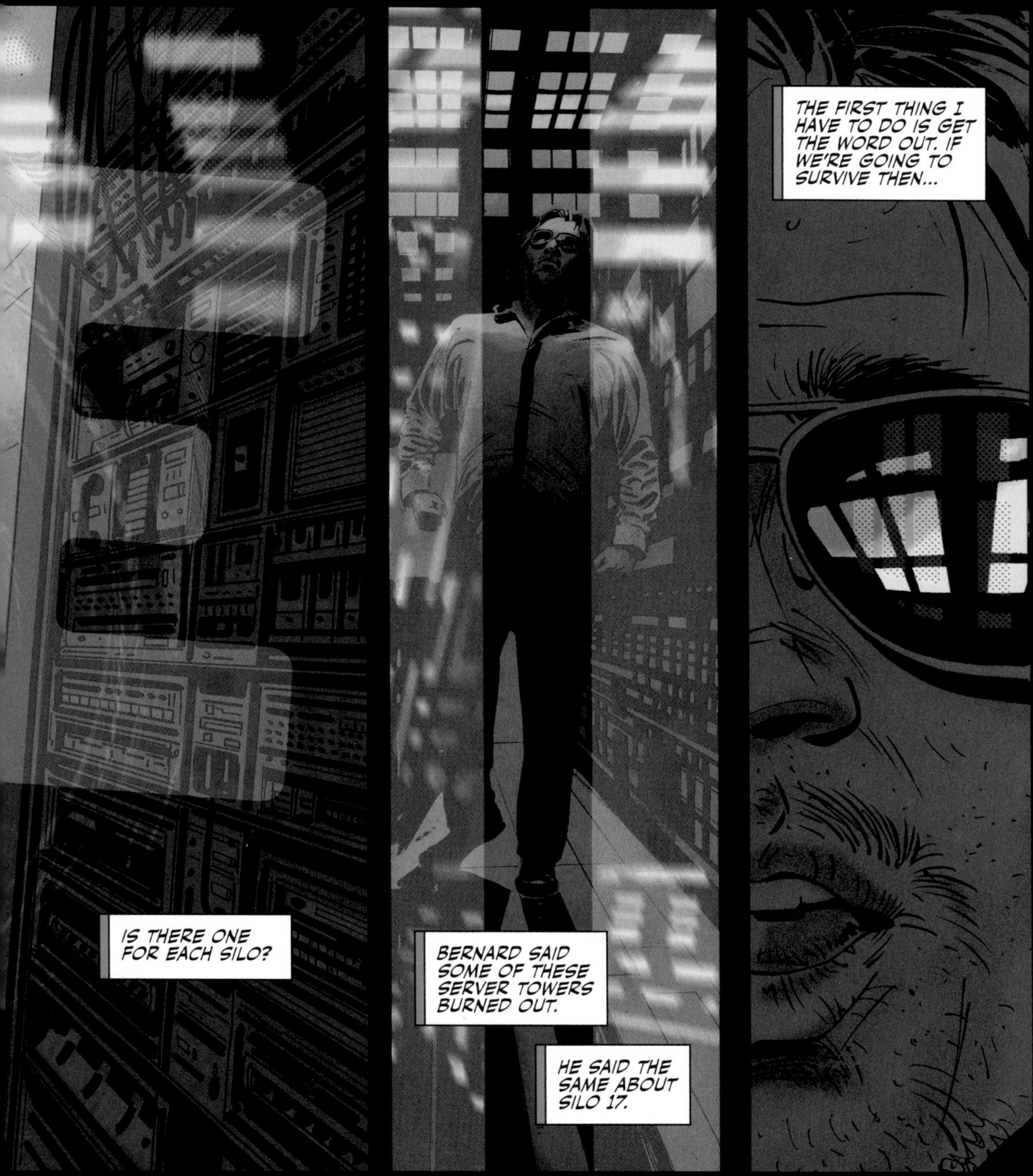
IS THERE ONE FOR EACH SILO?
BERNARD SAID SOME OF THESE SERVER TOWERS BURNED OUT.
HE SAID THE SAME ABOUT SILO 17.
THE FIRST THING I HAVE TO DO IS GET THE WORD OUT. IF WE'RE GOING TO SURVIVE THEN...

HOMECOMING

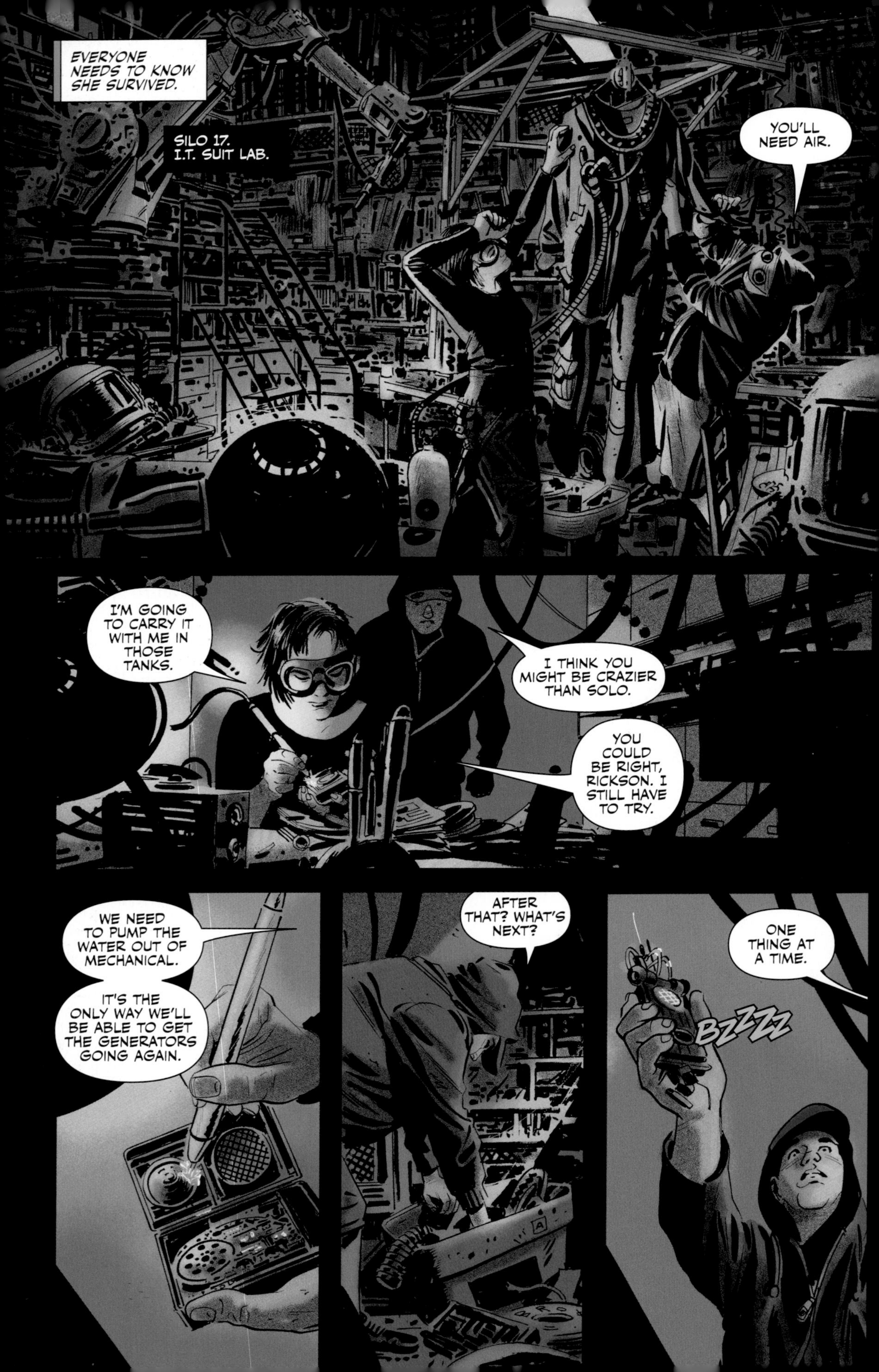
EVERYONE NEEDS TO KNOW SHE SURVIVED.
SILO 17. I.T. SUIT LAB.
YOU'LL NEED AIR.
I'M GOING TO CARRY IT WITH ME IN THOSE TANKS.
I THINK YOU MIGHT BE CRAZIER THAN SOLO.
YOU COULD BE RIGHT, RICKSON. I STILL HAVE TO TRY.
WE NEED TO PUMP THE WATER OUT OF MECHANICAL.
IT'S THE ONLY WAY WE'LL BE ABLE TO GET THE GENERATORS GOING AGAIN.
AFTER THAT? WHAT'S NEXT?
ONE THING AT A TIME.
BZZZZ

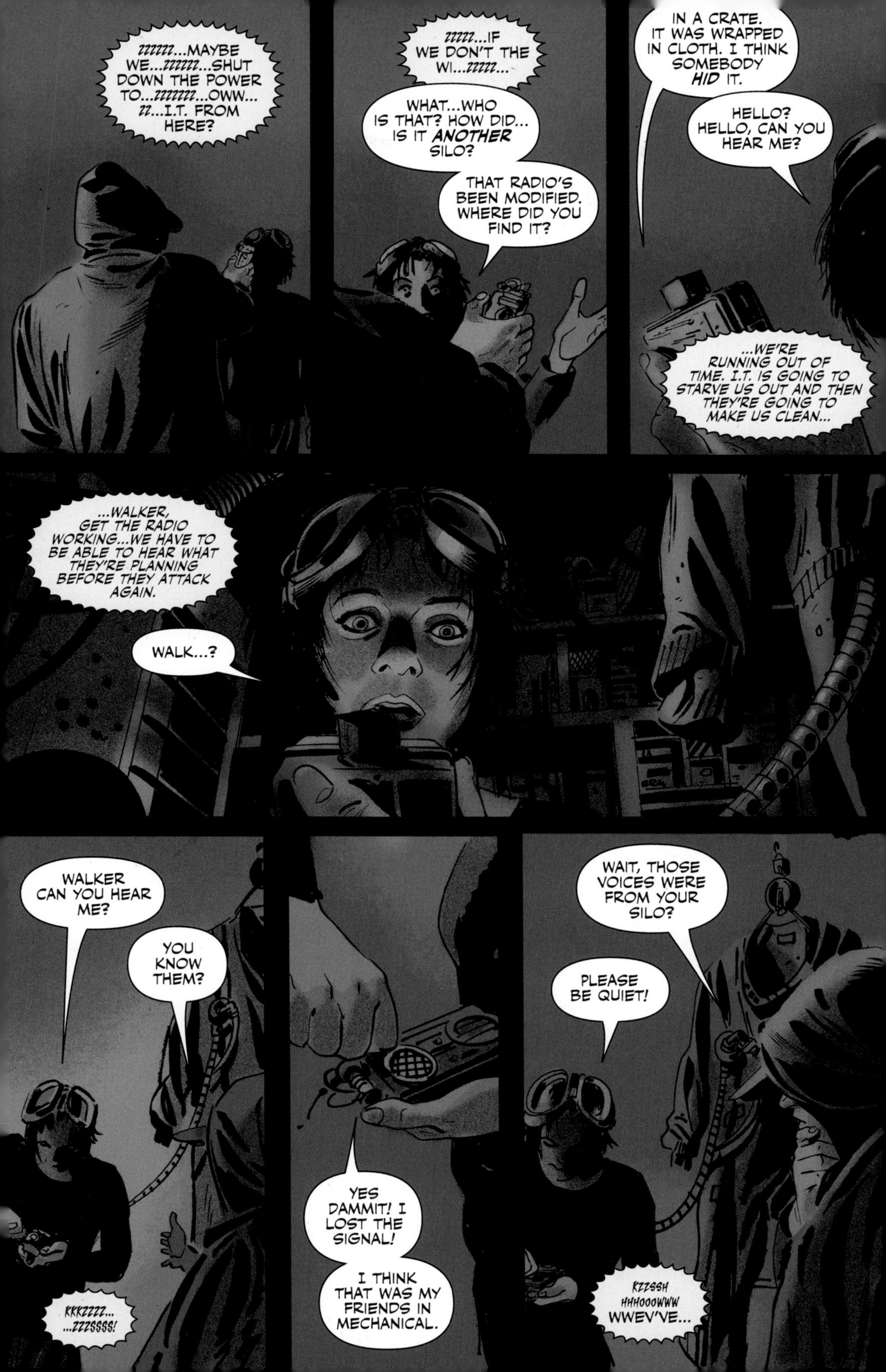

ZZZZZZ...MAYBE WE...ZZZZZZ...SHUT DOWN THE POWER TO...ZZZZZZZ...OWW... ZZ...I.T. FROM HERE?
ZZZZZ...IF WE DON'T THE WI...ZZZZZ...
WHAT...WHO IS THAT? HOW DID... IS IT ANOTHER SILO?
THAT RADIO'S BEEN MODIFIED. WHERE DID YOU FIND IT?
IN A CRATE. IT WAS WRAPPED IN CLOTH. I THINK SOMEBODY HID IT.
HELLO? HELLO, CAN YOU HEAR ME?
...WE'RE RUNNING OUT OF TIME. I.T. IS GOING TO STARVE US OUT AND THEN THEY'RE GOING TO MAKE US CLEAN...
...WALKER, GET THE RADIO WORKING...WE HAVE TO BE ABLE TO HEAR WHAT THEY'RE PLANNING BEFORE THEY ATTACK AGAIN.
WALK...?
WALKER CAN YOU HEAR ME?
YOU KNOW THEM?
KKKZZZZ... ...ZZZSSSS!
YES DAMMIT! I LOST THE SIGNAL!
I THINK THAT WAS MY FRIENDS IN MECHANICAL.
WAIT, THOSE VOICES WERE FROM YOUR SILO?
PLEASE BE QUIET!
KZZSSH HHHOOOWWW WWEV'VE...

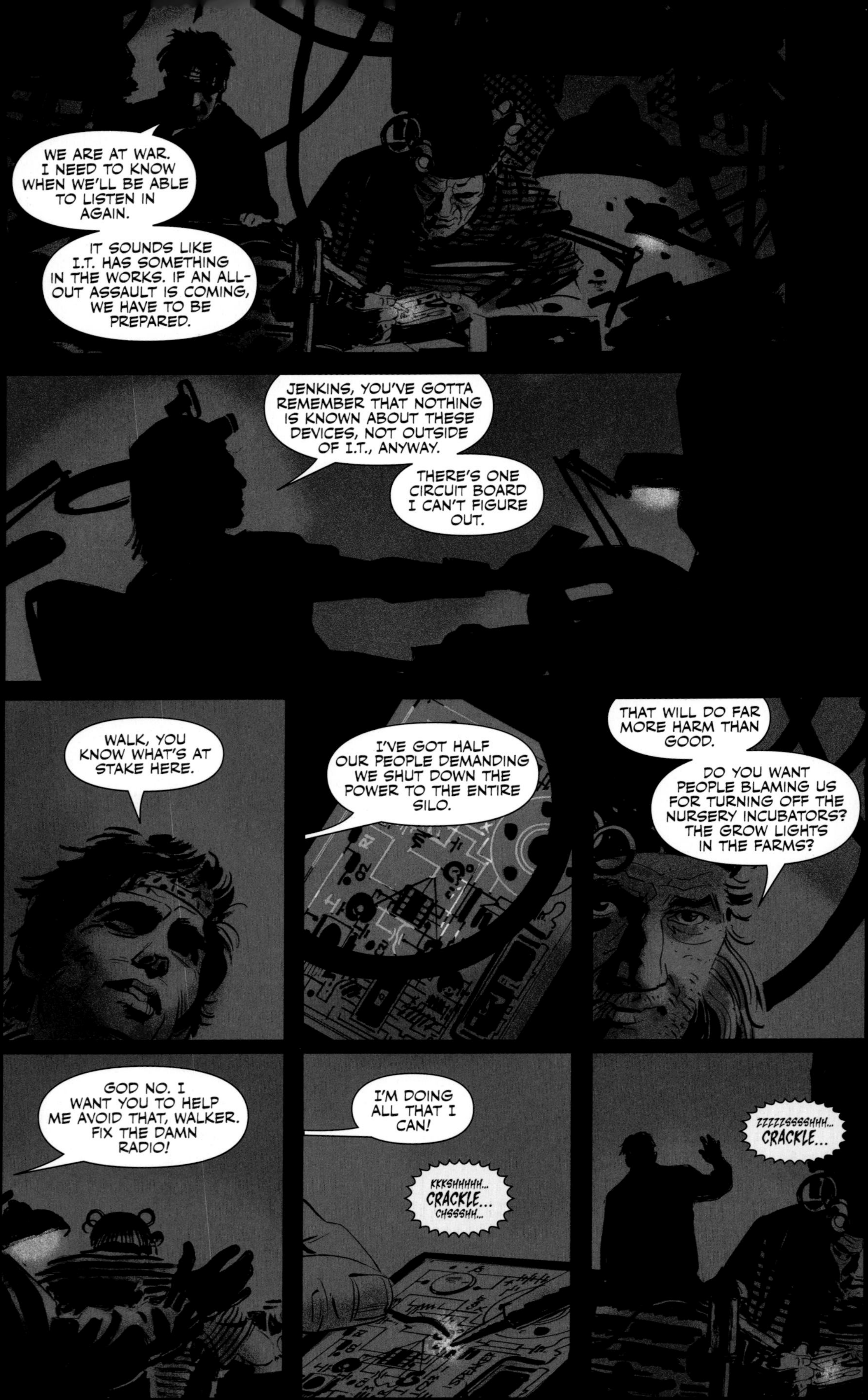
WE ARE AT WAR. I NEED TO KNOW WHEN WE'LL BE ABLE TO LISTEN IN AGAIN.
IT SOUNDS LIKE I.T. HAS SOMETHING IN THE WORKS. IF AN ALL-OUT ASSAULT IS COMING, WE HAVE TO BE PREPARED.
JENKINS, YOU'VE GOTTA REMEMBER THAT NOTHING IS KNOWN ABOUT THESE DEVICES, NOT OUTSIDE OF I.T., ANYWAY.
THERE'S ONE CIRCUIT BOARD I CAN'T FIGURE OUT.
WALK, YOU KNOW WHAT'S AT STAKE HERE.
I'VE GOT HALF OUR PEOPLE DEMANDING WE SHUT DOWN THE POWER TO THE ENTIRE SILO.
THAT WILL DO FAR MORE HARM THAN GOOD.
DO YOU WANT PEOPLE BLAMING US FOR TURNING OFF THE NURSERY INCUBATORS? THE GROW LIGHTS IN THE FARMS?
GOD NO. I WANT YOU TO HELP ME AVOID THAT, WALKER. FIX THE DAMN RADIO!
I'M DOING ALL THAT I CAN!
KKKSHHHHH... CRACKLE... CHSSSHH...
ZZZZZSSSSHHH... CRACKLE...

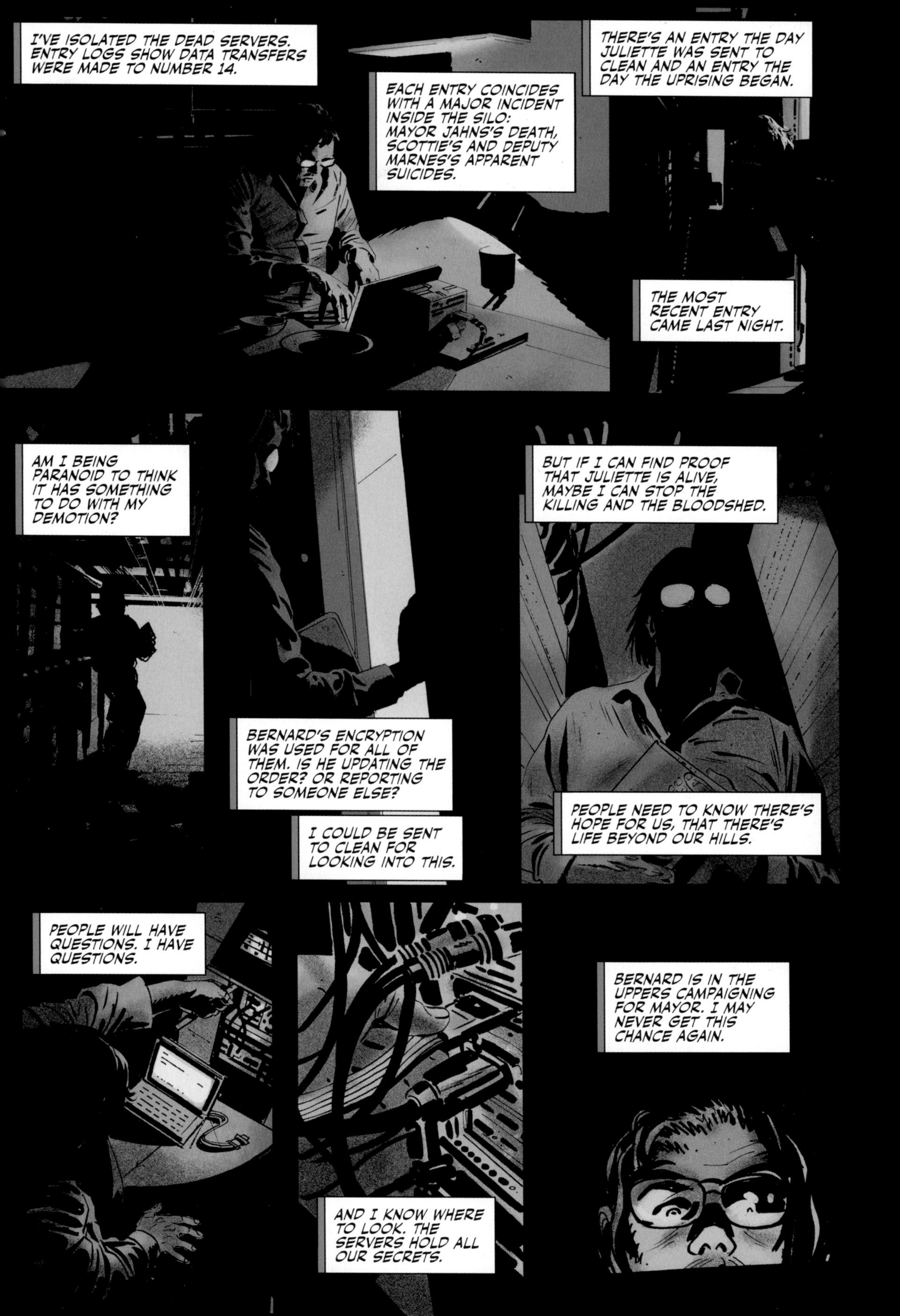
I'VE ISOLATED THE DEAD SERVERS. ENTRY LOGS SHOW DATA TRANSFERS WERE MADE TO NUMBER 14.
EACH ENTRY COINCIDES WITH A MAJOR INCIDENT INSIDE THE SILO: MAYOR JAHNS'S DEATH, SCOTTIE'S AND DEPUTY MARNES'S APPARENT SUICIDES.
THERE'S AN ENTRY THE DAY JULIETTE WAS SENT TO CLEAN AND AN ENTRY THE DAY THE UPRISING BEGAN.
THE MOST RECENT ENTRY CAME LAST NIGHT.
AM I BEING PARANOID TO THINK IT HAS SOMETHING TO DO WITH MY DEMOTION?
BERNARD'S ENCRYPTION WAS USED FOR ALL OF THEM. IS HE UPDATING THE ORDER? OR REPORTING TO SOMEONE ELSE?
I COULD BE SENT TO CLEAN FOR LOOKING INTO THIS.
BUT IF I CAN FIND PROOF THAT JULIETTE IS ALIVE, MAYBE I CAN STOP THE KILLING AND THE BLOODSHED.
PEOPLE NEED TO KNOW THERE'S HOPE FOR US, THAT THERE'S LIFE BEYOND OUR HILLS.
PEOPLE WILL HAVE QUESTIONS. I HAVE QUESTIONS.
AND I KNOW WHERE TO LOOK. THE SERVERS HOLD ALL OUR SECRETS.
BERNARD IS IN THE UPPERS CAMPAIGNING FOR MAYOR. I MAY NEVER GET THIS CHANCE AGAIN.

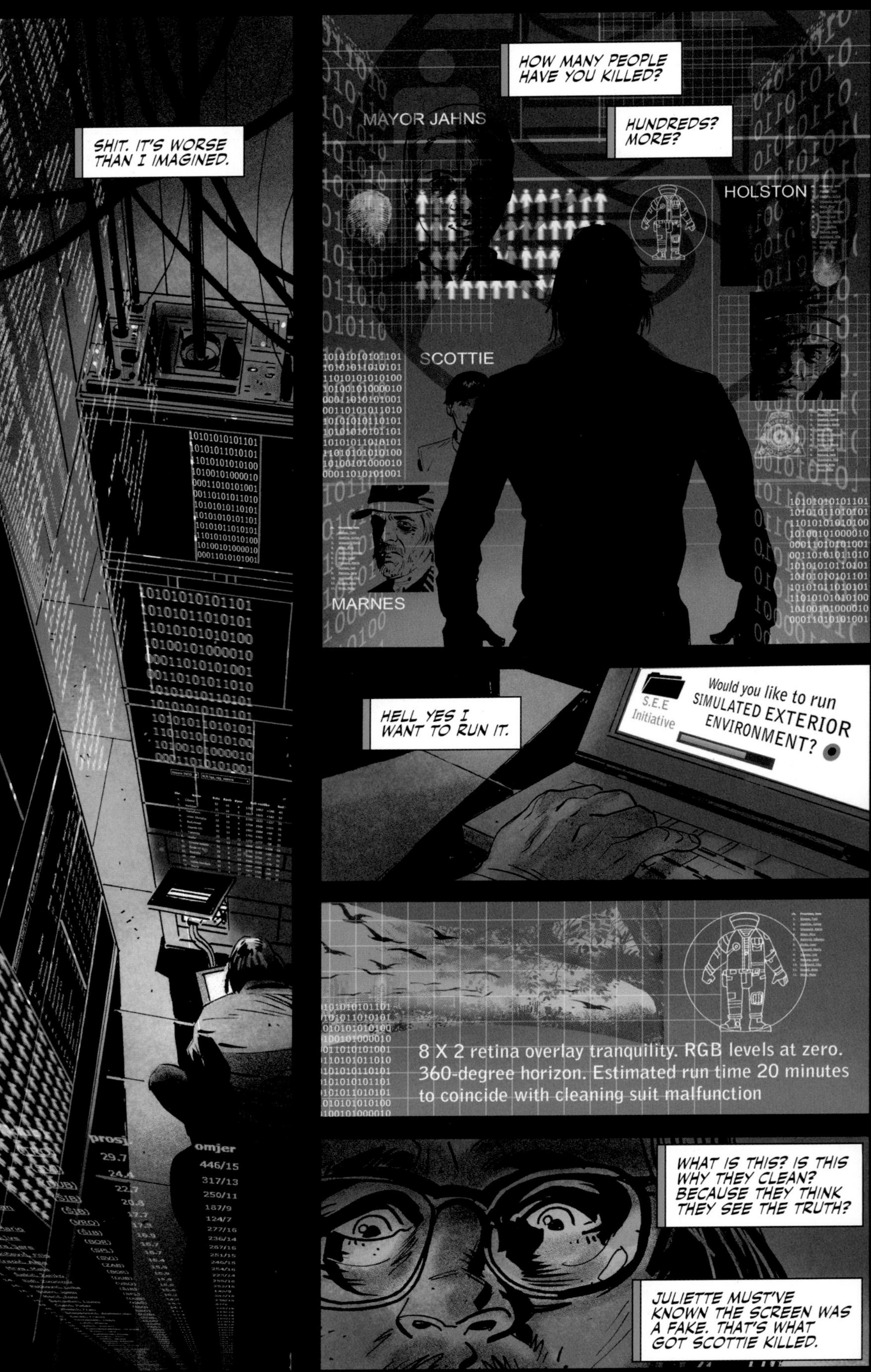

SHIT. IT'S WORSE THAN I IMAGINED.
HOW MANY PEOPLE HAVE YOU KILLED?
HUNDREDS? MORE?
MAYOR JAHNS
HOLSTON
SCOTTIE
MARNES
HELL YES I WANT TO RUN IT.
S.E.E Initiative
Would you like to run SIMULATED EXTERIOR ENVIRONMENT?
8 X 2 retina overlay tranquility. RGB levels at zero.
360-degree horizon. Estimated run time 20 minutes
to coincide with cleaning suit malfunction
WHAT IS THIS? IS THIS WHY THEY CLEAN? BECAUSE THEY THINK THEY SEE THE TRUTH?
JULIETTE MUST'VE KNOWN THE SCREEN WAS A FAKE. THAT'S WHAT GOT SCOTTIE KILLED.

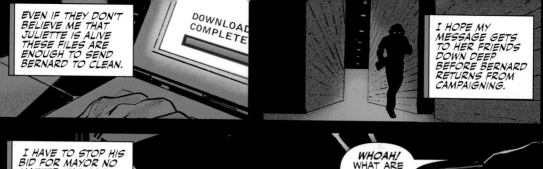

EVEN IF THEY DON'T BELIEVE ME THAT JULIETTE IS ALIVE THESE FILES ARE ENOUGH TO SEND BERNARD TO CLEAN.

DOWNLOAD COMPLETE

I HOPE MY MESSAGE GETS TO HER FRIENDS DOWN DEEP BEFORE BERNARD RETURNS FROM CAMPAIGNING.

I HAVE TO STOP HIS BID FOR MAYOR NO MATTER THE COST.

WHOAH! WHAT ARE YOU DOING, LUKAS?

UHNFF! SHIT!

PETER, NOW HOLD ON...

YOU'RE NOT SUPPOSED TO BE IN THAT ROOM.

I-I...IT'S NOT, LISTEN TO ME, BERNARD...

YES, BERNARD TOLD ME TO KEEP AN EYE ON YOU. HE SAID IF YOU WENT ANYWHERE NEAR THAT ROOM I WAS TO ARREST YOU AND CALL HIM IMMEDIATELY.

LISTEN TO ME. JULIETTE IS ALIVE. BERNARD POISONED MAYOR JAHNS AND MADE DEPTY MARNES' DEATH LOOK LIKE A SUICIDE. I CAN SHOW YOU...

I'M GONNA NEED YOU TO TURN AROUND SLOWLY WITH YOUR HANDS BEHIND YOUR BACK...

PLEASE JUST LISTEN! EVERYTHING IS ON THE LAPTOP. I CAN JUST SHOW...

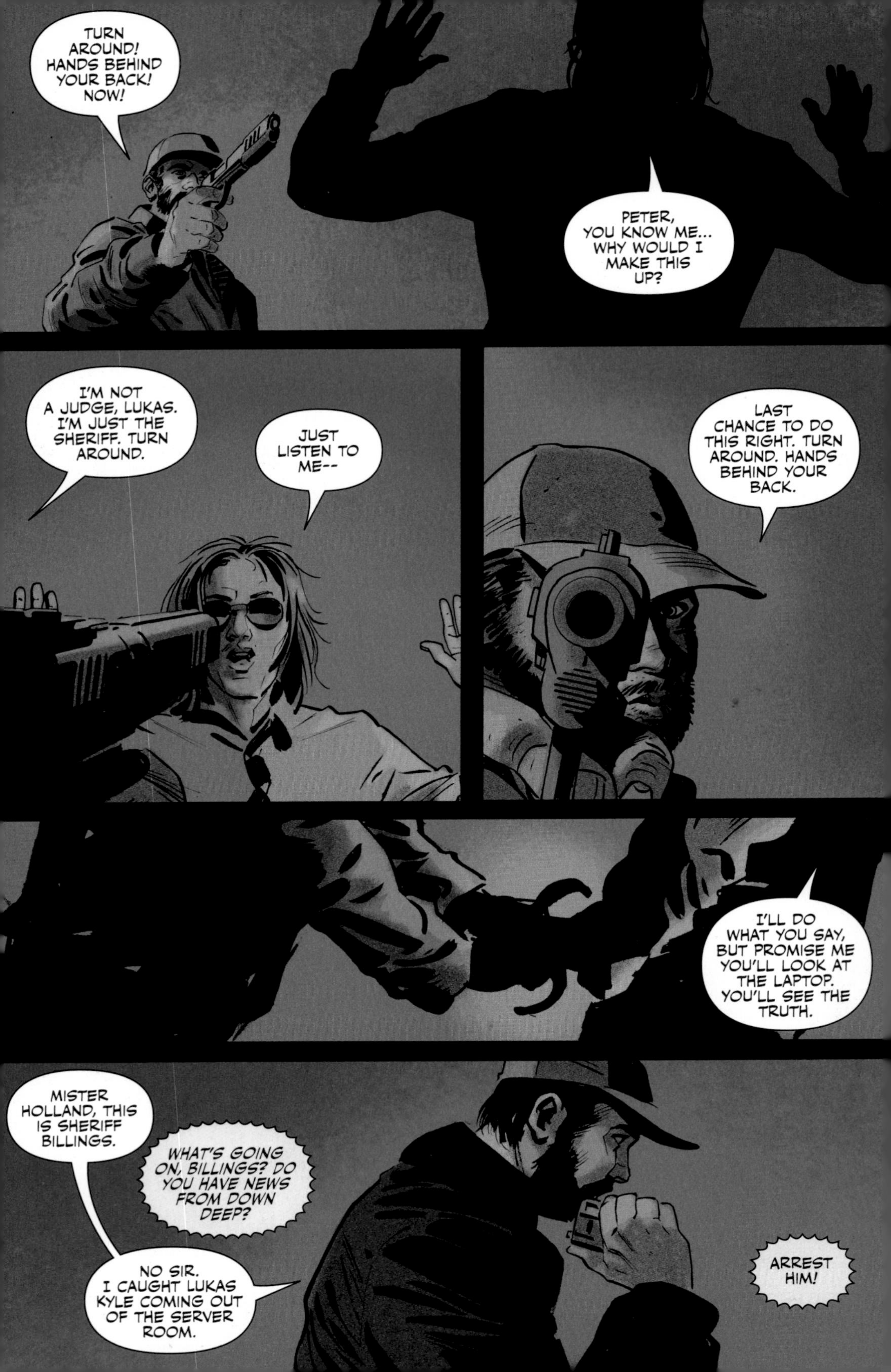
TURN AROUND! HANDS BEHIND YOUR BACK! NOW!
PETER, YOU KNOW ME... WHY WOULD I MAKE THIS UP?
I'M NOT A JUDGE, LUKAS. I'M JUST THE SHERIFF. TURN AROUND.
JUST LISTEN TO ME--
LAST CHANCE TO DO THIS RIGHT. TURN AROUND. HANDS BEHIND YOUR BACK.
I'LL DO WHAT YOU SAY, BUT PROMISE ME YOU'LL LOOK AT THE LAPTOP. YOU'LL SEE THE TRUTH.
MISTER HOLLAND, THIS IS SHERIFF BILLINGS.
WHAT'S GOING ON, BILLINGS? DO YOU HAVE NEWS FROM DOWN DEEP?
NO SIR. I CAUGHT LUKAS KYLE COMING OUT OF THE SERVER ROOM.
ARREST HIM!

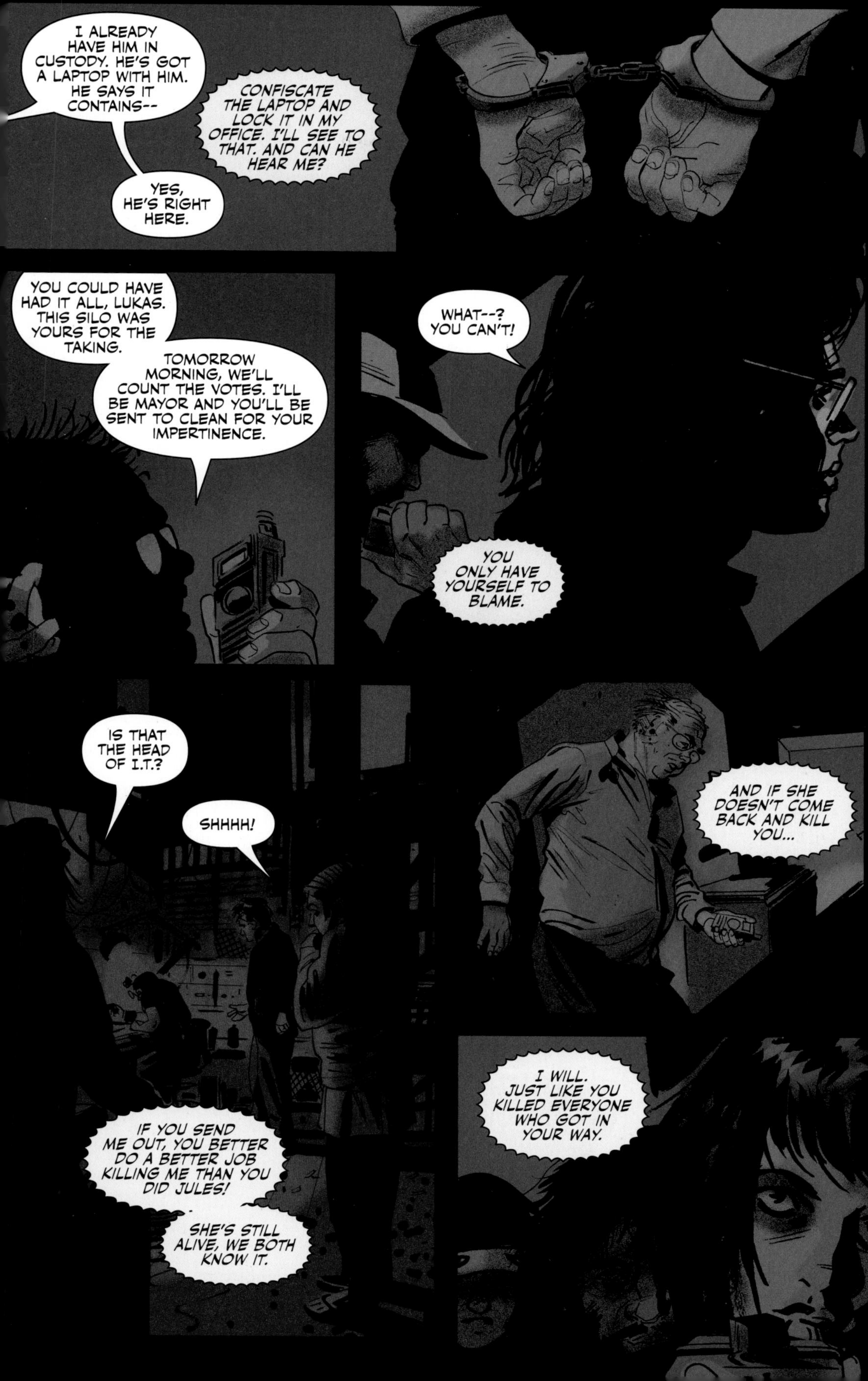
I ALREADY HAVE HIM IN CUSTODY. HE'S GOT A LAPTOP WITH HIM. HE SAYS IT CONTAINS--
CONFISCATE THE LAPTOP AND LOCK IT IN MY OFFICE. I'LL SEE TO THAT. AND CAN HE HEAR ME?
YES, HE'S RIGHT HERE.
YOU COULD HAVE HAD IT ALL, LUKAS. THIS SILO WAS YOURS FOR THE TAKING.
TOMORROW MORNING, WE'LL COUNT THE VOTES. I'LL BE MAYOR AND YOU'LL BE SENT TO CLEAN FOR YOUR IMPERTINENCE.
WHAT--? YOU CAN'T!
YOU ONLY HAVE YOURSELF TO BLAME.
IS THAT THE HEAD OF I.T.?
SHHHH!
AND IF SHE DOESN'T COME BACK AND KILL YOU...
IF YOU SEND ME OUT, YOU BETTER DO A BETTER JOB KILLING ME THAN YOU DID JULES!
SHE'S STILL ALIVE, WE BOTH KNOW IT.
I WILL. JUST LIKE YOU KILLED EVERYONE WHO GOT IN YOUR WAY.

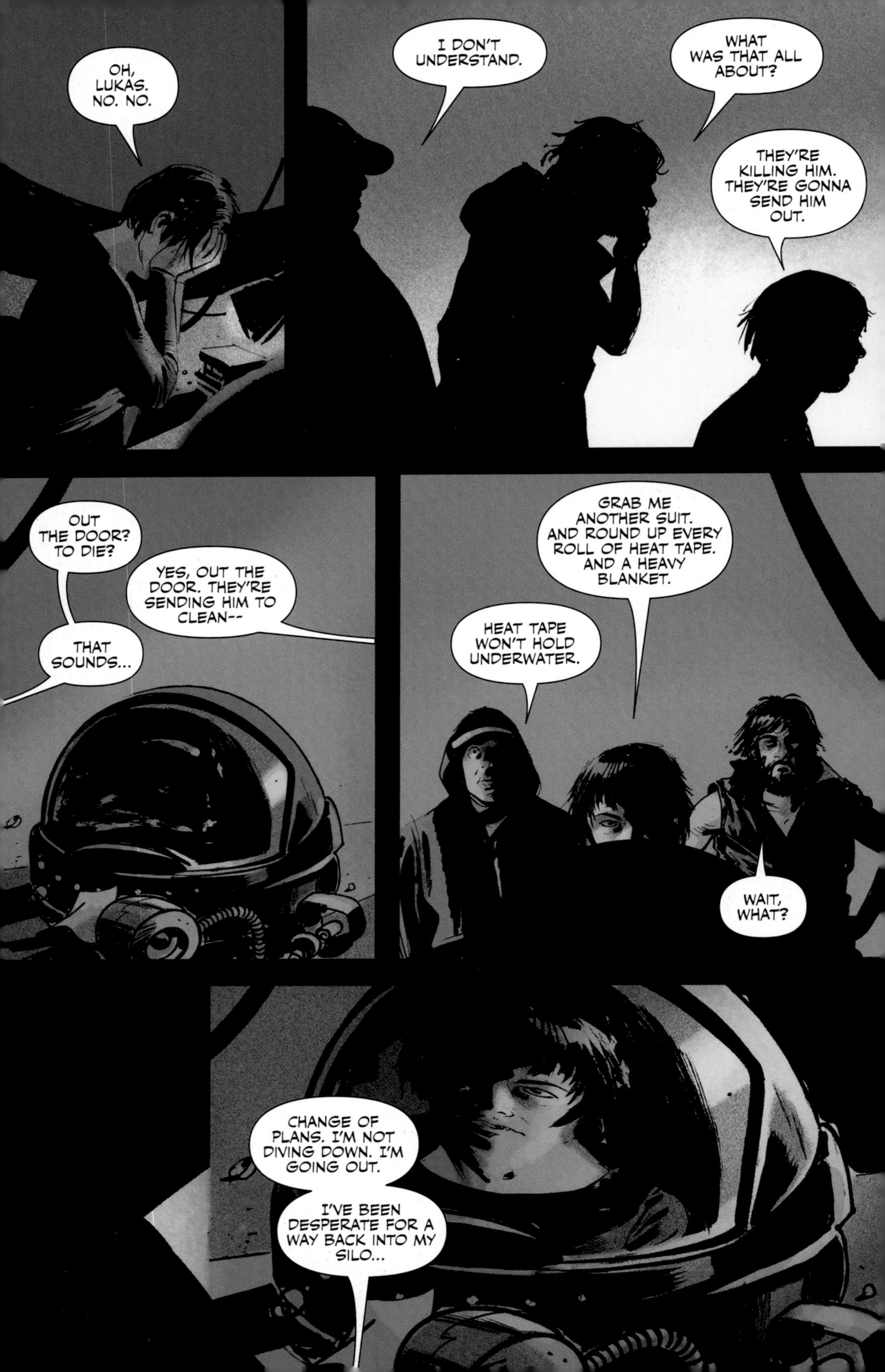
OH, LUKAS. NO. NO.
I DON'T UNDERSTAND.
WHAT WAS THAT ALL ABOUT?
THEY'RE KILLING HIM. THEY'RE GONNA SEND HIM OUT.
OUT THE DOOR? TO DIE?
YES, OUT THE DOOR. THEY'RE SENDING HIM TO CLEAN--
THAT SOUNDS...
GRAB ME ANOTHER SUIT. AND ROUND UP EVERY ROLL OF HEAT TAPE. AND A HEAVY BLANKET.
HEAT TAPE WON'T HOLD UNDERWATER.
WAIT, WHAT?
CHANGE OF PLANS. I'M NOT DIVING DOWN. I'M GOING OUT.
I'VE BEEN DESPERATE FOR A WAY BACK INTO MY SILO...

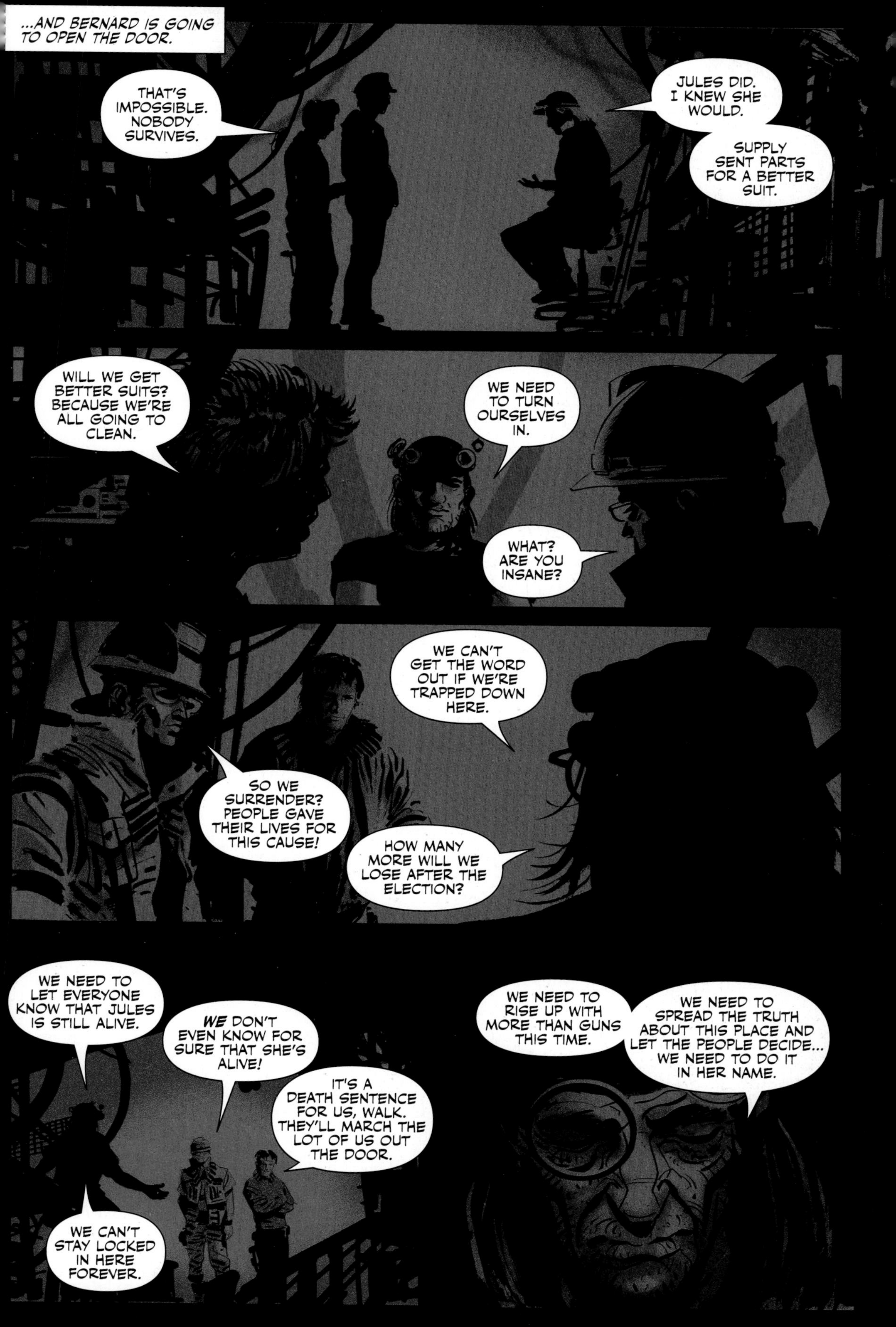
...AND BERNARD IS GOING TO OPEN THE DOOR.
THAT'S IMPOSSIBLE. NOBODY SURVIVES.
JULES DID. I KNEW SHE WOULD.
SUPPLY SENT PARTS FOR A BETTER SUIT.
WILL WE GET BETTER SUITS? BECAUSE WE'RE ALL GOING TO CLEAN.
WE NEED TO TURN OURSELVES IN.
WHAT? ARE YOU INSANE?
WE CAN'T GET THE WORD OUT IF WE'RE TRAPPED DOWN HERE.
SO WE SURRENDER? PEOPLE GAVE THEIR LIVES FOR THIS CAUSE!
HOW MANY MORE WILL WE LOSE AFTER THE ELECTION?
WE NEED TO LET EVERYONE KNOW THAT JULES IS STILL ALIVE.
WE CAN'T STAY LOCKED IN HERE FOREVER.
WE DON'T EVEN KNOW FOR SURE THAT SHE'S ALIVE!
IT'S A DEATH SENTENCE FOR US, WALK. THEY'LL MARCH THE LOT OF US OUT THE DOOR.
WE NEED TO RISE UP WITH MORE THAN GUNS THIS TIME.
WE NEED TO SPREAD THE TRUTH ABOUT THIS PLACE AND LET THE PEOPLE DECIDE... WE NEED TO DO IT IN HER NAME.

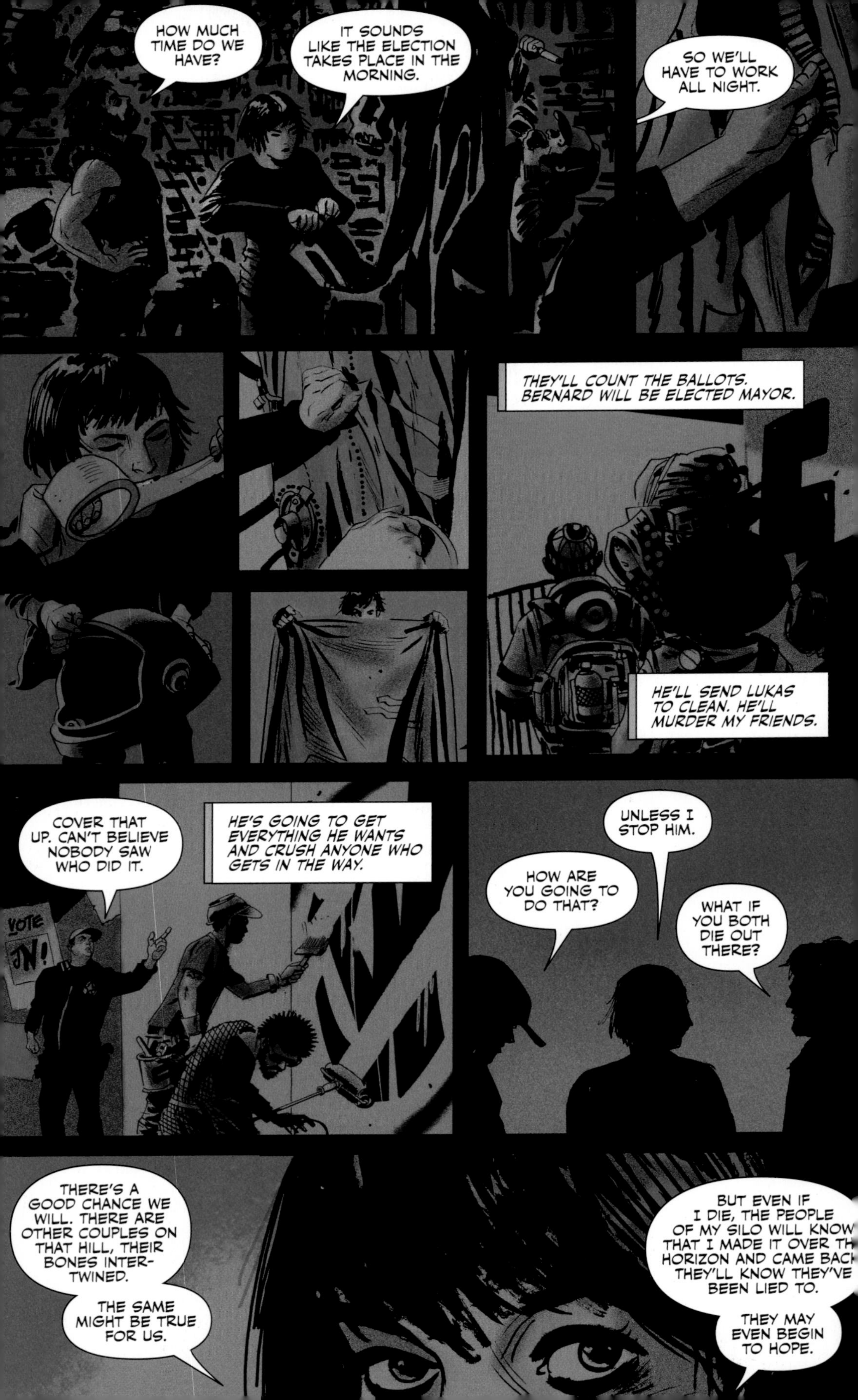
HOW MUCH TIME DO WE HAVE?
IT SOUNDS LIKE THE ELECTION TAKES PLACE IN THE MORNING.
SO WE'LL HAVE TO WORK ALL NIGHT.
THEY'LL COUNT THE BALLOTS. BERNARD WILL BE ELECTED MAYOR.
HE'LL SEND LUKAS TO CLEAN. HE'LL MURDER MY FRIENDS.
COVER THAT UP. CAN'T BELIEVE NOBODY SAW WHO DID IT.
HE'S GOING TO GET EVERYTHING HE WANTS AND CRUSH ANYONE WHO GETS IN THE WAY.
VOTE
UNLESS I STOP HIM.
HOW ARE YOU GOING TO DO THAT?
WHAT IF YOU BOTH DIE OUT THERE?
THERE'S A GOOD CHANCE WE WILL. THERE ARE OTHER COUPLES ON THAT HILL, THEIR BONES INTER-TWINED.
THE SAME MIGHT BE TRUE FOR US.
BUT EVEN IF I DIE, THE PEOPLE OF MY SILO WILL KNOW THAT I MADE IT OVER TH HORIZON AND CAME BAC THEY'LL KNOW THEY'VE BEEN LIED TO.
THEY MAY EVEN BEGIN TO HOPE.

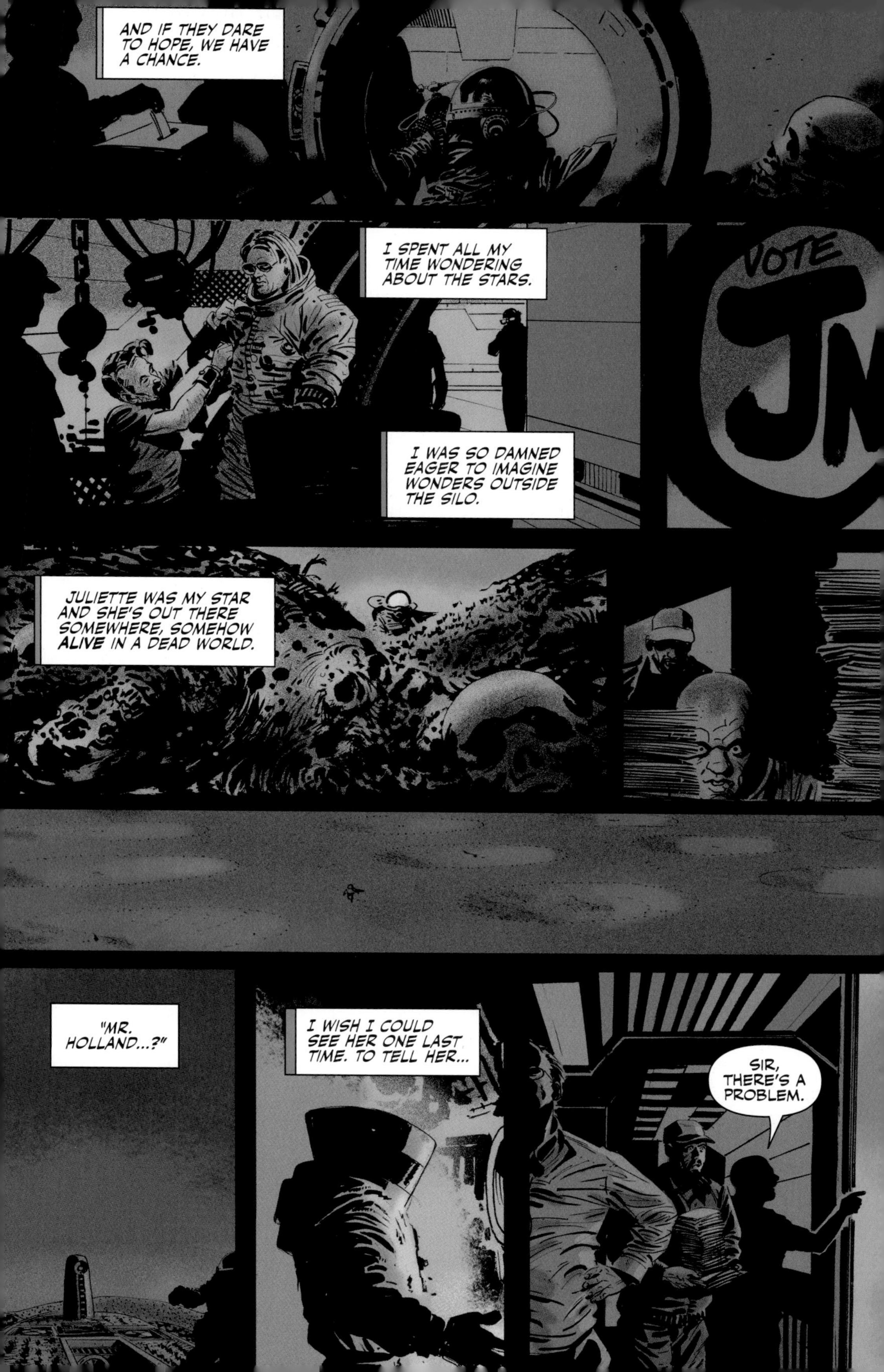
AND IF THEY DARE TO HOPE, WE HAVE A CHANCE.
I SPENT ALL MY TIME WONDERING ABOUT THE STARS.
I WAS SO DAMNED EAGER TO IMAGINE WONDERS OUTSIDE THE SILO.
VOTE
JULIETTE WAS MY STAR AND SHE'S OUT THERE SOMEWHERE, SOMEHOW ALIVE IN A DEAD WORLD.
"MR. HOLLAND...?"
I WISH I COULD SEE HER ONE LAST TIME. TO TELL HER...
SIR, THERE'S A PROBLEM.

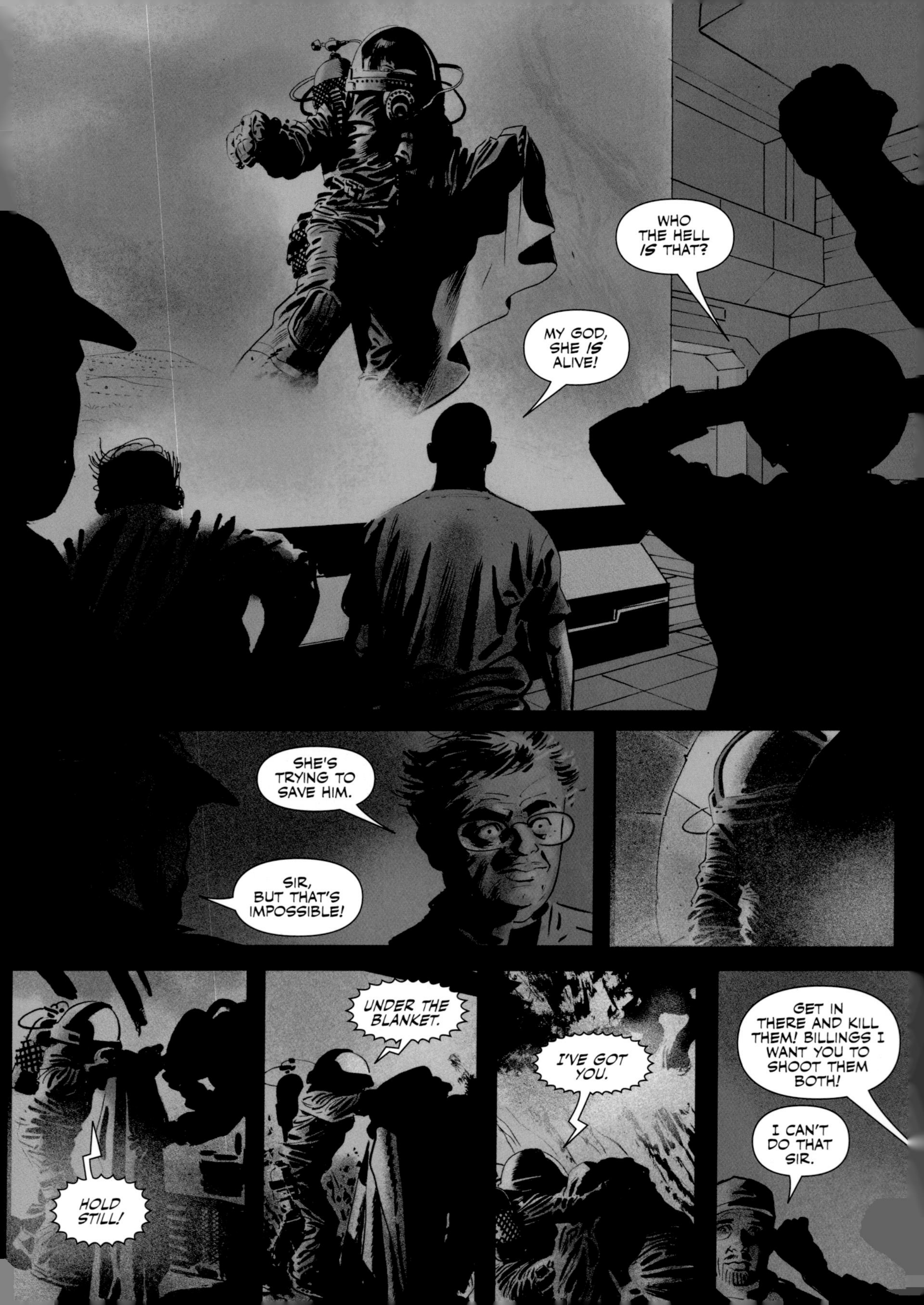
WHO THE HELL *IS* THAT?
MY GOD, SHE *IS* ALIVE!
SHE'S TRYING TO SAVE HIM.
SIR, BUT THAT'S IMPOSSIBLE!
HOLD STILL!
UNDER THE BLANKET.
I'VE GOT YOU.
GET IN THERE AND KILL THEM! BILLINGS I WANT YOU TO SHOOT THEM BOTH!
I CAN'T DO THAT SIR.

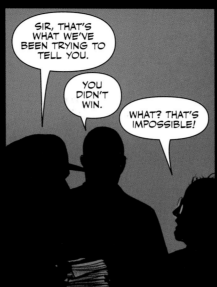

SIR, THAT'S WHAT WE'VE BEEN TRYING TO TELL YOU.

YOU DIDN'T WIN.

WHAT? THAT'S IMPOSSIBLE!

YES YOU CAN! I ORDER YOU! I'M THE MAYOR!

WHO DID?

SHE DID.

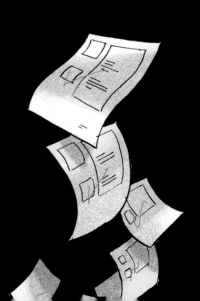

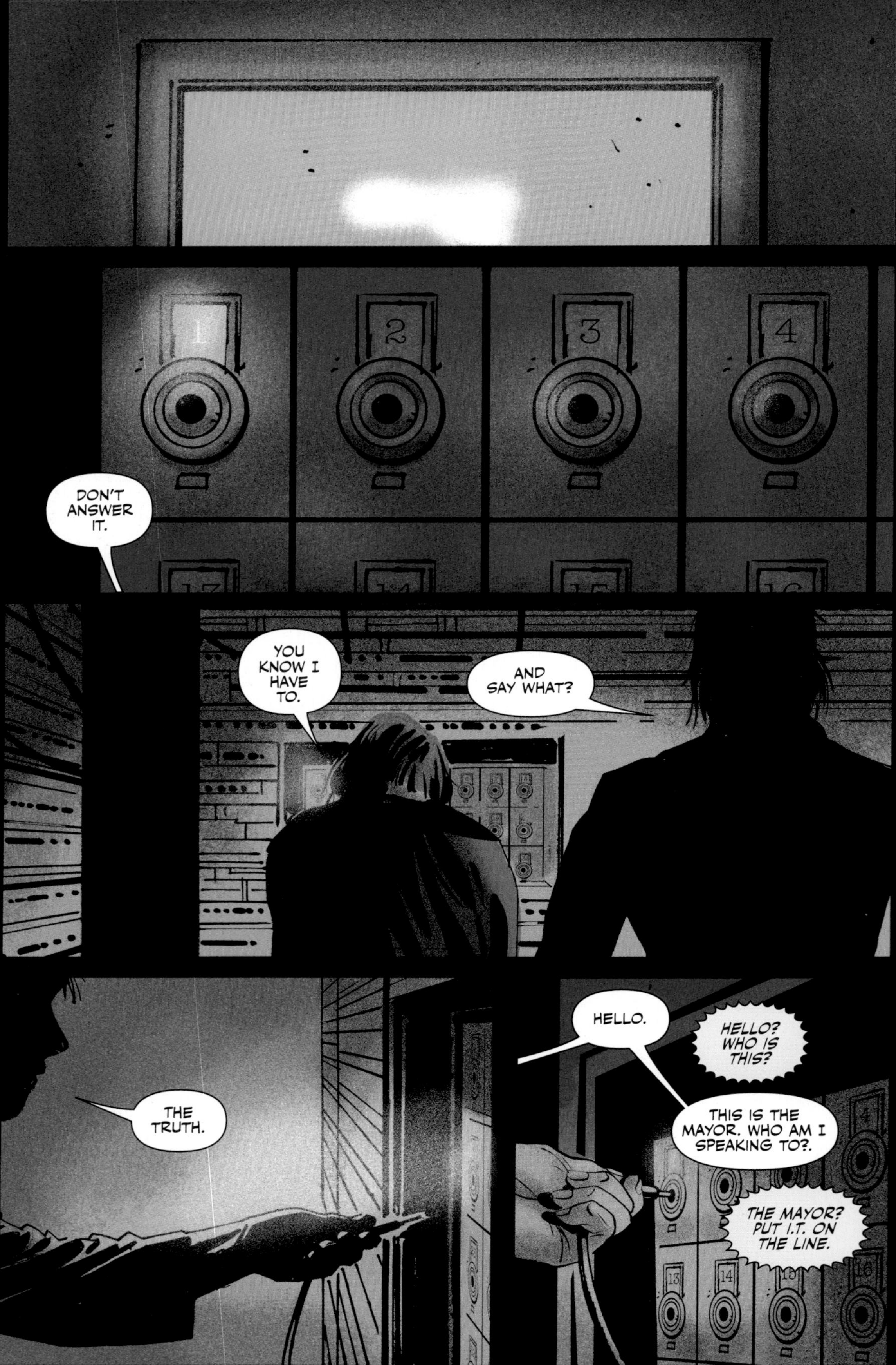
DON'T ANSWER IT.
YOU KNOW I HAVE TO.
AND SAY WHAT?
THE TRUTH.
HELLO.
HELLO? WHO IS THIS?
THIS IS THE MAYOR. WHO AM I SPEAKING TO?.
THE MAYOR? PUT I.T. ON THE LINE.

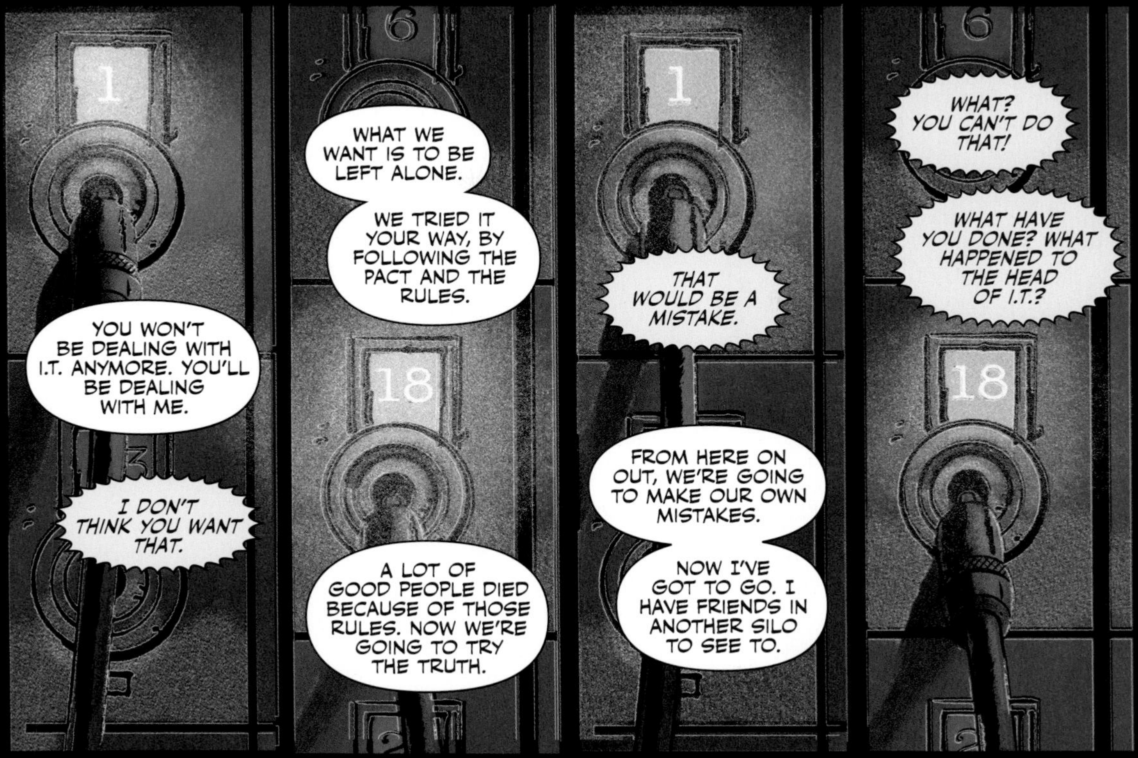
YOU WON'T BE DEALING WITH I.T. ANYMORE. YOU'LL BE DEALING WITH ME.
I DON'T THINK YOU WANT THAT.
WHAT WE WANT IS TO BE LEFT ALONE.
WE TRIED IT YOUR WAY, BY FOLLOWING THE PACT AND THE RULES.
A LOT OF GOOD PEOPLE DIED BECAUSE OF THOSE RULES. NOW WE'RE GOING TO TRY THE TRUTH.
THAT WOULD BE A MISTAKE.
FROM HERE ON OUT, WE'RE GOING TO MAKE OUR OWN MISTAKES.
NOW I'VE GOT TO GO. I HAVE FRIENDS IN ANOTHER SILO TO SEE TO.
WHAT? YOU CAN'T DO THAT!
WHAT HAVE YOU DONE? WHAT HAPPENED TO THE HEAD OF I.T.?

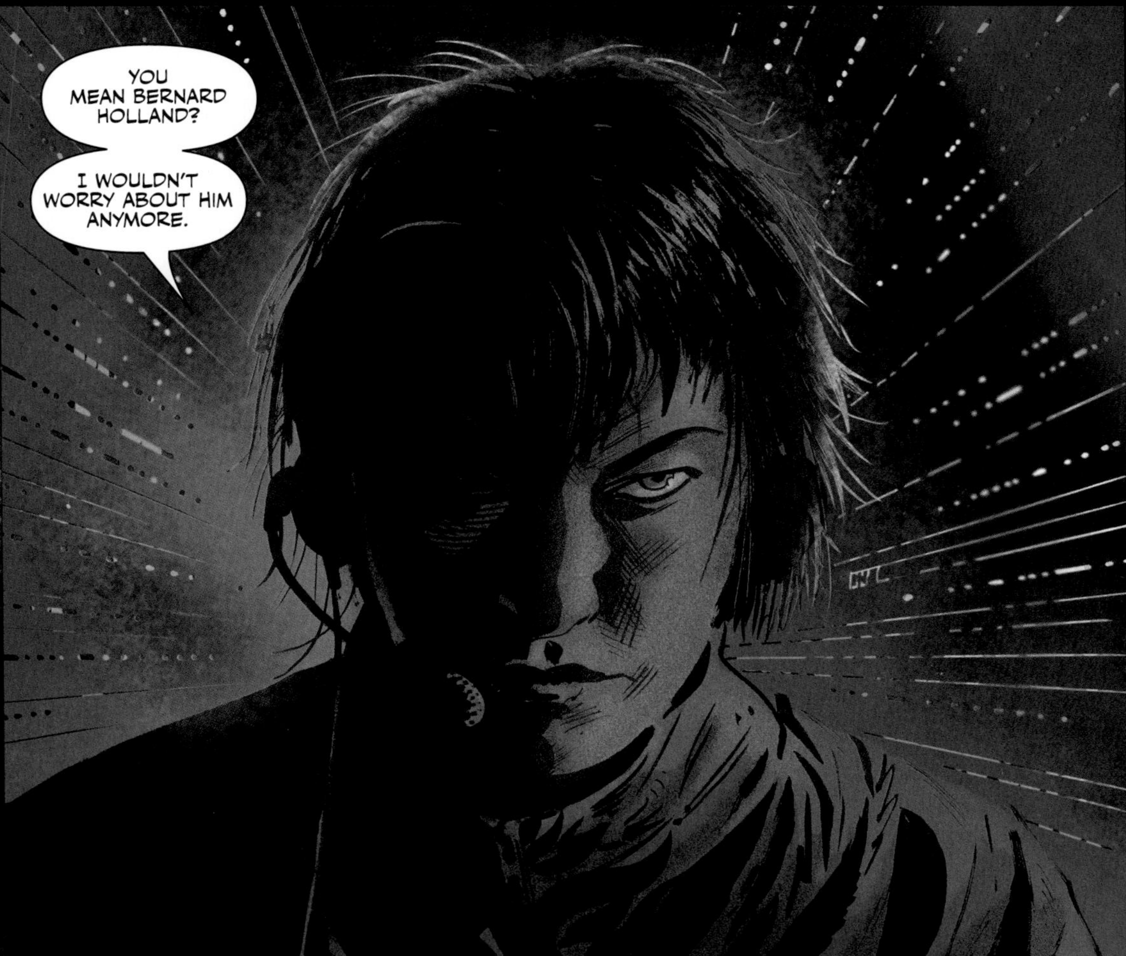
YOU MEAN BERNARD HOLLAND?
I WOULDN'T WORRY ABOUT HIM ANYMORE.

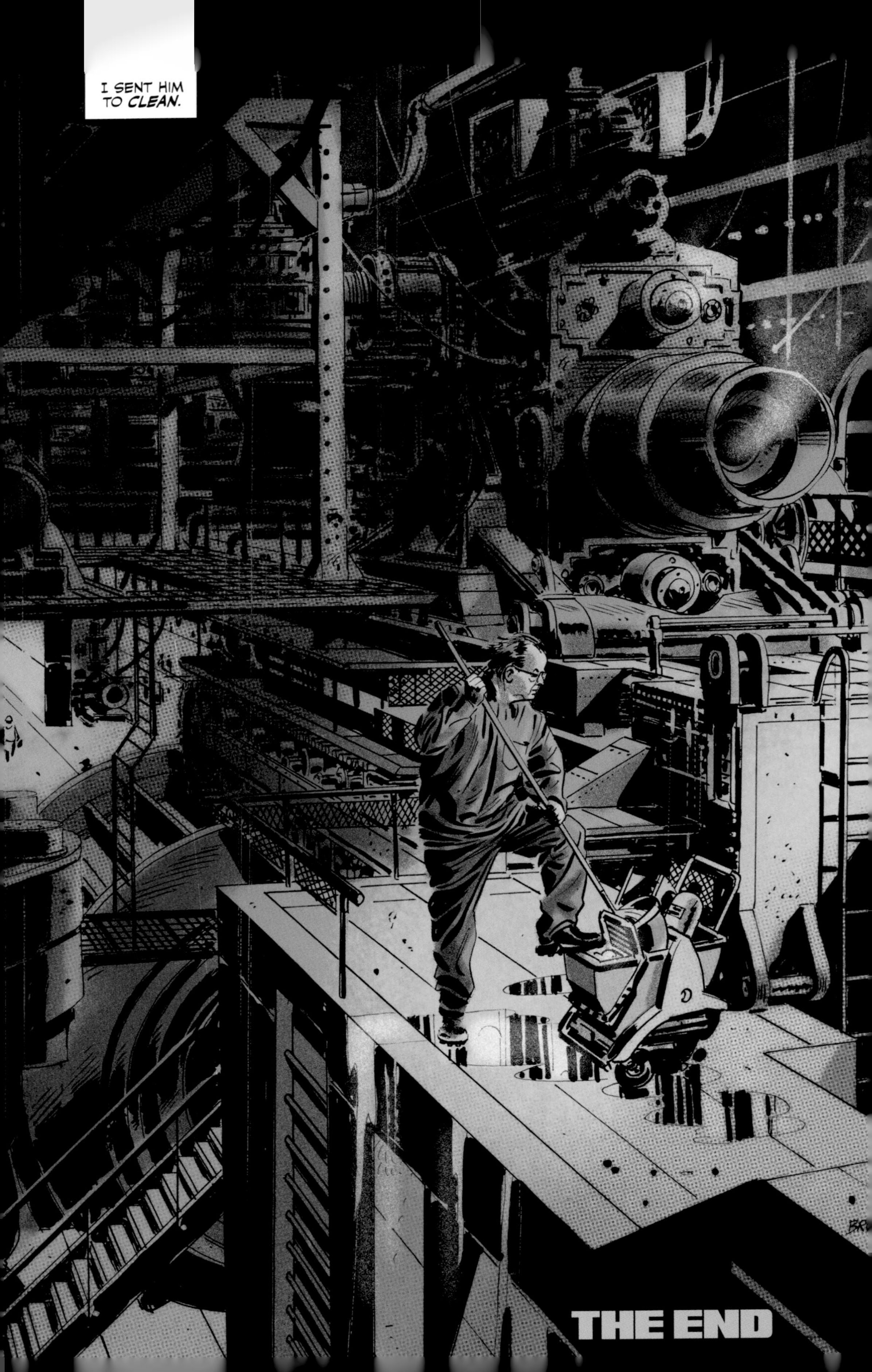
I SENT HIM TO CLEAN.
THE END

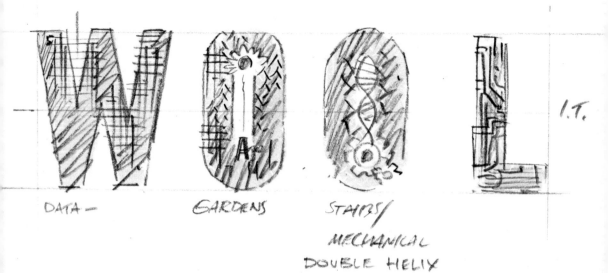

WOOL

DATA —   GARDENS   STAIRS/
MECHANICAL
DOUBLE HELIX

ARTIFACTS FROM THE SERVER

Variant covers plus sketchbook and inked pages by Jimmy Broxton

Cover Concepts by Darwyn Cooke

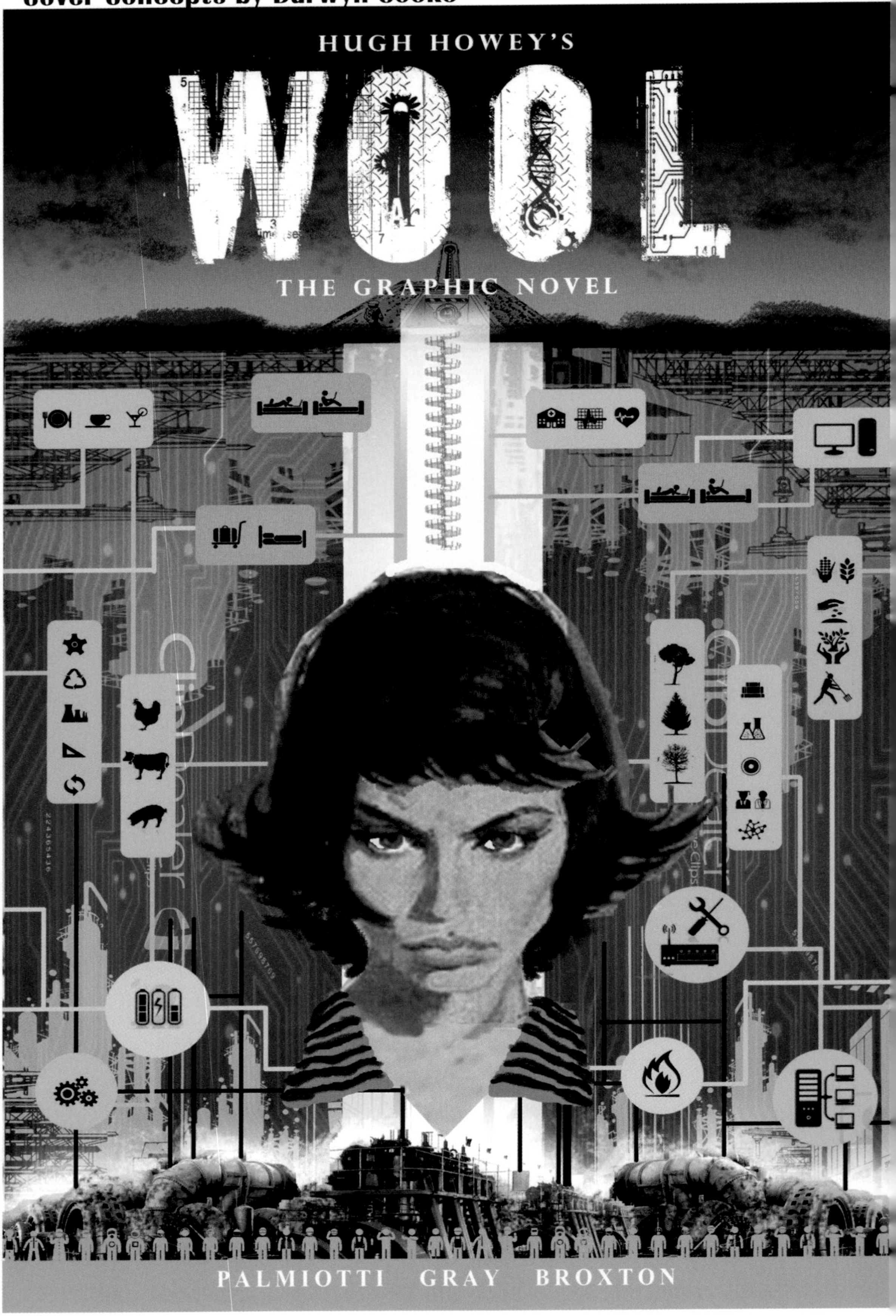
HUGH HOWEY'S
WOOL
THE GRAPHIC NOVEL
PALMIOTTI GRAY BROXTON

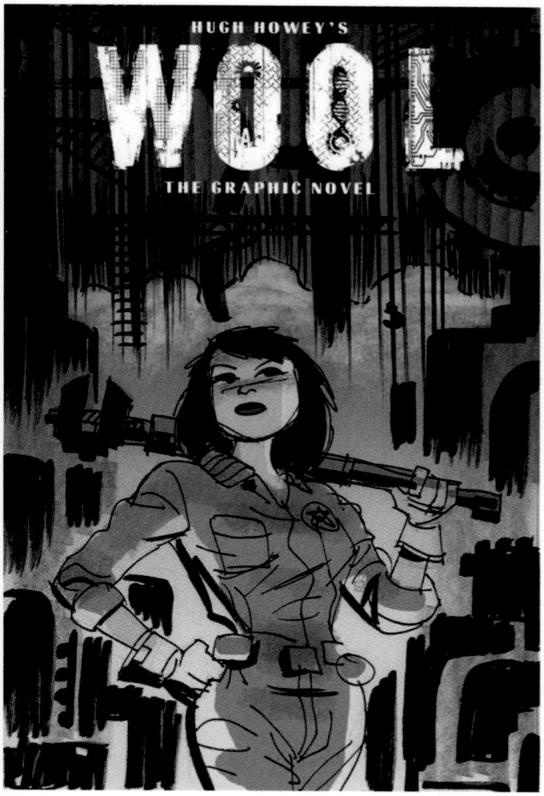
HUGH HOWEY'S
WOOL
THE GRAPHIC NOVEL

ISSUE ONE

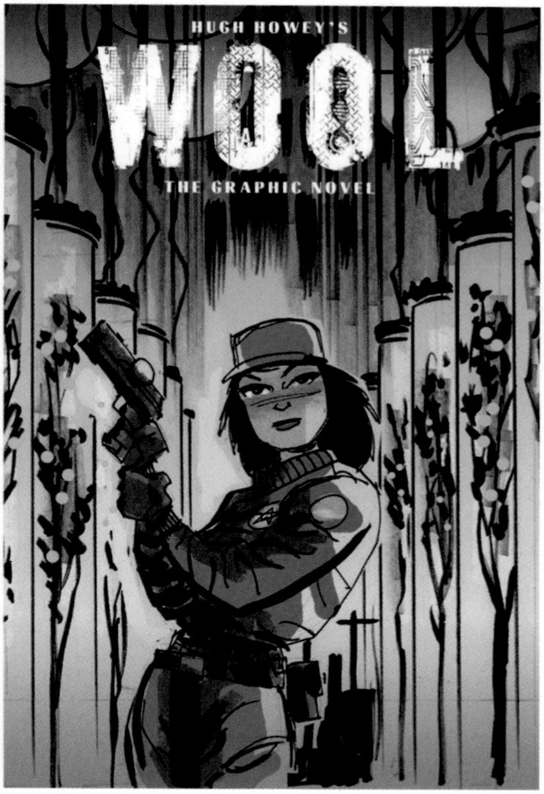
HUGH HOWEY'S
WOOL
THE GRAPHIC NOVEL

ISSUE TWO

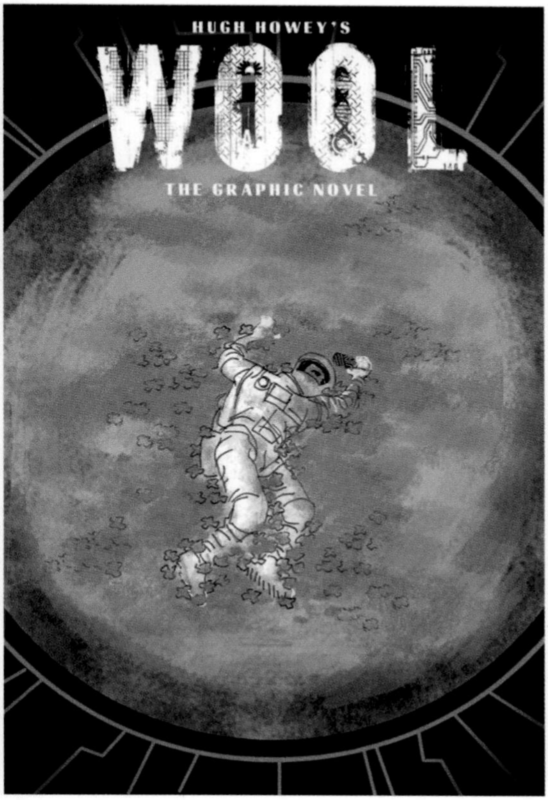
HUGH HOWEY'S
WOOL
THE GRAPHIC NOVEL

ISSUE ONE

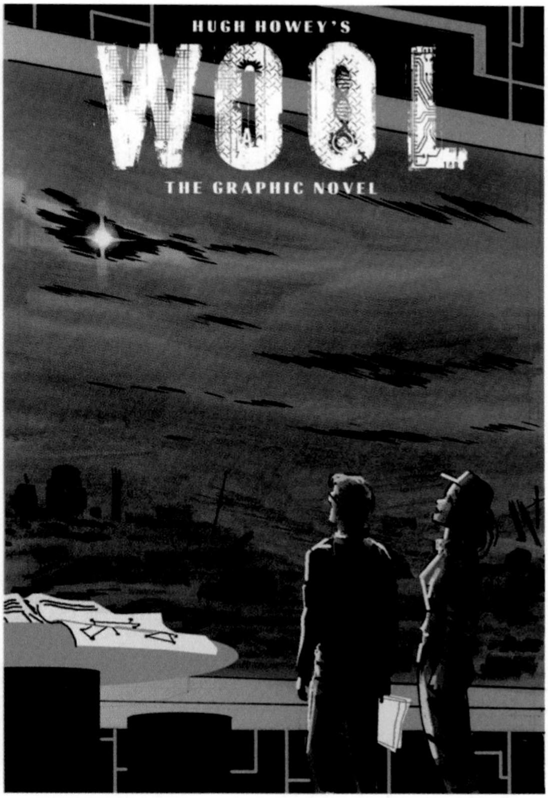
HUGH HOWEY'S
WOOL
THE GRAPHIC NOVEL

ISSUE TWO

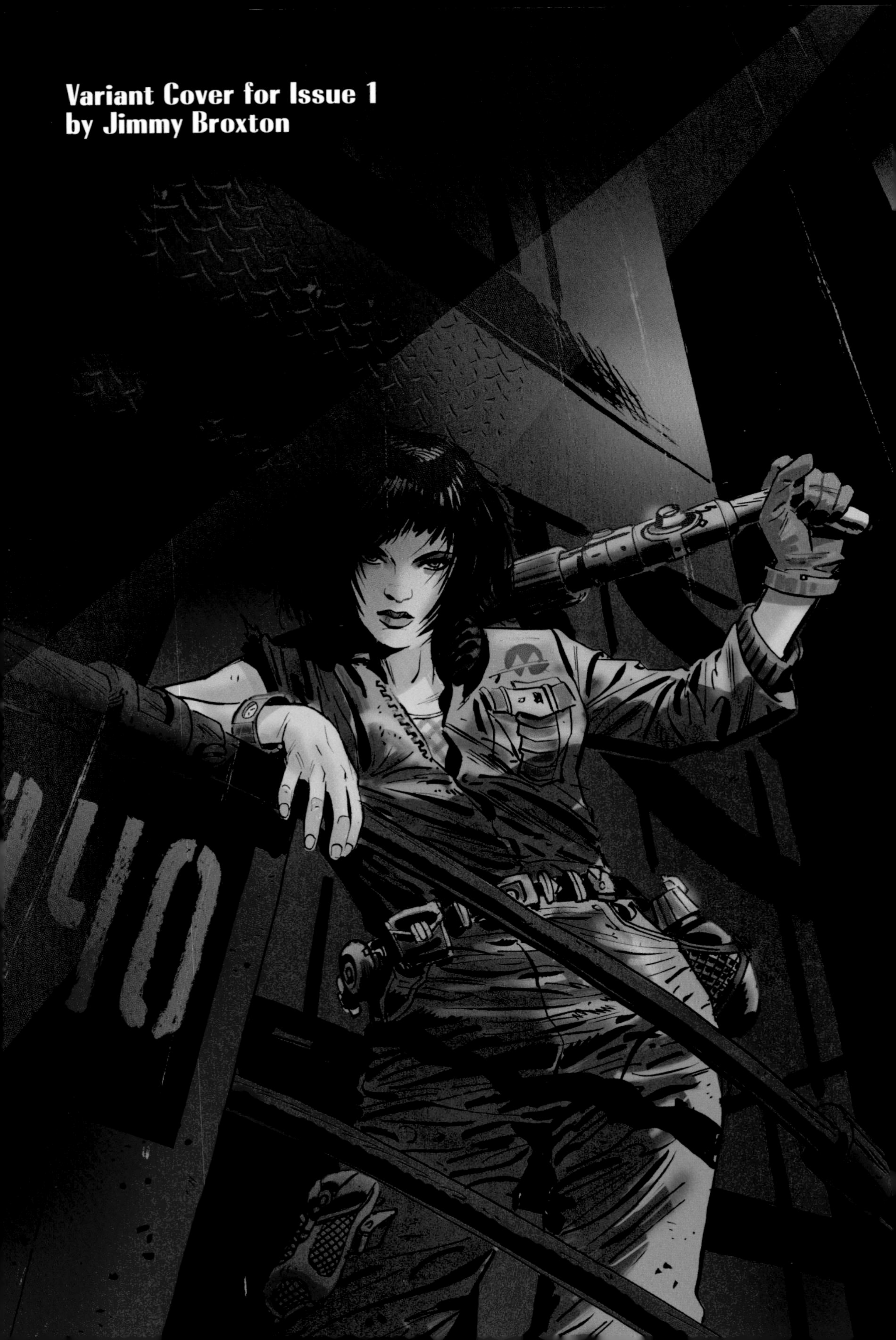

Variant Cover for Issue 1
by Jimmy Broxton

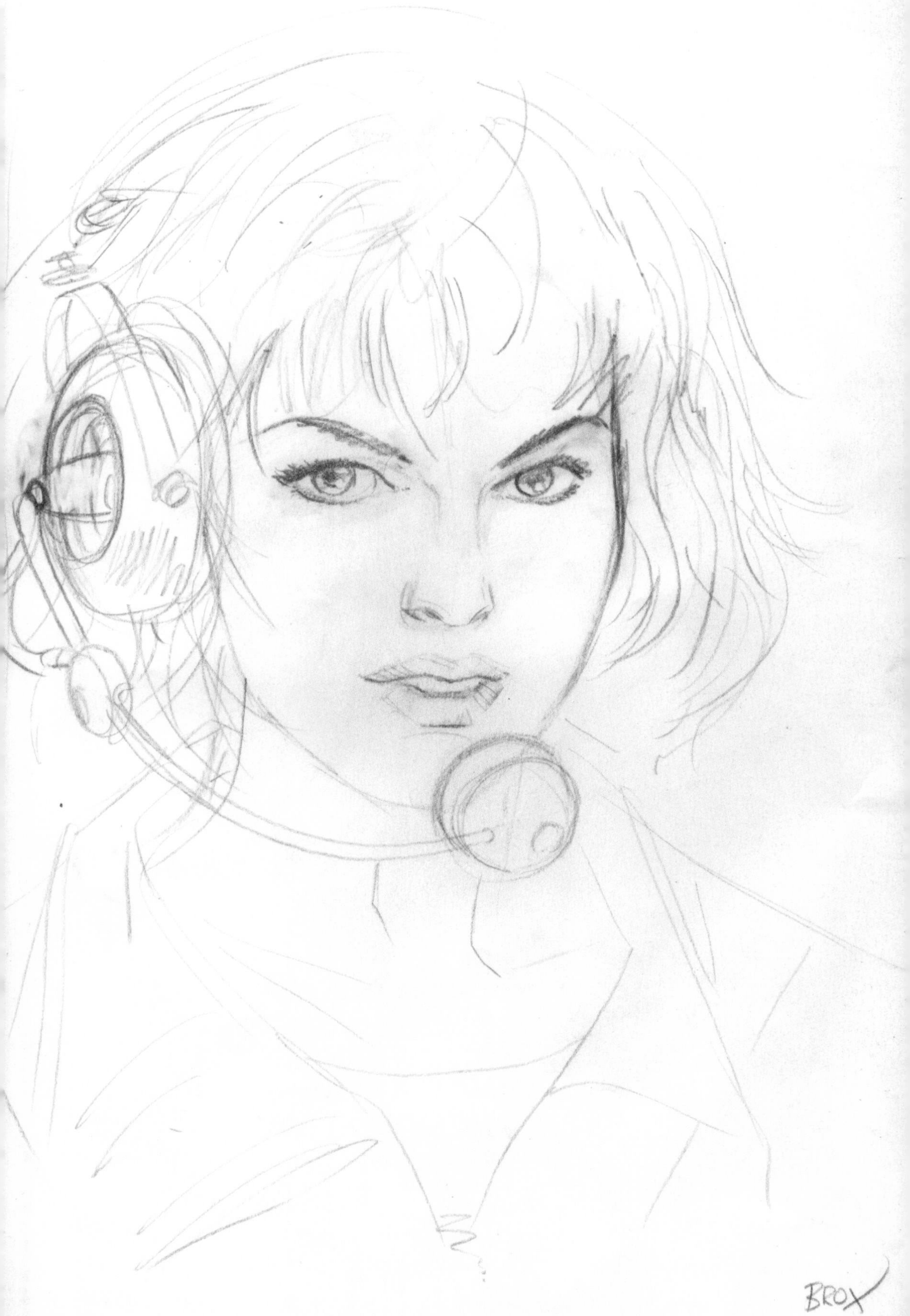
BROX

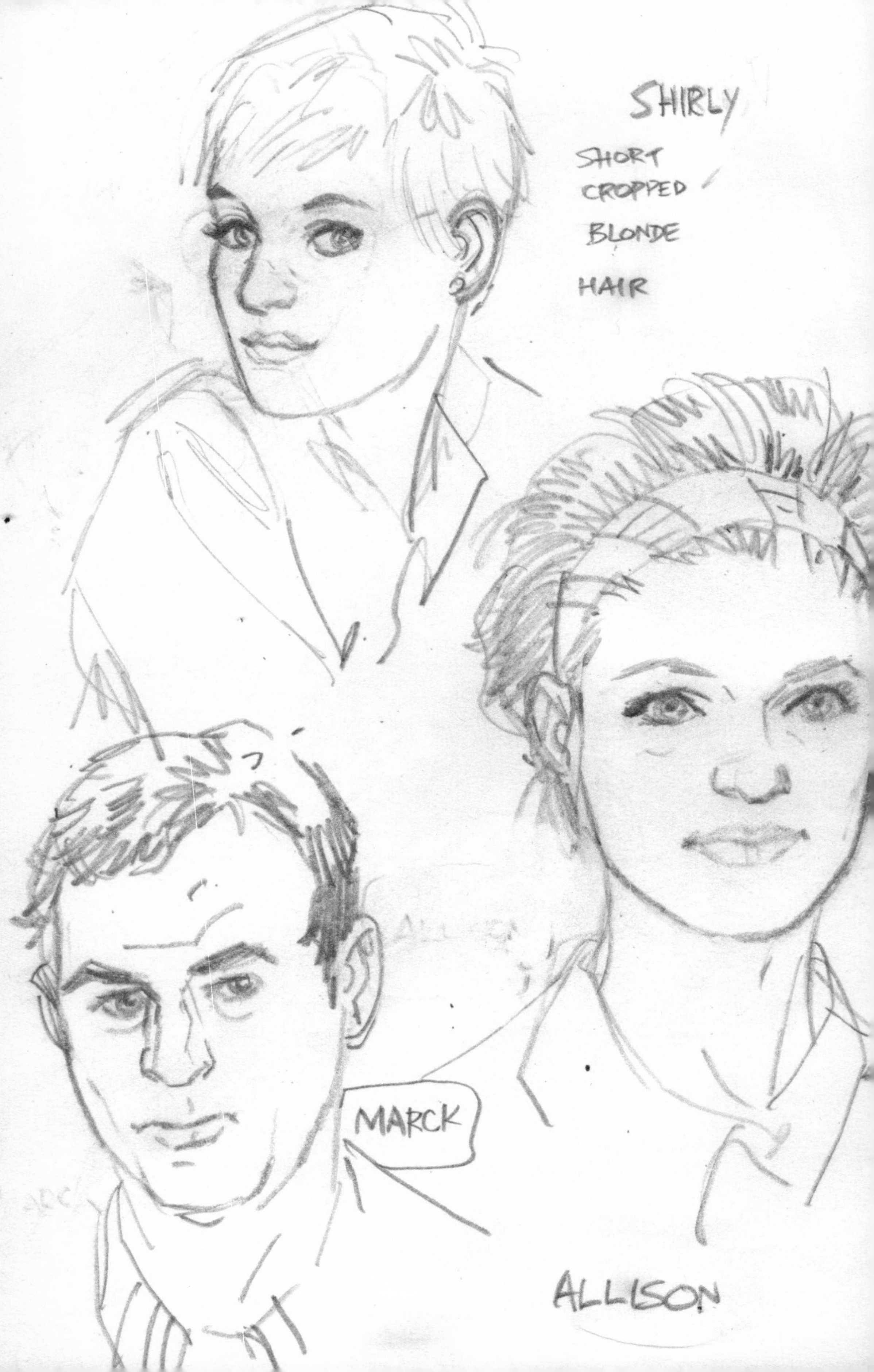
SHIRLY
SHORT CROPPED BLONDE HAIR
MARCK
ALLISON

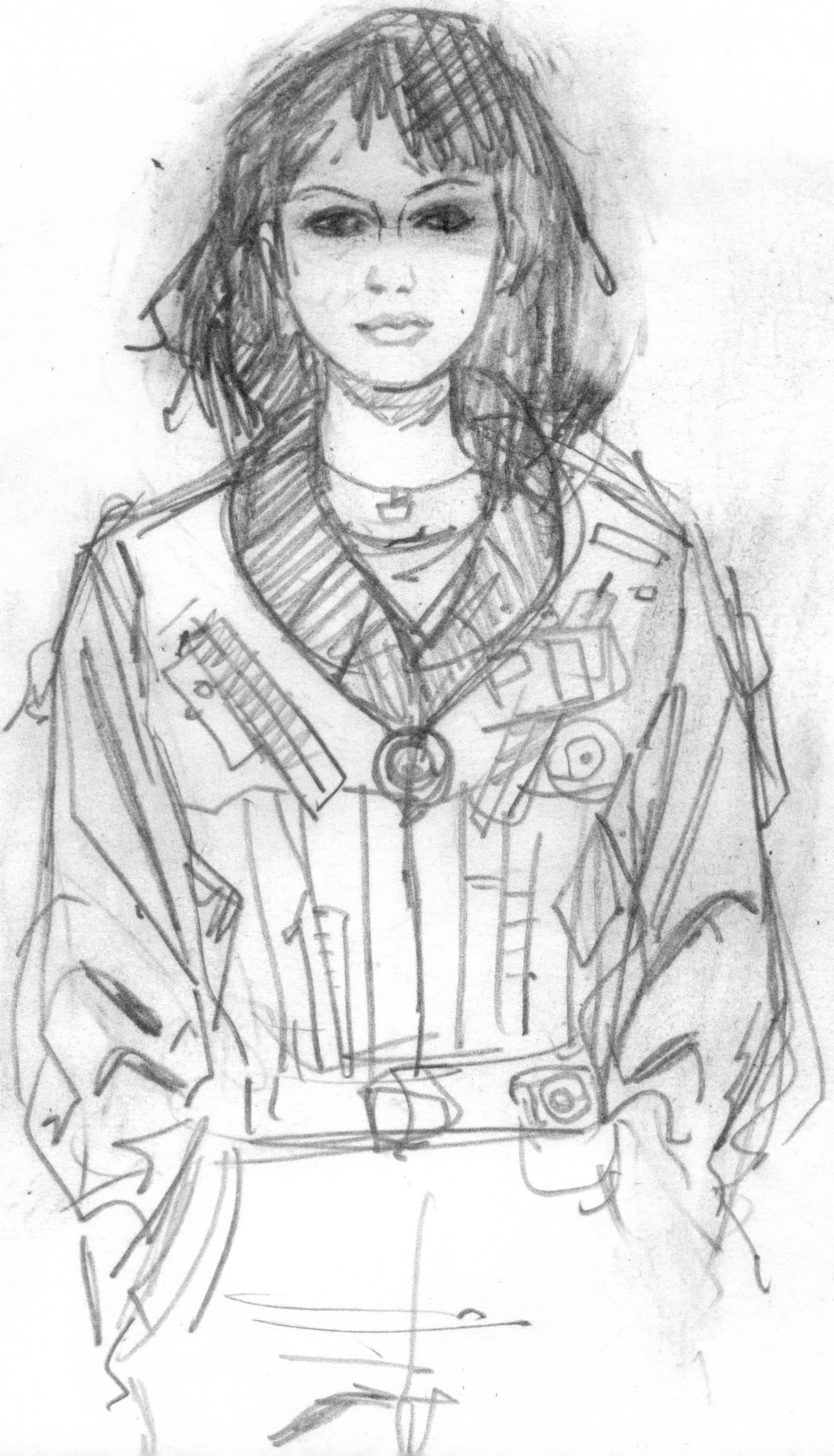

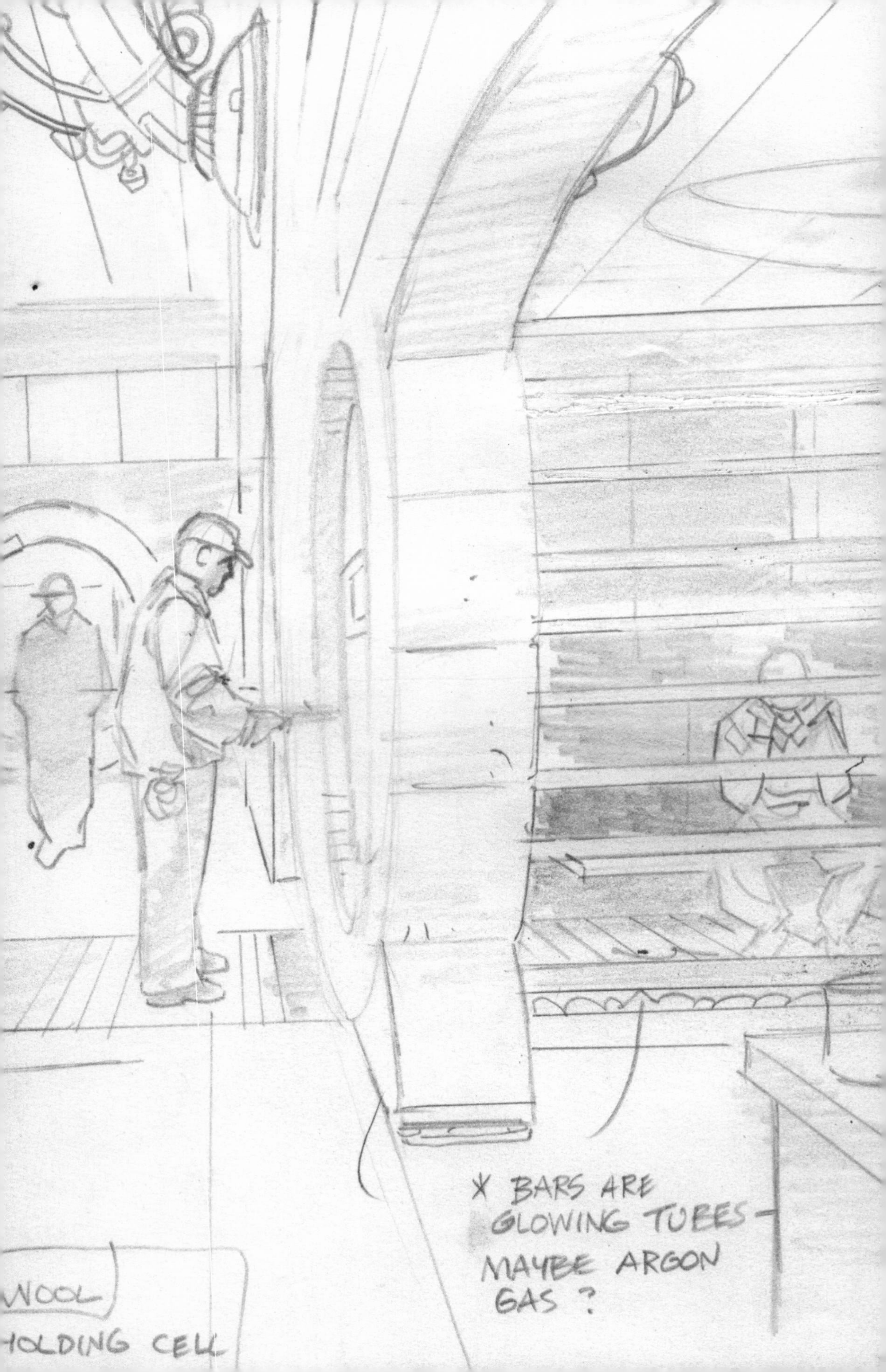

* BARS ARE GLOWING TUBES MAYBE ARGON GAS ?
WOOL
HOLDING CELL

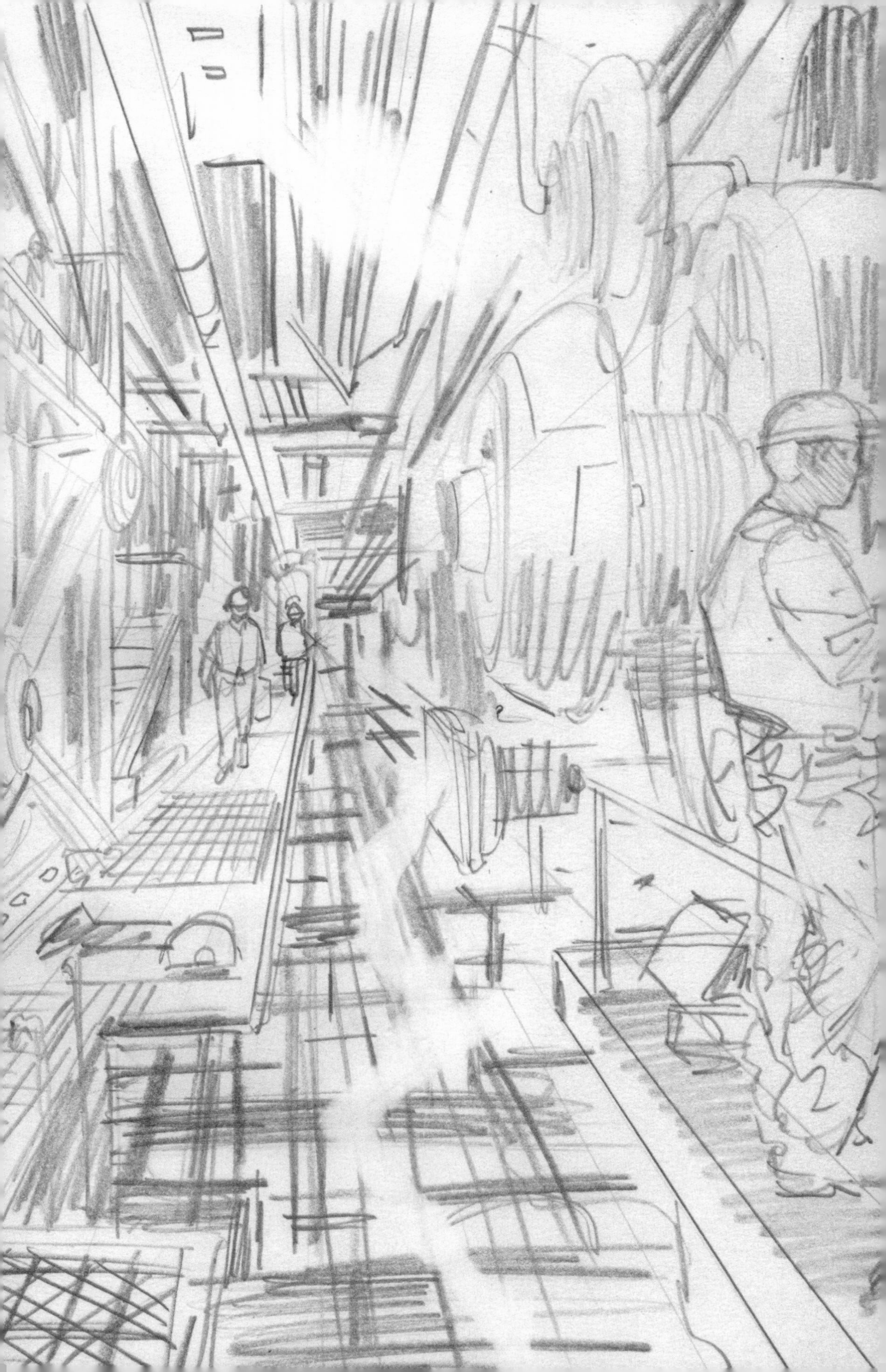

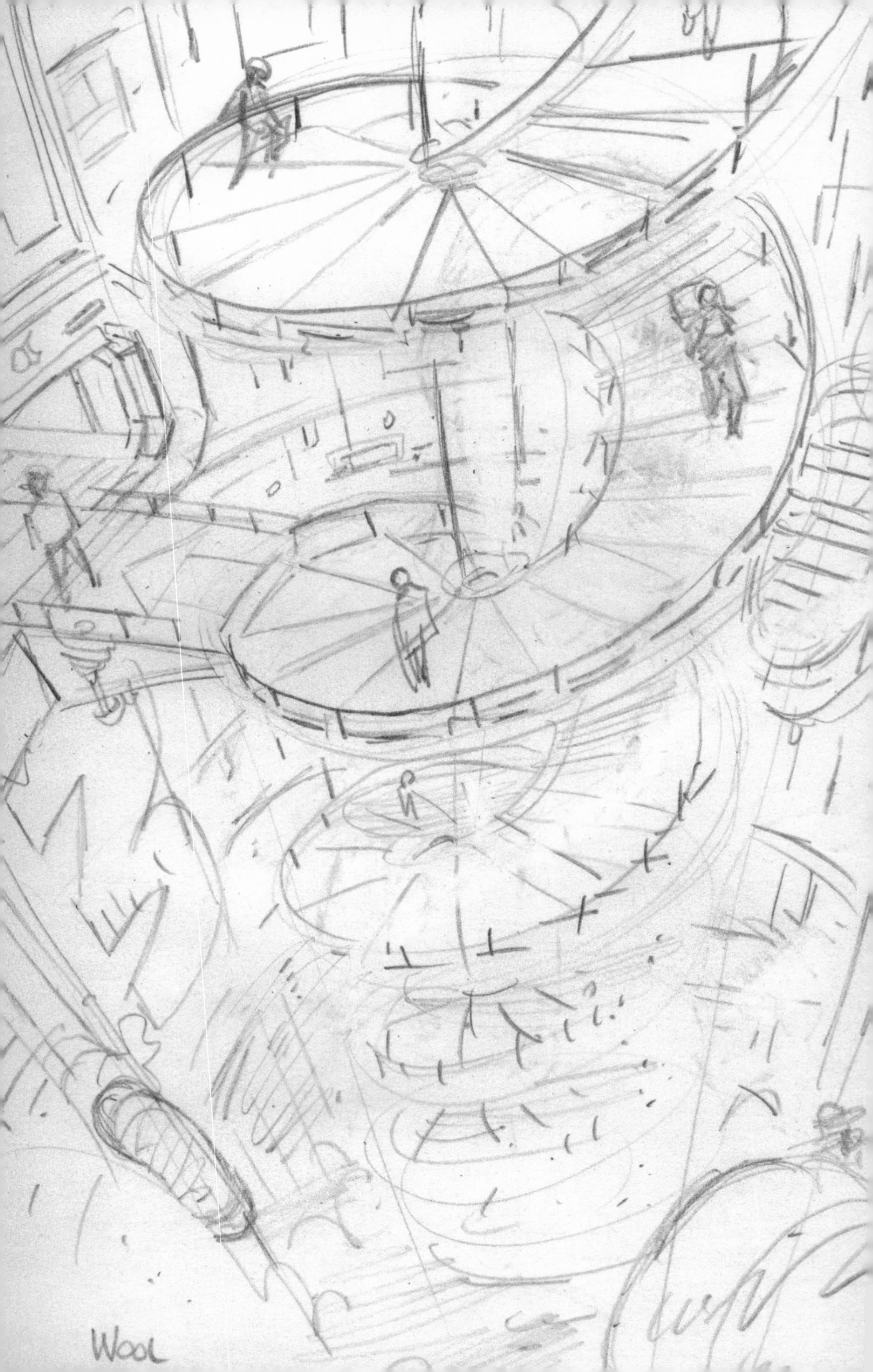
Wool

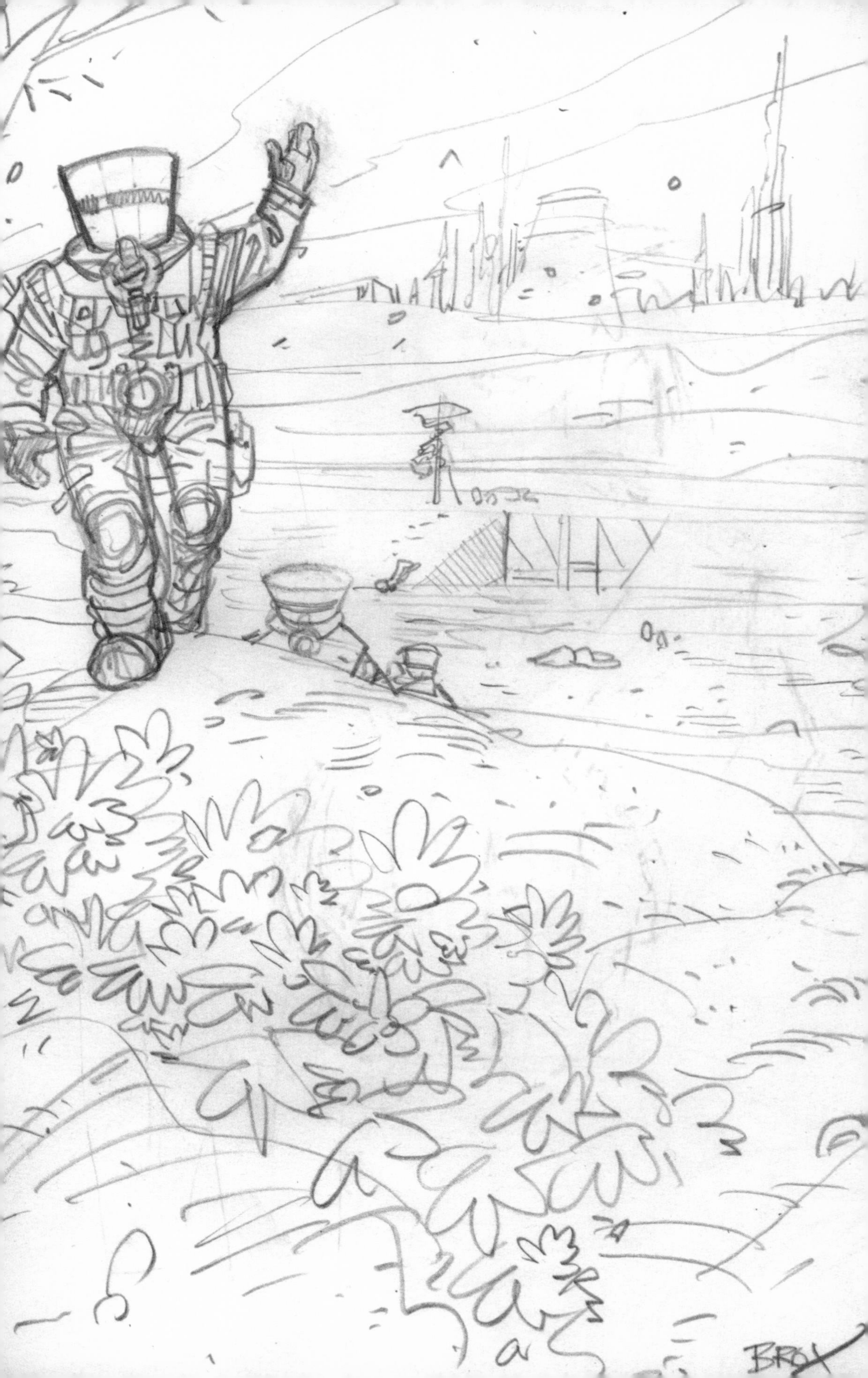
BROX

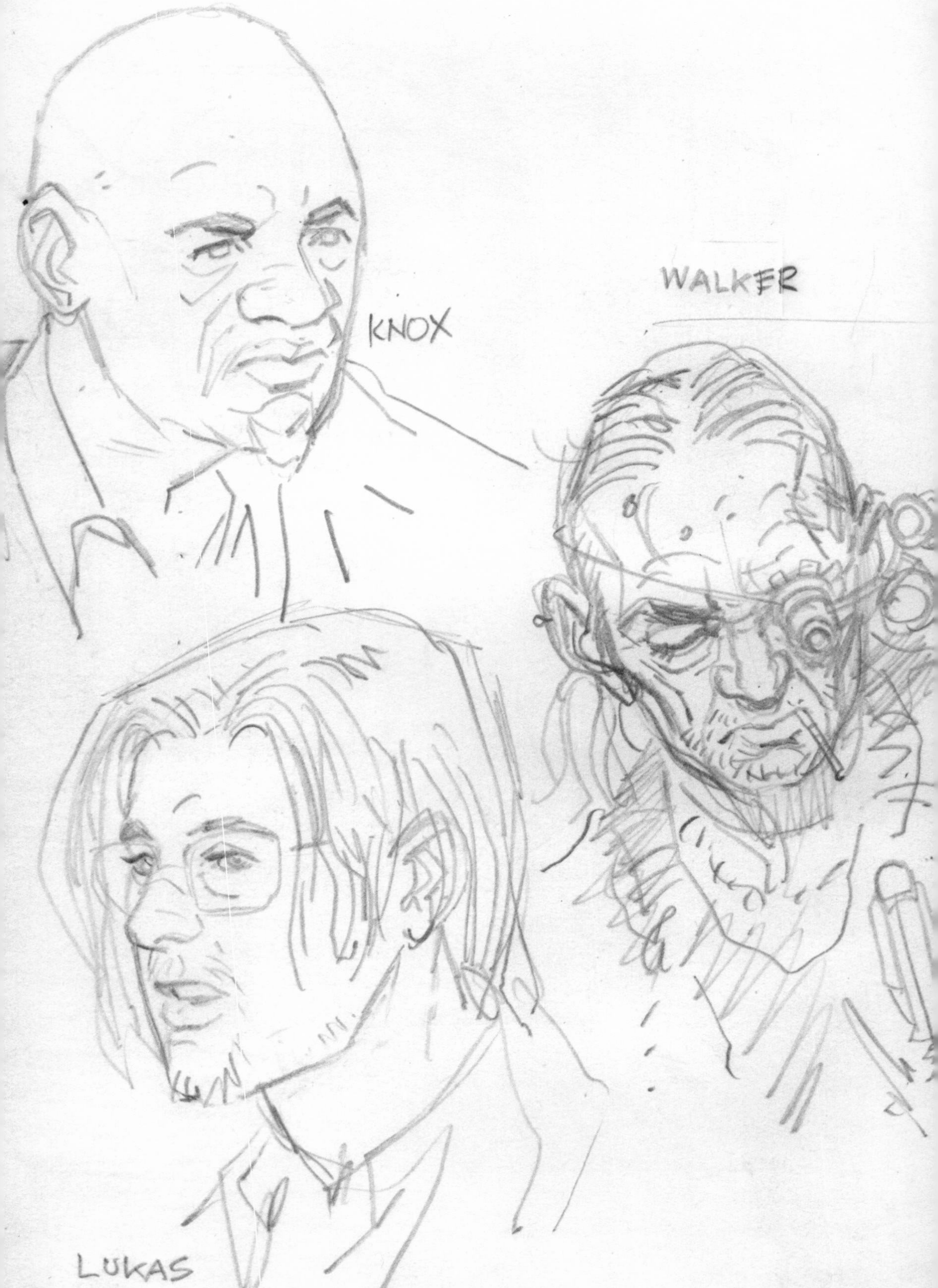
KNOX
WALKER
LUKAS

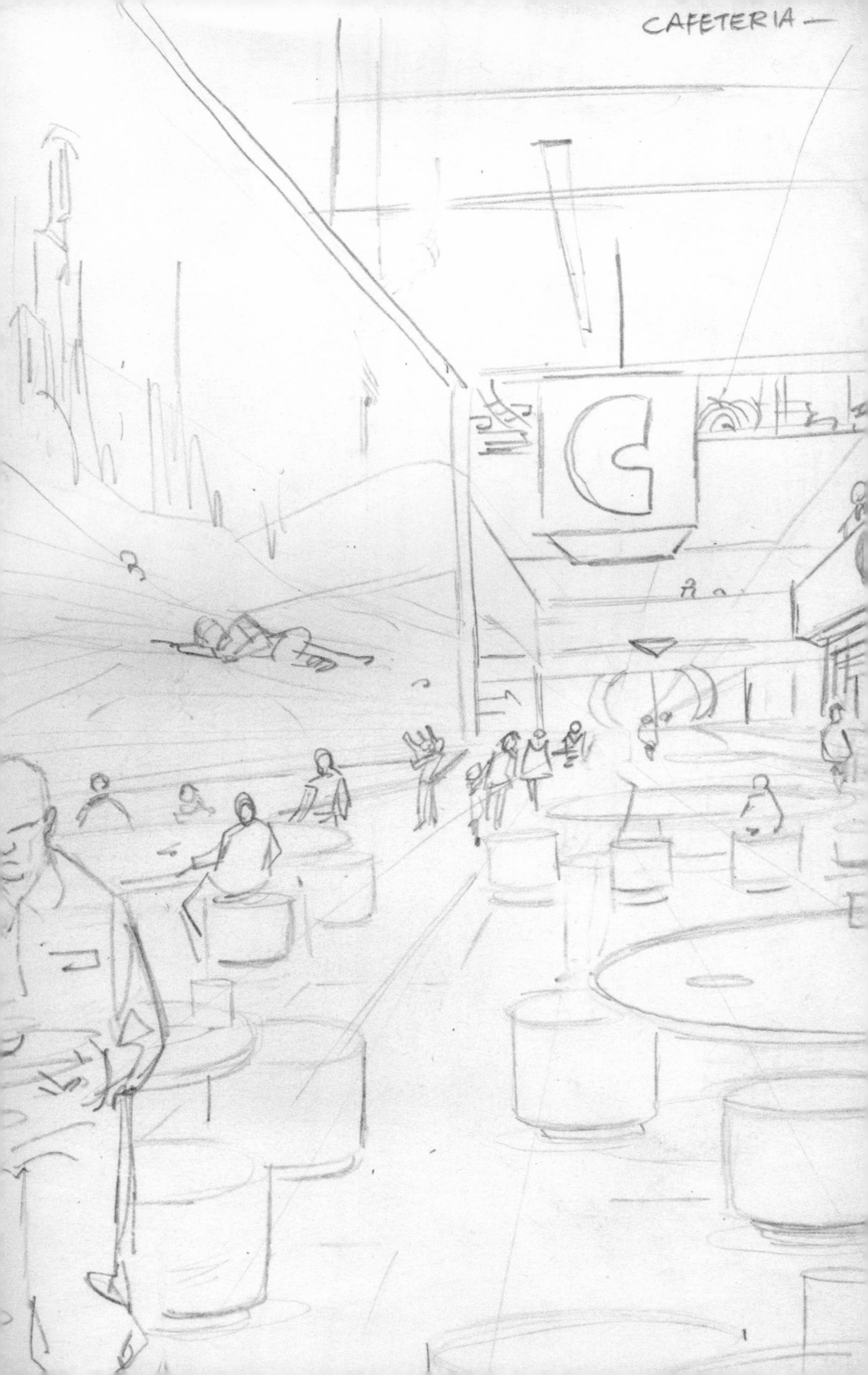
CAFETERIA —

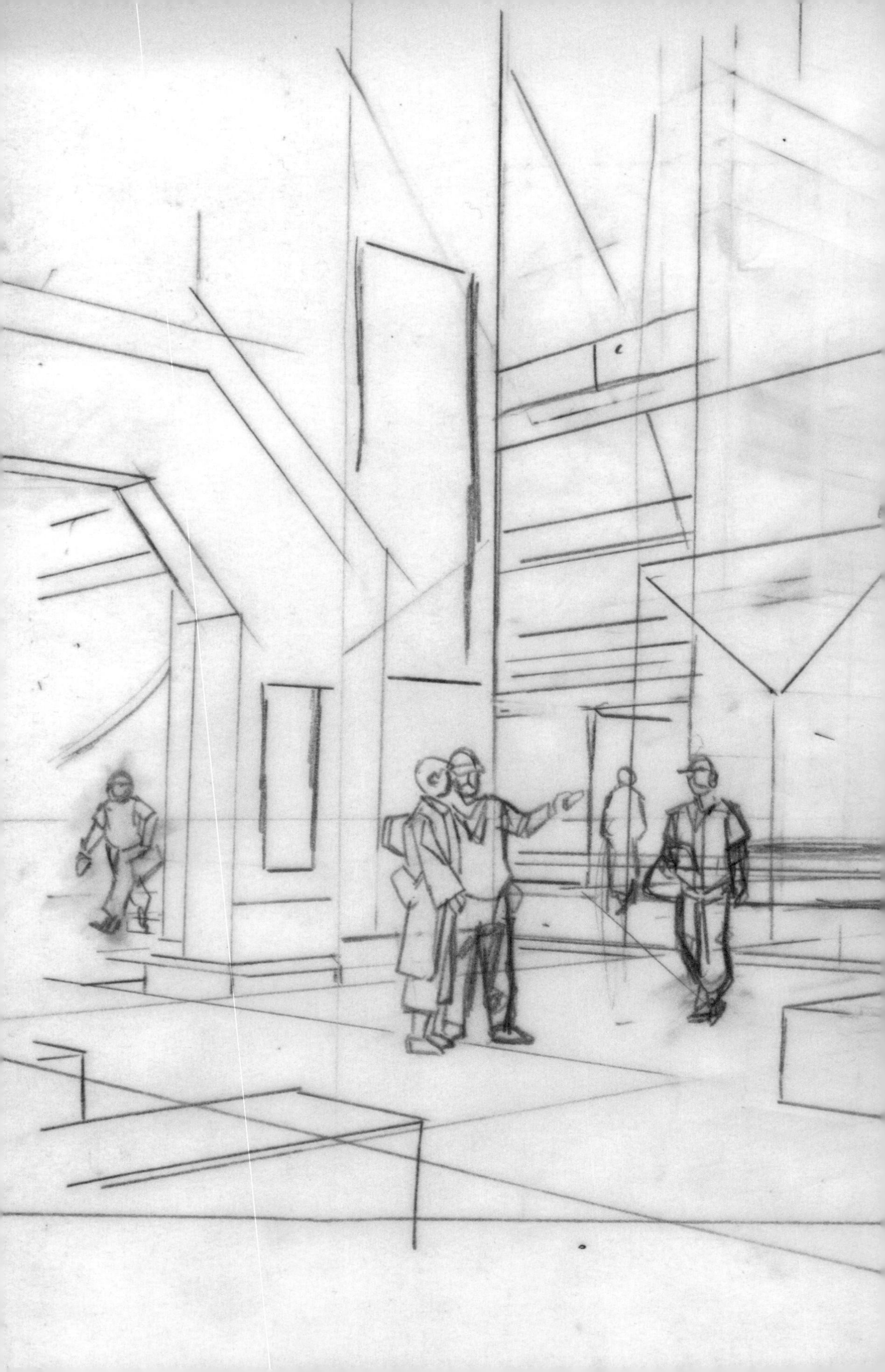

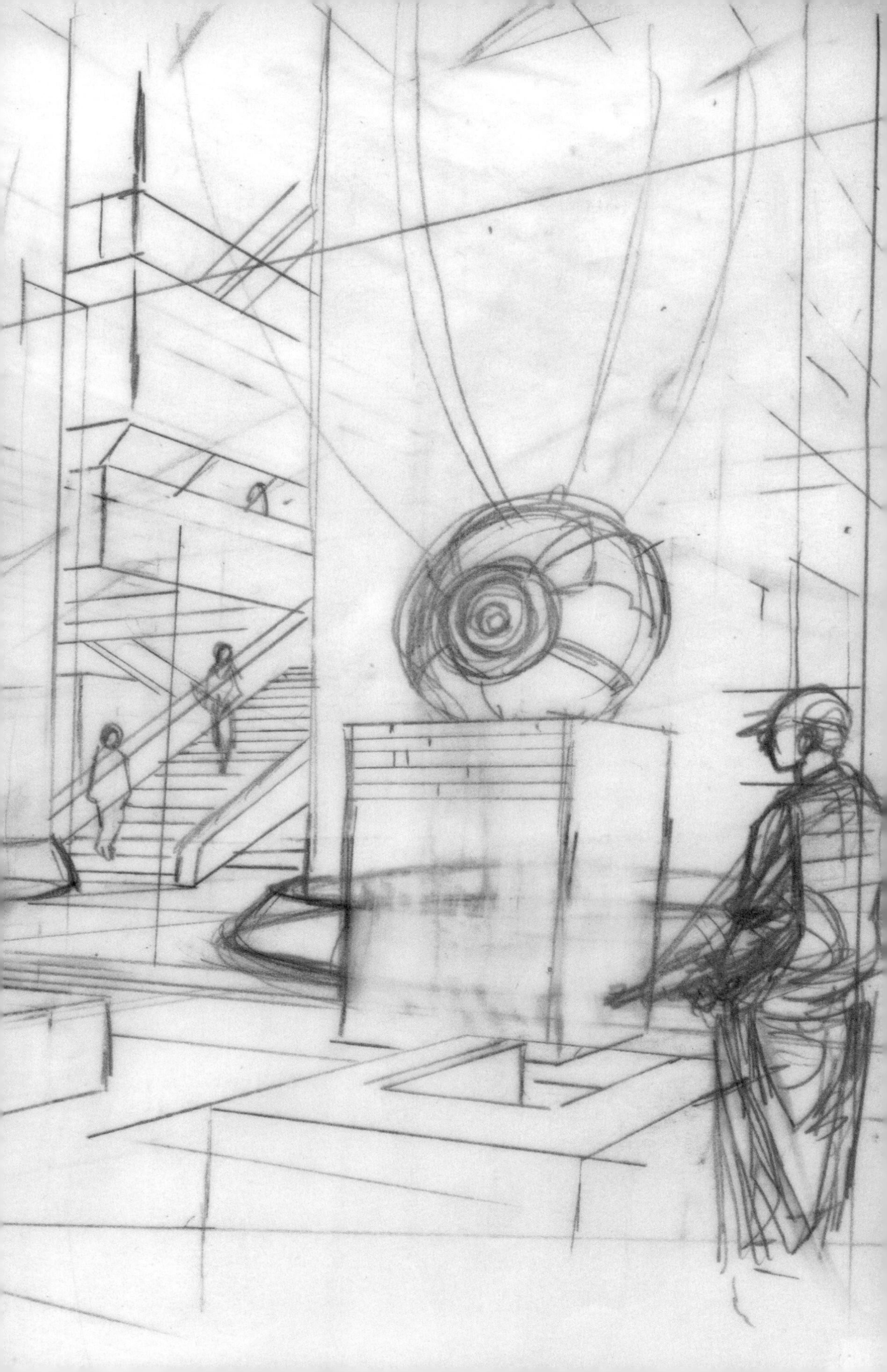

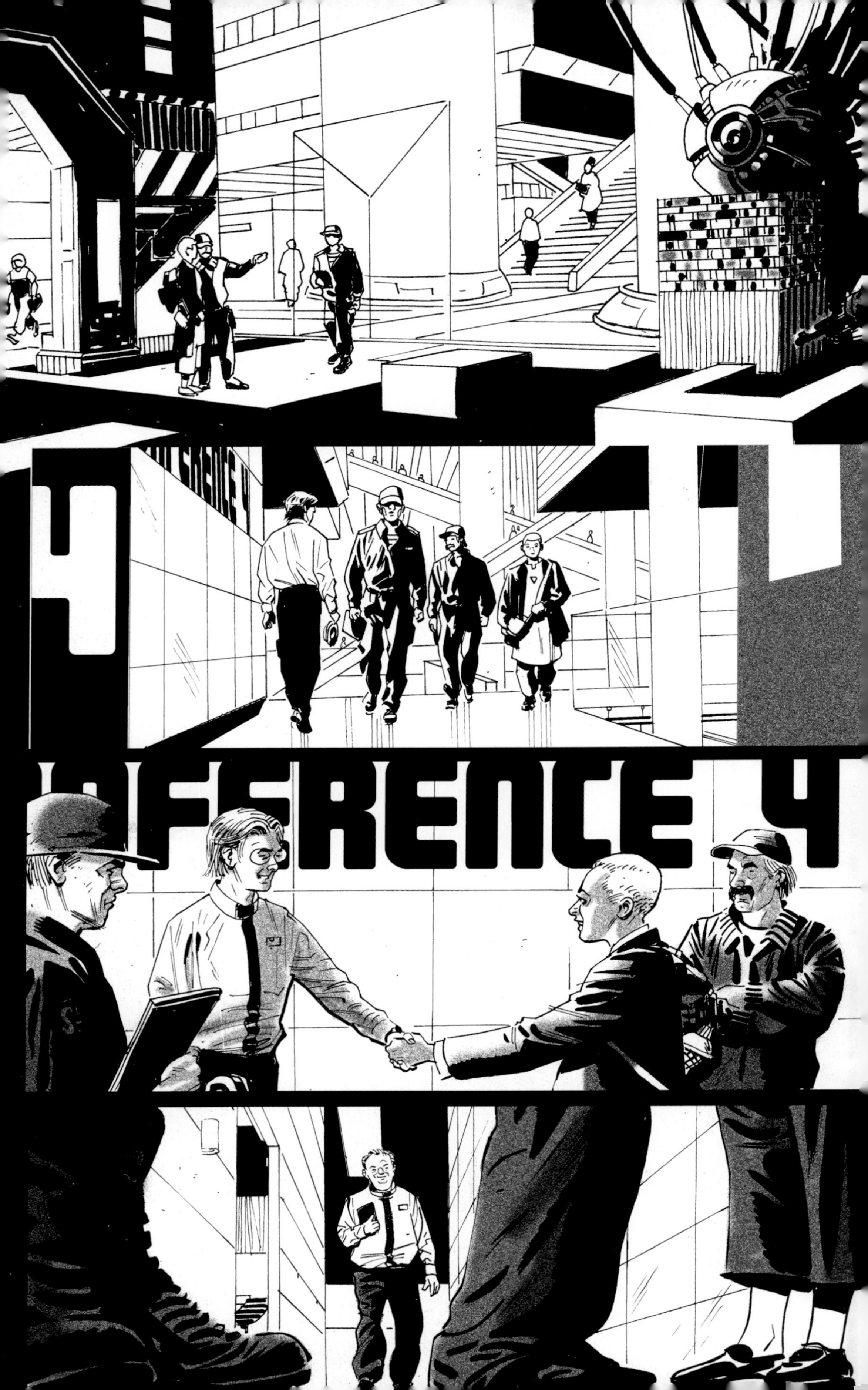
FERENCE 4

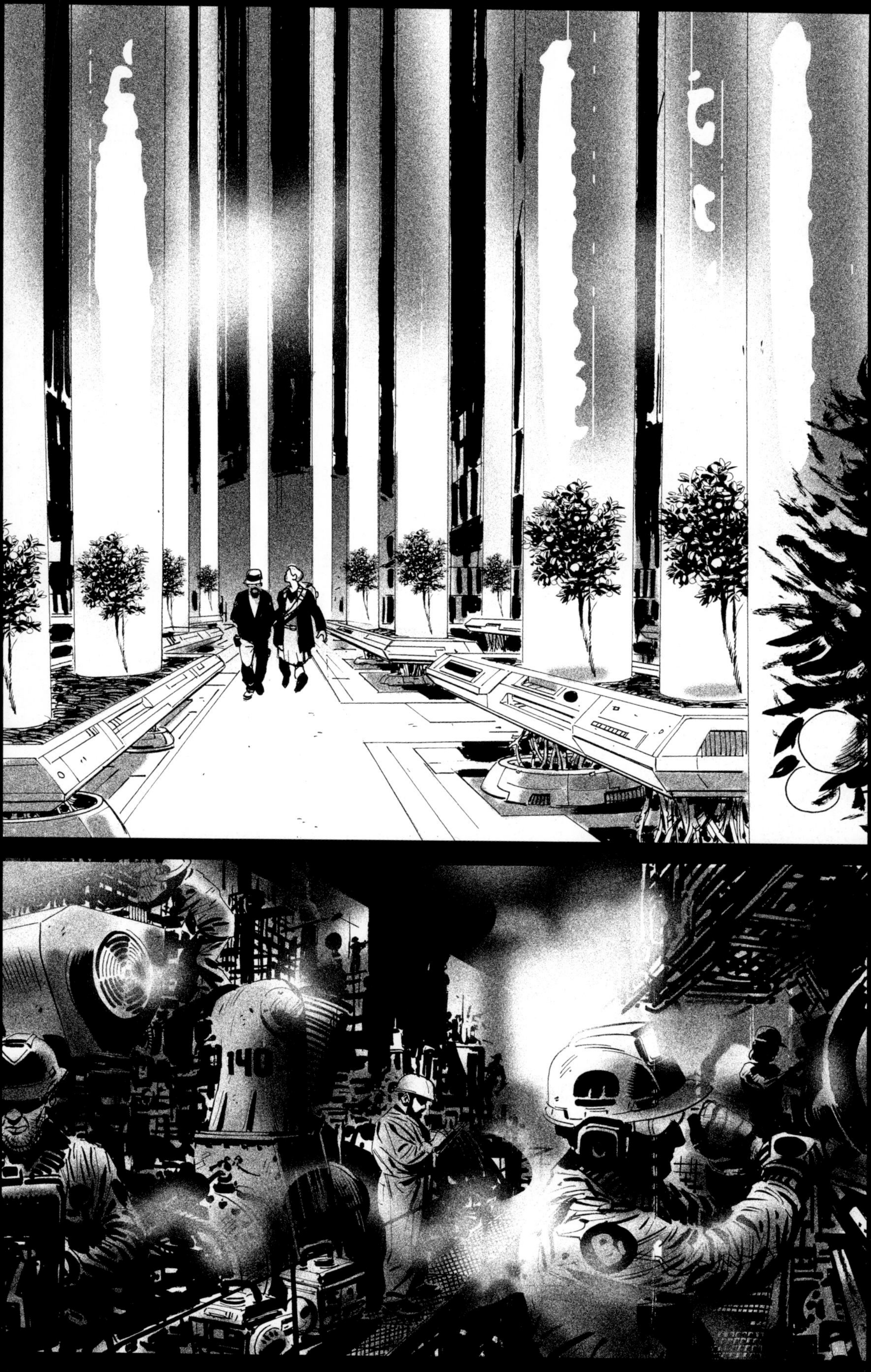
140

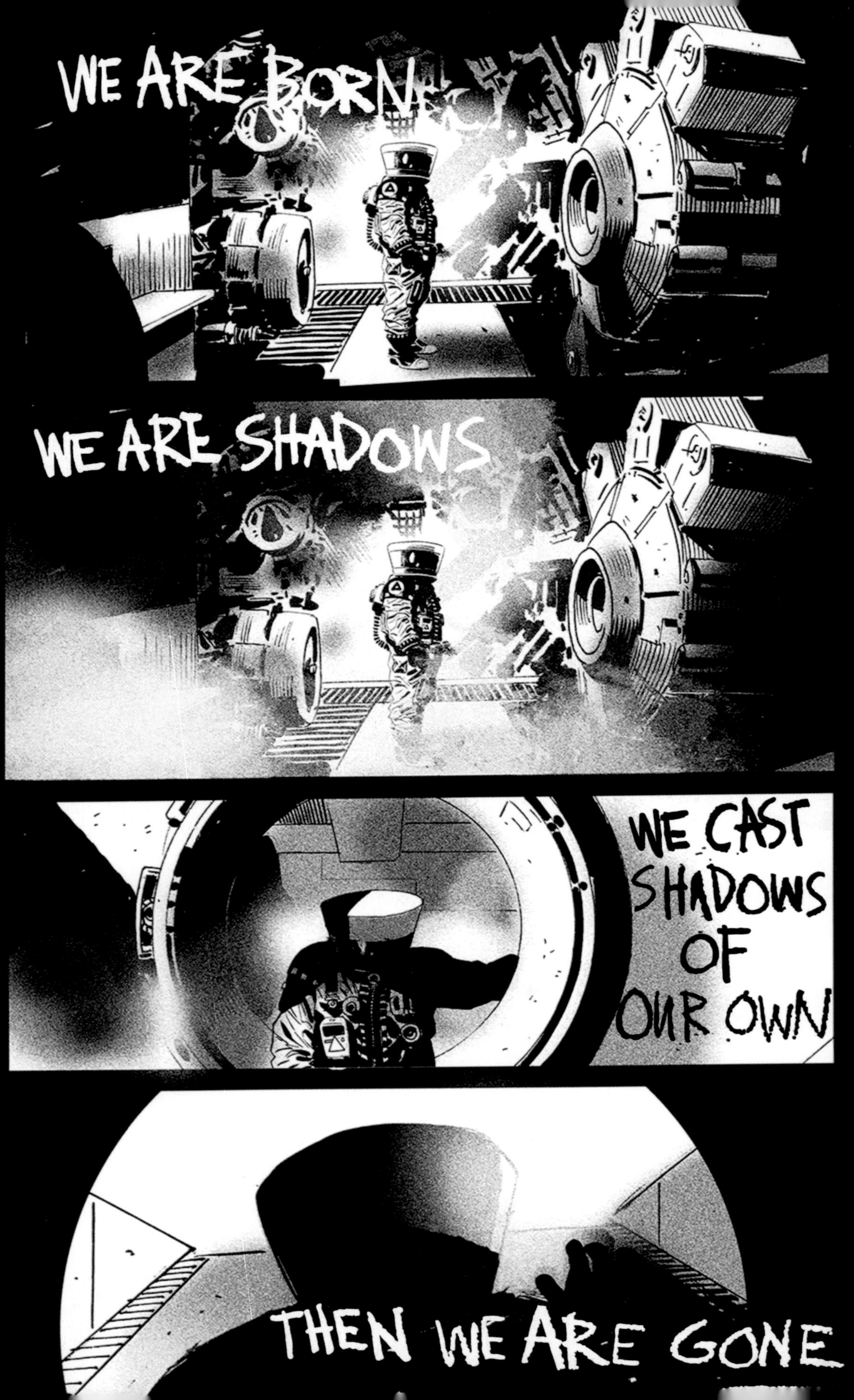
WE ARE BORN
WE ARE SHADOWS
WE CAST SHADOWS OF OUR OWN
THEN WE ARE GONE

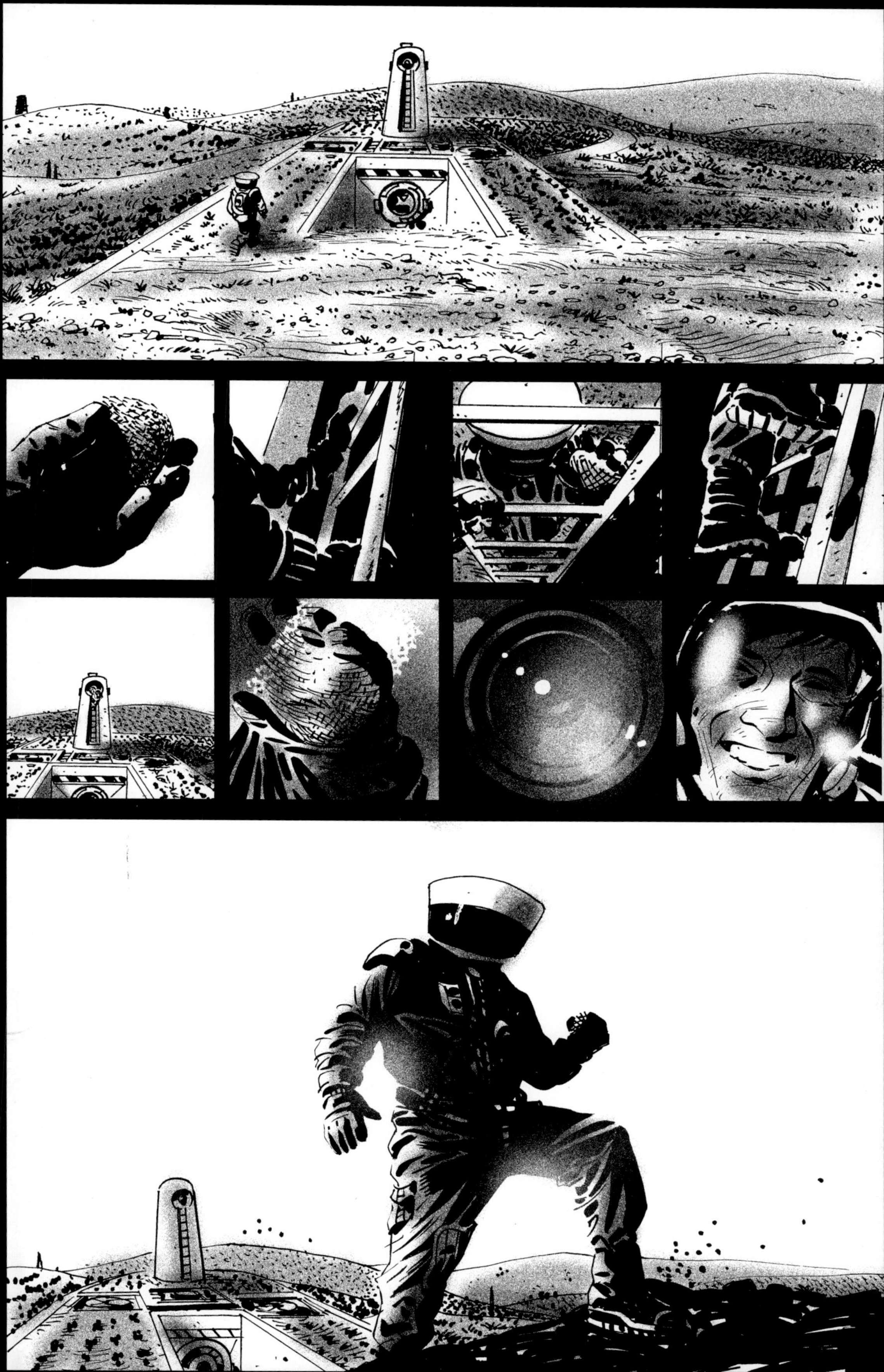

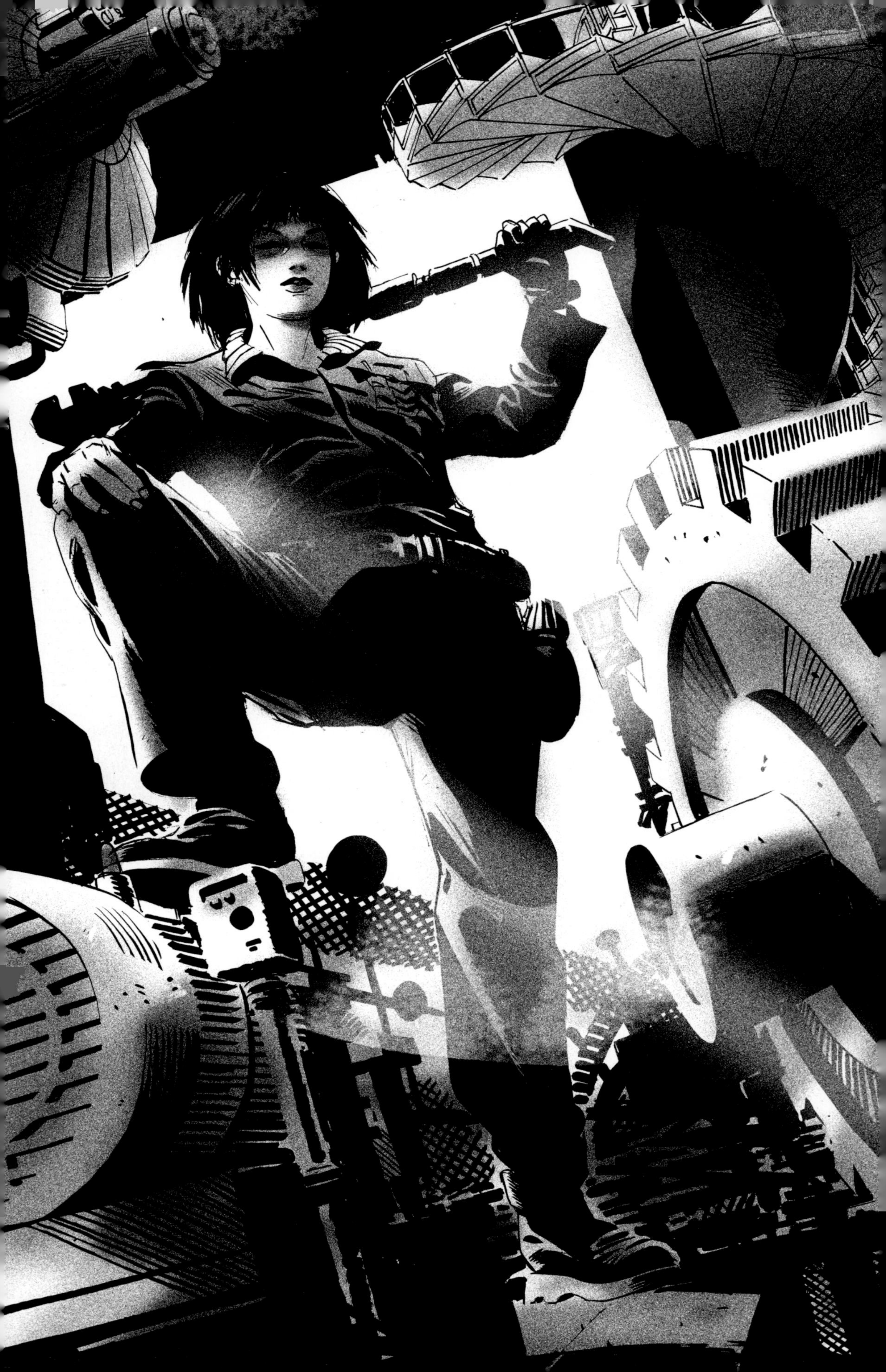

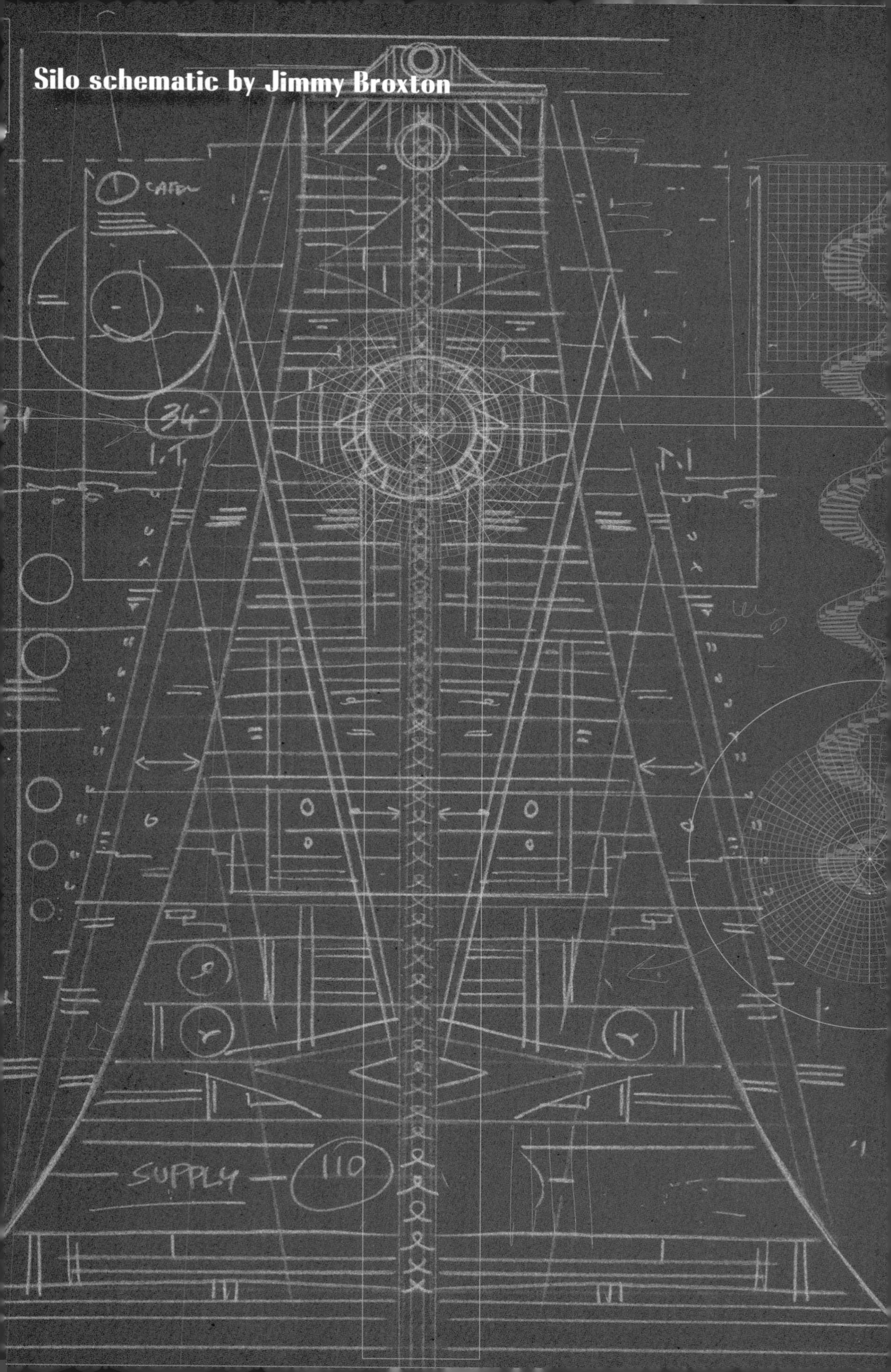
CAFE
34°
SUPPLY
110

Silo schematic by Jimmy Broxton

BIOS

HUGH HOWEY wrote Wool while working as a bookseller, writing each morning and during every lunch break for nearly three years. Originally self-published in 2011, Wool has grown into a New York Times blockbuster. He now lives in Jupiter, Florida, with his wife, Amber, and their dog, Bella.

JIMMY PALMIOTTI is a writer, editor, and creator—a multi award-winning character creator with a wide range of experience in advertising, production, consulting, editorial, film and comic writing, development and production, media presentation, and video game development.

JUSTIN V. GRAY is an author, graphic novelist, scriptwriter, and video game writer. He previously worked as an advocate for victims of crime, a chef, a fossil hunter, and a micro-photographer specializing in prehistoric insects and plants trapped in amber.

JIMMY BROXTON is a designer, illustrator, and comic book artist who cares way too much about "negative space," "pattern value," and the optimum consistency of waterproof drawing ink. He struggles daily to put the images in his head onto paper— his long-suffering partner and cats also struggle daily…just to put up with him.

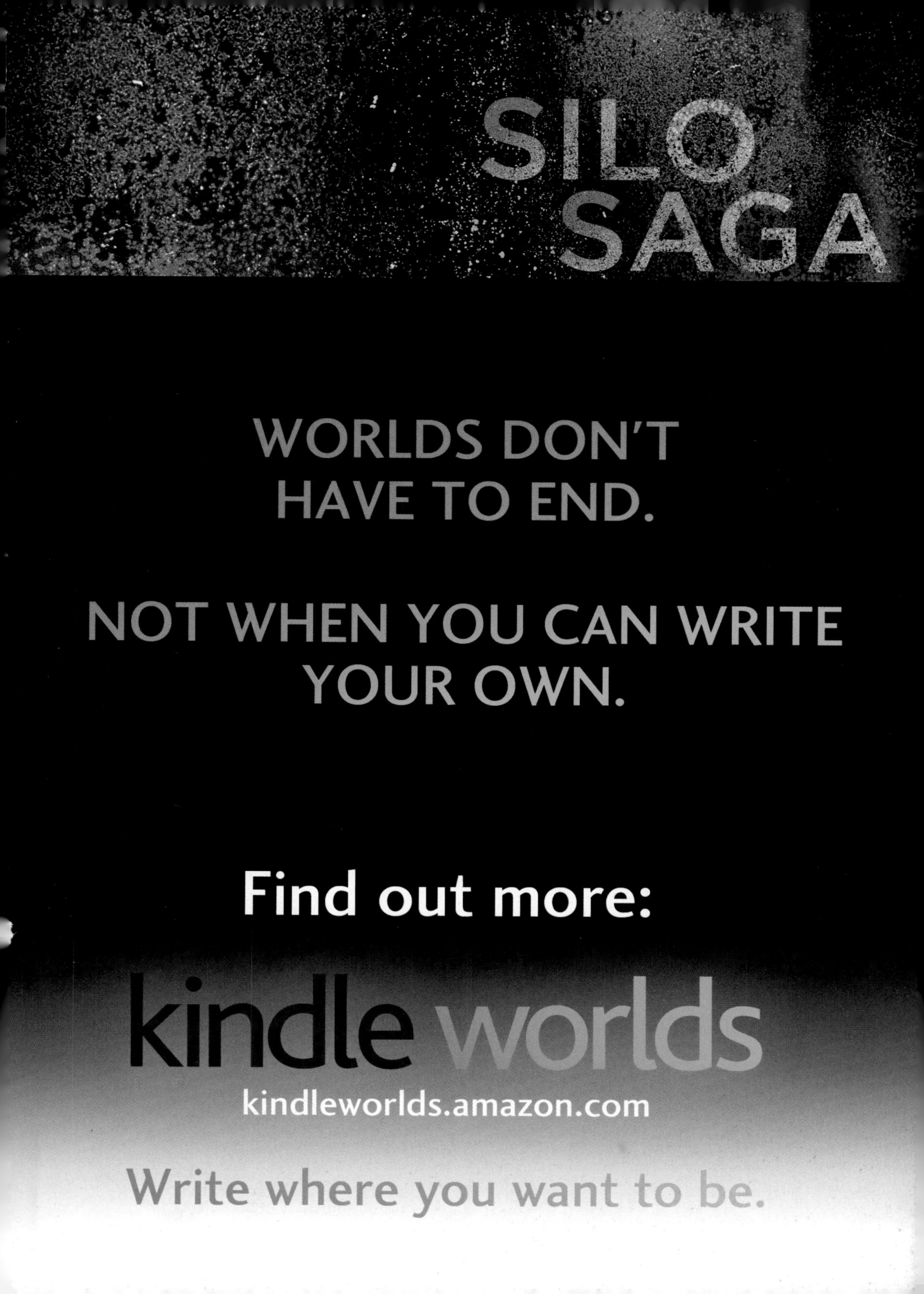
SILO SAGA
WORLDS DON'T HAVE TO END.
NOT WHEN YOU CAN WRITE YOUR OWN.
Find out more:
kindle worlds
kindleworlds.amazon.com
Write where you want to be.